STORY BIBLE
for Older Children

(New Testament)

Anne De Vries

STORY BIBLE
for Older Children

(New Testament)

Illustrations by
Cornelis Jetses

PAIDEIA PRESS
St. Catharines, Ontario, Canada

First published in Dutch as *Groot vertel-
boek voor de Bijbelse geschiedenis*, ©
J.H. Kok of Kampen. Translated by
Theodore Plantinga.

ISBN 0-88815-533-6
Printed in the United States of America.

Table of Contents

1: A miraculous message

The archangel Gabriel, God's holy messenger, flashed through the heavens like lightning and descended to the earth. He touched down in Jerusalem. He was in the temple, in front of the golden altar of incense in the Holy Place.

An old priest went about his work there quietly in the tender light of the seven lamps on the golden lampstand. Around him were walls inlaid with gold.

The priest's name was Zechariah. His home was in the hill country of Judea. He had come to Jerusalem with other priests to serve in the temple. When they cast lots to see who would be allowed to go into the Holy Place, Zechariah was chosen.

It was time to offer the morning sacrifice. The old priest scattered some aromatic herbs, incense and myrrh on the glowing coals of the altar of incense. He inhaled the sweet aroma and mumbled some prayers.

The people stood in the outer court. They were praying too. A cloud of the fragrant aroma and a cloud of prayers ascended to heaven.

Suddenly Zechariah saw the angel standing by the altar. His prayer broke off in mid-sentence, and his hands began to tremble. He was startled and shaken.

Zechariah was afraid of the heavenly figure.

The angel said to him, "Do not be afraid, Zechariah, for your prayer has been heard. Your wife Elizabeth shall bear a son, and you shall call him *John*."

His prayer had been heard? The angel was not talking about the prayer Zechariah had been mumbling at the altar; he was referring to a prayer prayed years before. When Zechariah was young and newly married, he had prayed repeatedly for a son. God had not been gracious to him; it was as if He had not heard Zechariah's prayer.

Zechariah and Elizabeth had grown old. They were lonely, for they had never had a child. This caused them great sorrow at first, but in time they became used to being alone. Now that they were old, it was no longer possible for them to have a child. They no longer prayed for a child or hoped for one. They had forgotten that prayer.

Could it be that the Lord still remembered that prayer? Was He now going to grant their request at last? In his great amazement, Zechariah forgot his fear. He shook his head in disbelief, and in his heart he laughed at the idea. No, that was impossible. An old, wrinkled woman like Elizabeth could not possibly bear a child. God could not be gracious to her now, after all these years.

Zechariah shook his head as he listened to the angel. The angel had more to say: he announced that an even greater miracle would take place.

"Your son will bring joy not only into *your* lives," said the angel. "There will be many who rejoice at his birth, for he will be a great servant of the Lord. He must not touch wine or strong drink. The Holy Spirit will dwell in his heart from the time of his birth. He will lead many children of Israel to repent and turn to the Lord their God. He will go before the Lord in the spirit and power of Elijah to prepare a people for the Lord."

Zechariah heard what the angel was saying, and he understood. His son was to be a great prophet. *His* son?

"No," said Zechariah, "that's impossible. I am old and my wife is old. How am I supposed to believe all this?"

The angel answered, "I am Gabriel. I stand in the presence of God. God Himself sent me to speak to you and bring you this joyful message. And behold, you will be silent. You will not be able to speak until the day this happens, for you have not believed my words, which will surely be fulfilled in their time."

The people waited in the outer court. They whispered to each other and watched the entrance to the temple closely. They were surprised at the priest. Why did he stay in the Holy Place so long?

At last they saw him coming, looking pale and perplexed. Humbly they bowed their heads, waiting for his blessing. But he said not a word. When they looked up to see what was happening, his trembling arms were extended and his lips moved, but no sound came from his lips. He couldn't speak.

Something strange must have happened to him in the temple, they thought; he must have seen something wonderful there. He tried to make signals to them, but the holy priest's blessing did not come from his lips, for those lips had uttered words of disbelief in the temple.

Zechariah soon left Jerusalem with the same priests with whom he had come. A different group of priests came to take their place. He hurried to his home in the hill country, where his aged wife was waiting for him.

That aged wife was to become young again, just as Sarah became young when she was old! A miraculous child was to be born! Yes, finally Zechariah could believe it.

He *had* to believe it. Even if he felt an impulse to say, "That's impossible," he would feel his tongue lying useless in his mouth. He was so happy that he wanted to sing, but he couldn't. He couldn't even tell Elizabeth what had happened. He had to inscribe it on a tablet for her to read.

"His name shall be *John*," he wrote. "That's what the angel said."

God is gracious—that's what the name meant.

Yes, God was indeed gracious. Although Zechariah and Elizabeth had forgotten their prayer, God had not forgotten.

Although His people had wandered from Him, He would show them love and grant them the greatest possible redemption. God's time had come.

2: The handmaid of the Lord

Six months later God again sent the angel Gabriel to the earth. This time he did not go to Jerusalem and the beautiful temple. He went to an insignificant corner of the country—a despised area known as *Galilee*.

The town of Nazareth lay on a hillside. The angel sought out a humble home in that little city and went inside.

A young woman named Mary lived in that house. Mary was really a princess, a descendant of King David.

David's royal family had fallen on hard times and was forgotten. Herod, a foreign king descended from Esau, was seated on David's throne in Jerusalem. Foreign people, the mighty Romans, had conquered God's people and now ruled their land.

Mary was a poor, simple girl. The man to whom she was engaged was a simple carpenter. His name was Joseph and he was also of the family of David.

Mary was alone in the house when the angel entered.

"Greetings to you who are so highly favored," he said. "The Lord is with you." The angel addressed her as if she were a queen!

Mary stared at the angel in amazement. What could that beautiful greeting possibly mean?

The angel said, "Do not be afraid, Mary, for you have found favor in God's eyes. Behold, you shall bear a son, and you shall call Him *Jesus.* Your son will be great and will be called the Son of the Most High. The Lord God will give Him the throne of His father David. He shall rule as King forever."

Rule as King forever on David's throne? That could only mean one thing, Mary concluded. Her son would be the Redeemer, the Messiah for whom the people had waited for centuries!

Would *she*, Mary, be the mother of the Redeemer? Had the Lord chosen her, poor and humble as she was?

Mary listened carefully, amazed and deeply moved. The miracle was too great; she could not comprehend it. But she did *not* say, "That's impossible." She *believed*, for she heard the Word of God.

She only asked, "How can this be, for I am not even married? Who will be the father of this child?"

The angel answered, "The Holy Spirit will come over you, and the power of the

Most High will overshadow you. God Himself will be the father of your child.
Therefore your son will be holy and will be
called the Son of God."

The angel also brought her news of
another miracle. "Elizabeth," he said,
"who is your relative, will also bear a son.
That's right—aged Elizabeth! Nothing is
impossible with God."

When Mary heard that, there was
nothing more for her to ask. Although it
was still a great riddle for her, she knew
that, with God, nothing is impossible. Was
God Himself willing to be the father of the
child? Then she would gladly be the

mother. She bowed her head obediently in
holy joy and said, "Behold, I am the hand-
maid of the Lord. May all of this happen
just as you have said."

Then the angel departed and left her
alone.

Mary was too excited to wait and rest
calmly. She was so happy that she had to
discuss the news with someone. She
couldn't discuss it with anyone in
Nazareth—not even Joseph, who knew
everything about her. Joseph would not
believe her, for this wonder was too holy
and too great.

She decided to visit Elizabeth, who had
also experienced a great miracle in her life.
She made a long journey across the country.
To reach Elizabeth's home in Judea took
three or four days. She wanted to reach
the house of the old priest Zechariah as
quickly as possible, to pour out what was
on her heart.

When Mary opened the door and greeted
Elizabeth, she didn't have to explain anything. Elizabeth jumped up with a cry of
delight and hurried to her. The moment she
heard Mary's voice she knew that Mary was
the mother of the Redeemer. God revealed
that to her.

"Blessed are you among women," cried
Elizabeth, "and blessed is your holy child.
What a joy for me that the mother of the
Lord has come to my home!"

When Mary heard that, she was overcome with joy. She, too, rejoiced. In her joy
she sang a song that welled up in her enrap-
tured heart—a song of praise to God. "My
soul praises the Lord," she sang, "and my
spirit rejoices in God, my Savior."

Mary stayed at Elizabeth's home for
three months. What better place was there
for her than this peaceful home? Where else
could she talk about the joy that filled her?

The two women waited in faith—the mother of the Redeemer and the mother of His prophet who would announce His coming.

3: Two joyful households

When Mary was back in Nazareth, Joseph the carpenter walked around with sadness written all over his face. His heart was so full of pain that he could hardly continue his work. His thoughts tormented him. What had happened to Mary, the young woman he was to marry? Why had she stayed in Judea for so long? Why did she act so silent and strange in his presence, as if she were hiding something from him?

Joseph soon discovered her secret: Mary was with child.

Joseph was shocked. To him it was horrible news, for he knew that it was not *his* child. Joseph and Mary weren't even married yet!

Mary must have deceived him in secret. Perhaps that was why she had stayed so long in Judea.

Joseph would never have suspected such a thing from Mary. Because he was a good and gentle man, however, he did not want to make a public issue of it. "I will not tell anyone how poorly she has treated me," he thought to himself. "I will leave her quietly and go somewhere else to live." But even as he made his new plans, he was in the depths of despair.

For the third time, an angel came to the earth from heaven. This angel addressed Joseph in a dream.

"Joseph, son of David," he said, "Mary has not deceived you. Take her as your wife, for the child in her womb is God's own child. You must name the child *Jesus*, that is, *Savior*, for He will free the people from their sins."

Joseph did just as the angel said. He did not understand what was going on, but he believed.

Joseph's joy returned—greater and more glorious than ever. Soon he and Mary were married. He brought Mary to his house and cared for her. Together they awaited the great miracle.

By that time, the miracle at Elizabeth's house had taken place. The child promised by God was born. All the neighbors and relatives joined the aged parents in their joy.

On the eighth day they came together to celebrate and to give the child a name. Everyone expected him to be named *Zechariah*, after his father.

Elizabeth shook her head. "No," she said, "he will be called *John*."

"John?" the people asked, surprised. "You can't call him *John*! There's no one in your family with that name. Just wait—we'll ask Zechariah. He'll know what to call him." But Zechariah took his tablet and wrote, "His name is John."

No one knew what to think of that. Just then Zechariah began to speak. His period of punishment was over. Everything had happened just as the angel had said it would, and Zechariah had obediently named the child *John*.

Zechariah finally had his voice back. All the words that passed over his lips were words of blessing. The Holy Spirit filled his heart. Zechariah became a prophet.

Like Mary, Zechariah sang a song of praise, a song in which he gave expression to his deep joy: "Blessed be the God of Israel, the Lord who has remembered His people."

All who heard Zechariah's song were

amazed. Throughout the country of Judea, people eagerly discussed the wonderful event that had taken place in Zechariah's house.

As the boy grew and walked through the hills, people watched him. They asked themselves, "What will he become when he grows up?"

When the boy became a man, the people hardly saw him, for he wandered in the wilderness. He waited there, alone, listening for the voice of God. He was waiting until his Master would need him.

4: Jesus' birth

Mary and Joseph slowly trudged down the dusty road that rose and fell through the hills of Ephrath. They were tired, for they had been traveling for days.

They were finally nearing their destination. Before them the white houses of Bethlehem shone in the bright evening sun.

They had not traveled all the way to Bethlehem for fun. They would rather have stayed quietly in Nazareth, for the promised child was to be born soon.

Mary and Joseph had no choice in the matter. The emperor Augustus, the mighty ruler of the entire Roman realm, had ordered a census taken of the whole empire. In Israel it was announced that each person must report to his own city to have his name registered.

No one dared to refuse when the emperor gave a command. Mary and Joseph had to make the long, difficult journey to Bethlehem, the city of David, because they were both descendants of King David.

As descendants of David, they were members of the royal family. Yet they had no money to buy transportation for that long journey.

They entered Bethlehem with a joyful sigh. At last they had arrived! They would soon find rest.

They passed through streets full of strangers who had come to Bethlehem from all directions. They went straight to the inn where they planned to spend the night. It was a big building that anyone could enter.

The inn was full of people and animals. Everywhere people were talking busily. They could not find a place for quiet rest, because other travelers had filled the inn before them. Vainly, they looked through the inn. There was no place left for the tired young woman and the carpenter. There was no place for the mother of the Lord.

At last they found a quiet corner for themselves—in a barn. The sheep were in the fields. The manger the sheep ate from was empty.

Mary and Joseph went into the barn. In the fading light they made a bed of straw for Mary. They sat down and ate their evening meal. They thanked the Lord for the food and for the humble lodgings they had found.

Soon it was dark. The stars beamed down from the sky. It was night in Bethlehem.

In the still darkness that night, in a hidden corner of the barn, the greatest miracle that could ever happen on earth occurred. The Son of God, who had been promised to mankind for centuries, came into the world as a baby—a small, tender baby. No one was present with Mary and Joseph when the Savior was born.

Mary kissed her child in her holy joy. Joseph caressed the baby with his rough hand. They had only their love to offer the

5: Shepherds and angels

In the darkness of the open fields near Bethlehem, shepherds kept watch over their flock that night. They had driven their sheep into an enclosure. They sat quietly near the sheep, grouped around a fire. They were silent—lost in their thoughts. Only the sigh of the night wind in the grass could be heard.

Whenever they heard the distant cry of some beast of prey, they raised their heads and listened carefully. If they heard

baby. They didn't even have a cradle. Mary wrapped the baby in cloths warmed by her body. Joseph put some hay and straw in the manger, and Mary placed her baby in it.

There lay the Son of God—in a feeding trough for animals. The King of heaven and earth was asleep in a barn. Who would ever have believed it?

nothing more, they let their heads sink again and drifted off in their thoughts.

Suddenly they jumped up with a cry. Standing in front of them was a shining heavenly figure—an angel of the Lord. With the angel standing before them, the glory of the Lord was all around them.

The shepherds threw up their hands to cover their faces. They sank to their knees, quaking with fear.

The angel addressed them in joyful tones, "Do not be afraid, for I bring you good news of great joy—good news for all the people. Today, in the city of David, a Savior is born to you, namely, Christ the Lord. And this will be a sign for you; you will find the baby wrapped in some cloths and lying in a manger."

When the angel had said this, the heavens became even brighter. Thousands of shining angels descended to the earth.

The sky was filled with angels. A great heavenly army hovered above the fields. In the stillness of the night the shepherds heard a beautiful song, more beautiful than was ever before heard on earth: "Glory to God in the highest, and on earth peace to men on whom His favor rests."

The shepherds understood those words. They listened in speechless awe.

The rejoicing choir of angels gradually disappeared into heaven. The sky grew dark again, and the heavenly music disappeared.

The heavens had closed above the shepherds. It was darker than before. The wind rustled through the grass. The angels with their heavenly message seemed to have been only a dream.

The shepherds stood looking at each other in amazement, not sure if they were in heaven or still on earth. "The Savior!" they whispered. "The Messiah has come!"

Finally one of them dared to speak aloud again. "Let's go straight to Bethlehem," he said excitedly, "to see what has happened there. Let's look into this news the Lord has told us."

Hastily they filed through the dark fields. They left their sheep in God's care. Soon they were in Bethlehem, and they found the barn. Hesitantly they went inside.

There they met Mary and Joseph, who were poor people just as they were. They saw the baby wrapped in cloths, lying in the manger. It was an ordinary baby, just like any other—small and helpless.

Yet the shepherds believed what the angel had told them. They believed that the helpless child in the manger was the Savior—Christ the Lord. The manger was His cradle, and the barn was His home.

The shepherds kneeled before the child, the one who had come to be their Shepherd. They bowed low, and pressed their brown faces to the floor.

"The holy baby Jesus!" they whispered reverently. "The Savior who will bring peace to earth!"

Tears of joy rushed to their eyes. They were the first to see the Savior of the world.

They were deeply moved as they told Mary and Joseph what the angel had said and what the heavenly host had sung. When they returned to their sheep, a new day was dawning. With husky voices they sang the song of the angels: "Glory to God in the highest, and on earth peace to men on whom His favor rests." Wherever they went, they told people about the special baby born in Bethlehem, for they were full of joy.

Mary let the baby drink for the first time as she lay on a bed of straw in the empty barn. She was almost bursting with joy. "My child!" she said in delight. "The

Redeemer!" she whispered reverently.

Yes, the baby was her child and her Redeemer. And she was allowed to care for Him and feed Him at her breast.

She was also permitted to kneel before Him and worship Him. The miracle became ever more great and glorious.

She stored in her heart all the words that the shepherds had spoken to her and pondered them often.

6: Simeon and Anna

After Jesus was born, the days slipped by one by one. The angels who sang on the night of His birth did not repeat their performance. People went about their work as they always had. The sun rose in the morning and set in the evening. The shepherds continued to pasture their flocks in the fields around Bethlehem. Life continued its usual course, just as if nothing had happened.

But Mary had a special child in her arms —the Redeemer of the world. Every day He drank from her breast.

Like any other child, the baby was given a name on the eighth day—*Jesus*, which means *savior*. Because He was the firstborn, Mary and Joseph brought Him to Jerusalem, which was two hours away from Bethlehem. This happened on the fortieth day.

Centuries before, when all the first-born in Egypt were put to death, God had spared the first-born of the Israelites in the land of Goshen. That was why the firstborn son was always brought to the temple. The first-born son was "presented" to the Lord. In other words, he was consecrated to the Lord.

The mother would show her baby to the priest so that the priest could bless him. She knew that God's eyes also looked down on the baby in love. Then the parents would offer a sacrifice. Rich people would offer a lamb; poor people would offer a pair of pigeons or turtle doves.

This was the first time that Jesus was in Jerusalem, the city of the Great King. No one recognized Joseph and Mary as they walked through the streets, and no one recognized the royal child Mary carried in her arms.

They entered the temple and offered the usual sacrifice for poor people. The priest approached them and unthinkingly laid his hands on the child. He had blessed the Messiah without realizing it.

Suddenly an old, gray man entered the temple with great haste. He hurried straight to Mary. *He* knew who the child was! Simeon knew because God had told him.

Simeon's only great desire in life was for the Messiah, the one who would redeem his people. Long ago, to comfort him, God had revealed to Simeon that he would not die until he had seen the Savior.

It was late evening in Simeon's life. The dark shadow of death had crept forward toward him. Simeon was living in dark times for the people of Israel. The people were oppressed by a powerful foe. But now the great day had finally come—the most beautiful day in Simeon's entire life.

Mary offered the baby to Simeon. Reverently the old man took the child in his arms. Full of joy, he praised God. "Now I can die in peace," he cried out, "for my eyes have seen Your salvation, O Lord."

Indeed, Simeon need not fear death, for this child he held in his arms would conquer sin and death.

Because the Redeemer had come, it didn't matter that Simeon lived in dark times. The Light of the world was finally beginning to shine.

Simeon sang of that light, the great and beautiful light that descended from heaven to beam down not only upon Israel but upon all the nations.

Simeon said that many would come to love this child and would receive happiness through Him. But there would be many others who would hate him. The child would cause some to fall and others to rise.

Simeon had more things to say. His aged eyes saw far into the future. He knew that Mary's joy was greater than anyone else's joy. But her *sorrow* would also be greater than anyone else's sorrow. She would suffer intense pain, as if someone had run a sword through her.

When Simeon fell silent, another voice was raised. The new speaker was an old, gray woman—the prophetess Anna. She was an 84-year-old widow who spent her time in the temple.

Anna came to stand by the baby Jesus. Like Simeon, she saw much more than a child six weeks old. They both saw Jesus as the Son of God. God had come so close to man that He now lay as a child in the arms of His mother.

Anna sang about this great wonder. From then on she told everyone she met that the Redeemer had come. All who looked forward to the coming of the Redeemer found rich comfort in this joyful message.

The finely clothed priests and the strict Pharisees were not among them. They had a different kind of Messiah in mind. They were not interested in a humble Messiah who came to earth as a child.

7: Wise men from the east

The caravan moved slowly through the wilderness. It was a caravan of rich, important men accompanied by their armed servants. They came from the east, perhaps from the land of the Chaldeans where Nebuchadnezzar had ruled, or perhaps from the land of the Medes and Persians, still farther away.

The wise men were on their way to Israel. They were looking for the king of the Jews, who had been born recently.

Somehow these wise men from a heathen land knew that a special child had been born in the land of the Jews. They knew that child would become a mighty king someday. The heavens had told them about the child.

The travelers were learned men. They had read many ancient books on wisdom. They followed the course of the stars through the heavens carefully. They believed that the stars unlocked the future and enabled them to foretell important events.

They had recently seen a bright new star in the heavens. There it was, suddenly, unexpectedly—a bright, shining light. That new star must mean a new human life on earth, they reasoned. Because it was such a beautiful star, the person just born must be someone very special, someone full of power and glory.

The wise men looked through their books, performed some tricky calculations, and concluded that a king must have been born in the land of the Jews. Perhaps Balaam's prophecy that a star would come forth from Jacob helped them reach that conclusion.

When they realized what the star meant, they had no peace while they remained in the east. Some force drove them to set out on a journey. They obeyed the silent compulsion in their hearts. They prepared their camels, assembled gifts to take along, and set out on a long journey westward.

They traveled through territory where they could be attacked by robbers and wild animals. They made the same long journey that Abraham had once made when he trusted in God's love to lead him to a new land.

At last, in the distance, the wise men saw Jerusalem with its hills, its high walls, its palaces, and its shining temple. *That* was their destination. Surely the king of the Jews was born in one of those palaces.

They entered the city's gates and began to ask, "Where is the king of the Jews who was born recently?" People stared at them in surprise and shrugged their shoulders. They didn't know anything about a new king.

"We saw his star in the east and have come to worship him," said the travelers.

Suddenly a gleam came into the eyes of the people. They began to look at each other in hope. The Messiah? Could it be?

No one could help the travelers. Disappointed, they moved down other streets, asking people the same questions.

The people of Jerusalem began to gather in groups. Could it be that the Messiah had come to deliver them from cruel Herod and to drive out the hated Romans? Could heathen travelers from a faraway land find out about the Messiah even before the Jews?

The news about the wise men and their strange question raced through the city. Soon all of Jerusalem was in an uproar.

8: Herod's hatred

Wise men from the east were in Jerusalem asking, "Where is the king of the Jews who was just born? We saw his star and have come to worship him."

Soon the news reached the palace, and King Herod heard it. It frightened him, and he trembled. A quiet fear that had tormented him as long as he had been king now flared up in his heart. King of the Jews? *Herod* was king of the Jews, and as long as he was around, no one else would be permitted to claim that title!

Herod had ascended David's throne through deceit. He had reason to tremble at the thought that someone might want to force him from the throne. Herod had murdered his own wife because he believed he couldn't trust her. He had also killed three of his sons. He had wiped out half of his own family. Many Jews had also fallen victim to his wrath.

All his life Herod had suffered a deep unrest. He had endured a long, bitter struggle to remain king over this people. Now, when he was old and sick and not far from the grave, was his throne in danger again?

The *Messiah* has come, the rumors whispered. Herod could clearly see how excited his servants were. He knew perfectly well that they hoped the rumors were true. They hated Herod, that foreigner, that cruel Edomite. All the Jews hated him. To win their favor, he had allowed them to rebuild their temple. It had done him no good. They still longed for the Messiah, the leader who would be a descendant of David. The Messiah could claim the throne occupied by Herod.

Herod hated the Messiah; he cursed Him. If the Messiah really had been born, Herod was not about to step aside for him.

This time, too, Herod would win; he already had a plan prepared. He called the chief priests and scribes, the men who knew the books of Moses and the prophets. He asked them if they knew where the Christ was to be born.

That was not a difficult question for these learned men. They thought back to a clear prophecy in Micah, "And you, Bethlehem, in the land of Judah—you are by no means the least among the leaders of Judah, for from you shall come forth a leader who will pasture My people Israel."

The priests and scribes laughed scornfully as they left the palace. *They* were the ones who knew all about the Messiah. They were not about to let a foolish rumor about the Messiah shake them from their rest. How could anyone believe that the Messiah might come without the priests and scribes knowing about it?

Herod summoned the wise men in secret and spoke to them in a friendly manner. He asked them when they had seen the star for the first time. What he really wanted to know was how old the child might be. He told them that they were looking for Bethlehem and gave them directions.

"Go there and search diligently for the young king," he said. "When you have found him, come back and let me know. I want to go there too and pay him my respects."

"I want to pay him my respects," the old king had said. Yet there was hatred staring at the wise men from those false eyes that tried to look friendly.

9: Worship and murder in Bethlehem

It was evening when the wise men left Jerusalem. The sun had already set, and darkness was creeping across the fields. Before them, in the night sky to the south, a bright star shone in silent majesty. It was the same star that the wise men had seen when they were in their own land. Now they saw it again—in the land of the Jews. The star went before them and hovered above the place where they could find the child.

Joyfully they hastened to Bethlehem. It did not take them long to find the house at which Mary and Joseph were staying.

They went inside, and there they found the child for whom they had made this long journey. They found the child in a modest house cradled in the arms of an ordinary woman without money or title. Could that child be the young king?

It was God who had led them to this child; therefore they *believed*. Those wise, powerful men kneeled before the child and

honored Him. They offered the simple child their royal gifts—gold, incense and myrrh. They laid the shining gold and costly spices at the child's feet as tokens of their esteem.

Then they were happy. Not because their clever calculations had proven correct, for with calculations alone they would never have found the child. They were happy because a great light had begun to shine in their hearts, the Light of which aged Simeon had sung. They were happy because they had found the Savior of the world.

That night God spoke to the wise men. He commanded them, in a dream, *not* to go back to Herod. They obeyed gladly and went home along a different route. They no longer had their gifts with them, but they took back a greater treasure—the peace and joy in their hearts.

Back in Jerusalem, Herod was almost consumed with anxiety. He waited in vain for the wise men to return. He was beside himself with rage when he finally realized that they had deceived him.

He would not allow the young king born in Bethlehem to escape him! Herod would still be the victor!

Quickly he sent his soldiers to the quiet town of Bethlehem. He ordered them to kill all little boys two years old and younger. The hated child would surely die, he reasoned. It was not that long ago that the wise men had first seen that strange star in the sky.

Herod's cruel soldiers obeyed, for they were not much better than their wicked master. A great cry went up in Bethlehem as the soldiers went about their murderous work, their swords red with blood. Herod didn't care about the pain suffered by the mothers in Bethlehem. He had just committed the most horrible, desperate act of his life, but he laughed and was at ease. He thought only of himself. He had won the battle, he believed. Now the cruel king on David's throne in Jerusalem could be sure of his power again.

Soon God knocked the blood-stained sword from Herod's filthy hand. Herod died of a horrible disease. There was no one on earth to punish him for his misdeeds. He had to face the One who avenges the innocent blood that is shed on earth.

The children of Bethlehem who had been murdered so cruelly were better off than Herod. They were snatched from their mother's arms mercilessly, but God's fatherly arms received them. They were in God's care. They were the first people on earth permitted to give their lives for King Jesus. They were martyrs.

One day Jesus would give His life for them. He was not dead—not at all! How could foolish Herod have thought that he could win his battle against the Messiah? When his soldiers marched into Bethlehem with their swords drawn, the baby Jesus was not there. He was far away, where He would be safe. An angel of the Lord had warned Joseph about Herod's plans, and told him to take Mary and the child to Egypt.

While Herod laughed about the murders in Bethlehem, Jesus was cradled in His mother's arms as she rode south on a donkey. Joseph and Mary were able to buy a donkey with gold that the wise men had given them. They traveled to Egypt on that donkey, and continued to live off the gold.

After Herod's death God told them to return to their own land. Joseph did not dare settle in Bethlehem, the city of his fathers. Archelaus, Herod's son, was king, and he was just as godless as his father. Joseph returned to the northern part of the country, to the despised area known as *Galilee*. He settled as a carpenter in the little city of Nazareth.

There had been no angels singing in Nazareth on the night of Christ's birth. No one from Nazareth had been present in the temple to hear what Simeon and Anna said about Mary's baby. When the people of Nazareth saw little Jesus, they never thought that He might be the Messiah.

10: Jesus as a boy

Jesus grew up in Nazareth, in the home of a simple carpenter. Joseph worked to support Him, and Mary took care of Him. She led and encouraged Him as He took His first steps. He learned His first words from her. He listened attentively as she told Him about heaven and about God.

As Jesus grew up, He learned to read and write. In his free time He wandered through Nazareth's narrow streets and in the open fields, where He observed and learned much.

He saw the shepherd go into the field with his flock and observed how deeply the good shepherd loved his sheep. He watched the vinedresser trim and prune vines that were to bear fruit. The wild branches that bore no fruit were cut off and thrown away. The others were purified and trimmed. When they blossomed, they bore heavy clusters of grapes.

Jesus watched as the sower sowed his grain. Some seeds fell on the pathway and were quickly eaten by birds. Some fell among thorns, and had no chance to develop into healthy plants. Other seeds fell on hard soil and were dried by the sun. Some seeds fell in good earth; they grew into plants that bore fruit. Sometimes a single kernel would multiply to become 30, 60, or even 100 kernels.

Jesus learned from everything He observed around Him. God put wisdom in His heart.

Jesus was carefree and happy, like any other boy. But He was also different from the others. The greatest difference was not that He was wiser and more sensible. The greatest difference was that He did no evil. He was born holy, and He remained holy all His life. He had become like other people in all things—except sin.

The people of Nazareth did not realize that. They thought they knew Him. "Jesus, the son of Joseph," they said, "the son of the carpenter." They did not know that Joseph was Jesus' foster father.

Mary knew. Did she remember always that Jesus was more than the son of Joseph?

When Jesus was twelve years old, a special day came for Him. He had looked forward to that day for a long time. For the first time, He was allowed to go to Jerusalem with Mary and Joseph to celebrate the Passover, the holy festival of deliverance.

The journey was long and very enjoyable. The fields lay green and shining under the spring sun. The grain was already developing, and the vineyards were blossoming on the warm hillsides.

Jesus, Joseph and Mary walked through the Valley of Jezreel with other people from Galilee. They crossed the Jordan and rested the first night in an inn. They traveled farther through the land east of the Jordan. The closer they approached Jerusalem, the busier the roads became. Pious people in festal garments came from all directions to the holy city. Their joyful singing could be heard far and wide across the sunny fields.

The people sang the songs of ascents, and Jesus joined with His holy voice: "I lift up my eyes to the hills; my help comes from the Lord." Indeed, there were mountains in the distance. The mountains behind which Jerusalem lay were on the horizon.

When Jesus and His companions had climbed the last hills, they saw the city before them. They saw thick walls with a set of towers, white houses among green trees, and a brilliant white marble temple with a golden roof. The temple looked like a mountain of snow with a fiery crown. The city was surrounded by hills—faithful watchmen. On one side of the city was the green hill known as the Mount of Olives; on the other side was a bare hill known as Golgotha. "As the mountains surround Jerusalem," sang the people, "so the Lord surrounds His people, both now and forever."

They hurried to reach the city. They entered the city gates rejoicing: "We enter your gates, O Jerusalem, city that we love."

A colorful stream of people poured through the streets. A boy in a white linen garment walked happily among them. He was the One for whom they were all waiting, the One of whom they all sang, the One who would make a much better Passover possible someday.

The Passover festival lasted seven days. During that time Jesus stayed close to Mary and Joseph. It was the most glorious event of His entire life. He stood by as the Passover lamb was slaughtered. He watched quietly as the blood drained into a basin— the precious blood that had preserved the people from death while they were in Egypt. He stood with the others by the table where He received the unleavened bread and dipped it in the bitter sauce. He also went to the temple and stood next to Joseph in the outer court. As He raised His eyes toward the blue sky He thought of His Father in heaven and sent up a silent prayer to Him.

Jesus joined the praying and singing. In fact, He participated with greater reverence than anyone else. No one knew better than He how great and holy the heavenly Father was. No one was more at home in the temple than Jesus.

11: Jesus in His Father's house

The Passover festival in Jerusalem was over, and the streets were no longer crowded. Mary and Joseph went through Jerusalem's gate with their travel companions. They did not have Jesus beside them, but that didn't worry them. They had not been able to locate Him in the crowd. He must have gone ahead of them with other people in their party. Jesus was always sensible and obedient; there was no need to worry. They would catch up with Him soon enough.

Mary and Joseph kept an eye open for Jesus as they walked. They asked people if anyone had seen Him. At last they became uneasy, for by evening they still had not found Him.

The anxiety in Mary's heart grew. She did not sleep that night. She *couldn't* sleep, for she couldn't get her missing son out of her mind.

Early the next morning Mary and Joseph went back to Jerusalem. They passed many groups of people on their way home from celebrating the Passover in Jerusalem. Mary and Joseph anxiously scanned each group, but by the time they reached Jerusalem's gate, they still had not found their son.

Mary allowed herself no rest. She hurried through the quiet city streets. Whenever she met people she knew, she asked, "Have you seen my son Jesus?" They all shook their heads and shrugged their shoulders.

Mary was crying, but she kept walking through the city's streets—down one street and up another. Again darkness descended.

It was a night of watching and praying for Mary, a restless night of tossing and turning. She simply didn't understand it. She was so tired and so afraid that she could hardly think.

Perhaps there had been an accident! Perhaps Jesus was dead! Or perhaps He had left the city after all. Why would He have stayed behind in the city after being so obedient all His life?

The next day she wandered through the city again, searching and asking questions. She was pale with fear and sorrow. Still her searching was in vain.

The third day she finally went to the temple. She had almost given up hope. Even the temple was quiet. Here and there a priest went about his work. A few pious people prayed quietly. The voices of scholars instructing their students in the law came from some rooms.

Mary and Joseph looked all through the temple. When Mary with tears in her eyes looked into one of the rooms, she almost cried out in surprise. There was her son! There He sat, calm as ever, with dignified scholars surrounding Him. He was exchanging ideas with them. The scholars were amazed at all that Jesus knew and at the answers He gave them.

Mary was deeply shaken when she saw how calmly Jesus was sitting there. *He* had

been peacefully conversing with old men in the temple while *she* had been suffering so much anxiety on His account.

Mary ran to Jesus and threw her arms around Him. "My child," she sobbed, "why have You done this to me? Your father and I have been worried sick about You!"

"Your father and I!" Like the people of Nazareth, Mary called Joseph Jesus' father.

Jesus had His answer ready. "Why were you looking for Me?" He asked in a friendly way. "Didn't you know that I must be busy in My Father's house?"

When Mary heard those words, she realized that her child had not been disobedient at all. It was not *Jesus* that had sinned but *Mary*. She had forgotten who Jesus' Father was. The Father could protect Jesus where ever He went.

Yet, Mary did not fully understand Jesus' words. It would not be the last time that she would suffer disappointment because she did not understand Jesus as He sought to do the will of His heavenly Father.

Jesus rose and went obediently out of the temple and along the city streets with Mary. Mary, Joseph and Jesus then went straight back to Nazareth, and arrived there a few days after the others who had attended the Passover festival in Jerusalem.

Joseph again took up his work as carpenter, and Jesus worked alongside him. He was obedient to Mary and Joseph in all things.

Jesus grew and became a man. He also grew in wisdom. People liked Him and thought well of Him. The Father in heaven looked down on Him in blessing.

For eighteen years Jesus remained a carpenter. But He knew that there was other work awaiting Him.

Jesus had come to earth not to make

tables and benches but to establish a *kingdom*. He had not come to be pleasant and friendly to people but to *save* them.

Finally the day arrived when Jesus would lay down His carpenter's tools forever and leave the home of Joseph and Mary. His time had come.

12: John the Baptist

When a king in the ancient Near East wanted to make a journey through his land, he would send one of his servants ahead to prepare the people for his coming. This forerunner would cry out to the people that the king was on his way. If the roads along which the king was to travel needed repairs, this could be done in time for his coming. That way the people would be ready to properly greet their sovereign.

The time had almost come for King Jesus to go out to His people. John, the son of Zechariah and Elizabeth, was to be the forerunner announcing His coming. He would be the royal herald who would prepare the people for the advent of the Messiah.

John had lived for years as a hermit in the wilderness, far away from people. During the daytime he wandered under the searing sun and sought his simple food—locusts and wild honey that he found in cracks in the rocks. At night, as he lay down somewhere in a cave or under the open sky, he could hear the cries of beasts of prey nearby.

John was safe under God's protection. God's voice had spoken to him in the lonely solitude and called him to be a great prophet. A desire to serve the Messiah burned in his heart.

When God's command to begin the work finally came, he hurried eagerly to the edge of the wilderness. He went to a spot where travelers often crossed the Jordan River. There he cried out to the people that the King was coming. He went to the people dressed just as he was dressed when he was alone. He was bareheaded and wore a rough garment of camel's hair which he fastened around his waist with a leather belt.

A herald? No, he didn't look much like the herald of an earthly king. But that's not what John was. He did not cry out to people that they had to repair the *roads* in their district. He told them that they should change their sinful *hearts* when the King came. They would have to become *new* people, people who hated sin, people with hearts full of faith, people eager to receive the Messiah.

"Repent!" he cried out. "Repent, for the Kingdom of heaven is at hand!"

People came from far and near. They crowded around John on the riverbank and listened in amazement to his preaching. Was the Messiah really coming? Was the One for whom the people had waited so long really as near as John said?

Some people who believed also knew that they were not yet in any condition to receive and welcome the Redeemer. They came to John penitently and told him how much evil they had done. They confessed their sins to God and to John.

John knew what to do with them: he baptized them in the name of the Lord. He took them into the water of the same river in which Naaman the Syrian was healed of his leprosy centuries before. There he dunked them. Just as the water washed the dirt from their bodies, it cleansed their souls of sin. That was what baptism

signified. Just as the people who were baptized went under the water, their old, sinful nature would go under. And just as they arose again from the water, new life would arise within them because they had repented and turned to God.

The news about John's preaching raced through the land. "A prophet has arisen!" people cried to each other. "He says that the Messiah is coming! He cries out for repentance!"

People streamed toward the Jordan from all sides. It had been 400 years since the voice of a prophet was last heard in Israel. Fishermen and farmers, shepherds from Judea, scholars from Jerusalem, nobles and poor people—a great host crowded around the prophet.

They saw him standing in his humble garment of camel's hair. They saw what a skinny, bony figure he cut. They saw his dark, sparkling eyes.

The prophet looked a little like Elijah. He was just as powerful, courageous and fiery as Elijah when he proclaimed the Word of the Lord. "Repent," he cried out, "for the Kingdom of heaven is at hand! The ax has been laid to the root of the tree. Every tree that does not bear good fruit will be cut down and thrown into the fire!"

The people understood these strange, threatening words, and they trembled with fear. Indeed, when the Messiah came, He would be a stern gardener. The people well knew how little good fruit they had brought forth in their lives. They had thought only of themselves, of their riches and honor. They had lived sinfully and forgotten about God.

"What must we do?" they cried in despair.

John knew their loveless, self-seeking hearts. Therefore he answered, "Repent! Anyone with two suits of clothing must share with those who have nothing. Anyone who has enough to eat must share with those who have nothing." That was how John preached.

13: A voice crying in the wilderness

All sorts of people came to listen to John the Baptist as he preached in the wilderness. Among them were tax-collectors. They were the people whose job it was to gather taxes and turn them over to the Romans.

The tax-collectors were hated by the people, for they often took in much more money than they were supposed to. They kept the extra money and became rich.

Even those selfish thieves came to John with fear in their eyes. They wanted John to baptize them. They asked him, "Master, what must we do?"

The prophet did not chase them away, for he saw that repentance was in their hearts. He said to them: "Do you really want to repent? Show that in how you go about your business. Be honest from now on, and do not wring more money than you are entitled to from people."

The power of John's words was so great that even soldiers came to him. Rough, crude men whom everyone feared stood before the prophet. Now they were afraid. They were afraid of the great day of which he spoke.

"What about us?" they asked. "What must *we* do?"

John knew perfectly well what godless lives these men had lived. They had often robbed people. No one was safe when they were around. He said to them, "Stop your plunder and extortion. Simply be satisfied with being soldiers."

John turned no one away, no matter how wicked he was, provided there was repentance in his heart.

Pharisees also came to John, but there was no repentance in their hearts. In their pride they believed they had not sinned. They hoped to *earn* a place in heaven through their good works.

They looked pious too. Moreover, they were scholars well versed in Scripture, and they kept the laws of Moses. In fact, they had even made up extra laws, which they also kept. In their clothes they had wide hems on which Bible texts were stitched. They prayed on street corners and they gave alms generously to the poor. But they did all these things only to be honored by men.

They needed that honor from their fellow men, for deep in their hearts lived a continual anxiety. The voice of their conscience accused them. But when people praised them, they no longer heard the voice of their conscience.

The Pharisees deceived themselves and the people. They had no genuine love in their hearts, and they were not truly pious. They were proud hypocrites.

Sadducees came too. The Sadducees were leading priests but they did not believe. They did not accept God's Word, and they rejected the idea of heaven and angels and eternal life with God.

"We only live once," they said. "Let's eat, drink and be merry, for when we die it's all over." Naturally, there was no repentance in their hearts.

Now these Pharisees and Sadducees, these blind leaders who poisoned the hearts of the people with their teaching, came to John. They saw how he baptized. They saw how the people honored him. Because the people thought so much of John, the Pharisees and Sadducees were willing to be baptized by him.

They didn't really need to be baptized, for they were pious Jews and children of Abraham. But surely they belonged to the Kingdom of which John spoke! In fact, they should be first in that Kingdom. John would surely feel honored if they came to him. He would bow before them and give them the best place, in the front row, close to him. The people would see once more how outstanding and how worthy of honor their leaders were.

What a hopeless misunderstanding! John did not bow before the Pharisees and Sadducees. There was no place for them in his circle—and no place for them in the Kingdom of heaven. John knew that there was no repentance in their hearts. He chased them away, lashing out at them with cutting words: "You brood of vipers! Who warned you to flee from the coming wrath? Show first by your works that you want to repent! Are you really Abraham's children? Then show that you have the same faith as Abraham. Do you suppose God needs you? I tell you that God can raise up children of Abraham out of these stones!"

No one had ever dared to speak to these mighty men in such tones before! Who was this man, that he had the nerve to do such a thing? He must be a great prophet, the people thought. They whispered to each other and looked at John with awe and respect. Could it be that John was the Christ, the one they all awaited?

John sensed this question in the people's hearts. "No!" he cried out. "I am not the Messiah. I am only a voice crying in the wilderness. The One who is coming is mightier than I am. He is so great that I am not even worthy to untie His shoes or to be His lowliest slave. I baptize you with water, but *He* will baptize you with the Holy Spirit and with fire."

14: The baptism of Jesus

One day, as John stood on the bank of the Jordan, he saw Jesus of Nazareth approaching. He eyes shone with joy, for he had heard about Jesus from his mother. He knew about the wonders that had surrounded Jesus' birth. John wanted to believe his mother when she told him that Jesus was the Messiah.

When Jesus declared that He, too, wished to be baptized, John was taken aback. He was puzzled. Must John baptize the King, the Holy One? No, that he would not do. After all, the Christ did not need a new heart; He had never committed a single sin. How could the Christ undergo such a humiliation? How could He allow Himself to be baptized just like a sinner?

John steadfastly refused. Reverently he said to Jesus: "I should be baptized by You instead. Why do You come to me for baptism?"

Jesus insisted. He wanted to be reckoned among sinners, for He was to be like other people in all things. If the people were being baptized, He, the head of the people, would also be baptized.

The people had come to John bearing the sins *they* had committed, but Jesus wanted to bear the sins of the entire world. Jesus was willing to suffer this great humiliation to bring happiness to His people. He said to

John, "I *must* be baptized, for in this way we will carry out God's will fully."

John hesitated, but finally obeyed. He went into the water with Jesus and baptized Him the same way that sinful tax-collectors and godless soldiers were baptized.

When Jesus came up again something wonderful happened. It cleared away all John's doubts.

The blue sky suddenly opened. A blinding light fell upon the earth. In that heavenly light the Holy Spirit descended in the form of a shining white dove and settled upon Jesus. John heard a voice from heaven that said, "This is My beloved Son in whom I take pleasure."

At that moment John knew for certain that Jesus was the Messiah. He knew because God had once said to him, "The one on whom you see the Spirit descend—He is the one." Now John had seen how God used the Spirit to anoint Jesus the King.

John had lived for this King and worked for His coming. Although he did not feel worthy to untie the King's shoes, he had been allowed to baptize Him in the Jordan!

John watched in delight as Jesus walked away into the stillness of the wilderness. He saw Jesus disappear beyond the rocks. He knew that his work as forerunner would soon be done. The King had finally come!

The people would quickly turn to Christ, and John would be forgotten. That didn't matter to John. "I must now become *less*," John thought, "because *He* must grow in power and glory."

John called the people together again. His eyes were shining with joy as he cried out to them happily, "Repent, for the Kingdom of heaven *has* come!"

15: Bread in the wilderness

Jesus was alone in the silent wilderness. Bare, gray rocks and dull sand surrounded Him. Only the blue sky provided color.

In that colorless desolation Jesus wandered around, just as John the Baptist had once done. Jesus was not looking for food; in fact, He wasn't even thinking about food. He was thinking instead about His Father, whose voice He had heard at the

Jordan. The Father had anointed Him with the Spirit, and now His soul was overflowing with holy joy. He also thought about the great work that lay ahead of Him. He had come to earth for that great work—to redeem the world from the power of satan. The road ahead of Him was long and difficult. As He traveled that road, He would be subjected to ridicule, scorn and shame. One day that road would lead Him into the dark valley of death. Beyond that valley lay triumph.

Jesus wanted to follow that road obediently to the end. He wanted to entrust Himself to the Father in complete obedience. Wild beasts prowled near Him while He was alone in the wilderness. But Jesus did not fear them.

Something else also prowled in the wilderness waiting for a chance to attack Jesus. It was a force much more horrible than an enraged lion or a poisonous snake. It was satan.

Satan knew Jesus. He knew that Jesus, the Son of God, was his greatest enemy. He knew that Jesus had come to conquer satan through obedience and to reclaim His people from satan's power.

Long ago satan had stalked someone who, like Jesus, was without sin. He had tricked that person into disobedience. That person was Adam. Adam had lived in a paradise, the Garden of Eden. All his needs had been supplied and he had lacked nothing as he lived in the midst of God's wonders.

But the person satan was now stalking was in a territory that looked as if it had been forsaken by God, a territory where there was nothing to eat or drink. Why shouldn't satan succeed this time, too, in his wicked work? Patiently he waited for an opportunity.

After 40 days it appeared that his opportunity had finally come. Jesus, lost in His thoughts all this time, finally realized how hungry He was and how much He needed food. There was no bread in the wilderness. There was only sand and rocks and loneliness.

Suddenly a voice near Him said, "If You are really God's Son, tell these stones to turn into bread."

The Son of God could easily do that. If He had been afraid that He might die of hunger and that His Father had forgotten Him, He could have turned the hard, gray stones at His feet into nourishing bread. He could put a quick end to His hunger. But He was not afraid, and He was certain that His Father in heaven would not forget Him. No, He would not allow anyone or anything to shake His confidence in His Father.

For 40 years God had taken care of His people Israel in the wilderness. His Word had caused more than enough bread to fall from heaven. Therefore Jesus, the Son of God, knew that He must wait patiently and obediently, listening for God's Word.

Jesus said to satan, "It is written, 'Man shall not live by bread alone but by every word that proceeds from the mouth of God.'"

Satan had failed in his attempt to make Jesus stumble and fall. But he was not yet finished!

16: Satan's defeat

Satan had tried to tempt Jesus, and Jesus had steadfastly resisted. Still, satan was not ready to give up hope.

He took Jesus to the holy city and climbed

to the top of the temple with Him. As Jesus stood on the roof of the temple, He could see the land around Jerusalem. He stood there between heaven and earth, between God and man.

The tempter made a cunning suggestion to Jesus: "If You are God's Son, throw Yourself down from above. It is written that God will command His angels to bear You on their hands so that Your foot will not be dashed against the stones."

That certainly sounded pious! Satan knew the Scriptures. He thought he had hit on just the right approach to overcome Jesus. Jesus had said that He wanted to trust in His Father. Well then, let Him show by this action how much He trusted.

Jesus knew perfectly well that the Father would always preserve Him. When wicked Herod tried to kill Him, the Father had saved Him. When the wild beasts prowled around Him, the Father had protected Him. If He had fallen off the temple, His Father's angels would surely have caught Him before He hit the ground.

But if He threw Himself off the temple, He would be deliberately endangering His life. By seeking danger, He would be *forcing* God to perform a miracle. Was that obedience? Was that trust?

Indeed, He was God's Son, but He did not have to prove that to satan. Satan knew that perfectly well, and he trembled at Jesus.

Calmly Jesus replied, "It is also written, 'You shall not tempt the Lord your God!' " Then He walked to the stairs and climbed down from the temple. Satan's second attack had also been stopped with the help of God's Word.

Satan's foolish hopes still were not extinguished. He went up a high mountain with Jesus and showed Him all the kingdoms of the world in some miraculous manner. He did not let Jesus see all the misery he had caused everywhere. All he showed Jesus was the *glory* of the world's kingdoms.

The Savior had come to earth to save the world. He would do this by giving Himself to the world. He would follow a long, difficult road of scorn and shame, of pain and suffering, in obedience unto death. After that He would be King over the whole world.

Perhaps it could be done in a different way. Perhaps Jesus could become King of the entire world in an instant, without suffering and dying. It all hinged on forgetting God.

Satan whispered, "I will give all of this to You—provided that You bow down and worship me."

Jesus did not hesitate for a moment. He turned around and said, "Get away from Me, satan, for it is also written, 'You shall worship the Lord your God and serve Him only.' "

Satan trembled and fled, leaving the Savior in peace for a while. Now he knew that Jesus was stronger than he was, and that Jesus would someday strip him of his power. Yes, one day satan would have to kneel before Jesus!

The outcome in the barren wilderness was different from the outcome in Paradise. In Paradise *Adam* was driven out, but here *satan* was defeated and driven out. In Paradise satan had caused a curse to fall on Adam and his descendants. But now, out in the wilderness, blessing had the upper hand again. When Jesus was alone, God's angels descended from heaven. They surrounded their Lord and served Him.

One day the whole world would know that Christ had defeated satan and won a great victory for His people.

17: The first disciples

Six weeks had passed since Jesus was baptized in the Jordan. John the Baptist still preached at the Jordan every day, crying out happily to the people that their King had come. He did not stop, for he simply could not be silent about Jesus. From far and near people streamed to the Jordan to listen to Him.

Some men who listened to John did not want to leave him. They stayed with him and became his disciples. They were not scholars, nor were they highly respected among the people. They were simple men with rough, calloused hands—poor fishermen from Galilee. But their hearts were upright and pious and full of yearning for the Savior. They had been baptized by John and had confessed their sins to him. Now they were ready to receive their King. Where could they better wait for Him than here, next to His herald, who already knew Him? They listened eagerly to John whenever he spoke of the Savior. They never tired of hearing about Him.

One day, as John stood by the Jordan preaching, he saw Jesus approaching again. Happily he threw up his hands and pointed to Jesus.

"Look!" he cried out. "Here comes the Lamb of God who takes away the sin of the world. He is the one who I said was coming. I have seen the Spirit descend like a dove out of heaven and rest upon Him. This is the one who baptizes with the Holy Spirit. This is the Son of God!"

All the people who listened to John that day now knew Jesus. He stood among them, listening silently as John spoke. And then He left again, just as quietly as He had come.

The next day, when two of John's disciples were present, Jesus came again. John saw Him walking along the river, as if He were waiting for someone. John looked at his two disciples and said, "There is the Lamb of God!"

He nodded to them. "Go!" he was telling them. "Don't worry about me. It doesn't matter that I am left alone."

The two disciples left their master and followed Jesus. They walked behind Him silently, their hearts pounding with joy. Yet they did not dare address Him.

Suddenly Jesus turned around and looked at them. In a friendly way He asked them, "Whom do you seek?"

They stammered, "Master, where are you staying?"

Their hearts were overflowing. There was so much more that they wanted to ask Him, but they could not find the words.

He answered, "Come along, and you will see."

They went with Him and saw where He lived. From that day on, they stayed with Him. By evening of that unforgettable day, they knew that they would never leave Jesus. They had become His first disciples.

One of the two was named *Andrew*. The other bore the same name as Jesus' forerunner—*John*.

Andrew had a brother named *Simon*, who was also a fisherman. He immediately went to find his brother, for he could not remain silent about his great happiness. "Simon!" he cried out. "We have found the Messiah, the Christ!"

Andrew brought Simon to Jesus. Jesus looked at Simon. He looked right into his heart. It was a heart full of love and zeal, but it was not always strong and faithful. Simon loved nothing more than to serve God, but too often he forgot. Jesus knew

that this man would be His most courageous and fiery disciple when the power of God's Spirit came into his heart.

Jesus said to him, "You are Simon, the son of John, but you shall be called *Peter.*"

Peter! That name meant *rock*. There was no name Simon would rather have borne.

18: Can anything good come from Nazareth?

The next day Jesus and His three disciples made a journey to Galilee. While they were on their way, they met a man who came from Bethsaida, the same city that Andrew and Peter came from. The man's name was Philip.

Jesus said to him, "Follow Me."

Those two words were enough for Philip. He obeyed. Soon he knew he would be following Jesus all his life.

His happiness was so great that it was almost too much for him. He just *had* to let others share in it.

Philip had a friend with whom he had already spoken about the coming Messiah. This friend lived in Cana, a small village in Galilee, near Nazareth. He looked for his friend, because he knew that he was longing for the Savior too. Eagerly Philip told him the good news.

Philip's friend, who was named Nathanael, was in the garden, sitting in the shade of a fig tree. He had sought out a quiet place to pray by himself and to think.

Suddenly he saw Philip standing in front of him. Philip cried out, "We have found the one of whom Moses and the prophets wrote—Jesus, the son of Joseph, from Nazareth!"

Nathanael looked at Philip suspiciously. There was no joy in his eyes. Sadly he shook his head. He would have liked to believe it, but he couldn't. He was an honest, upright man, and he did not seek to hide his disappointment.

"Nazareth?" he asked. "Can anything good come from Nazareth, that despised city?"

What could Philip answer? He didn't know what to say, for he knew very little about Jesus. His joy about Jesus was too great for him to jump into an argument.

"When he meets Jesus," Philip thought to himself, "he'll surely believe, just as I did." Therefore he said, "Come with me, Nathanael. Come and see!" That was the best answer he could think of.

Jesus saw Nathanael coming and said, "Look, here comes an Israelite in whom there is truly no deceit."

"How is it that You knew me?" Nathanael asked, amazed.

Jesus answered, "Even before Philip called you, I saw you sitting under your fig tree."

All the doubt disappeared from Nathanael's heart, and was replaced by joy. Someone who knew all about him in advance—wouldn't that have to be the Messiah? Then He wasn't the son of Joseph, as Philip had said.

Nathanael, deeply moved, bowed before Jesus and cried out, "Master, You are the Son of God, the King of Israel!"

Jesus answered, "You believe simply because I said to you that I saw you when you were sitting under the fig tree. I tell you, you will see much greater things than that."

From then on there were five men following Jesus wherever He went—five simple, true friends. They were the first of Jesus' disciples.

19: Water and wine

There was a wedding in Cana, the little village in Galilee where Nathanael lived. The whole house was filled with music and sounds of joy. A young man and a young woman sat next to each other in their most beautiful clothes. They were happy and thankful, for they were beginning a life together. They had invited their family and friends to join them in the feast. Mary, the mother of Jesus, was there too.

Jesus had not been in Galilee long when this wedding was held. He and His disciples were invited to the wedding. The people here knew Nathanael, but the other disciples were also welcomed heartily, for they were with Jesus.

At this joyful wedding feast, Jesus sat in the midst of the guests and ate and drank with them. Repeatedly Mary's eyes wandered to the figure of her grownup son, who had already left her household to take up God's work. She noticed how humbly He sat at the table among all the guests.

But when the feast was in full swing, it appeared that the joy would suddenly be spoiled. The servants who circulated among the guests pouring wine were huddled together in earnest discussion. The bridegroom, who had been so happy only a few moments before sat staring straight ahead, looking embarrassed.

Mary soon figured out what was wrong. The poor bridegroom! She could certainly sympathize with him. He had been hospitable enough to invite all these people to his feast. Now, the feast was not nearly over and all the wine was gone. The bridegroom couldn't buy any more, for he was not wealthy. What would the guests say if there was such an early, disappointing end to this joyful feast? People would never forget it, and the bridegroom would feel ashamed all his life.

There was only one person who could help, Mary thought. Jesus, her son, was always wise and good. He would know what to do. But He could see for Himself what was wrong. Why didn't He do something about it? Why did He stay sitting where He was?

Mary went over to Jesus. In her concern for the embarrassed bridegroom, she forgot that Jesus was much more than her son. She whispered to Him, "They have no wine!"

But Mary could no longer tell Jesus what to do. Jesus had begun His divine work. Now He had to obey only one person—His Father in heaven. His Father would know when it was time for Jesus to step in and help. No one could come between Jesus and His Father—not even His mother Mary.

Jesus spoke to her in a friendly but determined way, "Woman, why do you bother Me with this matter? My time is not yet come."

"Not yet," Jesus had said. That made Mary feel better. He did want to help. He would not disappoint those who fixed their hopes on Him!

Mary went to the servants and pointed to Jesus. "Do whatever He tells you," she whispered.

There were six water jars near the servants. They were great stone pots; each one had a capacity of about 100 liters. The water in the pots was used to clean the vessels and to wash the guests' hands.

There were *six* water jars, and there were *six* unexpected guests at the feast—Jesus and His five disciples.

The Savior spoke to the servants, "Fill those jars with fresh water."

Immediately they obeyed, for there was plenty of water. They filled the jars to the brim.

Then Jesus said calmly, "Draw some out and take it to the master of the banquet."

The master of the banquet was a friend of the bridegroom. He was in charge of all the arrangements. He showed the guests to their places and tasted the wine before it was served to the guests.

"What is he supposed to do with the water?" thought the servants. They looked at Jesus with puzzled faces. They remembered what Mary told them, so they obeyed.

Quietly, so quietly that no one noticed, a divine miracle had happened. The servants had poured *water* into the stone jars, but they drew out *wine*. Now there was an abundance of wine in the house. Not even a wealthy man would have that much wine on hand.

The master of the feast tasted the wine without knowing where it had come from. He cried out to the bridegroom in amazement, "People usually put their best wine on the table first and save the poorer wine for later. You have kept your best wine back until this moment!"

Soon all the guests knew what had happened. They were awe-struck as they drank the wine, with their amazed eyes fixed on Jesus. Who was this man who had done such a great miracle in their presence?

The disciples knew who He was, and their hearts were bursting with joy. They were delighted to have Jesus as their Master. They no longer had to take John's word that Jesus was indeed the Messiah. With their own eyes, they had witnessed a demonstration of His power.

When they were with John they had fasted and mourned on account of their sins. Now that Jesus was their Master, their sadness and longing were turned into joy, just as the water was turned into wine. As long as the disciples stayed with Jesus, they could celebrate a continuing feast in their hearts.

20: The cleansing of the temple

It was again time for the Passover feast. The people of God came streaming from all directions along sunny roads toward Jerusalem singing songs of praise. Jews even came from such faraway areas as Egypt, Greece and Asia Minor. They entered the city's gates rejoicing and hurried happily through the streets until they reached the temple, their destination. For months they had yearned to be in God's house.

When they passed through the temple gate and stood in the outer court, they found themselves in the midst of a tumult as boisterous as a marketplace. Cattle and sheep stood tied together in rows. Doves fluttered and flapped their wings in baskets. Everywhere merchants noisily extolled their sacrificial animals. Money-changers sat near tables which were piled high with glistening coins. These money-changers were tricky, greedy men who exchanged the heathen money of the visitors for holy Jewish shekels.

The house of God? A holy place? The ground was filthy, and the air was filled with bleating, lowing, shouting and cursing. The racket beat against the temple walls. The pious had to pass through this tumult on their way to worship God.

The people were used to this scene. They were so used to it that they almost thought it was proper. The priests saw what was going on, but did nothing to stop it. After all, the people could hardly be expected to take their own sacrificial animals from home. Here they could buy good, sound animals without a blemish for sacrifices. Wasn't that a worthy service? How could Jews from faraway lands buy animals for sacrifices if there were no money-changers?

Every Jew had to put half a shekel in the offering box every year. The priests could not allow heathen Roman coins with an image of the emperor or of some idol—among the holy temple treasures. Moreover, great profits could be made by selling the sacrificial animals and exchanging money. Therefore the priests were happy to allow the noise of commerce to disturb the peace of God's house. They saw it as a benefit.

Jesus came with the pious people from Galilee for the Passover. He came every year. When He entered the outer court of the temple, He was not surprised at what He saw. It had always been this way. For eighteen years He had watched as His Father's house was profaned. It had always pained Him, but He had suffered in silence. Now, since He had begun His work, He could tolerate it no longer. Now His hour had come.

He knotted a couple of ropes together to make a whip. Holy wrath blazed in His eyes. He walked among the frightened merchants with His whip. He cut a frightening, awesome figure as He stood before them and ordered them out.

Unwillingly they yielded to His amazing power. They grumbled, but no one dared

to disobey. He drove them all out of the temple, along with their sheep and cattle. He overturned the money-changers' tables and scattered their coins over the floor. To those who sold doves He said, "Get all that stuff out of here. You are not to turn My Father's house into a marketplace."

Every last one of them left. They were gripped by a mysterious fear of the man who addressed them as if He were their king.

At last, it was quiet in the outer court of the temple. The people stood staring silently at the mighty stranger, wondering who

He was. He seemed more powerful than anyone they had ever met.

The priests, who had observed the whole scene, approached Him as a group. They were hesitant and afraid, but there was pride and defiance in their eyes. They were not about to buckle under to Him.

What did that Galilean want? Where did He get the nerve to give orders around here? Weren't *they* the masters of the temple?

Indignantly they asked Him, "Who gives You the right to chase those merchants away? If You are a prophet, then give us a sign. What miracle can You perform to show us that You have the right to act this way?"

Jesus looked at them and read the hatred in their eyes. That hatred would grow so great that they would kill Him one day. Did they want to know who He was? Did they want to see a miracle? The greatest miracle possible on earth would happen right in this city. Here He would triumph over death. Here He would arise from the grave three days after He died. Then they would know who He was.

Jesus said to them, "Break down this temple, and within three days I will build it up again."

They did not understand that He was talking about His body. His holy body was also a temple, filled with the Holy Spirit. They looked up at the immense walls of God's house, against which the sun shone brightly, and laughed scornfully. "It took 46 years to build this temple," they said. "You mean to say that You will rebuild it in three days?"

Although Jesus' disciples did not understand these strange words, they did not join the laughter. They knew that every word spoken by their Master was truth. They stored His statement in their minds. Later, when He had arisen from the grave, it came back to them.

The disciples *believed* in Jesus. Many others who had come to Jerusalem for the Passover also believed, for the Savior performed miracles before their eyes. The sick were healed and cripples were helped. No one who came with his suffering to Jesus went away disappointed.

The priests and scribes who had asked for a miracle wanted nothing to do with Jesus. Their proud hearts were already blinded by hatred and unbelief.

21: Nicodemus

One night, when the streets of Jerusalem were dark and quiet, a leader of the Jews went to the house where Jesus was staying. He was a Pharisee named *Nicodemus.*

Nicodemus had witnessed some of Jesus' miracles. After seeing the miracles he had no rest. He did not believe that Jesus was the Messiah, for the Messiah would surely come in a much different way. He would be a mighty king who would chase out the Romans with the sword. He would judge and punish all heathen nations. The Messiah would not be a poor, simple, gentle person. And He would surely not come into the world as a carpenter's son!

Yet, there was something about Jesus that he could not understand. That made Nicodemus uneasy. Nicodemus always wanted to *understand* things, for he was a typical Pharisee. That's why he went to Jesus to talk with Him. He chose to see Jesus at night—perhaps because he was afraid that other Jewish leaders would laugh at him. Perhaps he simply wanted to talk to Jesus under peaceful circumstances.

Jesus was willing to meet with Nicodemus. In the quiet of the night they talked together. The Savior who had come to earth for sinners talked with the rich, prominent rabbi who felt virtuous and upright because he obeyed the law of Moses.

Nicodemus believed that God simply *had* to love him because he was pious. Surely he had earned himself a place in God's Kingdom!

Jesus told him something different. If Nicodemus wanted to enter heaven, he should start over, at the very beginning, with his life. The way he was living was all wrong. He should begin a *new life* and leave his pride behind him. He should become like the simplest of Jesus' disciples, who had confessed their sins to John the Baptist and had been baptized by him. The Holy Spirit would then come into his heart and make him a new man.

Jesus therefore told him, "Truly, truly, I say to you, unless a man is born again, he cannot see God's Kingdom."

Born again? Although he was a scholar, Nicodemus had no idea what Jesus was talking about. Surely he could not become a small child or a baby again. He was already a grown man!

Jesus explained it to him. Nicodemus should become just as humble and pure in heart as a small child. That was only possible through the Holy Spirit.

Nicodemus still didn't understand. But there was no need to understand the part about the Holy Spirit. No human being can understand the work of the Spirit, just as no one knows where the wind comes from and where it goes. Nicodemus should believe, even if he did not understand.

When Israel was punished in the wilderness with poisonous snakes, Moses made a bronze snake, attached it to a pole, and placed it in the midst of the afflicted people. Anyone who looked at the elevated snake in faith was healed of his poisonous snakebite. Anyone who tried to understand the miracle and refused to believe died of his snakebite.

Jesus said, "Just as Moses lifted up the snake in the wilderness, so the Son of man must be lifted up. Everyone who believes in Him will have eternal life."

It was all so strange and wondrous to Nicodemus. Was Jesus, the Son of man, to be lifted up? What did that mean? Would He be fastened to a pole, just like the bronze snake? Would that somehow give eternal life to all who believed in Him? No, Nicodemus did not understand.

If Nicodemus had known how wicked and sinful his heart was, he would surely have understood! He would find it even stranger that God could love him anyway. If only he would believe, eternal joy would be his.

Jesus spoke some glorious words to Nicodemus, "God loved the world so much that He sent His only Son. All who believe in Him will not perish but have eternal life."

It was late night when Nicodemus finally went home through the quiet streets of Jerusalem. Jesus' words were still ringing in his ears: "God loved the world so much . . . ."

It was still dark in Nicodemus's soul—just as dark as the streets of Jerusalem. The first red rays of light were starting to appear on the eastern horizon. A new day was dawning. It would not always be night.

"God loved the world so much that He sent His only Son . . . ."

Had God *already* sent His Son? Who was the Son of God? Could it be Jesus of Nazareth?

"Yes!" said a voice in Nicodemus's heart. "*He* is the one! He is the Messiah!"

One day that voice would grow much stronger and drive away Nicodemus's doubt and unbelief. The light would break through fully in Nicodemus's heart.

When that happened he would come to Jesus openly, in the daylight rather than in darkness. He would come without shame or fear. But that day was still a long time away.

When Jesus was fastened to a pole—the cross—like the bronze snake fashioned by Moses in the wilderness, then Nicodemus would think back to that night. Then, at last, he would believe. Then he would finally understand what Jesus meant when He talked about being born again. The love of God, which he could never understand but only accept, would finally allow him to see the Kingdom.

22: Jews and Samaritans

The sound of bubbling water came from deep in the well. Jesus could hear it clearly. There was cool, fresh water deep in the old well, and Jesus was thirsty.

It was very warm, for it was the middle of the day. Jesus could see the outlines of two mountains—Mount Ebal and Mount Gerizim—against the clear blue sky. One was bare and rocky; the other had some green growth on it. The two crowns looked down on a fruitful valley. In the distance, beyond fruit trees and vineyards, Jesus could see the bright sun beating down on the white houses of the little town of Sychar.

This was the place where Abraham had lived, between the terebinths of Mamre. Jacob had set up his tents here upon returning to Canaan after his years with Laban. Jacob had also dug the well by which Jesus now sat.

Here, by these mountains, Joshua had called the people of Israel together when he was told to say goodbye to them. Now the One on whom all those Old Testament believers had fixed their hopes had come. He sat alone, tired and dusty from the long journey He had made.

The disciples had gone to the city to buy food. They had followed their Master when He left Judea. They were going to Galilee, but the Savior had chosen a route that took

them through the land of the Samaritans. This was something He had to do, He had told them. The disciples didn't understand, but they went along.

There was an age-old hatred between the Jews and the Samaritans living in Palestine. Each looked down on the other from the day they met.

The day had come when the Jews, who had just returned from exile in Babylon started rebuilding their temple. The Samaritans came and offered their help in the rebuilding project. The Jews declined the offer, for they regarded the Samaritans as a heathen people. The Samaritans said that they wanted to serve God, but they went about it in their own way.

That was the beginning. The Samaritans had made rebuilding the temple almost impossible. They had harrassed the Jews night and day, and had even tried to get the Persian authorities to intervene.

The Jews never forgot what the Samaritans had done. Later they destroyed the temple that the Samaritans had built on Mount Gerizim.

The old hatred and contempt still flared up whenever Jews and Samaritans came into contact. Neither side passed up an opportunity to lash out against the other. They cursed and scorned each other and would not receive each other in their homes. There could be no friendship between Jews and Samaritans.

Jesus' disciples were not very happy, then, when their Master told them that they would be passing through Samaritan territory. What was Jesus up to?

23: Living water

Jesus sat by Jacob's well near the Samaritan town of Sychar. He was thirsty. He could see a woman walking down the road. She was coming toward the well, carrying a water jar on her head.

The woman walked past Jesus without greeting Him. She had a small pail attached to a rope. She lowered the pail into the well and used it to fill her jar with water.

She looked at Jesus curiously out of the corner of her eye. Although she could see that He was tired and thirsty, she was going to go home without saying a word to Him.

Suddenly she heard Him saying to her in a friendly voice, "Give Me some water to drink."

She looked at the stranger in amazement. Was she hearing things? The man was a Jew, yet He had spoken to her in a friendly way. A Jew never accepted a drink from an impure vessel belonging to a Samaritan!

No, she would not give Him any water. Instead she asked Him, almost frightened, "How is it that You, a Jew, ask me, a Samaritan woman, for water to drink?"

Jesus answered, "If you knew *who* just asked you for water to drink, you would have asked *Him* for water, and He would have given you living water."

Living water? The woman didn't understand what Jesus was talking about. The warmth in the stranger's eyes melted her hatred and distrust. No, she did not know who He was, but the friendliness and earnestness of His words made her respect Him deeply.

"Sir," the woman said politely, "You have no pail to draw water, and the well is deep. How, then, could You give me living water? Or do You perhaps mean some other kind of water? Is this water, which even our father Jacob, his sons and his flocks drank, not good enough?"

Jesus responded with some wonderful words, "Anyone who drinks of *this* water will thirst again. But whoever drinks of the water that *I* give him will never thirst again."

That was puzzling language. The woman did not know that Jesus was talking about the Holy Spirit, who could quench the thirst of her heart forever. The Spirit can make people happy forever, so that they never desire anything else. All she knew was that that living water must be something very special, something glorious.

She did not quite know what to make of the stranger's words. She laughed as she thought how easy life would be if she had some of that wonderful water. She said, "Sir, give me some of that water, so that I never have to come to this well again and draw water."

Jesus was willing to do so. Although she really knew little of that living water, He was willing to give her some. First she would have to recognize her sins and repent of them. Only then could the Spirit of God come into her heart. Therefore Jesus said to her, "Go home and summon your husband."

The woman acted embarrassed. "I have no husband," she said.

Jesus replied earnestly, "You are right when you say you have no husband. You have had five husbands, and the one you have now is not your husband. In this you have spoken the truth."

The woman turned pale with fright. She felt the eyes of Jesus penetrating the depths of her soul, and she trembled with shame. She knew what a wicked life she had led. Her life was one long story of sin and faithlessness. She was very unhappy and had wanted to change. In her soul was a burning thirst for purity and true joy. She had prayed to God at the ruins of the temple on Mount Gerizim, but it had done no good. It seemed that God simply did not hear her.

Did this amazing man she was talking to know that? He seemed to know everything else about her life. He must be a great prophet, a servant of God!

"Sir," she said, "I see that You are a prophet. Our fathers always prayed on this mountain, but you Jews say that Jerusalem is the place where people must pray . . . ."

Jesus told her that the Father in heaven always listens to prayer, no matter where it comes from—as long as it is *true* prayer arising from an upright heart. She should tell her sins to God and hide nothing from Him. If she would only do that, she would learn that God wanted to love her and had already been waiting for her for a long time.

The woman looked at Jesus in awe. She had never heard anyone talk about God so beautifully. A thought suddenly occurred to her, a thought that made her so happy she trembled. Could this man, who knew all about God and all about people, possibly be the Messiah?

She did not dare ask Him directly. Her heart was pounding. Cautiously she said, "I know that the Messiah is coming, who is called the Christ. When He comes, He will explain everything to us." She waited.

Jesus removed the last of her doubts as He said to her, "*I* am the one of whom you speak."

The joy and surprise were almost too great for her. The Messiah had come, and He had spoken with her! Now there would surely be much better times ahead.

She turned around and hurried away, leaving her water jar behind. She passed the disciples, who were on their way back from the town, where they had bought food.

When she reached the town, she cried out to the people about the good news: "Come with me and see the man who told me everything I ever did. He must be the Christ!"

24: Harvest in Sychar

The people of Sychar were surprised. The woman who had spoken with Jesus at the well was completely changed. They had never seen her so happy.

They followed her down the path to the well, back to the place where Jesus was waiting.

Meanwhile, the disciples had surrounded Jesus and laid the bread they had bought before Him. They had been amazed when they saw Him speaking with a despised Samaritan woman. They did not dare ask what He had said to her. Why wasn't their Master eating? Why did He sit so quietly, obviously happy, staring straight ahead?

"Master, eat some of this food," they urged.

Jesus shook His head. His thoughts were not on eating and drinking. He was thinking only about the work which the Father had given Him to do.

He said to them, "I have food to eat of which you know nothing."

The disciples looked at each other in surprise. "Did someone else bring Him food?" they whispered.

Jesus said, "My food is to do the will of Him who sent Me and to finish His work."

By then He could see the people of Sychar approaching. He had sowed the seed of His Word in the heart of one woman. Now the seed had already sprouted and borne fruit. It was to bear much fruit here in Sychar.

There was a rich harvest of many thankful souls.

"Look!" he said. "The fields are white with the harvest."

Then the disciples saw the Samaritans coming. They watched in amazement as the Samaritans crowded around their Master and listened to every word He spoke. The miracle that no one would have thought possible had happened. There was no anger and no contempt in those eyes fixed on Jesus. An age-old enmity had suddenly vanished. The hatred had been overcome by Jesus' love.

The people even asked Jesus and His disciples to remain with them. He stayed in their city for two days.

By the time He continued His journey to Galilee, there were many who knew what the living water was. They would never thirst again.

They said to the woman who had met Jesus at the well, "First we believed because of what *you* told us. Now we have heard Him ourselves; we know that He is truly the Savior of the world."

The Savior traveled farther through the land, sowing the seed of His holy Word. Wherever He went, He carried on the work to which His Father had called Him.

25: The healing of the official's son

Jesus traveled through the land with His disciples. Wherever He found hearts open to Him, He sowed the seed of His Word. The seed had already sprouted in the hearts of the Samaritans and borne fruit abundantly. How would it go when Jesus reached Galilee, the area where He had grown up?

Things looked so promising! The news of

His coming had raced through the country ahead of Him, and the people came out joyfully to meet Him. Many of them had been present at the Passover feast in Jerusalem and had seen the miracles He had performed there. He had cleansed the temple all by Himself. He had healed the sick.

The people who had witnessed these things did not forget. What a great wonder-worker Jesus of Nazareth was! The stories were told and retold, and they spread from village to village.

People followed Jesus wherever He went. They stared at Him and waited. Surely He would perform miracles in their town too!

People came from all over. They came to *see* Jesus, but they did not come to *listen* to Him. They were much more interested in His *miracles* than in His words. They were not really interested in Jesus Himself.

When the Savior came to Cana where He had changed water into wine, people were waiting to see the miracles they had heard so much about. But Jesus did not perform miracles simply to entertain people.

A seven-hour journey from Cana, a father sat by his child's sickbed. This father and child lived in Capernaum, a city on the Sea of Galilee.

The boy was gasping for breath. His little chest was rising and falling rapidly, and his sunken cheeks were red with fever. The anguished father held the boy's glowing hand and saw death rapidly approaching. The boy did not seem to have more than a day to live. Death would claim him, and the father would no longer have a son.

The father was in despair. He had done what he could, sparing no expense. He was a rich and prominent man—an official who served at the court of King Herod Antipas. But what good did his money and connections do him now? Death does not care

about such things but carries away rich and poor, old and young.

There was no more hope for the child; there was nothing more he could do—that was the worst part of all for this father. His heart was throbbing with pain.

The news that Jesus was now in Galilee had also reached Capernaum. The official heard it, too, at his son's bedside.

His dull eyes began to shine again, and he jumped up. Jesus of Nazareth was the only one who could help in this situation, for He possessed miraculous power. He was in Cana, people said. Cana was a long way from Capernaum, but that didn't matter to the father. He was willing to walk to the ends of the earth if it would save his child.

Once more he bent over his son. If only he could manage it in time! If he could find Jesus quickly and persuade Him to come along at once, there might be hope for the boy yet.

The official hurried out of his house and set out on the winding, rising path that ran into the hill country. He undertook a long, difficult journey. He left his home early in the morning, but the sun was already in the west when he got to Cana.

He found Jesus preaching, surrounded by people. Were those people any better than the unbelieving priests in Jerusalem, who also asked for a miracle before they would believe? The Samaritan woman had not seen a miracle, but she had believed. Her heart was open to the seed of Jesus' Word. But these people's hearts were hard. Their hearts were not fertile soil open to Jesus' Word; they were hard as bedrock, like the rock on which the people built their houses.

As Jesus was preaching, a man forced his way through the crowd. Sweaty, dusty, gasping for breath, he bowed before Jesus. "Sir," he begged, "my child is about to die.

Come with me to my house and save my child."

Again Jesus was confronted by someone asking for a miracle! The people crowded closer. They craned their necks to see better. Eagerly they waited. Now they would surely see a miracle! Even if they had to go all the way to Capernaum, they wanted to be there when that child was healed.

The Savior shook His head sadly. "Unless you people see miraculous signs and wonders, you will not believe," He said.

The official didn't understand what Jesus was getting at. All he could think about was his boy back in Capernaum. How was the boy doing? Was he still alive? He wrung his hands in great anguish and begged, "Sir, please come with me, for my son is dying."

The Savior looked at him carefully. He saw in the official's heart the same faith He had found in the Samaritan woman—the true faith that can live without wonders.

Jesus said to him, "Go home. Your son will live."

Those simple words were enough for the official. He believed. Tears of joy and gratitude filled his eyes. His child would live! His child was saved! He did not doubt Jesus' words for a moment. Rejoicing, he set out for home following the same winding path.

When he approached Capernaum the next day, he found his servants coming out to meet him. "Your son lives!" they cried.

The official asked when the boy began to get better. The servants said, "Yesterday, at about four o'clock, the fever left him."

That was the very same time when Jesus had said, "Your son will live." Even though Jesus was a long way away from the child, He had been able to heal him.

The official and his whole family then knew that Jesus was indeed the Messiah, the Savior who was to come into the world. They all believed in Him.

There had been a miracle, after all. It had taken place in such a way that the curious crowd trailing Jesus had not been able to observe it. Jesus did not want to be regarded as a wonder-worker. He had not come into the world to entertain people. He had come to save sinners.

But the greatest wonder of all, the saving of sinners, could only take place if they were willing to listen to His Word in faith.

26: Isaiah's prophecy fulfilled

While Jesus was in Galilee, He also went to Nazareth, where He had been raised. All the people there knew Him. They saw Him walking through the streets again, just as He used to do. On the sabbath, He joined them in the synagogue, the building where the people came together to praise God and be instructed by the scribes. It was as if nothing had changed.

Some amazing rumors circulated in Nazareth about great things that Jesus had done in other places. "Who would ever have thought such things of this carpenter?" the people asked.

Yes, Mary's son must be someone special. The people of Nazareth agreed on that, and they were proud to say that Jesus came from their town. Some people even claimed that Jesus was the Messiah.

A carpenter's son was the Messiah? No, that was impossible. The Messiah could not be someone who had lived among them, and had worked like any other person. The Messiah would have to be someone much greater than an ordinary man. They would soon know if He were capable of doing

miracles. If He had performed miracles in other places, why not in His own hometown?

He sat among them in the synagogue, humble and still, just as He had sat every sabbath day for years. When it was time to read from the prophets, Jesus stood up and took the scroll from the hand of the servant. He opened the scroll, stood before the lectern, and began looking for the passage to be read. It was deathly still in the synagogue.

Jesus had the book of the prophet Isaiah in His hands. He read, "The Spirit of the Lord is upon Me, for He has anointed Me to bring the gospel to the poor. He has sent Me to proclaim freedom for the prisoners and sight to the blind, to release those who are oppressed and to proclaim the year of the Lord's favor."

Those were beautiful words, and the people understood them. Isaiah was talking about the glorious time that would come when the Messiah appeared. The Messiah would bring the joyful gospel of God's love to the poor and the humble.

The oppressed, those who were unhappy, would then be happy. The Messiah would release all who were held in the grip of sin. That year of the Lord's favor, that glorious year of Jubilee—how long would the people have to wait for it?

Jesus had given the scroll back to the servant. He sat down to speak. That was the custom in the synagogue; one *stood up* to read the Word of God aloud and *sat down* to address the congregation.

All eyes were focused on Jesus. The people were curious. What would He say about this passage that spoke of the Messiah?

The people listened intensely. They were amazed. Never before had they heard anyone speak so simply and beautifully about God's Word.

Where had the carpenter learned that? He spoke about Isaiah's prophecy with great conviction and certainty, almost as if He knew better than Isaiah what the prophecy was about.

Listen! What was He saying now?

"Today this prophecy from Scripture that you just heard has been fulfilled."

What was that supposed to mean? Was it now suddenly the year of the Lord? Had the Messiah come? But who, then, was the Messiah? Was it Jesus, the son of Joseph?

27: Rejection in Nazareth

The people in Nazareth's synagogue were speechless. Jesus, a man who had grown up in their town, had read aloud one of Isaiah's prophecies about the Messiah. Then He told the congregation that the prophecy had been fulfilled right then and there. What did He mean?

People began to whisper to each other. Some scoffed at Jesus. Others grew angry.

"He claims that He's the Messiah! Where does He get such an idea? He's no better than we are! He thinks *He* can bring us all those blessings of which Isaiah speaks. Is *He* going to perform all those miracles? Why doesn't He show us that He's the Messiah? Why doesn't He perform a miracle right now?"

Their hearts were full of pride and unbelief. Jesus could easily see this. He was surprised that the people of Nazareth reacted so strongly. When He began to speak again, there was sadness in His voice. He now spoke harsh words.

The Savior taught them that no prophet had ever been honored in His own land. Long ago, in days of the great drought and famine, where was the prophet Elijah sent by God to find refuge? There were many widows in Israel who could have taken care of him, but he did not go to them. Instead he went to a heathen woman in Zarephath. That woman was blessed by God.

Later, in the days of Elisha, there were many lepers in Israel. Not one of them went to the prophet to ask for healing. But Naaman the Syrian did! On that occasion, too, deliverance bypassed unbelieving Israel and was given to a Gentile instead.

When the people of Nazareth heard this, they jumped up, enraged. Did that carpenter think He could say whatever He pleased here? Were the Gentiles better than the Jews? Did they have more faith than the Jews? Did the carpenter mean to say that when the Messiah came, He would bypass the Jews? Away with Him if that was what He thought!

The people grabbed Jesus and dragged Him out of the synagogue. They pushed Him down the road that led out of the city.

Their wrath grew even greater when they saw Him walking before them silent and defenseless. Had they admired *Him* and been proud of *Him*?

Jesus was a deceiver, a blasphemer who dared to say that He was the Messiah! He must be punished. Never again would He be allowed to chastise them with His words. Never again would they listen to Him!

They pushed Him to the edge of the plateau on which the town was built. They wanted to throw Him over the cliff so that His body would be broken on the rocks.

The Savior could have easily destroyed His enemies in a flash. He could have called down fire from heaven to punish them for their unbelief. Instead, He let Himself be pushed ahead by those rough hands. He was as quiet and submissive as a lamb. Although they scorned and despised Him, He loved His enemies. Giving them time to reconsider, He waited as long as He could before reacting.

At the edge of the cliff He stood still and turned around. It was enough; His hour had not yet come. Suddenly all the people He looked at fell back in fear. Their hands hung limp at their sides. No more threatening, scornful language came from their lips.

Jesus walked right between them like a king, erect and majestic. He left Nazareth unhindered. A mysterious fear stayed behind with the people.

The people had seen a miracle after all—when they did not expect to see one. But the miracle had separated them from the Savior.

28: The Holy One of God

It was the sabbath day in Capernaum. All work had come to a halt. The fishermen's boats were drawn up on the beach. The farmer's plow stood waiting by his furrow. The blacksmith's fire was put out.

On this day of the Lord, the people walked through the silent streets toward the synagogue—fishermen and farmers, merchants and shepherds, rich people and poor people, men and women. A colorful crowd went into the house of prayer.

After they had prayed, Jesus stood up to read the Word of God, just as He had in Nazareth. He also addressed some words to the congregation. But in Capernaum there was no whispered scorn and anger. The people listened reverently, in joyful amazement. What they heard that day was news to them.

The prominent rabbis and scribes had never spoken the way Jesus did. They usually talked about the laws of Moses and other strange laws that they had instituted themselves. Anyone who did not obey those laws would be punished. The scribes and rabbis placed burdens almost too heavy to bear on the people.

This rabbi, the one called Jesus, took those burdens away. He did not threaten the people. He offered comfort to all who were distressed because they had not kept God's law. He spoke of God's love for poor sinners. He brought the joyful news of God's grace for all who repented of the evil they had done. He promised rest to all who were tired and burdened.

The people had never before heard such glorious words. They were deeply moved. It was still in the synagogue. Only the voice of the Savior was heard.

Suddenly another voice began to shriek, frightening the people. It was a harsh, grating voice.

A man had stood up. His eyes were flashing angrily. Apparently he could no longer bear to listen to Jesus' words about love and blessing. Angrily he shook his fist at Jesus. With fear in his voice he cried, "What do You want with us, Jesus of Nazareth? Have You come to destroy us? I know who You are: You are the Holy One of God!"

The people looked fearfully at the man who had so rudely broken the spell in the synagogue. They knew who he was. He was a most unhappy man that no one was able to help. He was possessed by the devil. An evil spirit had penetrated his soul and now had the man completely in its power. The poor man was a slave to the devil that lived within him. That devil tormented him daily.

The evil spirit had spoken out against Jesus. The man himself did not know what he was doing. The evil spirit used his hands and his mouth to do whatever he wanted.

Jesus, who knew what was going on, was not angry with the man. He had compassion on him. Jesus had come to strip satan of his power. That was why this evil spirit was now raging against Him.

Jesus stood up. His voice was strong and authoritative as He said, "Be still and go out of him."

The unclean spirit had no choice but to obey. It seemed as if he were ripped out of the man. He threw the man to the floor and scattered the people, but he did not harm the man further.

The man lay on the floor silently. When he stood up, he seemed to have awakened from a deep, frightening sleep or a nightmare. He looked around in amazement.

His eyes were now clearer than anyone else's and could see more. He was fully healed. He could return to his home as a free and happy man.

The people of Capernaum who had witnessed this miracle looked at Jesus in amazement and awe. "Who is He, then," they asked each other, "that even the evil spirits obey Him?"

They knew the answer: Jesus was the Holy One of God. That was all they talked about from then on. In all the surrounding towns and villages, people were told about Jesus' great power.

29: Healings in Capernaum

Jesus and His disciples left Capernaum's synagogue and went to the home of Simon Peter and Andrew. There was sorrow in the house, for the mother of Peter's wife lay in bed sick. She was in the grip of a burning fever.

When Jesus found out, He went to her bed, took her hand in His, and got her to sit up. At once the fever disappeared.

The woman was able to get out of bed. Feeling strong and fit again, she was soon busy in the house with her usual activities. She prepared food for Peter, Andrew and the guests.

The sabbath was drawing to a close. The tops of the mountains surrounding the Sea of Galilee shone in the evening sunlight, but it was already twilight on the water, in the valley and in the quiet town of Capernaum.

Then the people came down the streets and alleys. They came from all corners of the town toward the house where Jesus was staying. A strange-looking crowd gathered in front of the house.

Blind people were led to the door. Cripples hobbled on crutches. Those who were possessed by demons were tied up and brought to Jesus. People who were too sick or wounded to walk were carried.

All that day, after they heard what had happened in the synagogue, these unfortunates had waited for a chance to go to Jesus. Because they feared the strict scribes and rabbis, they had not dared to go to Jesus for healing while it was still the sabbath.

But now, at last, the sabbath was officially over. Now a pitiable group stood outside the house and cried out for Jesus. All the misery of the town was brought together at His door.

Then Jesus came outside. He moved among the unfortunates and touched them with His special hands. When He touched people, pain went away and sickness fled. Even the cripples were restored. Eyes that had been shut for years were opened. Useless legs suddenly became strong. The dumb began to speak.

When He finally finished this mighty work, a crowd of happy, healthy people stood before Him. Rejoicing, they went

their way. The cripples danced through the streets, the blind walked boldly back to their homes, and the sick carried the stretchers on which they had been borne. This was the great sabbath of their lives, the day of the Lord that they would never forget.

What happened that day in Capernaum had been foretold long before by the prophet Isaiah: "He had taken our diseases upon Himself and borne our pain."

Late that night, when everyone was sleeping, the door of the house where Jesus was staying swung open. The Savior stepped outside alone. He walked through the quiet, dark streets. He walked along the Sea of Galilee, where the waves shimmered softly in the first rays of morning light. He went into the dark hills and sought a desolate place. There, alone between the rocks, Jesus kneeled and prayed.

Above Him the sky grew pale. A bird began to sing.

On the horizon, silent and majestic, the sun slowly rose. A new day was dawning. What new difficulties would it bring?

30: Fishers of men

After the evening in Capernaum in which Jesus had healed so many people, word had spread through the region. Early each morning people began to seek Jesus out, and they followed Him around all day. More and more people came to Him from all villages in the area.

One day, Jesus stood by the Sea of Galilee, near Capernaum. On this day, too, people crowded around Him eagerly. No one wanted to miss a word He said. They almost forced Him into the water.

There were two little boats on the shore near Jesus. The boats had just returned from a fishing expedition on the lake, and the fishermen were busy cleaning their nets. One of the boats belonged to Simon Peter, the other to Zebedee, the father of James and John.

Jesus stepped into Peter's boat. He asked Peter to row a few feet away from the shore and anchor the boat there. Sitting in the boat, He went on speaking to the crowd. Now the people on the shore could calm down, for they could all see Him clearly.

Jesus' voice resounded across the water as He spoke of the eternal blessings for which they all longed. It was completely quiet on the shore. The people were caught by Jesus' words.

He finally finished His address to the people at noon. The sun was high in the sky.

"Now go out to the deep water," Jesus said to Peter. "Put your nets in the water to catch some fish."

Peter was surprised at what he heard. Go

fishing in the middle of the day? That was not a good time to catch fish!

"Master," he answered, "we worked hard all night long, but we caught nothing." He stopped suddenly, ashamed. He looked down and said, "But if You say so, we will set out our nets again."

Peter and Andrew raised the pointed sail. Peter took hold of the rudder and steered the ship to the middle of the lake, where the water looked blackest because of the depth. They set out their nets and waited. There were doubts in Peter's heart. Would they be able to catch fish during the hottest part of the day?

Suddenly he noticed that all the floats attached to the nets had been pulled down. The lines from the ship to the net were taut. He grabbed one of the lines so that he and Andrew could haul in the nets. There was so much movement and splashing that the water seemed to be boiling. He saw the silvery gleam of the fishes' scales as they flopped furiously back and forth.

The net was so full that Peter and Andrew could not lift it out of the water. They tried, and it began to rip.

The fishermen's hearts were pounding with excitement and joy. They shouted and signaled to the fishermen in the other boat. They needed help. They filled both boats so full with fish that they almost sank.

Finally the fishermen stood on the shore again. Amazed, they stared at their enormous catch taken in such a short time.

Peter was so ashamed that he hardly dared raise his eyes to look at Jesus. Had the Master seen all those fish in the depths of the sea? Then His holy eyes would also see the doubt and sin in the dark depths of Peter's heart!

Peter did not feel worthy to be in Jesus' presence. He fell down at His feet and cried

out, "Lord, go away from me, for I am a sinful man."

Jesus laid His hand on Peter's head and said, "Don't be afraid. From now on your job will be to catch people." He said to the other fishermen, "Follow Me, and I will make you fishers of men."

Fishers of men? Were they to go into the world, that great sea of nations, some day to catch people with the Word of God and bring them into His Kingdom? Would they become emissaries of Jesus and talk about the great things Jesus had done?

There was nothing that Peter and the others wanted more! Peter and Andrew, James and John tied up their boats on land. Then they left everything behind—home and family and even all the fish they had just caught—to follow Jesus.

From then on they gave up their work as fishermen. There was a much greater and more glorious calling awaiting them. If Jesus led them in that work, their net would surely be full again.

31: Sinners and apostles

Soon more people wanted to follow Jesus wherever He went. They were all simple people. They were not rich in learning, but they were certainly rich in love. They were better off that way, for love is greater than learning.

Among them was a tax-collector, a contemptible sinner whom the Pharisees would not allow into the synagogue. His name was Levi. Jesus spotted him sitting in his tax office. He knew that this man's heart yearned for the Messiah.

He said to Levi, "Follow Me." Levi obeyed without hesitation. First he held a great banquet at his home and invited all his friends, who were also tax-collectors. Other people came too. The doors of Levi's house were open to all. In the midst of all the guests sat Jesus and His disciples.

When the Pharisees found out, they threw up their hands in amazement and indignation. They would never touch food offered to them by a tax-collector! In fact, they wouldn't even enter a tax-collector's house. They were pure and pious and righteous, and therefore would have nothing to do with sinners.

How could the man who taught the people to come to God dare defile himself by contact with tax-collectors?

Sternly the Pharisees asked Jesus' disciples, "Why does your master eat with tax-collectors and sinners?"

Jesus overheard the question. Calmly He answered, "It is not the healthy who need a doctor but those who are sick. I did not come to call the righteous but sinners, to repentance."

Jesus continued to spend time with tax-collectors and sinners. He belonged with sinners just as a doctor belongs with sick people.

The Pharisees simply did not believe that Jesus was the great heavenly physician who had come into the world to heal the sick and mend sinful hearts. These proud fools did not realize that they, with their hearts of stone, were the sickest people of all. Scoffing at Jesus, they went their way.

That same day something truly miraculous happened: the tax-collector Levi left his house and his money to follow the Savior as a poor wanderer. This actually made him richer than ever.

A little later, Jesus spent an entire night in the mountains alone, praying. After that He picked twelve men from among His followers to be His *disciples*. Seven of the twelve had already been called: Simon Peter and Andrew, James and John, Philip and Nathanael, who was later called Bartholomew, and the tax-collector Levi, who was later called Matthew.

The other five disciples were: Thomas, a quiet, melancholy man; James, the son of Alphaeus; Judas, who was also called Thaddeus; Simon the Zealot, who had once been a member of the Zealots, the group that wanted to force the Romans out of Palestine; and another Judas, known as *Judas Iscariot*.

From that day those twelve men followed Jesus wherever He went. They were friends He could count on when His enemies surrounded Him. Sometimes He sent them out to preach on their own in various villages. One day they would be apostles.

Apostles, ambassadors, fishers of men!
All of them?
Only Jesus knew for sure.

32: The law of love

Jesus went through all of Galilee with
His disciples. He proclaimed the good news
of the Kingdom that was coming, and He
healed the sick.

The news of His miracles went beyond
Israel's borders. More and more people
came to Him. Whenever He approached a
village, they waited along the road and
followed Him in great numbers.

It seemed as if a king were passing
through the land with a great retinue of

followers. He was indeed a king—but a different kind of king from what people expected.

The people knew so little about Jesus!
Not even the disciples knew Him well.
Because the people had received much instruction from the scribes and the
Pharisees, they expected strange things of
Jesus. They had been taught that the
Messiah would establish a new, powerful
kingdom and drive out the Romans. He
would then rule all the nations with
strength. The scribes and Pharisees taught
that anyone who wanted to be a good
citizen of that kingdom would have to live
as they did and keep all the laws they had
made.

Despite all their learning, those wise
scribes really understood nothing of the

new Kingdom that Jesus was bringing.

One day, when there was a great crowd of people surrounding Him again, Jesus decided to speak to His disciples and followers about His Kingdom. He climbed up a mountain and sat on the slope. His twelve disciples were at His feet. The others sought places for themselves on the grass or on a rock. All looked reverently toward Him.

The sun was shining. A bird was singing in the bushes. The voice of the Savior was calm in that peaceful setting.

In a long, beautiful address, Jesus taught His disciples that His Kingdom was not of this earth. It was the *Kingdom of heaven*. It was not a kingdom of power and force but a *kingdom of love.*

There would be no Pharisees among the citizens of that Kingdom. The Kingdom was not for the proud, who felt themselves richly blessed. It was for the poor in spirit, who awaited all things from God.

The Kingdom was not for those who lived carefree, thoughtless lives. It was for those who mourned on account of their sins.

It was not for those who were satisfied with themselves. It was for those who yearned to be delivered from their sins.

The Kingdom was not for cruel, callous people. It was for the merciful.

It was not for deceivers. It was for the upright, the pure of heart.

It was not for troublemakers but for peacemakers.

It was not for those who oppressed and persecuted others. It was for martyrs, those who suffered on God's account. All such people would be blessed as citizens of the Kingdom.

Jesus declared, "Blessed are the poor in spirit, for theirs is the Kingdom of heaven.

"Blessed are those who mourn, for they shall be comforted.

"Blessed are the meek, for they will inherit the earth.

"Blessed are those who hunger and thirst for righteousness, for they shall be satisfied.

"Blessed are the merciful, for they will be shown mercy.

"Blessed are the pure in heart, for they will see God.

"Blessed are the peacemakers, for they will be called sons of God.

"Blessed are those who are persecuted for the sake of righteousness, for theirs is the Kingdom of heaven.

"Blessed are you when people scorn you and persecute you and speak all sorts of evil against you on My account. Rejoice and be glad, for your reward will be great in heaven. So, too, they persecuted the prophets who were before you."

The Kingdom of the Messiah would be a much different kingdom from the one the wise rabbis talked about. The rabbis taught that there were many laws. In the Kingdom of heaven there was only one law, the law of love. That law requires that we love all kinds of people, good and evil, friends and enemies.

The scribes said to the people, "An eye for an eye, and a tooth for a tooth. If someone hits you, hit him back. If someone hates you, you should hate him."

Jesus taught, "You have heard that it is said, 'An eye for an eye, and a tooth for a tooth.' But I say to you, Do not resist evil people. If someone strikes you on one cheek, turn the other cheek to him also.

"You have heard that it was said, 'You shall love your neighbor and hate your enemy.' But I say to you, Love your enemies, and bless those who curse you. Do good to those who hate you, and pray for those who persecute you, so that you may be children of your Father Who is in heaven. Your Father makes the sun shine on the evil and the good, and He makes rain fall on the righteous and the unrighteous.

"If you love those who love you, what reward do you deserve? Don't the tax-collectors do the same? If you greet your brothers, what are you doing out of the ordinary? Don't the pagans also do so?

"You must strive to be perfect, just as your heavenly Father is perfect."

33: The Lord's prayer

When Jesus talked to His disciples and followers, He stressed that they should not look to the Pharisees as examples. When such hypocrites gave alms for the poor, they didn't have compassion on the poor. They only wanted people to see how kind and good they were.

Jesus said, "See to it that when you do good, it is not in order to be seen by others. Give your alms in such a way that the left hand does not know what the right hand is doing."

Jesus also talked about prayer. The Pharisees liked to pray in public, on street corners. People would notice what they were doing there and praise them for it.

That was not true prayer. It was only a stream of words that would not be heard.

Jesus said, "When you pray, go into your inner room, shut the door, and pray to your

Father in secret. Your Father, who sees in secret, will reward you.

"When you pray, do not go on and on and on, the way the pagans do. They believe they will be heard because of all their words. Do not be like them, for your Father knows what you need even before you ask Him."

The disciples were told that they must learn to pray just as a child speaks to his father—simply and full of trust. The Father in heaven would surely hear their prayers, for He loves His people even more than a father loves his children.

Jesus said to them, "Ask, and it will be given to you. Seek, and you will find. Knock, and it will be opened to you. For everyone who asks, receives; everyone who seeks, finds; and to everyone who knocks, the door will be opened.

"Which of you, if his son should ask him for bread, would give him a stone? Or if he asks for a fish, would give him a snake? If you, sinners that you are, know how to give good gifts to your children, how much more will your Father in heaven give good things to those who ask for them in prayer?"

Jesus also taught a prayer to His disciples. It is such a simple prayer that any child can learn it. Yet it is such a full, complete prayer that there is really nothing more to pray for. It is a perfect prayer, the best and most beautiful prayer that anyone has ever prayed: "Our Father in heaven, hallowed be Your name. May Your Kingdom come and Your will be done on earth just as in heaven. Give us this day our daily bread, and forgive us our sins, just as we forgive those who sin against us. And lead us not into temptation but deliver us from evil. For Yours is the Kingdom, and the power, and the glory, forever. Amen."

Jesus also talked about true riches. Many people thought that money and property would make them happy. They sweated and saved to become rich. They wanted to love God too, but money was more important to them.

What anxious lives such people led! Day and night they worried about their earthly treasures. Mammon, the idol of money, was a harsh master.

Levi the tax-collector, one of Jesus' disciples, had given up all his money and property to follow Jesus. Yet now he was richer than ever.

Jesus said, "Do not gather treasures for yourselves here on earth, where moth and rust cause decay and thieves break in and steal. Lay up treasures in heaven instead, where moths and rust will not make them decay, and there are no thieves to break in and steal. Where your treasure is, there will your heart be also.

"No one can serve two masters. He will hate one and love the other, or he will cling to one and despise the other. You cannot serve God *and* Mammon."

34: Seek first the Kingdom

Jesus wanted to say much more to His disciples and followers. He told them that those who wished to serve God alone—and not money—did not have to worry about suffering need. They should simply entrust themselves to God's fatherly care.

"Therefore I say to you, do not be concerned about your life, what you will eat or drink, or what clothes you will wear. Isn't life much more than food, and isn't the body much more than clothing?

"Look at the birds of the air. They do not

sow or reap or store food in barns. Yet your heavenly Father feeds them. Are not you of much greater value than those birds?

"Which of you, by being anxious, can add even a single hour to his life?

"Look at the lilies of the field—how they grow. They neither toil nor spin. Yet I tell you that even Solomon in all his glory was not arrayed like one of these.

"If God so clothes the grass of the field, which is here today and is thrown into the fire tomorrow, won't He also clothe you, you people of little faith? The pagans worry constantly about such things.

"Rest assured that your heavenly Father knows exactly what you need. Seek first His Kingdom and His righteousness, and all these things will also be yours."

If the people would only do as Jesus said. If they would only seek the Kingdom of God, they would not be so busy finding fault with each other and complaining about each other. They noticed every little sin, every little shortcoming in their neighbor. Their own sins and shortcomings, which were often much greater, escaped their attention.

Jesus said, "Why do you worry about the splinter in your brother's eye but pay no attention to the plank in your own eye? How can you say to your brother, 'Let me take the splinter out of your eye' while there is a *plank* in your own eye? You hypocrite! Take the plank out of your own eye first! Then you will be able to see properly to remove the splinter from your brother's eye."

Jesus emphasized to His followers and disciples that they must not be only *hearers* of the Word. They must become *doers* also if they were to be good citizens of the Kingdom. To drive this point home so that they would never forget, He told them a parable.

It was a story of two men. Each man built a house. One was obedient; he went to work just the way he was taught. The other was careless; he did not worry about what he had been taught.

Jesus said, "Everyone who hears My words and acts on them is like the sensible man who built his house on a rock. When a great storm struck, when the rain fell and the wind blew fiercely, the house was not swept away. It was built upon a rock.

"But whoever hears My words and does *not* act on them is like the foolish man who built his house upon the sand. When a great storm struck, when the rain fell and the wind blew fiercely, the house collapsed. It fell with a great crash."

Then Jesus was silent. The people were silent too. They were dumbfounded. Never had they heard anyone speak so beautifully, so truly, and with so much power.

If Jesus could speak about the Kingdom of God in this way, could it be that He was the King? Awe-struck, the people followed Jesus as He walked down the mountain.

35: Unclean! Unclean!

All alone beyond the city wall lived a man with a very serious disease—leprosy. His whole body was covered with large sores that grew deeper and deeper into his flesh. He suffered pain constantly.

The leper was not allowed to come into the city. Whenever someone came near him, he had to cry out and warn that person about his horrible illness: "Unclean! Unclean!"

People stayed out of his way. They circled around him and turned their faces away from him. Not even the members of his family dared to come close to him. They brought him food daily, but they put it some distance away from him, as if he were a dangerous animal. People feared and abhorred him.

The leper spent all his time alone. Healing was out of the question for him. The disease would affect him more and more as time went on. The rest of his life would be one long bout of torment and anguish, ending in death. Wouldn't it be better for him to die than to live a leper's life?

Still, the leper dearly loved life.

One day the news of Jesus' miracles penetrated even the world of this lonely leper. His family told him about the great things Jesus had done. People on the road freely discussed Jesus.

Hope was born anew in the poor leper's heart. He had never heard of a leper being healed, and his *mind* told him it was impossible. But his *heart* told him that it could be done. And his *faith* said that Jesus could do it.

He had no rest. He simply *had* to go to Jesus.

He stumbled along the roadway on his diseased legs. He had nothing to show for himself but his filthy, tattered rags. The bottom part of his face was covered with a piece of cloth. The law required this of lepers whenever they came near normal people. "Unclean! Unclean!" he cried out in his hoarse voice whenever anyone came near.

He was trembling with joy and expectation, for soon this would no longer be necessary. Jesus was going to help him! Or would Jesus turn away from him in disgust, the way other people did?

The leper knew perfectly well that he was not worthy to have Jesus bother with him. But he *had* to go to Jesus, for only Jesus could help him.

He stumbled on, breathless and excited. He looked around him with his half-blinded eyes. Where was Jesus?

Jesus had come down from the mountain where He had been teaching His disciples and followers. He was in the city. The leper found Him there. In his deep yearning for healing, he had dared to go past the city gate and into the town. That was strictly forbidden in the law. He was terrified that he might be chased out before he could find Jesus. He stumbled down the streets as quickly as his weak legs would carry him—anxious, trembling, crying out hoarsely, "Unclean! Unclean!"

The people of the town were frightened at the sight. They kept out of his way, but they also yelled angrily at him. They told him to go away. How did this horrible, frightful man dare to break the law by entering their town?

The leper managed to find Jesus before the people could drive him out of town. He fell at Jesus' feet and worshiped Him. He lay his aching head down on Jesus' feet.

"Sir," he stammered, "if it is Your will, You can make me clean."

Jesus did not shrink back in horror or become angry at the leper. He had just told His disciples to be merciful, and His own heart was full of mercy when He saw this poor leper.

He bent over the leper and stretched out His hand toward him. The people around Him cried out in dismay when they saw what Jesus was doing. Jesus was touching the man! He laid His hand on the leper's oozing, diseased head and said, "It is My will. Be clean!"

At once the man was healed. A stream of

that there was hardly room for Jesus. He
went out to an open field, where droves of
people came to Him to listen and to be
healed.

Sometimes He drew back into the
stillness of the wilderness. There He could
be alone and pray to His Father.

36: The centurion's faith

In Capernaum there lived a man who
was a lot like the leper Jesus had healed. He
was not sick and miserable; he was strong
and healthy. He was a Roman centurion, a
captain over a hundred soldiers.

People did not fear and abhor this centurion; they loved and honored him. Still,
he was a lot like the leper, for he also had
great faith in Jesus' power and regarded
himself as unworthy.

Most Romans despised Jews, but the centurion did not. He loved that oppressed
people. He knew that the pagan idols could
not make him happy. He wanted to serve
the Lord.

When the Jews yearned to build a
synagogue in Capernaum but didn't have
enough money, the centurion had the
synagogue built. The Jews loved him
because of this.

The centurion was a noble man. Other
pagan masters were often harsh and cruel
to their slaves, but *he* was kind to them.
One day, one of his slaves became sick and
hovered on the brink of death. The centurion was as sad as if he were about to lose
a friend.

He had heard about Jesus, for all of
Capernaum was talking about His
miracles. The centurion firmly believed
that Jesus could heal his servant.

energy surged through his body. He felt no
more pain, for he was completely healed.
He threw himself down at Jesus' feet in
gratitude.

Jesus forbade him to tell anyone how he
had been healed. He did not want people to
think of Him as a wonder-worker. People
already followed Him around too much
in hopes of seeing Him perform a miracle.

Jesus sent the man to show the priest that
he had been healed. He would then offer a
sacrifice for his healing. That's what the
laws of Moses demanded.

The man joyfully promised to do just as
Jesus had said. But he had not gone far
before he forgot what Jesus had told him.
His joy was too much for him; his happiness
overcame him. He could not keep his news
to himself; he had to tell others how he had
been healed.

Then even greater numbers of people
came running to Jesus. The city was so full

He did not go to Jesus himself. Because he was a Gentile, he did not regard himself as worthy of contact with Jesus. Instead he sent some friends, who were Jewish elders. They approached Jesus and urged Him to help the centurion.

"He deserves it," they said. "He loves our people and has built a synagogue for us."

Jesus went with them. When the centurion heard that Jesus was coming, he was frightened. Would the mighty prophet come into *his* house, the house of a Gentile? The centurion knew himself better than the Jews knew him; he knew that he was not worthy to receive Jesus!

Quickly he sent other friends with a new message. These friends approached Jesus respectfully and said, "Sir, the centurion has sent us. He says, 'Don't trouble Yourself, for I am not worthy to have You come into my house. Simply say the word, and my servant will be healed. You have the power to command sickness and death, just as I command my soldiers. I tell them to come and go, and to do this and that, and they obey.' "

When Jesus heard that, He was amazed. He knew that many of His own people who had seen His miracles still did not believe. But this Gentile believed that Jesus was the heavenly king whom even sickness and death must obey. He believed without even seeing Jesus!

Jesus turned around and said to the people who were following Him, "I tell you, in Israel I have not yet found such great faith as this. I tell you, there are many who will come from east and west to take their place in the Kingdom of heaven. But the children of the Kingdom will be cast out."

There again, were those strange words that sounded so sad and somber! Would

God forsake His own people and receive the Gentiles as His children?

The people who didn't love and believe in Jesus had no idea what He meant. They shook their heads. Their eyes flashed with anger at the thought that the Jews might be rejected.

Jesus then turned to the messengers and spoke to them in a friendly way, "Go and tell the centurion, 'It shall be as you wish.' " When the messengers arrived at their friend's house, they found that the slave was already recovering.

The leper and the Gentile centurion both expected a great deal of the Savior, but they did not expect too much. Faith can *never* expect too much of the Savior. Those who believe in Jesus are never put to shame.

37: A funeral procession interrupted

The sun shone brightly in the clear blue sky. Sweet-smelling flowers raised their heads towards the sun. But a procession of silent, sorrowful people came from Nain's city gate. Slowly the procession moved down the hill on which the city was built.

Four somber men carried a stretcher.

The body of a young man lay wrapped up on the stretcher. His face was covered. The young man was dead. At the head of the procession the young man's mother walked, weeping and wailing.

The mother was heartbroken. Her husband had died some time before that, leaving her with only one son. That son had worked and sweated for her and was a great comfort to her in her old age. Now that son had been taken away from her. She had once brought her husband to be buried in a dark cave in the side of a hill. On this horrible day she would have to bury her son, within hours of his death.

The woman had nothing left, no husband and no child for her to lavish her love upon. Who would work to put bread on her table? The future looked dark for her; it would be full of sorrow and worries.

She wept as she walked. Her neighbors and friends went with her. They joined her in mourning.

Eyes blurred with tears and heads bowed in anguish, they moved ahead slowly. The sun shone brightly overhead and the fields were in bloom.

There was also a procession coming *up* the hill. It was just as large as the funeral procession. The second procession moved to the side and stood waiting reverently to let the funeral procession through. The tearful mother didn't even see the second procession.

The second procession was made up of Jesus, His disciples and other people who were following Him. They watched sympathetically. They were moved by her heart-rending sobs. The disciples and the other people present, including the people of Nain, could feel only *part* of the mother's great pain. Jesus, who knew her as He knew all human beings and loved her as he loved the whole world, felt her pain as keenly as she did.

The grieving woman did not know that Jesus stood before her. Neither did she know that He had come to Nain for her sake and for the sake of her son. He had set out on this journey while the young man was still alive.

She asked him nothing, preferring instead to pass by in silence.

Jesus said, "Do not weep."

All heads were raised and all eyes were fixed on Jesus. Do not weep? Who could say such a thing in this sorrowful situation?

Jesus walked over to the stretcher. He laid His hand on it, and the bearers stood still. Then He addressed the dead person as if he weren't dead. "Young man, I say to you, get up!"

At once there was movement on the stretcher. The dead person sat up and began to speak haltingly, as if he had just woke up from a deep sleep.

Jesus took him by the hand and led him to his mother. It had all happened so quickly that people didn't quite know if they were dreaming or awake. Paralyzed with fear and amazement, they stared at the young man, who was already locked in his mother's embrace.

The realization finally dawned on them. This was no dream, the mother really had received her son from the clutches of death. They rejoiced and praised God for the great miracle.

"A great prophet has arisen among us!" they cried out to each other. "God has been gracious to His people." Rejoicing, they crowded around Jesus as He walked on and entered Nain's city gate.

The mother and her son walked arm in arm, among the happy people. They looked at each other constantly in love.

The stretcher lay forgotten on the sunny path outside Nain's wall.

38: Lowered to Jesus' feet

Jesus was in Capernaum again. From all sides people streamed toward the house where He was staying. People came from all over the land to listen to Him. Some came out of curiosity, like certain scribes and Pharisees.

The house was full, and the inner court was full. People even crowded around the door in hopes of hearing a word from Jesus' mouth or catching sight of Him for a moment.

Four men came walking toward the house with an unusual burden. They were carrying a bed, a mattress. On that bed lay a sick man.

The sick man lay so still that he seemed to be dead. There was life only in his eyes. Those eyes were shining with joy and hope because he was going to Jesus.

He could never have gotten to Jesus alone. He was paralyzed; he couldn't move any part of his body. The poor man needed

constant attention; he had to be fed like a baby.

Worse than the disease ravaging his body was the unrest in his heart. The burden of his sins weighed on him even more heavily than the burden of his suffering.

Often during long, still nights, he thought about how he, with all his sins, would have to appear before God someday. When he thought about this he was too frightened to sleep. His life was a constant torment for him, and death terrified him. He was sick in both body and soul.

Who could possibly heal him? The people he lived with did their best to care for him, but they couldn't heal him. His friends came to offer him comfort, but their words did him little good.

Only Jesus could help him. That much he knew. His friends thought that too. Now those faithful friends brought him to Jesus. They had already approached the house where Jesus was staying. Everything would turn out well after all!

But people crowded around the door, and no one would step aside for them. There was no way to get through.

What should they do? Bring their friend back to his room, with his hopes dashed? They didn't even consider it. They *had* to bring him to Jesus.

Suddenly a plan occurred to them. They whispered; they pointed; they nodded happily. Sure! That would work!

This house, like every other house, had a stairway leading to the flat roof. The four men carried their friend up the stairs on his bed. They were panting when they reached the roof.

Now they could see into the inner court, which was full of people. They were so close to Jesus that they could hear His voice! They could tell exactly where He was stand-

ing. When they lifted up one of the roof tiles, they saw Him below!

Eagerly they removed more and more tiles. They made a great opening in the roof right above the place where Jesus stood. They tied ropes to the four corners of their friend's bed. With pounding hearts they carefully lowered him through the opening. Slowly he descended; he was lowered to Jesus' feet.

Jesus stopped talking to the people. He saw that the man on the bed had raised his eyes to Jesus in supplication. He looked up and saw four faces looking down at Him, four pairs of hopeful eyes.

Jesus knew exactly what was going on. The life of the paralyzed man was an open book to Him.

He healed the man's soul first. He said to him, "Take courage, My son. Your sins are forgiven."

The scribes who were watching Jesus were shocked. They did not notice that the sick man was beaming with joy. They only heard Jesus' words. They thought to themselves, "How does He dare say such a thing? He is blaspheming! Who but God can forgive sins?"

Jesus was watching them. They could sense that He knew what they were thinking.

Jesus said to them, "What are you thinking about in your hearts? Is it easier to say, 'Your sins are forgiven' or 'Get up and walk'?"

The scribes said nothing. They were confused and embarrassed. Then Jesus showed them He was not a deceiver but that His Word was always truth. He said, "You shall know that the Son of man has power to forgive sins on earth."

He turned to the paralyzed man and said, "Arise, pick up your bed, and go home."

The man who could not move a single part of his body suddenly jumped up. Rejoicing and thanking Jesus, he picked up the bed on which he had lain motionless for so long. He went his way, healthy and strong.

The people stepped aside and let him through this time. Amazed and almost afraid, they stayed out of his way.

The scribes were even more confused and perplexed. They did not dare raise their eyes to Jesus. They had seen how great His power was.

Couldn't someone capable of banishing paralysis in an instant also forgive a person's sins? Wouldn't such a man have to be the Messiah, the Son of God?

No, Jesus was not guilty of blasphemy. The doubting, unbelieving scribes were the guilty ones!

The man who had been healed returned to his house with his friends, carrying his bed on his shoulder. He was so happy that he danced in the streets.

His life was no longer a daily torment. It would be a festival. He was no longer afraid of death, for his sins had been forgiven!

Both his soul and his body had been healed. The Savior had made all things well.

The people of Capernaum said, "We saw something unbelievable today!"

39: A welcome for Jesus

Simon the Pharisee was giving a banquet at his house. The tables in the banquet room were set, and the couches were ready for the guests to recline on. The doors were open wide, and the servants stood prepared to serve the prominent guests.

Simon knew what was expected of him as a host. He showed honor to his guests as they came in. He had their feet washed and their heads anointed with a sweet-smelling oil. He even had their clothes sprinkled with scented water. He embraced his friends one by one and led them inside. He showed each one personally to his place at the table.

Then Jesus arrived. He, too, had been invited by Simon. Actually, that simple rabbi from Nazareth did not belong in such refined company. He should consider Himself fortunate that Simon had bestowed such an honor upon Him.

Simon wanted to have a quiet talk with Jesus sometime; he really did not know what to think of Him. The people said that He was a prophet. Great numbers followed Him. But the scribes declared that He was a deceiver and a false teacher. Simon wanted to form his own opinion of Jesus. Therefore he invited Him to this banquet.

Jesus accepted the invitation, although He knew exactly what Simon was up to. Simon did not make much of a fuss over his simple guest. He received Jesus in a cool, distant manner. He did not summon a servant to see to Jesus' needs. Instead Simon led Jesus into the banquet room just as He was, hot and dusty from His journey. He pointed to a place at the far end of the table and left Jesus alone. He didn't want that carpenter's son to think He was just as important as the other guests.

The banquet began. The guests lay around the table on long couches. They leaned on one arm and stretched their legs behind them.

There was Jesus among all these rich, proud people. He was just as calm and friendly as He had been when invited to eat with the sinners and tax-collectors in Matthew's house. He knew what the other guests thought of Him, but He said nothing. Their proud contempt and the insulting reception of His host did not hurt His feelings.

The platters were passed. Wine was poured into the cups. Conversations were struck up.

Poor people from the street crowded together at the open door to see the wealth and luxury inside the home of this wealthy man. That was the custom in those days: the poor people were allowed to gather at the open door.

Then something happened that shocked the guests and onlookers. A woman pressed through the crowd at the door and walked into the banquet room. She fell down at Jesus' feet and wept.

No one knew what this meant, but Jesus understood. He knew that this woman was deeply unhappy because of the sin in her life. She was a sinner whom everyone looked down on and hated. She had heard Jesus preach in the city, and she yearned for Him. She believed that only He could save her. Therefore she had bought myrrh for Him and some expensive oil in an alabaster jar. When she heard that Jesus was a guest in this beautiful house, she came inside. She felt she simply had to get to Him quickly. Now she had found Him, and now she could speak to Him about what was in her heart.

Her tears dripped on His feet. She wanted to dry them, but she had no towel. Therefore she dried Jesus' feet with her long hair. She kissed His feet repeatedly and anointed them with the oil she had brought.

That way she showed her repentance and love. At the same time, she demonstrated her faith in the Savior.

Such was the welcome Jesus received at Simon's house.

40: Two debtors

Jesus was a guest at Simon's banquet. The banquet was interrupted when a woman came in unexpectedly and fell down at His feet. She wet His feet with her

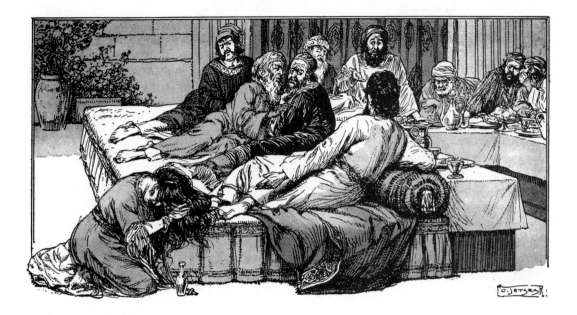

tears, dried them with her hair, and anointed them with oil.

Simon and the other Pharisees watched indignantly, for they knew who the woman was. Whenever they saw her on the street, they crossed to the other side to stay out of her way. Simon would not want that sinful woman touching *his* feet. He would have kicked her and chased her away! But Jesus did nothing. He didn't even seem to realize what a horrible sinner the woman was. Surely He was not a prophet after all!

Jesus knew what proud thoughts were running through Simon's mind. "Simon," He called out, "I have something to say to you."

The Pharisee answered proudly, "Say it, Master."

Jesus told the proud Pharisee a story. He said, "There were two men who owed money to a certain moneylender. One owed him 500 silver coins, and the other owed 50. When they could not pay, he canceled the debts of both these debtors. Which of the two loved him more?"

Simon knew the answer. That wasn't hard. He said, "I suppose the one with the bigger debt."

Jesus said, "That's right."

Then it became apparent that this was not an ordinary story. This was a *parable*, a story with a meaning.

Jesus turned to the woman who still lay at His feet. In a friendly way He said to Simon, "Do you see this woman? I have come as a guest in *your* house, but you did not give Me anything with which to wash My feet. She has now washed My feet with her tears and dried them with her hair. You did not kiss Me, but she has not stopped kissing My feet since she came in. You did not anoint My head with oil, but she has anointed my feet with myrrh."

The Pharisee looked down in deep shame. Jesus continued, "Therefore I say to you that her many sins are forgiven, for she has shown much love. But those who are forgiven little show little love."

Yes, the Pharisee had shown Jesus very little love. Little was forgiven him. Was that because he had hardly sinned at all? Or did he still have a great debt to pay?

Simon was the debtor who owed 50 silver coins. In other words, he was a sinner. That was what Jesus was getting at. Simon, too, had to ask for forgiveness.

The woman had done just that. She was the debtor who owed 500 silver coins. Her debt was great, but so were her faith and love. Therefore Jesus said to her, "Your sins are forgiven."

That was the most glorious thing anyone could ever say to this woman. Joy as she had never known before came into her heart. She continued to lie in adoration at Jesus' feet.

There was anger and indignation in the guests' eyes. "Who is this man," they said to themselves, "that He also forgives sins? Only God can do that!"

Jesus said to the woman, "Your faith has made you whole. Go in peace."

The woman went away overjoyed. She had become a different woman. Now she could set out on a new, pure life. She was poor when she came to Jesus. Now she was rich.

The other debtor stayed at the same table with Jesus. Now he knew who Jesus was: He was more than a prophet!

What friendly, gentle treatment Jesus had given Simon! If only the rich Pharisee would now see how poor he really was! If only he would see his great debt!

41: Bethesda

Bethesda was a pool close to the Sheep Gate in Jerusalem. Five porticos had been built around it. The name of the pool meant *house of mercy*.

It looked like an ordinary pool with quiet, cloudy water. Sometimes, suddenly, water would come up, surging and whirling, from the mysterious spring that fed it. After the turbulence, the water would soon be calm again. It would swirl and splash for a few minutes, and then the surface would be completely still once more. But during those few minutes of motion, the water had a miraculous power to heal. Anyone who could get into the water to bathe while it was turbulent would be healed, regardless of the disease he might be suffering from.

"An angel sometimes descends to stir up the water," people said reverently. Many people lay in the open porticos waiting for the coming of the merciful healing angel. Some were blind; some were crippled; some were lame. All sorts of diseases were represented. People waited and hoped, sometimes holding their breath to listen more intently. They didn't want to miss the angel's coming. Day and night they waited expectantly.

As soon as the mysterious gurgles from the depths were heard, the horrible race to the pool began from five directions. Some sick people could hobble along on their own; others crawled on hands and feet; the blind stumbled ahead with their hands thrust out before them; the lame were sometimes carried by their friends. Every sick person there wanted to be first into the pool.

When that happened, Bethesda no longer looked like a house of mercy. People elbowed each other and pushed each other aside in their eagerness to be first. Each one thought only of himself. Most got into the pool too late. A few might leave the pool to begin a new, healthy life. The rest would have to lie down again with a sigh and wait for the next time.

At such times many would give up hope and become indifferent to everything around them. When asked if they still wanted to be healed, they might not even answer.

Among all these unfortunate people was a man who had been sick for 38 years. He had lived a wicked life and ruined his health.

Now he was lame. He could hardly move as he lay waiting by the pool. No one paid attention to him anymore; he had no friends or relatives to help him. He was always one of the last people to reach the pool when the water became turbulent.

For 38 years he had suffered his punishment. What penance he had to do for his sin! He had almost become an old man in that time. But still he had not completely given up hope. He continued to hope that God would be gracious to him one day.

It was the sabbath day, and there was a festival in Jerusalem. A large, happy crowd surged through the streets and offered sacrifices in the temple. There was music and singing everywhere.

It was busy in Bethesda too. Friends and relatives of the sick people had come to visit them.

No one came to visit the lame man. He lay there just as lonely as he was any other day. Of all the people who had come to Jerusalem for the festival, who would think of him? They had come to the festival looking for *joy!*

Still, that day was different, for someone had come to seek that which was lost.

A man walked quietly along the pool and stopped at the lame man's bed. The lame man was already moved by the way the stranger looked at him. In the 38 years of his illness, no one had shown him compassion. A love and mercy he had never

before encountered shone in the stranger's eyes.

"Do you want to be healed?" the stranger asked.

Now the lame man's eyes were shining. He sensed that the stranger was not asking the question from curiosity, for his voice and eyes were full of truth and goodness.

The lame man felt he had to speak to this stranger very respectfully. Still, there was sorrow reflected in his answer.

"Sir, I have no one to throw me into the pool when the water starts to move," he said. "While I am working my way to the water, others go in before me."

The stranger said, "Arise, pick up your bed, and go your way."

Those words were a command.

Who could possibly resist that voice? Who could say no when such eyes looked down on him in love?

The sick man didn't hesitate a moment.

He didn't say, "I can't walk! Surely you can see that." He simply stood up and picked up his bed.

Only then did he realize what a great divine miracle had happened in his life. His legs supported him again as he walked among the sick people and away from the pool! No, he wasn't dreaming. His legs, once useless, would continue to support him as he entered a life of health and freedom!

42: Enemies of Jesus

After 38 years of waiting and hoping, the lame man by Bethesda's pool suddenly was able to walk again. Where was that stranger who had healed him, who had saved him from his plight? He was gone. He had disappeared as silently as he had come, without waiting for a word of thanks.

The man's heart overflowed with gratitude. He went outside. The sun beamed down on him, and the wind caressed his skin. Delirious with joy he put his bed on his shoulder and walked through the city gate and down the city streets. All around him were people who had come for the joyful festival. He was so happy that he laughed and cried.

Suddenly someone stopped him. A group of well-dressed men, scribes and Pharisees, stood before him. They looked at him sternly, with frowns on their faces.

"It's the sabbath today," they said to him indignantly. "You're not allowed to carry your bed today. Shame on you, you godless man! You're working on the sabbath!"

The poor man was both frightened and amazed. Was it really the sabbath day? Yes, come to think of it, it was. But for him it was much more than the sabbath. For him it was the day of deliverance, the day of God's mercy! Was it wrong for him to walk and carry his bed? It felt so glorious to be able to walk and carry something! The stranger who healed him had told him to carry his bed. Surely it wasn't wrong!

Happiness beamed from the man's face as he answered, "The stranger who healed me said, 'Arise, pick up your bed, and go your way.' "

That he had just been healed made no difference to the scribes. They had caught him carrying his bed on the sabbath day! The frowns on their proud faces deepened. They nudged each other.

"Who is this man who said to you, 'Arise, pick up your bed, and go your way'?" they asked sternly.

The man felt sad that he couldn't tell them. Quickly he went his way, for he couldn't stand to look at those sour faces on this glorious day.

He put his bed down finally, for he had to go to the temple. If there were one person in Jerusalem who should be in the temple, surely he was that person.

Joyfully he entered the outer court. He gave thanks as he bowed before God. When he straightened up again, who was standing before him? Could it be? It had to be! He would never forget those eyes and that voice as long as he lived!

There stood the stranger who had healed him. The stranger said, "Now that you have been healed, sin no more, so that nothing more will happen to you."

Those were stern, sober words, but the stranger did not speak like the scribes and Pharisees. There was love in that sternness. The man bowed deeply before the stranger who had healed him.

"Does he know all about my life?" he asked

himself in amazement. "Who is he?"

Suddenly it dawned on him. All the people in Jerusalem knew about this man. His name was Jesus.

Jesus. Savior. What a beautiful name! It was the finest and sweetest name imaginable.

The man hurried back to the scribes who had stopped him when he was carrying his bed. He wanted those scribes to know about Jesus the Savior too.

"Jesus!" he said respectfully, his eyes beaming. "Jesus healed me!"

The scribes and Pharisees hated that name. Their eyes glowed with wrath. They already suspected that He was the one. Now they were sure. Jesus had dishonored the sabbath and led others to do the same.

The scribes and Pharisees went to Jesus and denounced Him for violating the sabbath. They used sharp, angry words. But Jesus looked at them calmly and said, "My Father is working still, and I am working too."

What fools! Didn't they know that even on the sabbath the Father in heaven is busy watching over them? Did they think they could give orders to Jesus, the Son of God?

The learned rabbis couldn't win when they matched wits with Jesus, for He was blessed with divine wisdom. Finally they gave up and slipped away. But their hatred of Jesus had grown even greater.

"He says that God is His Father," they said indignantly. "He puts Himself on the same level as God. He breaks the sabbath and He blasphemes God!"

From then on they watched Jesus closely for an opportunity to get back at Him. They would have killed Him if they could get away with it, for He was their enemy!

Their *enemy*? If only they knew how much He really loved them!

43: Hardened hearts

The leading Jews hated Jesus more and more as time passed.

If there had been just the smallest amount of love for God in their hearts, that would never have happened. But they honored God with their *lips* only. In their hearts they stayed far away from Him.

Those leaders only loved themselves. All their piety served to make them honored and praised among men.

As they recited their long prayers, they said to themselves, "Do the people notice how *pious* we are?" And as they made a great show of giving alms, they wondered, "Do the people notice how *merciful* we are?"

When the sabbath came, they gave instructions to the people in the synagogue. They taught them more and more new laws. The people had to live by many commandments and rules. Did the people honor the rabbis enough for all their learning and virtue?

The people really did respect these pious, stern, well-dressed rabbis. Willingly they shouldered the heavy burdens laid upon them. The poor, simple people did not know what awful hypocrites the rabbis were.

When Jesus came, things began to change. Jesus did not teach the people harsh laws. He spoke of God's love and mercy, of faith and the forgiveness of sins.

He did not revere the scribes and Pharisees. He warned the people about them. He said openly that they were pretenders, hypocrites who were only interested in winning the praise of men.

Many people followed Jesus. They stood in awe of the simple preacher from despised

Nazareth. If that situation continued the day might come when no one would listen to the scribes and Pharisees!

When the rabbis thought about this, their hearts burned with jealousy and hatred. They were the bosses, and they wanted to remain in charge. They were so proud that they could not live without people honoring them.

They began to make wicked plans designed to pull the people away from Jesus. They wanted the people to listen to *them* and no one else.

They were blinded by their hatred. Nicodemus, who was also a Pharisee, had been amazed at the wonders Jesus performed. These rabbis were not struck by such signs.

Nicodemus had gone to Jesus during the night to learn from Him. These rabbis were not interested in learning from Jesus. The voice of their conscience may have warned them that they were doing wrong, but they silenced that voice. They hardened their hearts. They deliberately closed their hearts to God and to His Word.

There was room in their hearts for only wickedness and hatred. From then on, the rabbis were ready to try anything. No plan was too wicked or corrupt for them. They wanted only to do something about Jesus.

44: The sabbath is made for man

The rabbis watched Jesus daily. They hoped He would do something wrong. They were determined to catch Him in the act. Then they would tell the people about it so that the people would not listen to Him any longer.

They watched Jesus for a long time, but in vain. He did nothing wrong. No curse or foul language came from His lips. Everything He did was holy and good.

Finally, on a certain sabbath day, they observed something. They caught Jesus in the act!

The sabbath was the day of the Lord. God had given that day to people as a day of joy. The rabbis had made it a day of unhappiness, a day of heavy burdens.

They had made numerous foolish laws about the sabbath. Everyone was supposed to observe those laws. No one was allowed to wear a hat with a rim of more than three centimeters. He would be working by carrying a burden. No one was to wear shoes with nails. That, too, was carrying a burden. No one was to pick any fruit. That was harvesting. No one was allowed to carry a needle. A needle was a tool.

Those pious scribes even debated whether one were allowed to eat an egg that had been laid on the sabbath! They had made a day of rest into a day of cares with special burdens of its own, a day that brought sorrow. They had turned the blessing of the sabbath into a curse!

One sabbath day, Jesus and His disciples were walking along a grain field. The grain was almost ripe. The heavy ears with their sweet, tender kernels bent the stalks.

The disciples were hungry. They plucked some of the ears of grain. They crushed them between their hands, blew away the chaff, and ate the kernels. The owner of the field didn't mind. In those days, anyone who passed a field was allowed to help himself to a bit of the harvest if he was hungry. That's what the law of Moses said.

The rabbis had their own laws that they had added to Moses' laws. To pluck ears was a form of *harvesting*, and to crush the ears between one's hands was really

threshing. Jesus' disciples were working on the sabbath!

The rabbis went to Jesus and acted indignant. A wicked joy was in their hearts. "Look!" they said sternly. "Your disciples are doing something that's not permitted on the sabbath."

Jesus defended His disciples. He asked, "Have you never read what David did when he suffered hunger and want while fleeing from Saul? Don't you remember how he went into the house of God and ate the showbread that only the priests are allowed to eat? Don't you realize that even the priests work on the sabbath? They offer sacrifices in the temple. Yet we don't accuse them of violating the sabbath!"

The rabbis said nothing so Jesus continued. "The sabbath is made for man—not man for the sabbath. The Son of man is lord over the sabbath!"

The wise rabbis did not know how to answer Jesus. They were bitter when Jesus and His disciples went their way. But they did not give up the battle. They followed Jesus wherever He went. Soon they saw something else that gave them a chance to speak evil of Jesus. Again it happened on a sabbath.

Jesus had gone into the synagogue to talk to the people. Among the people listening to Him was a man with a withered hand.

The Pharisees watched this man closely. Would Jesus heal him? If He did, He would be violating the sabbath!

Jesus knew what wicked thoughts they were thinking. Suddenly He told the man to stand up. The man obeyed, and Jesus asked the Pharisees, "Is it permitted to do good on the sabbath? Or is one only allowed to do evil on the sabbath? Is it permitted to heal a man? Or must we let him go on suffering?"

He looked straight at them. He looked right into their eyes. They were silent.

Jesus continued, "Who among you, if his sheep were to fall into a pit on the sabbath day, would not pull it out? Isn't a human being of much greater value than any sheep?"

Again He looked straight at the rabbis, with both anger and sadness in His eyes. He was angry because the rabbis were false, and sad because their hearts were hard.

They were still silent. Jesus said to the man with the withered hand, "Extend your hand."

The man obeyed. He stuck his arm straight out. The hand was suddenly healed. It was just like his other hand.

The people who were watching were amazed. They looked at Jesus in awe. The rabbis were beside themselves with anger. Jesus had challenged them. He had deliberately humiliated them while all the people watched.

That day they began making new plans. They wanted to kill Jesus. They would accept help from anyone. They even went to the Herodians, the followers of the godless king Herod Antipas for help.

It was the sabbath day, a day to serve God and think about Him. But the rabbis were serving satan, for they were thinking about murder.

Who was violating the sabbath, Jesus or the rabbis?

45: Jesus and Beelzebul

The rabbis hated Jesus so much that they would stop at nothing. It no longer mattered to them how rotten they were inside. After all, the people didn't know what really lived in their hearts. As long as the *hands* of the rabbis were clean, the people would not protest. As long as they *looked* pious and religious, they could safely *be* full of evil.

The rabbis made sure that their hands were always clean. They washed them many times each day—always before and after they ate. They complained that Jesus' disciples did not follow their example. Jesus said, "What defiles a person is not what goes *into* his mouth but what comes *out of* his mouth. A person is defiled by the bad words and wicked thoughts that issue from his heart."

The rabbis said that Jesus was a glutton and a drunkard, a friend of tax-collectors and sinners. They believed they were much better than Jesus, for they lived by strict laws. They wanted to make the people bend again under the heavy burden of their laws.

Jesus said, "Come to Me, all you who are weary and burdened, and I will give you rest. Take My yoke upon yourselves and learn from Me, for I am gentle and lowly of heart. You will find rest for your souls, for My yoke is easy and My burden is light."

Again and again, when the rabbis came to Jesus to argue with Him, they were silenced by His calmness and His wisdom. They wanted to put Him to shame before the people, but *they* were put to shame each time instead.

Finally they slandered Jesus in a horrible manner. One day when He stood in a house preaching, a miserable, unhappy creature was brought to Him. The man was blind, unable to speak, and possessed by an evil spirit. Jesus healed him in an instant, using His divine power. The man came to his senses; he could see again, and he could speak.

The people who observed this miracle were amazed. They shouted in delight, "This man must be the Son of David! Jesus must be the Messiah!"

The Pharisees, pale with fear and anger, jumped up and screamed, "He is not the Son of David! He is a deceiver, and His power is of the devil. He has driven out the evil spirit with the help of Beelzebul, the chief of all evil spirits."

That was the most horrible accusation they could possibly make. That accusation was such an awful, frightful sin that it could only have arisen in their wicked hearts, which had been hardening for so long.

Jesus knew what severe punishment they deserved for those horrible words. He was very sad for them. He warned them that they would have to render account to God one day for what they had said.

Then Jesus proceeded with His divine work.

46: My mother and My brothers

As Jesus went about His work, He wouldn't even let His own family stand in the way. One day His mother and His brothers asked to see Him. They had heard in Nazareth how the Jews hated Jesus and fought Him every step of the way. They had come out of concern and wanted to take Him back home with them. They thought they had to protect Him.

They did not take His work very seriously, then. His own brothers didn't even believe in Him. Mary, His mother, had already been worried about Him years before, when He stayed behind at the temple for the first time as a boy of twelve. At that time Jesus had asked her, "Don't you know that I must be busy with the things of My Father?" Now she was concerned again. She was afraid things weren't going very well with her oldest son. She was convinced that He was not supposed to follow a path that led to so much hatred and danger.

Jesus' mother and brothers were standing at the edge of a great mass of people who crowded around Jesus. Because they couldn't get through, they sent Him a message that they wanted to talk to Him.

Someone said to Jesus, "Look! Your mother and Your brothers are out there in the crowd."

Jesus knew why they had come. Although they meant well, they were working against Him as He sought to do the will of His Father in heaven.

He knew He had to obey His heavenly Father more than His mother on earth. If His brothers did not believe in Him, they did not belong with Him.

He answered, "Who is My mother, and who are My brothers?"

Stretching out His hand towards His disciples, He said, "These people are My mother and My brothers! Whoever does the will of My Father who is in heaven is My mother and sister and brother."

The disciples were the ones who belonged with Jesus! They did not hinder Him in His work; they helped Him. While the rabbis slandered Him and tried to stir up the people against Him, He went through the land, blessing people, helping them, and preaching the good news of God's grace for all who were willing to listen.

Jesus knew that the Pharisees wanted to kill Him, but He did not let that stop Him. His work was not finished; His time had not yet come.

When the time finally came, He still would not be afraid. He would do the will of His Father even to the point of death. It might *appear* as if the rabbis had won the battle, but after three days He would arise from the grave. He knew all this in advance.

One day the Pharisees said to Him, "Give us a sign that You are the Messiah."

He answered, "A wicked generation demands a sign, but it will receive no other sign than the sign of Jonah the prophet. Just as Jonah was three days and nights in the belly of a huge fish, so the Son of man will be in the heart of the earth for three days and nights."

At the time no one, not even the disciples, understood what Jesus meant. They simply *could not* understand it yet. Their Master's life would be so different from what they expected.

Still, they remained faithful to Him, for they believed in Him. While enemies watched Jesus carefully wherever He went, His disciples surrounded Him with their love.

The love of those disciples must have been a glorious comfort to the Savior. And yet—Jesus was the only one who knew this from the beginning—there was one disciple who did not truly love Jesus. That disciple would betray Him some day.

47: The parable of the sower

Jesus was sitting on a ship tied up by the shore of the Sea of Galilee. On the bank before Him stood people who listened carefully to every word He said. All sorts of people were present—farmers and fishermen and merchants, men and women, faithful disciples and rabbis who hated Jesus.

Jesus looked into all the eyes that were focused on Him—cold, indifferent eyes, curious eyes, eyes full of concern, eyes full of love and longing.

He knew what was in the hearts of the people. He saw the enmity and hatred in some hearts, in others He saw faith and a longing for God. He knew which people wanted to receive His Word with reverence.

He had so often spoken to all these people about the Kingdom of heaven. He had addressed them clearly and simply. They may all have believed that they understood Him. But the rabbis argued with Him about what He had said. Other unbelievers also made fun of Him thoughtlessly. They had really understood nothing of what He had said.

They had ears to *hear* what He said, but their hearts were closed, for they had no faith. Therefore they did not understand Him. What poor souls they were!

If only they knew the truth about them-

selves. If only they knew how poor they really were, perhaps they would open their hearts.

That's why the Savior spoke to them in a different way this time. He told them a story. It was not an ordinary story; it was a parable.

He said, "One day there was a sower who went out to sow. Some of the seed he sowed fell on the path. It lay on the hard, compact earth, but it could not sprout. The birds came along and ate it. It was lost.

"The rest of the seed fell in the field. It did not all fall in good soil. In some places the ground was not suitable. There only a thin layer of topsoil covered the bedrock.

The seeds that fell there sprouted quickly. Tiny plants soon sprang up. When the hot sun beat down, the thin layer of earth quickly dried up and the small plants perished. Their roots could not receive any nourishment from the rock. That seed, too, was lost.

"Some of the seed fell among thorns. It sprouted and started to grow, but the thorns and other weeds grew faster, strangling the young plants. Again, the seed was lost.

"But some of the seed fell in good, fruitful earth. It was hidden in the dark furrows where the birds could not find it and eat it. The little plants sent their roots deep into the soft, moist ground, and the hot sun did not make them wither. This seed was not lost. Instead it grew and blossomed and bore fruit richly. Some seed multiplied a hundredfold, some sixtyfold, and some thirtyfold.

"He who has ears to hear, let him hear," said Jesus, bringing His parable to an end.

48: Richer and poorer

Jesus had just told the parable of the sower to the people gathered around Him as He sat in a little boat. When He was finished, He simply looked at the people silently. The people looked back at Him—cool and curious, concerned and respectful.

Jesus said nothing. He was waiting. Like the sower in the parable, He had sowed His seed, the seed of His Word. Now He was waiting to see if it would sprout and take root.

Jesus had told a simple story. The people had all seen a sower at work at one time or other, and they knew that the seed didn't all land in the right place.

The people were well aware that Jesus had not just told them an ordinary story. There was a *meaning* to His story. Jesus wanted to teach them something, but they did not know what.

There they stood. Suddenly they all realized how little they really understood of the Kingdom of God. They realized how poor they really were.

Anyone who truly yearned for God would ponder this story and ask Jesus what it meant. Soon the first people came.

Not all who had heard the parable came. The unbelievers, the enemies of God, and the indifferent people stayed away.

Only a small group of people stood before Jesus asking for an explanation. Jesus could read respect and love in all the eyes now fixed on Him. All those hearts yearned to hear more from Jesus.

Jesus now explained His parable to His disciples and friends.

The seed is the Word of God. The sower is anyone who speaks to people about the Kingdom of God.

Jesus was a sower, as the disciples would see for themselves. The seed is good, but it cannot sprout just anywhere. The hearts that are to receive the seed are not always fruitful earth.

Some hearts are hardened and closed, just like a pathway of hard, compact soil. People with such hearts hear the Word but do not understand it and a little later forget it. Satan takes it away from them.

Some other hearts may *look* fruitful, but from within they are hard and unrepentant. The people listen curiously, and they're happy when they hear about God's Kingdom. But they are people of the moment. The seed cannot grow in their hearts for long. As soon as things become difficult, they show that they have little trust. They forget God. The plant of their faith, which had just started to grow, dies. It is like a little plant which dies when the noonday sun begins to beat down on it because it is rooted in only a thin layer of topsoil.

Some other hearts are full of worldly concerns and desires. They are like fields full of weeds.

Such people hear the Word and think about it, but they think even more about themselves. They want to love God. They are also eager to get rich, and they have many other wishes! They do not want to give themselves *completely* to God. They become so busy with other things that soon there is no time left for God. They forget about Him. The seed of God's Word is strangled by their worldly concerns.

In all these people, the seed sown by the sower is lost.

There are also hearts that are fruitful fields. The people hear the Word and understand it. When things become difficult for them, they trust in God. In love they surrender their lives to Him. They have only one great desire—to live close to Him always and be His children forever. They serve the Lord in love and gratitude. They are like the seeds that bear a rich harvest, some thirtyfold, some sixtyfold, some a hundredfold.

Jesus explained all this to His friends and disciples. They had come to Him in faith to ask for more wisdom.

As they learned more and more about the Kingdom of God, they became richer and richer. Those who did not ask what He meant, because they had no faith, became poorer and poorer.

Jesus said, "Those who have will be given more. As for those who have nothing, even what they think they have will be taken away."

49: Good seed and bad

A man once sowed grain in his field. The seeds fell all over that fruitful field and were soon covered by moist earth.

At night, when the sower was asleep, his enemy went into the field and sowed bad seed among the good seed.

Now good seed and bad seed were mixed together in the field. Both sprouted and plants sprung up. The two kinds of plants looked so much alike that there was no way to tell them apart at first. But when both blossomed and bore fruit, the difference quickly became apparent.

The ripe ears that grew from the bad seed were scattered through the heavy ears of grain which grew from the good seed. They swayed just as gracefully in the wind and bowed their heads just as humbly because of their great weight. Yet, their seeds were black and poisonous.

The man's servants finally realized the field had been spoiled. They went to their master with their frightening discovery and asked him, "Sir, didn't you sow good seed in your field? Where do all these bad plants come from?"

He replied, "Some enemy must have done this."

"Do you want us to pull out all the bad plants?" the servants asked.

The master said, "Let them both grow together until the harvest. Then I will say to the harvesters, 'First gather the bad plants and tie them in bundles to be burned. Then bring in the harvest and put it in my barn."

This was a parable Jesus told the people. Again His disciples asked Him what it meant. Jesus gave them an explanation.

The Son of man, Jesus, sows the good seed. The field is the world. The good seed represents the people who love God. The weeds are the people who hate God.

The enemy, the devil, sowed the bad seed. He is prowling around the world unnoticed, doing his best to ruin God's work. Just as in the man's field, there is good and bad living side by side in the Kingdom of God. The good and bad people often look a great deal alike. No one on earth can say for sure if his neighbor really is a child of God. But *God* knows. God lets them live side by side. He lets His sun rise on both the evil and the good and sends rain on both the righteous and the unrighteous. But they will finally be separated one day, when the time of harvest comes.

The harvest time is the great day when Jesus will return to judge the living and the dead. He will send out His angels as harvesters. They shall remove all the deceivers and evildoers from His Kingdom. The wicked will receive their punishment, but the righteous will shine like the sun in the Kingdom of their Father.

"He who has ears to hear, let him hear!" declared Jesus.

That was what Jesus meant by the

parable of the bad seed sown among the good seed in the field. To make sure that the disciples would never forget the point He was trying to teach them, Jesus later told them another parable that made the same point, the parable of the fishnet.

One day the disciples would be fishers of men. Using God's Word as their net, they would catch people and bring them to God. They would find that there were some people who would let themselves be dragged along by the Word but who would not love God uprightly. Some would act as if they belonged to God's Kingdom, but would never really enter it.

Jesus said, "The Kingdom of heaven is like a net that is set out in the lake. All sorts of fish get trapped in the net. When the net is full, the fishermen haul it on the shore. Then they sort all the fish, throwing the good ones into baskets. The unclean fish, the poisonous ones and the ones that are no good to eat they throw away.

"That's what will happen when the world comes to an end. The angels will go out to separate the wicked people from the righteous among whom they have been living."

50: The Kingdom of heaven

As yet, not many people followed Jesus or wanted to love Him. His Kingdom, the Kingdom of heaven, was only beginning. How small and insignificant it was, compared to the great Roman empire! But it would grow and expand; it would become greater and mightier than any other kingdom on earth.

Jesus taught His disciples this through the parable of the mustard seed. He said to them, "The Kingdom of heaven is like the little mustard seed which a man took and planted in his garden. It is the smallest seed of all seeds, but when it is full grown it is the largest of all the garden plants. It becomes a tree; the birds can nest in its branches."

Anyone who enters the Kingdom of God becomes a wholly different person. God's Spirit comes into that person's heart and works quietly there. The Holy Spirit permeates that person's entire life and makes all of it holy, good and rich. Wherever the Kingdom of God is, everything changes.

Jesus taught His disciples this by way of the parable of the yeast. He said that a woman once wanted to make bread. She took flour and kneaded the dough. She did not put the dough in the oven right away. If she had, the bread would have been hard and tasteless. She mixed a small amount of yeast through the dough. That little bit of yeast or leaven quietly affected the whole lump of dough. It gave the bread a flavor and made it rise. The yeast made the bread soft and tasty.

Then Jesus said, "The Kingdom of heaven is like that bit of yeast. A woman mixes it into three measures of flour, and the whole lump of dough is leavened."

It is glorious to belong to the Kingdom of heaven, for this Kingdom brings the greatest happiness possible on earth. The greatest treasure of all is to be a child of God. Many walk right past that treasure without realizing it. A person who has once caught sight of that treasure's heavenly gleam will never have peace again until he makes it his own. He will spare no effort and expense to get it. This, too, Jesus taught His disciples.

He told them the story of the treasure hidden out in the field. A man was busy digging one day. His shovel hit something hard. He was curious, so he dug all around. He found a great treasure that might have been buried there for centuries. He threw up his hands in delight, but then he realized that the treasure could not be his. The field belonged to someone else. But he *had* to have that treasure; he couldn't get it out of his mind.

He buried the treasure again and went home. He sold everything he owned; only then did he have enough money. With that money he bought the field that had the treasure buried in it.

Jesus told another parable to make the same point. He told His disciples about a merchant who was looking for beautiful pearls. One day the merchant found a pearl that was bigger and more beautiful than any he had ever seen. That pearl captured his imagination so much that he no longer cared about his other treasures. He sold everything he owned and used the money to buy that one special pearl. Only then did he have peace.

The two men in those parables—the merchant and the man digging in the field—both had to lose everything. All they had in the end was their pearl, their treasure.

Anyone who has found the happiness that Jesus brings for us on earth is like those men. Although he loses everything, he still is rich. The heavenly treasure is worth much more than any other treasure and can never be lost.

51: Jesus stills the storm

Evening fell on the Sea of Galilee. The sun sank behind the mountains by Capernaum. The blue water turned black, and the mountain wall in the east, on the far side of the lake, slowly darkened. At first the top of that wall continued to shine in the sun, but the twilight rose slowly to banish the sun's last rays.

The water was still and smooth. As the light faded away, the evening breeze caused only a few ripples. The day was almost over.

Jesus was in a small ship, the same ship in which He had stood to speak to the people. The ship was gliding gently over the shimmering waves on its way across the lake. A few other boats trailed behind Jesus' boat.

Jesus worked all day. It had been a tiring day for Him. He had been busy among the people from early morning. He had taught and admonished them, and He had healed their sick. He had spoken to the crowd in parables, and later He had explained to His own disciples what the parables meant. He had talked about the sower, about the bad seed sowed in the field, and about the beautiful big pearl. He had been a sower Himself, for He had sowed His seed in the hearts of the people. He loved the people who came to Him. He loved all of them—even those who were indifferent and those who opposed Him. All day long He tried to help them.

Now it was evening, and He was exhausted. The people had continued to crowd around Him. They would allow Him no rest as long as He made Himself available. Therefore He said to His disciples, "Let's go over to the other side of the lake."

They agreed readily and quickly set out in the ship. The Master was exhausted from His day's work. Jesus could rest on the other side of the lake, in the hill country of Gadara.

The little ship glided silently in the twilight. The first stars were already gleaming in the night sky. Jesus lay down in the back part of the boat with His head on a cushion and went to sleep. Only the little waves washing up against the bow, the gentle fluttering of the triangular sail, and the subdued voices of the disciples could be heard.

Halfway across the lake everything suddenly changed. It seemed that a storm had been lurking behind the mountain wall. Now the storm moved in on the little ship. It began to howl and whistle. The stars disappeared from the heavens as heavy, black clouds moved in. The water began to heave, and the wind picked up.

As quickly as a bird of prey attacking his victim, the howling storm swept down on the lake and the little ship.

There was no more rest for the disciples. They quickly took down the sail and began to row. Most of them were fishermen and had spent half their lives on the water. They had been through many unexpected storms.

Such storms were common in Galilee. The Sea of Galilee lay so low between the surrounding mountains that there was really no horizon to be seen. On a warm day it sometimes seemed as if the wind were coming into that deep valley from all directions at once.

The disciples rowed as hard as they could. They battled to stay afloat while Jesus lay sleeping in the back of the ship.

This was the worst storm the disciples had ever seen. The waves were towering walls of water and foam. They took turns rumbling toward the ship and assaulting it. They threw themselves at the sides of the ship as it pitched to and fro on the water. The sides of the wooden boat creaked and groaned.

The storm continued to scream and howl as it clutched the little ship in its invisible claws and threw if off course. The wind shook the ship so hard it seemed about to break into pieces. Although the disciples struggled hard, they felt they could not win the battle against this awesome power.

The sea was so wild that the waves were washing right into the ship. The ship seemed to be part of the sea. It drifted helplessly in the darkness, lashed by one giant wave after another. But in the back part of the ship, Jesus still slept soundly, as if there were no danger.

The disciples had given up all hope and courage. They were trembling with the fear of death. How could their Master lie sleeping as they struggled to save their lives and His life? They cried out in fear as they staggered along to the back part of the ship to Him.

"Master, help us!" they screamed. "Master, Master, we're drowning! Master, don't You care if we drown?"

Jesus woke up. He heard the storm and the wild waves, and He felt how the ship trembled. There was no trace of fear in His eyes.

He asked, "Why are you so afraid, you men of little faith?"

Then He stood up. He stood calmly in the howling storm and stretched out His hand, ordering the raging sea to calm. He rebuked the wind for threatening their lives and the sea for acting as their enemy. The wind and the water heard His voice, and they obeyed. They had to.

The rumble of the storm suddenly ceased. The wind subsided. It was as if a frightened animal crept back into his lair. The lake was still not completely calm; it continued to howl and heave. Jesus said, "Peace! Be still!" He meant it as a stern command. The waves immediately subsided. They lay down before Him. It was completely quiet again.

The disciples trembled as they watched. They were so amazed that they couldn't speak.

They heard their Master's voice ask them in a friendly way, "Where is your faith?" Then they bowed their heads in shame.

Soon the sail was hoisted, and they were gliding across the calm water of the lake. The stars were once again twinkling in the sky. The disciples whispered to each other, "Who is He, that even the wind and the waves obey Him?"

52: My name is Legion

In the hill country of Gadara, east of the Sea of Galilee, lived a horrible creature. He was a frightening, raging man feared by everyone. This man had originally lived in town, but he became a danger to everyone around him because of his wild fits of rage. The people had tried binding him hand and foot, but with his superhuman strength he broke free and ruined the chains.

Now he wandered around in the wilderness alone, living in caves that had been cut out of the rock. If people knew where he was, they stayed far away from him. They fled as soon as they heard him come, running and screaming. He terrorized the whole area and plagued the people. He hardly ever wore clothes, and he rarely seemed to eat. A furious wrath seemed to hold him in its grip, making him rage against anyone who came near him. Sometimes he even raged against himself.

Occasionally people saw him standing high up on top of the rocks, outlined against the blue sky. He was a horrible sight as he struck himself with stones. He would scream and continue to strike himself until he finally disappeared behind some rocks, where he would go on shrieking. Even the stillness of the night would be shattered by his voice coming from the rocks as he wandered in the darkness. He was always uneasy, always tormented, always driven by a strange, horrible power.

Jesus had now come to this area. After the horrible storm on the Sea of Galilee, He and His disciples had landed safely on the coast. Early in the morning they walked along the rocks near the caves. Jesus knew that the frightening man lived here, but He did not make a detour. Jesus was not afraid of him. He knew that the poor man was in satan's power. He was possessed; evil spirits lived within him. They were destroying his body and tormenting his soul. They caused him anguish day and night.

The raging, half-naked possessed man suddenly came running toward Him, shouting and screaming. Jesus did not flee. He stood calmly before His frightened disciples. His eyes were full of compassion as He looked at the poor man.

The evil spirits shrank back before Jesus' gaze. Love and compassion were horrible to them.

The possessed man fell on the ground before Jesus and cried out with a loud voice, "What do You want with me, You Son of the most high God? I beg You, do not torment me!"

Jesus was not there to punish anyone; he was there to deliver the poor man from the power of satan. That's why He had come to this area alongside the Sea of Galilee.

Jesus asked, "What is your name?"

The man could not speak for himself. The evil spirits answered the question instead.

"Legion!" cried the voice. "My name is Legion." This meant that there were many evil spirits within the man.

Jesus ordered the evil spirits to leave the man. He permitted them to go into a great herd of pigs that were feeding on a plateau above the lake.

The madness that had held the man in its grip was suddenly transferred to the pigs. Groaning and crying out in great confusion, they stampeded across the plateau to the cliff.

Jesus made sure that the evil spirits would not torment them for long. The pigs ran straight over the cliff, fell into the water below, and drowned. It was an amazing sight. The men watching over the pigs fled in great fear.

The disciples looked at their Master in awe. Was there no limit to His divine power? Not only the wind and the water but even the evil powers of hell were at His command!

53: A living sign

Jesus had just performed another amazing miracle; He had ordered some evil spirits to leave a poor man whom they had tormented for a long time. He allowed them to go into a great herd of pigs instead. The pigs promptly ran headlong into the water and drowned.

Not only the disciples had watched this wonder in amazement. The man seated at Jesus' feet—the man Jesus had just delivered from the power of the evil spirits—also watched with wide eyes.

It was clear from the man's eyes that he had returned to his senses. The evil powers that had driven the pigs into the water were the same ones that had so long tormented him. Now he was free of them; he had seen them disappear. *Jesus* had delivered him. He bowed before Jesus in adoration.

The man was happy to sit at Jesus' feet. By the time people arrived from the little town of Gadara, he was clothed and looked almost normal again.

The people from the town owned the pigs. The men who had fled had told them what had happened. They looked at the man who had caused them so much trouble in the past. Now he was a normal person again, free and happy. No one need fear him. He no longer clenched his fists as soon as he saw others. His bright eyes looked around.

The people were not concerned with the happiness of the man who had been delivered. To Jesus, a human soul was worth much more than a herd of pigs, but that wasn't how they saw it. "Our pigs!" they groaned. "Our money! Everything we own! What a pile of money went over the cliff!"

They were now delivered for good from

the wicked man who had long terrorized them, but that did not matter much to them. They were even willing to put up with the wild man again if they could have their pigs back.

The people of the town were now afraid of Jesus. They feared it would cost them even more money if He stayed around. Therefore they begged Him to leave their region.

Jesus did as they asked, for He never forced Himself on people. He and His disciples started to walk back to the ship that was tied up by the shore. The man freed of the evil spirits followed them. When Jesus climbed aboard, the man begged to be allowed to come along. He wanted to stay with Jesus always.

Jesus said no. He still loved the people in this region, even if they were selfish and enslaved to money. The man should go on living in the area as a living sign of God's power and mercy.

Jesus said to him, "Go back to your house and tell everyone what God has done for you." The man obeyed. As the little ship bobbed forward on the lake, heading west toward Capernaum, he went back home.

He traveled all through his area, telling people how Jesus had delivered him. All the people were amazed.

54: Healed by faith

One day, as Jesus stood preaching on the shore near Capernaum, a man pushed his way through the crowd around Jesus. He fell down in despair at Jesus' feet.

"Master," he cried out, "my daughter is about to die. Come quickly and lay Your hands upon her, for then she will be healed and live."

Jesus knew the man, and so did the people who crowded around Him. It was Jairus, one of the most important men in Capernaum, a leader in the synagogue. He had heard Jesus' words on the sabbath days and had seen His miracles. He remembered the miracles more than the words.

"Master, come and lay Your hands upon her," he begged.

Jairus did not have the same kind of faith as the Gentile centurion who turned to Jesus for help when one of his servants fell ill. The centurion believed that even a single word from Jesus' mouth could hold back sickness and death.

Jesus did not let Jairus plead in vain. He went with him at once. The people who had heard Jairus's request did not stay behind. They followed, excited at the prospect of witnessing a miracle.

People crowded around Jesus as He headed toward Jairus's home. They wanted to stay as close as possible to Jesus. But they were in the way. Jesus and the despairing father could not advance very well with all those people in front of them. The people were not concerned about that.

The small streets of Capernaum leading to Jairus's house were crowded. It was taking Jesus a long time to get there. Jairus wrung his hands in anguish. The little girl was his only child! If Jesus came too late, he would have nothing left.

Among the people jostling and crowding around Jesus was a pale, emaciated woman. Her hollow eyes were fixed upon Him with great longing. She wanted to be alone with Jesus to tell Him about her suffering and her cares, and to beg Him for healing.

For twelve years she had suffered a disease that had robbed her of almost all her strength. She had sought treatment from all sorts of doctors. This had cost her a great deal of money, but it had not helped her. In fact, the illness became worse. The doctors had made her poor, but they had not healed her.

She was now following Jesus because she was convinced that only He could heal her. She was sure of it. But she did not dare to speak to Him in the street and tell Him all about her disease, with all the people listening. She simply followed Him around, not sure what to do next, full of both fear and faith. She would make sure she stayed close to Jesus.

"Perhaps if I touched His cloak," she thought, "just touched it, maybe then I would be healed."

Soon she had her opportunity to touch Jesus unobserved. Her heart pounded as she bent over and reached out to touch the hem of Jesus' cloak with her fingers. Immediately she felt a surge of energy passing through her wasted body, and she knew she was healed.

But that same moment she had a shock. Jesus turned around and asked, "Who touched My cloak?"

Peter was puzzled. He said, "Master, don't You see that the people are crowding around You? How, then, can You ask, 'Who touched My cloak?'"

But Jesus said, "I know someone touched Me, for I could feel power flowing from Me."

His eyes had already found the woman. He looked at her expectantly.

The woman realized that she could hide nothing from Jesus. Trembling, she fell down before Him and told Him everything.

Jesus said, "Daughter, your faith has healed you. Go home in peace and be healed of your disease." That woman had been healed *by faith*, not by touching Jesus' cloak.

The woman went her way thankful and happy. She was delivered from her suffering at last.

55: Jairus's daughter

Jairus was growing more nervous and afraid by the moment. His daughter was on the brink of death. Jesus had agreed to come, but He was held up first by the crowd milling around Him and then by a woman seeking to be healed of some ailment. Now Jesus might be too late to heal his daughter!

Jairus saw one of his servants pushing through the crowd. From the somber look on the man's face, Jairus could already tell what sorrowful message the servant had come to bring. "Your daughter is dead," the servant said. "It's no use to bother the Master anymore."

Was it really too late? Jairus could not quite believe it. In despair He looked at Jesus. The Savior gave him an encouraging smile. There was no sadness in Jesus' eyes. "Don't be afraid," He said. "Just believe, and your daughter will be restored."

Jairus didn't know what to think, but Jesus' words brought marvelous comfort into his heart. He walked on next to Jesus, trusting blindly in Him. That was all he could do; there was no other way out. Stubbornly he clung to the belief that Jesus could make everything turn out well in the end.

The people following Jesus crowded Him even more when they reached Jairus's house. Jesus did not allow anyone inside except Jairus and three of the disciples—Peter, James and John. They locked the door to keep the crowd out.

The house was full of crying and wailing. The hired mourners who had been waiting outside the house before the little girl died went about their work. That was the custom those days: when someone died, the family would hire some women to mourn. They would wail and create a great commotion, although there was no real grief in their eyes.

Jesus asked, "Why all the wailing? Why are you weeping? The child is not dead; she is asleep."

The mourners looked at Him in surprise. They were irritated and angered by His comments. They didn't know what He was talking about, so they laughed at Him.

Jesus sent them all outside so that there would be silence in the house. Then He went upstairs with the father and the mother and His three disciples. They went into the room where the dead child lay on her bed. She was only twelve years old, and now she was gone. She had fallen asleep.

That's all death was for Jesus, it was a sleep. He took the girl's limp hands in His and gently woke her, just as a mother would awaken her child in the morning. "Talitha cumi," He said. "Little girl, get up."

The little girl opened her big eyes and looked around in amazement. She got up from her bed and walked over to her mother as Jesus held her hand.

The happy mother folded the girl in her arms with a cry of joy. Her head was spinning. She could hardly believe that she really had her daughter back! The father and the three disciples were awe-struck as they stared at Jesus.

But Jesus was thinking about the child. The little girl had been sick and had not eaten in a long time. She was very hungry. Jesus, in His love, felt her hunger and ordered that food be brought for her.

He told Jairus and the three disciples not to tell anyone what had happened. He did not want people following Him around just to see Him perform miracles.

The *Word* He proclaimed was worth much more than the *miracles* He performed. Jairus knew that. It was His Word that had awakened the little girl from her sleep of death.

Jesus' Word had taken away Jairus's fear when He said, "Don't be afraid. Just believe." Jairus never forgot that glorious, divine Word!

56: John the Baptist in prison

A man in a camel's hair coat with a leather girdle around his waist sat trapped in a dark prison cell. He couldn't even move his feet; they were in blocks. There was no sunshine in his cell and no sound to disturb the deathly silence.

Sometimes the iron bars would be removed and a soldier would come in with a piece of bread and a jug of water for John. When the soldier left, he would shut the heavy door and put the bars back in place. Then it would be just as still as before.

The air was stale and musty. The silence was oppressive. The blocks opened sores on the man's feet. The man trapped in his dark, dirty cell suffered a great deal, but he did not complain.

The man did not deserve this punishment. He was not a criminal. He was a good and righteous man, guilty only of doing the work God had called him to do. In fact, his freedom had been taken away because of the upright, courageous way he went about that work. John the Baptist was in prison because he obeyed God more than man.

John had continued his work after he baptized Jesus in the Jordan and some of his disciples left him to follow Jesus. He simply couldn't stop crying out to people that the King had come to establish His kingdom. The King would punish all the godless and wipe out His enemies, but all who loved Him would find happiness with Him. The King was the great heavenly harvester, and He would want to start on the harvest soon.

"His winnowing fork is in His hand," John had cried out. "He will clear His threshing floor and bring the grain into the barn. He will burn the chaff with a fire that cannot be put out."

John continued to cry out to people that they should repent of their sins, so that they would be *wheat*, not chaff. He went on baptizing them in the Jordan when they repented. He baptized first in Judea and later more to the north, in Aenon, which was near Salim. The disciples who stayed with him followed him everywhere.

One day when John was at Aenon, his disciples came to him, fearful and concerned. "Master," they said, "we heard some news about Jesus, who came to you at the Jordan. He, too, has started preaching. His disciples are also baptizing people. The people are flocking to Him in great numbers."

John's disciples had not understood much of what their master was saying. They thought they were bringing him bad news. They thought that John would be jealous of Jesus. The truth, however, was that they could hardly have brought him more wonderful news.

"This is just what I've been hoping for," he cried out. "Jesus must become greater, and I must become less. The people should all follow *Him* and forget about me. You know that I have said, I am not the Christ but have been sent ahead of the Christ to prepare the way for Him. I am only a man; I am no more than a servant. *He* has come from heaven; *He* is the Son of God. Whoever believes in the Son has eternal life!"

Eagerly John went ahead with his work of leading people to Christ. Fearlessly he pointed to sin wherever he saw it and appealed for repentance. His cutting words spared no one, not even the king.

The king was Herod, the son of the

Herod who had murdered the children of Bethlehem. This Herod ruled over Galilee and Perea. He had heard of John and wanted to see him. He was a wicked man, almost as wicked as his father. He had stolen Herodias, his brother Philip's wife, and had sent his own wife away. Now Herodias and her daughter lived with him in his palace. Herodias had left her husband to become Herod's queen.

John knew this. The whole country knew, but no one dared to say anything about it. Everyone trembled at the king's power and his wicked wife's cruelty.

John served the King of kings, and therefore he was not afraid. When he stood before Herod, he looked just as bold and proud as Elijah had when he stood before Ahab. He was not overwhelmed by the king's beautiful clothes, his power, or all his courtiers who constantly flattered the king. He saw only a man, a weak, sinful man who would have to repent to be happy. He saw a man in need of forgiveness.

John said straight out what others didn't even dare to whisper. He chastised the king in powerful language for all the wicked things he had done. He also said, "You may not take your brother's wife as your wife."

These bold words cost John his freedom. When Herodias heard what he had said, she was beside herself with rage. She would not rest until she could take revenge. John would have to die, she was unshakable on this point.

Yet Herod knew that the people honored and feared the prophet. There would be an uproar if John were put to death. Therefore he had John arrested and locked in a dark cell. Although Herodias had not gotten her way completely, the mouth of the faithful prophet had been stilled.

57: Doubts about Jesus

John the Baptist sat chained and imprisoned as if he were a criminal. The man who had lived in the wide open wilderness and had slept under the starry sky was now confined to a dark cell.

Sometimes his disciples were allowed to visit him. When they sat by him, they could see how much he was suffering. They tried to comfort him. They told him what they had heard about Jesus, and about the enmity and opposition Jesus had to endure.

When they were gone and John was alone in the silence with his thoughts, he rested his head against the wall. John was sad and disappointed. Certain thoughts began to torment him.

His thoughts were always about Jesus and His work. Were the deeds Jesus performed really the deeds of a *king?* Jesus preached, just as John had done, and He healed the sick. But what about the Kingdom? Why didn't He strike down His enemies and rescue His servant John from prison? Surely He had that power! Why didn't He make the people of Israel great and powerful again if He was really the long-awaited Messiah?

Had John been wrong about Jesus? Surely John had spoken God's words, and not just words he had made up himself. He had cried out to the people that the Messiah would come as a stern judge and that He would judge all of them. But now someone had come who had shown the people nothing but *mercy!* John had preached that the heavenly harvester was coming with His winnowing fork in His hand to begin the harvest. But Jesus had come as a sower!

John simply didn't understand it. Those thoughts tormented him. When his

disciples came to visit him again, he instructed two of them to go to Jesus and ask
Him if He really was the Messiah.

They obeyed. They traveled to the area
where Jesus was. They found Him busy
with His work, with a great crowd of
people around Him. The sick and the lame
were being brought to Jesus from all directions. The great helper moved among all
those unfortunate people and healed them.
He went to the cripples and they stood up
rejoicing. He touched the eyes of the blind,
and they were delirious with joy when the
light came streaming in. He extended His
hands in blessing to the lepers, and they
were healed. He approached demon-
possessed people who screamed wildly
when they saw Him and tugged at the ropes
with which they were bound, and they
suddenly became calm. He cast out evil
spirits and gave such people back to their
families again in sound mind.

John's disciples interrupted Him with
their question. "John the Baptist has sent
us," they said. "He asks, 'Are You the one
who was to come, or are we to wait for
another?'"

What a foolish question to ask in the
midst of all those miracles! How could anyone who had seen all those things doubt that
Jesus was the Messiah?

But Jesus understood John's question. He
knew how much His faithful servant was
suffering in prison, and He was filled with
compassion. He wanted to help John, but
not by simply assuring him in words that He
was indeed the Messiah. That would not be
enough. Jesus' *works* would speak for Him
and testify about Him.

He said to the two disciples, "Go back
and tell John what you have heard and
seen. The blind see, the lame walk, the
lepers are healed, the deaf hear, the dead
are raised, and the poor have the gospel
proclaimed to them."

Were there some other wonders that
John had been expecting the Messiah to perform? He would have to believe on the basis
of these miracles and the testimony of his
disciples. Then Jesus added something to
the message, "Blessed is the man who takes
no offense at Me."

John's disciples were gone, but Jesus'
thoughts stayed with His servant. Jesus
loved John. He loved him as much now as
He had before, although the prophet had
almost given up hope.

Jesus talked about John the Baptist to the
people who stood before Him. He said that
this simple man whom they had seen by the
Jordan in his cloak of camel's hair was the
greatest prophet who had ever lived. He
praised John more than He had ever praised
anyone else.

John's disciples reported to their master
the answer Jesus had given them. They
were excited as they told him about all the
miracles they had seen.

Even then John did not fully understand.
There were still questions on his mind. But
these questions were stilled by a song he
began to sing in his heart, a song that Jesus
was the Messiah after all! Who could do
such works but the Son of God? No, John
took no offense at Jesus. In the darkness of
his cell he worshiped Him.

John did not know what awaited him,
but he was not afraid of the future. He
believed firmly that Jesus would rule as
King one day. And John would be with
Jesus in His Kingdom.

58: A grisly gift

To the very end, John the Baptist remained a faithful witness to his Master. Sometimes he was taken out of prison for a little while and brought to Herod. He would speak as courageously as ever, and it would seem that he had influenced the king. Herod would listen very carefully. Fear would come into his eyes when John spoke of the punishment the king would receive on account of his sins.

The king was willing to do much to escape that punishment, but John demanded that he send away Herodias, his brother's wife. Herod would not do that. Still, he liked listening to John and seemed to fall more and more under the spell of his words.

Herodias sensed this, and she looked down on Herod in scorn and contempt. Hatred grew in her heart. The prophet's imprisonment was not enough for her. She knew that she would never be secure while John the Baptist was alive and could speak boldly to the king.

John would have to *die*. Only then could Herodias be sure that she would remain queen. She tried to convince the king to put John to death, but Herod resisted. He realized that John was a righteous and holy man who should really be set free.

The king had the power to release John, but he did not dare because of Herodias. "Put him to death!" urged Herodias, flattering the king. "Do it for me."

Herod simply didn't dare. He was a weakling. He wavered between the voice of his conscience, telling him to do what was right and the scorn of his wife, urging him to do wrong.

Herodias did not give up. She did not forget her enemy in prison. She waited patiently for her opportunity.

Finally her chance came. She would never have a better opportunity.

It was Herod's birthday, and he was celebrating with his officials and captains and leaders in Galilee. He served a sumptuous banquet in the palace. Wine made the hearts of the guests joyful.

Herodias was not in the room. Usually, women were not present on such occasions. She watched from behind a curtain, for she recognized her opportunity. The king was in a good mood, and the wine had excited him.

Now was the time!

Herodias summoned her daughter and told her to go and dance among the men. That was contrary to custom, but Herodias did not care. She was concerned only about reaching her horrible goal.

"Dance the most enticing dance that you can," she whispered. "If the king asks how he can reward you, come to me and I'll tell you what to say."

The girl swept into the banquet room scantily dressed and danced a beautiful dance before all the men. The king was delighted. "She's doing this for *me*," he thought. "She has come here for *me*."

He called the girl over when her dance was finished. "Ask me for anything you want," he called out enthusiastically, "and I will give it to you."

He raised his hand as if swearing an oath. His eyes were shining. His face was red from the wine.

"I give you my word," he declared proudly. "I give you my word, my daughter. Whatever you ask, I will give it to you, up to half of my kingdom."

The girl did not know what to ask for,

but her mother seemed to know. She went to her mother to find out.

That was the moment Herodias had been waiting for. The king had given his word; he could not take it back.

"Ask for the head of John the Baptist," Herodias told the girl.

The girl did not waver; she was a true daughter of Herodias. She skipped into the banquet room and bowed before the king. She smiled and said, "I want you to give me the head of John the Baptist here on a platter."

A deathly silence filled the hall after those horrible words. The king was pale; he somberly stared straight ahead. Now he understood why the girl had come in and danced for him. She had not done it to please him but to please *Herodias. Herodias* was really asking for the head of John the Baptist.

Could he refuse this request? He looked at his guests with shame in his eyes. They were waiting to see what he would do. Would he give the girl the grisly gift she asked for?

What would the guests say if the king did not keep the promise he had backed up with an oath? "He is a coward," they would say. "Herod is a weakling. He swore he would do it, but he is afraid to go through with it."

John's life was not so important to Herod that he would allow people to think of him as a weakling and a coward. He was unhappy about it, but he had to go ahead. He sent a soldier out and told him to return with the head of the prophet. The soldier did as he was commanded. He beheaded John in prison.

59: No rest for Herod

Herodias had her way at last. The troublesome prophet was silenced because the king had made a rash promise.

The bloody head of John the Baptist was brought on a platter to Herodias's daughter. The girl brought it to her mother. Now there would be rest for Herodias, for she wouldn't have to worry about the prophet anymore.

The stern eyes of the prophet were closed for good. The mouth that had spoken only truth would speak no more.

What would Herodias say when God called her to account for this horrible deed? God would surely give this matter His attention, for the blood of His children is precious in His eyes.

Herodias held the platter with John's head on it, but John was already with God. He had completed his work. He had worked humbly and faithfully, and now his suffering was over.

Instead of being confined to a dark cell, he enjoyed the glory of being in God's presence. While Herod celebrated his godless feast with his rich, powerful friends, John joined the great festival above.

John's disciples mourned as they came to the prison to claim his body and lay it in a grave. They no longer had a master. They went to Jesus and told Him what had happened. Jesus gave them comfort and rest.

But there was no rest for Herod. Repeatedly he saw the head of John the Baptist dancing before him. It hovered before him in his dreams. During his waking hours he was consumed with regret.

Later, he heard about Jesus and the miracles He performed. Herod heard that one of his own servants' sons had been called back to life by Jesus' Word. Herod became frightened. He said to his servants, "John the Baptist has arisen from the dead. That's why this man is capable of such things."

Herod's servants assured him that Jesus was really Elijah or another prophet. But Herod remained firm. "John the Baptist, the man I beheaded, has risen from the dead."

Although Herod was afraid of Jesus, he was eager to see Him. He wanted to know if Jesus was really John the Baptist.

One day he got his chance to see Jesus. Jesus stood before him, bound and silent. That moment could have provided rest for Herod's troubled soul. But he scorned the Savior and made fun of Him. Herod sent Him away in shining garments intended to mock Him. There would be no rest for Herod, the coward.

Not long afterward, the emperor of Rome took away Herod's crown. Herod lived the last years of his life in exile.

John, the courageous servant of the Lord, enjoyed the rest that is reserved for the people of God. He had been faithful unto death. Now he enjoyed the crown of life.

60: No rest for Jesus

Jesus visited all the towns and villages in Galilee. He taught in the synagogues. He also preached the joyful news of the Kingdom of heaven in the streets. He healed the sick and infirm people brought to Him.

People could easily see where Jesus had passed, for pain and worry fled before Him. Everywhere He left joy in His wake.

When Jesus saw the people streaming toward Him, He was moved with compassion for them. He saw eyes full of yearning focused on Him. He saw hearts full of questions and cares. Many people waited for Jesus in cities and towns throughout the land. Hundreds and thousands of people no longer knew where to turn with their sins and sorrows. People had long sought rest for their hearts but had not found it. No one could lead them and help them. They were exhausted and worn from all their fears. They were like sheep without a shepherd.

Jesus could not let them wander any longer. He needed helpers to do His work. He called His disciples together and laid His hands on them in blessing. He gave them the power to heal the sick and drive out evil spirits. Then He sent out all twelve of them, in pairs, to preach that the Kingdom of heaven was coming. He sent them out to the lost sheep of Israel to show them the way to the Father's house.

They were not to accept any gifts or rewards for the deliverance they brought. Salvation had come to them as a free gift, and they were to pass it on freely to others. But they were not to take food or money with them on their travels. Wherever they stayed for a while, the local people would look after them. The laborer was worthy of his keep. Peace and joy would descend on any house that received them. But people who did *not* want to receive them as God's emissaries and did *not* want to listen to what they had to say would surely be punished for their godlessness.

The disciples set out in pairs, going in all directions. They obeyed the instructions their Master had given them. They looked like paupers; each carried a staff as his only possession. But they carried with them a great treasure that was worth more than all the gold in the world.

They gave of this treasure generously, but their supply never dwindled. They went through the villages, proclaimed the gospel and healed the sick wherever they went. They, too, left blessing behind them as they traveled through the land.

When they finally rejoined Jesus at Capernaum, they told Him excitedly what they had done and learned. Jesus could see how tired they were, and He knew that there would be no rest for them there. Already, a great crowd was gathering because of Jesus' presence. There was so much activity that there wasn't even time to eat.

Jesus wanted to take care of His disciples. He took them to the lakeshore, where the small ship they had used so often lay waiting. He said, "Let's sail away and rest for a while."

They sailed toward a deserted spot on the other side of the lake. In that peaceful setting, they could be alone with their Master and receive new strength. Jesus also yearned for peace and rest. John the Baptist's disciples had come to Him in Capernaum with the news of John's death. Jesus was still grieving for His faithful servant.

The ship glided slowly across the shining blue waves, and the disciples had some glorious hours together. But even before they arrived at the far shore, their rest was interrupted. The people had seen Jesus sail away and had followed the little ship with their eyes as they walked along the shore. They did not let the Savior out of their sight. They walked around the lake. The quickest ones even beat the boat to the far shore. They stood waiting, with a triumphant gleam in their eyes. When the boat arrived, they were tired and sweaty from the long difficult journey, but that didn't matter. They had shown that they would go to great lengths to be with Jesus again. They wanted to see His miracles and listen to His words. For that, they were willing to leave their houses and their work unattended.

Soon the crowd began to swell. People arrived from all the towns around the Sea of Galilee.

When Jesus climbed a hill and sat down with His disciples, they crowded around Him again. They voiced their concerns and questions and showed Him the sick and infirm people they had brought along.

Jesus forgot His own sorrow. He spoke to the people to comfort them and told them about the Kingdom of God. There was no rest for Jesus that day.

61: The feeding of the five thousand

Jesus had sailed across the Sea of Galilee with His disciples to get some rest and spend some time alone with them. But the people had followed Him, bringing Him their sick and begging to hear more about the Kingdom of God. He could not turn them away.

It was starting to get late. The sun was sinking slowly. The disciples watched as it hovered above the hills on the far side of the lake, casting ever longer shadows.

The disciples were worried about the time. The people were listening to Jesus so intensely and watching Him with such amazement that they had no idea how late it was. Yet they had made a long journey and had been away from home all day. Soon they would become hungry and they would feel how tired they were. Where would they eat, and where would they find shelter?

The Master should not hold the people any longer, the disciples thought. They went to Him and told Him what was on their minds. But He was already aware of the problem. He asked Philip, "Where shall we buy bread so that these people can eat?" He said this only to test Philip, for He already knew what He would do.

Would Philip now remember that the Master was the Son of God? Would he remember that Jesus could command the wind and the waves, and could chase away sickness and death? Could the one who had changed water into wine also take away hunger? What would Philip say? "Lord, You can do all things. Tell these stones to turn into bread, and it will come to pass."

No, that was not what Philip said. It didn't even cross his mind.

He started to figure instead. How much money would he need if he were to buy bread for all those people? Then he said, "Even if we spent 200 silver coins, it would not be enough for each person to receive a small piece of bread."

The other disciples had nothing better to suggest. "Send the people away," they said. "They can go to the towns and villages around here to buy food." They did not consider how poor the people were and

how hungry they must be by this time.

Jesus, however, thought mainly of the people. "It is not enough to send them away," He said. "*You* give them food to eat."

What a strange thing to say!

The disciples didn't understand what Jesus was talking about. Jesus asked them, "How many loaves do you have? Let Me see."

Andrew, Peter's brother, had been looking for food and had found something. "Here is a boy with five barley loaves and two fishes," he said. "But what good does that do when we have so many people to feed?" He pointed in despair to the thousands of people.

Jesus said, "Bring Me the loaves and the fishes."

That was fine with the boy, so the food was brought to Jesus. The food was put down in front of Him, five flat loaves, and two small baked fishes.

Jesus said, "Have the people sit down on the grass in groups of about 50."

The disciples obeyed, although they did not understand what their Master was doing. They walked through the crowd, counting the people and dividing them into groups. Soon all the people in their clothes of many colors were arranged neatly on the hillside. From a distance it looked like a colorful array of flowers in the green grass of the hillside.

When the disciples returned to their Master and had taken their places again, they witnessed a miracle like nothing they had seen before. Jesus looked up to heaven to thank the Father for the good gifts. He spread out His hands in blessing over the small supply of food. Then He took the loaves and began to break them. He broke the fishes too. The pieces He dropped into baskets placed before Him by the disciples.

Jesus kept on steadily with the work. Pieces of bread and fish kept falling from His holy hands into the baskets. And the disciples went to the people with the heaping baskets of food. They returned to Him with their baskets empty, and He filled them again.

All the people—5000 men, not counting the women and children—ate and were satisfied. They ate silently, for they were awe-struck. It was almost like they were dreaming. The dream-like state continued as the disciples went among the people to gather the remaining crumbs and uneaten pieces. The master had given them strict orders that there was to be no food left on the ground.

The disciples brought twelve full baskets back to Jesus. There were twelve baskets of leftovers when Jesus had started with five loaves and two fishes. And that was after 5000 men along with the women and children, had eaten. How was it possible?

62: A kingdom of love

Thousands of people were seated before Jesus in groups on a hillside. They had followed Him and listened to Him all day. Then, instead of sending them home so they could eat, Jesus and the disciples had fed all of them miraculously, using five small loaves and two fishes.

It seemed like a dream, but slowly it began to sink in to the people that it was not a dream. It really happened!

The people's excitement and joy knew no bounds. Their eyes shone and their faces beamed in the light of the setting sun. The people whispered to each other excitedly. There were cries of amazement, and people extended their arms to Jesus joyfully. They cried out to each other, "This is truly the prophet who was to come into the world! He is the Messiah! He is the King we have been waiting for so long!"

They were sure that the glorious time for which Israel had yearned so long, the year of Jubilee, the time of freedom, had finally come! The Romans would be chased away. The old kingdom of David and Solomon would rise in glory. What a powerful Messiah this Jesus would be! How rich and happy the people would be under His rule!

It would soon be time for the Passover feast. At that holy feast of deliverance, Jesus would be crowned in Jerusalem.

What if He didn't want to be king? He was so modest and humble. But He had to! If need be, they would forcibly drag Him to Jerusalem to be proclaimed king. His disciples would agree to help. Their eyes shone too, and their hearts pounded with joyful expectation. They, too, began to whisper about the great plan, and they were just as excited as the others.

Jesus knew what the people were thinking, and there was sorrow in His heart. Didn't His disciples know Him better by now? He had not come to establish an earthly kingdom. He had come to establish the Kingdom of heaven, which is not a kingdom of power and might but a kingdom of *love*.

Jesus called the disciples together and pointed to the ship. He told them to start sailing to the other side of the lake while He sent the people on their way. The disciples had to obey, although they were deeply disappointed. They entered the ship reluctantly. Why did Jesus send them away when everything promised to become so glorious? Sadly they set sail, leaving their Master, their King, behind.

Jesus sent the people to the surrounding villages. They had been strengthened by the food He had miraculously provided. They could now undertake the journey.

The people obeyed Jesus. They had to. Like the disciples, they were unhappy and disappointed. Still, they did as Jesus said.

Jesus remained behind alone. It became dark and still. In the stillness of the night He climbed one of the mountains. High on the peak, in the darkness above the lake, He kneeled down to pray.

63: Jesus walks on the water

The sun had set. Darkness covered the earth. It was nighttime.

On a dark hillside east of the Sea of Galilee a lonely figure kneeled between the rocks. It was Jesus. He was praying.

The stars glittered over His head. Their light was reflected in the dark waters of the lake. The hours slipped by but He seemed not to notice.

Then the wind picked up and rumbled across the hills. It grew in force and came sweeping down at the lake. It whipped up the waves until they looked like mountains of water with frothy tops of foam. The weather was bad, but the lonely figure praying on the hillside seemed not to notice.

Whenever Jesus prayed, He was very close to His Father. It seemed as if His soul had been taken up into heaven.

Finally Jesus stood up, strengthened and encouraged. He was in a howling storm, surrounded by thick darkness. But as He looked around, nothing was hidden from His eyes. He saw the lake and the foaming waves. Far away, in the middle of the lake, He saw a little ship. In that ship twelve men were doing their best to row against the wind. They sweated and toiled, but made little progress.

The darkness was so deep that the men in the little ship could hardly see each other. But the darkness was no barrier to Jesus. As He watched, He could see the fear in His disciples' eyes.

Jesus started down the dark path that led from the hillside to the shore. His eyes were fixed on the little ship, and His heart was with the disciples. Was there anything to stop Him from going to them now?

Jesus' feet had carried Him all the way to the water. Now the turbulent waves bowed their frothy heads before their Lord and Master. They fell down before Him to bear His full weight. Across the waves, through the dark night of the storm, Jesus walked toward the little ship.

When the disciples had reluctantly obeyed their Master's command and went into the ship, they stayed close to the shore after setting sail. They thought that Jesus would probably join them in the ship before long.

They were even more discouraged when He didn't come. They had it so good with their Master! They wanted to work for a glorious future for themselves and for Him. They wanted Him to win the honor and fame rightly due Him. He had refused. Didn't He trust them? Had He now forgotten them?

It was a cold, raw night. The wind suddenly picked up. A strong headwind made the waves splatter as they struck the bow. They still had to make it to the other side, for that was where the Master had told them to go.

They rowed with all their strength, but they hardly made any progress. After more than half a night of rowing and sweating profusely, they had only advanced some five or six kilometers. By the time it was three o'clock at night, they were still in the middle of the sea. Would they ever reach their goal?

The disciples began to think about another night when they had an even bigger storm to contend with on the Sea of Galilee. They had been terrified that night, but there had been no reason to be afraid. Jesus was with them that time; He had been sleeping quietly in the back of the ship. When they finally woke Him, He calmed the wind and the water with a single powerful command.

This time Jesus' place was empty. This time He had left them alone, at the mercy of the furious storm. They were at the mercy of the dark, evil powers that raged against them.

Look! What was that? A white figure seemed to be hovering over the dark water a distance from the ship. How could the figure of a man appear over the waves?

The disciples were terrified. "A ghost!" they screamed. "It's a ghost!"

A friendly voice cried out to them, "Have no fear! It is I. Be not afraid."

That familiar voice calmed their fears instantly. "The Master!" they stammered at last. "The Master is coming!"

The disciples no longer worried about the wind and the waves. The Master was with them! He had not forgotten them after all. Would He come across the water to the boat? Who was He, anyway, that He could do such a thing?

Peter managed to speak up first after this incredible surprise. Great joy and fiery love arose in his heart. The Master had not left them alone. Peter wanted to be with the Master again, for he yearned for Him earnestly. The Master was coming, but Peter couldn't wait; he simply *had* to go to Him.

"Lord," he cried out, "if it is really You, command me to come to You across the water."

Jesus said, "Come!"

It was only one word. But for Peter, whose faith had suddenly become great and strong, that one word was enough. Without fear, without thinking twice, Peter climbed over the side of the ship and lowered himself to the water. He kept his shining eyes fixed on Jesus. Firmly, without hesitation, he started walking on the water. And the water supported his weight! Jesus was Lord even over the waves. Peter, through his faith, now also had power over the waves.

Suddenly it occurred to Peter how miraculous this really was. At first he had not thought about it; he had thought only of Jesus. Now he looked in amazement at the black, living floor of water under his feet. Could that water really support his weight? He listened to the howling of the

wind. How the wind whipped up the waves! Mountains of water rolled toward Peter.

Finally, Peter forgot about the Master. He saw only himself and the water all around. He thought only of the danger.

Now, just as suddenly as his faith had become strong, fear arose within him. At once he began to sink into the water.

"Lord, save me!" cried Peter, stretching out his hands toward Jesus.

Immediately he felt the Master's hand taking hold of him and pulling him up. He heard the Master ask him, "You man of little faith, why did you doubt?"

They walked, hand in hand to the ship and climbed aboard. The wind died down, and the surface of the water became as calm as a mirror.

The disciples threw themselves down before Jesus because of this new miracle and stammered, "Truly, You are the Son of God!"

As the first rays of morning light colored the tops of the mountains, they moored their little ship safely on the shore.

64: The bread of life

Jesus and His disciples were passing through the land of Phoenicia, which lay north of Israel along the Mediterranean

Sea. This was the land of Tyre and Sidon, the native land of Jezebel, the heathen queen who had brought the priests of Baal to Israel. It was also the land in which the prophet Elijah had hid during the great drought. Elijah had stayed with a widow in Zarephath.

Why had Jesus forsaken His people to go to this foreign, heathen land? Because His people had forsaken Him and no longer wished to listen to His words.

The people's feelings about Jesus became clear in Galilee, the day after Jesus miraculously fed thousands. On the morning of that day, the people Jesus had sent away the previous evening to find lodgings returned to the spot where they had been fed. They assumed that Jesus was still there, because there had been only one boat tied by the shore, and the disciples had set off in that boat without Jesus.

The people looked everywhere for Jesus, for they hoped He would give them bread again. It was a shame that He could not be found.

As they stood on the shore of the Sea of Galilee, they saw fishermen's boats from Tiberias. The fishermen were fishing close to the shore. Since Jesus was no longer where they had expected Him, the people hailed the fishermen to bring them to the other side of the lake. Soon they were in Capernaum.

Look! There was Jesus! They found Him in the midst of His disciples, as if He had not been separated from them for a moment. How had He managed to get to this side of the lake so quickly if He was not with the disciples when they sailed across? The people simply couldn't understand it. Surprised and happy, they walked up to Him.

"Rabbi," they asked, "when did You get here?"

Jesus was disappointed as He looked at them. He saw the desire and excitement in their eyes. He knew *why* they had come. They sought Him because they wanted more bread and miracles. They did not seek Him for His own sake. They did not believe that He could bring them eternal joy. If He would *continue* to give them bread and perform other miracles, they would love Him and follow Him everywhere.

But Jesus had really come to give them the bread of life—the Word of God. It was His task to satisfy not the hunger of their bodies, but the hunger of their souls.

But there was no hunger in their souls. There was no genuine longing for God in their hearts. There was so little faith.

Jesus was sad when He saw how little faith they had. He had been in Galilee for over a year. Was this the fruit of His work? There was only one way left to save the people: they would have to hear *the truth*. So Jesus told them the truth, although it was not pleasant for them to hear.

"I tell you the truth," He began earnestly, "you seek Me because you have eaten your fill of the bread I gave you yesterday. Do not work for the food that spoils, but for the food that endures to eternal life, which the Son of man will give you. *I* am the bread of life. Anyone who comes to Me will never suffer hunger again, and anyone who believes in Me will never thirst, for I have come down from heaven to do the will of My Father."

When they heard this, the people made it apparent that they had no faith, for they started to grumble. They said to each other, "Isn't that Jesus, the son of Joseph, whose father and mother we know? How can He say, 'I have come down from heaven'?"

When Jesus went on speaking and they saw that He did not intend to give them any more bread, they started to leave. They said, "This is a hard teaching. How can we possibly accept it?"

Some who had been with Jesus for a long time and called themselves His disciples also left Him. When they finally realized that Jesus was not going to give them any earthly benefits, they had no more need of Him. They forsook Him.

Yet Jesus was not left all alone. The twelve disciples remained with Him. But He knew that among them, there was one who, had he been honest with himself, would have forsaken Him too. There was one among the twelve who stayed with Jesus only because he awaited riches and earthly advantages. The other disciples did not know that. Only Jesus knew what lived in the heart of Judas Iscariot.

Jesus spoke to His disciples with sadness in His voice, "Don't you want to go away too?"

Peter answered resolutely, "Lord, where could we turn? *You* have the words of eternal life!"

Judas was silent.

Jesus warned them once more. He said, "Have I not chosen all twelve of you? Yet, one of you is a devil."

Still Judas remained silent. He went with the others when Jesus left Galilee and set out for the land of Tyre and Sidon.

65: Crumbs from the master's table

Jesus and His disciples had gone north to the land of Tyre and Sidon, leaving their own land behind them. Perhaps if the people did not see Jesus for a while or hear Him talk, they would begin to yearn for Him again.

Because Jesus loved His people, He did not want to leave them. He wanted them to repent and turn to Him.

Jesus and His disciples had settled into a house in Phoenicia. Here Jesus could enjoy the rest that He had vainly sought in Galilee. Here He would have time to give His disciples some instruction.

He did not preach in this heathen land, although He did not despise the Gentiles, as the Jews did. Later, when His own work on earth was finished, His disciples would go into the world to spread the happiness He had brought for *all* peoples. But God's time had not yet come for the Gentiles.

Yet the Samaritan woman in Sychar had already shown her faith in Jesus and had been blessed by Him. Here, too, in the land of Tyre and Sidon, a drop of God's grace fell.

Jesus did not want anyone in the area to know who He was, but He could not keep His identity hidden. A woman started following Jesus and His disciples. She had heard about the miracles He had performed in Israel.

"Lord, Son of David," she cried, "have mercy on me. My daughter is deathly ill. She has an evil spirit."

Jesus kept on walking and acted as if He had not heard her pleading with Him. But the woman did not give up. She kept walking behind Him, begging Him to help her child: "Lord, Son of David!"

The disciples were irritated. Soon all the people would know who Jesus was, and then He would have no rest.

"Send her away," they said to Jesus, "for she keeps crying out after us."

Jesus answered, "I was sent to the lost sheep of the house of Israel." Yet He did not send her away. He wanted to test her faith.

The woman kneeled before Jesus. "Lord, help me!" she cried.

Still Jesus acted as if He didn't want to help. He said, "It is not good to take the bread from the children and throw it to the dogs."

The woman understood what He meant. The children were the people of Israel, and the dogs were the Gentiles, including herself. The Messiah had been born an Israelite and His blessing was first of all for Israel. But couldn't He spare a few crumbs for her?

She said, "Yes, Lord, but even a dog is allowed to eat the crumbs that fall from the master's table when the master gives bread to his children."

Jesus was delighted with this answer. "Woman," He said, "great is your faith! Your request is granted."

At that very moment her daughter was healed.

66: Jesus in Decapolis

Jesus made a long journey outside Galilee. From Phoenicia He went east with His disciples, entering the hill country. The blue water of the Mediterranean Sea shimmered behind them. Later the gospel would be carried across that sea to people in the west.

When Jesus and His disciples passed through the hill country, they found themselves by the Jordan River. It foamed and surged as it snaked a path through the valley. The Jordan was narrower here than in Judea, and not as deep. Therefore they could cross it easily.

Jesus and the twelve were in Decapolis, the area of the ten cities. It was a partially heathen area not far from the Sea of Galilee. Wherever He went in this area, Jesus demonstrated love and patience as He helped people.

One day the people brought Jesus a man who could not hear and could hardly talk. Jesus took the man to a quiet place. When He was alone with him, Jesus made it clear to him what was to happen and that God could heal him. Thus he first aroused faith in the man's heart.

Jesus placed His fingers on the man's ears and touched his tongue. This meant that the ears and the tongue would have to be healed. Jesus looked up to heaven and sighed. This meant that the Father in heaven would provide healing.

Then Jesus said, "Ephphatha. Be opened." At once the man's ears were opened, and his tongue shook free. He could hear and speak. He heard the songs of the birds and the wind rushing through the trees. The man now spoke clearly, and rejoiced with the people who followed Jesus around. "He makes the deaf hear and the dumb speak," people said. "He has made all things well."

Jesus ordered the people not to tell anyone about this. He did not want the people here seeking Him out because of His miracles as had happened in other places.

Despite Jesus' command, the people could not keep silent. From all sides people streamed toward Him with the crippled, the blind, the dumb, the lame, and people with all sorts of diseases. When He healed them, they glorified the God of Israel.

Here, in Decapolis, Jesus also fed a large crowd. The people had stayed with Him for three days. When they had nothing left to eat, He did not want to send them home with empty stomachs. They might have fallen ill from hunger and exhaustion.

In His mercy Jesus performed the same great miracle He had once performed for the people in Galilee. There were only seven loaves of bread and a couple of fishes available. But 4000 men, not counting the women and children, ate and were satisfied, and seven baskets of food were left over.

67: Signs of the times

Jesus was close to His own people again, and His heart yearned for the lost sheep of Israel. He crossed the lake and returned to Galilee.

It was only a short visit. He was hardly back after His long absence when He found the Pharisees and Sadducees standing before Him, ready to argue with Him again. They asked Him to perform a miracle, to give them a sign from heaven to prove God had really sent Him.

What fools! If they saw a red sun setting in the evening, they could be sure the weather would be nice the next day. But if the sky was red and overcast in the morning, they knew there was rough weather ahead. They knew all about the signs telling them of the weather. But what about the other signs? The blind could see, the cripples could walk, the lepers were healed, the deaf could hear, the dead were raised, and the gospel was proclaimed to the poor. Unlike John the Baptist, who knew the Messiah had come when he heard what Jesus was doing, the Pharisees and Sadducees still did not know.

Jesus sighed deeply, and then He said, "You know how to interpret the signs you see in the sky. Do you not know how to read the signs of the times?"

He would not give them the sign for which they asked. He would give them no other sign than that of Jonah the prophet. Three days after His death He would arise from His grave.

Again Jesus left His own land, greatly disappointed. The hatred and enmity of the Jewish leaders had not grown any less. That hatred blinded them. Jesus knew that, one day, that hatred would drive them to have Him nailed to the cross.

But the time had not yet come for Jesus to suffer and die. Therefore Jesus began to tour His own land again. He went to Bethsaida, on the eastern shore of the Sea of Galilee, and healed the eyes of a blind man there. He also took that man to a solitary place, leading him by the hand outside the village. He put some spit in the man's eyes and laid His hands over them in blessing.

When He took His hands away, He asked, "Can you see anything?"

The man saw the world as if he viewed it through a mist. Trembling, he answered, "I see people, but they look like trees walking around."

Then Jesus laid His hands over the man's eyes once more. When the man looked up again, he could see everything clearly. He was completely healed, and his joy knew no bounds.

Jesus sent him home at once. "Don't even go into the village," He said. Jesus was trying to shield Himself from the people's gossip. The man could best thank God in silence for the miracle.

Then Jesus sought silence and solitude Himself. He took His disciples to a place where they could be alone, for it was time to teach them something very difficult.

68: You are the Christ!

Jesus and His disciples went far north where the snow-covered tops of the Hermon range shone in the distance. Here the Jordan was only a small stream.

They were on their way to the villages around Caesarea Philippi. Jesus chose this moment to tell His disciples what was going to happen to Him, for He knew their expectations were wrong.

He began by praying under the open sky. Then He asked the twelve, "Who do people say that I am?"

They answered, "Some say that You are John the Baptist, who has arisen from the dead. Others say Elijah, for they believe that he will come again before the Christ comes. Still others say Jeremiah, or one of the prophets . . . ."

Jesus nodded. He knew perfectly well what people were saying about Him. Then He asked, "But what about you? Who do *you* say that I am?"

Again Simon Peter answered for all of them. Without hesitating a moment, Peter said forthrightly, "You are *the Christ*, the Son of the living God!"

There was joy in Jesus' heart. He knew that this faith was not just an opinion that Peter and the others had reached on their own. He knew that God had opened their hearts. With this unshakable faith they would one day go into the world as apostles.

"Jesus is the Christ, the Son of the living God!" That's what they would preach everywhere. That would be the bedrock foundation of their confession.

All who shared that confession would be true disciples of Jesus. Together they would form Jesus' church. Faith would be the rock on which the church of Christ was built. That faith came from God.

Therefore Jesus said, "Blessed are you, Simon, son of Jonah, for flesh and blood has not revealed this to you but My Father who is in heaven. You are Peter, the rock, and on this rock I will build My church."

Jesus then ordered His disciples not to tell anyone that He was the Christ. When His earthly work would be finished they would be allowed to proclaim the message to the entire world. If they would do it now, they would hinder Him in His work. The people would again want to make Him their king, just as they did that day after He miraculously fed 5000 people by the Sea of Galilee. That would never do.

They could be certain that Jesus' Kingdom would come. But it would come in a different way from what people expected. Jesus would have to follow a pathway of suffering before He ascended the throne.

69: Get out of My sight, satan!

Jesus had asked His disciples who they thought He was. Peter had given a glorious answer: "You are the Christ, the Son of the living God."

When this faith was firmly rooted in the disciples' hearts Jesus told them some things they found hard to understand and accept. He told them that He would have to go to Jerusalem and suffer much at the hands of the chief priest and scribes. He would even be put to death and buried. After three days He would rise from the grave. The prophets had already foretold this. The Messiah would willingly suffer all of this.

The disciples stared at their Master in fright and dismay because they still cherished their beautiful dream of an earthly kingdom. Could it be that their dream would never come true? That was really what Jesus had told them!

Must the Master they loved so dearly really suffer and die? Surely that could never be permitted! In their hearts they were set against the idea that their Master must die.

Peter, who so often spoke without thinking and was always first to act, took his Master aside. Perhaps he was filled with pride after the beautiful words Jesus had spoken to him on account of his confession that Jesus is the Christ.

Peter admonished Jesus as if *he* were the master. "God forbid," he said. "This shall never happen to You!"

Then he suddenly shrank back in fear, for the Master's eyes were full of wrath as He glared at Peter. Jesus gave Peter a harsh, stern answer, as if Peter were no longer His disciple. "Get out of My sight, satan! You are a stumbling block to Me. You do not have the things of God in mind but the things of man."

Actually, Jesus didn't address Peter, He spoke to the devil, who occupied an invisible spot next to Peter. It was the devil who had whispered those awful words to Peter. He was trying to tempt Jesus again, just as he had done in the wilderness.

Pale and bewildered, Peter rejoined the other disciples. He was deeply ashamed that he had been a tool of satan.

But the Savior's voice was friendly again. Soon He called together all the people who were with Him and began to teach them. He told them that if they were to be His disciples, they, too, would have to suffer.

Jesus said, "Anyone who wants to follow Me must deny himself, and take up his cross."

Yes, Jesus' disciples would have to be willing to *die* for Him. Then they would find eternal life. "Anyone who wants to save his life will lose it, but anyone who loses his life for My sake and the sake of the gospel will find it."

Jesus told His followers not to dream about wealth and prominence anymore. That was not the way of true happiness. "What good would it do you if you gained the whole world but lost your own soul?"

These words gave the disciples fresh hope, for the Master also said that there were some who would not die before they saw Him come in His royal majesty.

They did not fully understand much of what Jesus said. Often this became apparent. Yet they continued to follow Him toward Caesarea Philippi, silently and reverently. They wanted to follow Him all their lives, wherever He might lead them. They knew that Jesus was the Son of God. His Kingdom would surely come!

70: The Mount of Transfiguration

Less than a week before, while they were on their way to Caesarea Philippi, Jesus had spoken with His disciples about His coming suffering. But a few hours ago something beautiful and amazing had happened which seemed to contradict what Jesus had said. The three disciples who observed it remembered it clearly all their lives.

Jesus and His disciples had come to a high mountain. Jesus followed a twisting path up the mountain, for He wanted to be alone and pray. He ordered nine of the disciples to wait below. Peter, James, and his brother John were permitted to come with Jesus.

It was evening. The sun had set by the time they reached the top. Night covered the earth with a dark veil. In the stillness of the night Jesus kneeled down.

Peter and the other two disciples sat down a little distance away. They may have prayed too, but they could not pray as fervently as their Master. They were tired from the long climb, and their eyes were heavy with sleep. They rested their tired heads on the rocks and fell asleep.

A bright light awakened them. Was it daytime already? The valleys were still carpeted with the darkness of night, for the sun had not risen yet.

The bright, shining light was right before them, where Jesus was kneeling. And there was their Master!

But was it really Jesus? He seemed to have been transformed; He didn't look like a human being. His face shone like the sun, and His clothes were bright as the light and whiter than snow. They were whiter than any amount of washing on earth could possibly make them.

There were two heavenly figures standing with Jesus. Moses and Elijah had come down to earth from heaven and were talking with Jesus about Jerusalem and what would happen to Him there.

It was such a wondrous, sublime scene that the disciples did not dare to say a word. They sat and watched, trembling in awe and fear. It seemed as if heaven itself had come down to earth.

When the heavenly messengers were leaving Jesus, Peter could not restrain himself any longer. Peter wanted to cling to this divine miracle. He wanted this bit of heaven to remain on the earth. He didn't know exactly what he was saying when he stammered, "Master, it is good that we are here. If you wish, we can set up three tents —one for You, one for Moses, and one for Elijah."

While Peter was still speaking, a bright cloud came down from heaven and covered the three shining figures. A voice spoke from the cloud and said, "This is My Son, My beloved, in whom I am well pleased. Listen to Him!"

It was God's voice. When the disciples heard it, they threw themselves to the ground, quaking with fear. They did not dare look up again until a hand touched them and the familiar voice of Jesus said, "Stand up. Don't be afraid."

When they opened their eyes, they saw only Jesus. They looked timidly in all directions; there was no one but Jesus with them.

Still, they had not dreamed. They had actually witnessed this miracle, and their respect and love for Jesus had grown even greater. Now they knew once and for all that He was the Son of God.

Their hearts were full as they climbed down the mountain. The early morning light beamed down on the earth, but their Master had been much more radiant than the sunlight. The bright sun climbed above the eastern horizon, but Jesus had been brighter by far. Now He walked with them again in His ordinary clothes, looking like an ordinary person.

They heard Him say that they should not tell anyone what they had seen until He had risen from the grave. They puzzled over what He meant by rising from the grave.

Less than a week before, the Master had spoken to them openly about how He would have to suffer and die in Jerusalem. Only a few hours ago they had heard Moses and Elijah discussing it with Him on the mountain. Still, they had not understood the truth. Was the Son of God supposed to suffer and die?

They could not accept the idea. That miracle was too great and too horrible for them.

71: Jesus heals an epileptic boy

The disciples were still weak and powerless without Jesus. They were not yet prepared to get along without Him.

When Jesus, Peter, James, and John came down from the Mount of Transfiguration, they found the other nine disciples standing together in the middle of a noisy crowd. The disciples didn't know what to do as they listened to the mocking voices of some scribes who had come to argue with them.

When Jesus approached, everyone fell silent. The people walked toward Him and greeted Him respectfully. He asked the scribes, "Why are you arguing with them?"

Before anyone could answer, a man from

the crowd fell down on his knees at Jesus' feet and cried out, "Lord, have mercy on my son. He is my only boy, and he is deathly ill. He is deaf and dumb, and he has horrible fits. There is an evil spirit living in him. I begged Your disciples to drive out the evil spirit, but they couldn't."

Jesus was disappointed. What a contrast to the mountaintop! Just a few hours ago He had been surrounded by heavenly glory. Now He was surrounded by people with their sins and suffering and unbelief. It was indeed a difficult path that He had to follow.

Jesus sighed, "O unbelieving generation! How long must I still stay with you and put up with you?"

Still, He was ready to help at once. He said to the man, "Bring your son here."

The man brought him, with some help, for his son was already quite grown up. While he was standing before Jesus, he had another one of his horrible fits. He fell on the ground, pounding with his hands and feet. His mouth was foaming.

Jesus asked, "How long has he been doing this?"

"From childhood," replied the father. "He has often fallen into the fire or the water." The man stretched out his arms to Jesus. There was despair in his eyes as he begged for help. "If You can do something," he pleaded, "help us and have mercy on us."

"*If* you can," the man had said. Didn't he know Jesus?

"What do you mean, 'If you can'?" said Jesus. "Everything is possible for him who believes."

The father wondered, did his son's healing depend on his faith? He wanted to believe. But he knew how weak he was. Such a faith was beyond him.

"I believe, Lord!" he cried. "Help me overcome my unbelief!"

That was enough. Jesus rebuked the evil spirit and said to him, "I command you, go out of the boy and do not go back in."

The boy screamed, and then suddenly lay still. He was pale, and his eyes were closed.

"He's dead!" cried the people who crowded around from all sides. Jesus took the boy by the hand, raised him to his feet, and brought him back to his father, completely healed. Thankful and happy, the two went away together.

Jesus went away too. His disciples walked silently behind Him. Three of them were still deeply under the impression of the miracle that had taken place on the Mount of Transfiguration. The other nine were filled with shame at their own powerlessness.

When they were alone with their Master again, they asked Him, "Why weren't we able to heal the boy?"

"Because your faith was too small," Jesus told them. "If your faith were great enough, you could even move mountains."

Once, when Jesus had sent out the disciples in pairs through the land, they had healed the sick and had cast out demons through their faith in their Master, who had told them to do so. Where had that faith gone? Once more the disciples saw how much they needed Jesus.

Jesus and the disciples went farther through the land. The one who had enjoyed the glory of heaven walked along the road like any other human being, patiently teaching His disciples. He would follow this pathway to its end. He would remain obedient to the Father to death.

72: True humility

It required a great deal of Jesus' patience to put up with His disciples. They understood so little of what He was talking about! Sometimes it seemed as if they didn't *want* to understand.

He had said, "Blessed are the peacemakers." But the disciples had a hard time putting up with each other and often quarreled over little things. He had said, "Whoever would come after Me, let him deny himself." The disciples did no such thing. They were too concerned with their own honor and their own rights and their own advantage. They were often so jealous and so proud! Jesus had said, "Love one another." But the disciples loved *themselves* too much for that.

They traveled together through Galilee, along quiet, hidden paths. When they were on their way to Capernaum, Jesus spoke to them openly once again about the suffering He would have to undergo. He said, "The Son of man is to be delivered into the hands of men. They will put Him to death, but after three days He will rise again."

Those were somber words. The disciples had heard them before, but they still didn't know what Jesus meant. There were a lot of questions they would have liked to ask, but they didn't dare. They would rather forget about the whole matter.

Suffering? Dying? They had better, more beautiful things to think about. They would rather think about Jesus' Kingdom, which would come one day. In the Messiah's mighty realm they, the disciples, would be the most important people. They would be right next to Jesus.

Who would be the greatest among the disciples? Who would be second only to Jesus when the Kingdom came?

They busily discussed the question of who was the greatest among them. Each of the disciples believed he could claim this honor for himself. Was it Andrew? Or perhaps John? Weren't they the first disciples to come to Jesus? Or could it be Simon Peter? He was also one of the first disciples, and he had been given a new name. Then there was Judas, who was entrusted with all the money.

Which disciple had given up the most for Jesus? Matthew! He had walked away from considerable wealth and a secure position as a tax-collector. Each disciple could find something special on which to base his claim.

They walked behind Jesus and argued with each other, exchanging some harsh words. No one wanted to be regarded as less important than another. No one wanted to humble himself before another. They were in a surly mood as they walked together.

Jesus walked ahead of them and said nothing, although He knew exactly what was going on. But when they came to the city, He gave His disciples a lesson in true humility.

A few men came up to Peter. They were citizens of Capernaum, and they were collecting the temple tax. Each year every Israelite had to give half a shekel, in the form of a silver coin. Everyone except Jesus had paid already.

The men asked, "Doesn't your master pay the temple tax?"

Peter answered, "Certainly!" Of course Jesus would pay the tax just like anyone else, thought Peter. Why should his pious Master not want to pay His share of the tax for the temple?

Peter went into the house Jesus had en-

tered and wanted to talk about the temple tax. Jesus beat him to it with the question, "What do you think, Peter? On whom do earthly kings levy taxes, on their own sons or on others?"

"On others," Peter answered.

Jesus nodded and said to him, "Then the sons are free."

Peter understood Jesus' point. He had not thought through the matter of the temple tax properly. The temple was the house of God and Jesus was the Son of God and the Lord of the temple. Therefore Jesus was not

obliged to pay the tax. He had the right to refuse to pay it.

Jesus did not refuse to pay, however. He did not want to be a stumbling block to others, so He did not claim His rights. He said, "So that we will not give offense, Peter, go to the lake and throw out a fishing line. Pull in the first fish that bites. When you open its mouth, you will find a silver coin inside. Take the coin and pay the temple tax for Me and for you."

Never had this fisherman made such a

strange catch. It all happened just as Jesus said it would. The first fish Peter pulled out of the lake had a shining coin in its mouth. With his heart full of amazement, Peter brought that coin to the men who were collecting the temple tax.

Jesus had shown that He was the humblest of them all. He was not too proud to pay the temple tax, although He had the right to refuse.

The disciples were together in the house. Suddenly their Master asked them, "What were you talking about on the way over here?"

No one said a word. The disciples were embarrassed and looked down. They heard Jesus say, "Whoever seeks to be first will be last and will be the servant of all the others."

Nothing remained hidden from Jesus. The disciples knew this. Therefore they finally admitted that they had been discussing who would be the greatest in the Kingdom of heaven.

At that point they saw Jesus call a little boy to Himself. The child came to Jesus gladly, for no child was ever afraid of Him. He placed the boy in the midst of His disciples and put His arms around him. The disciples no doubt looked down on that child in their great pride, but that child was not at all concerned about honor and prominence. That child, said Jesus, was an example to the disciples. "Truly, I say to you, if you do not repent and become like children, you will not enter the Kingdom of heaven. Whoever humbles himself like this child is the greatest in the Kingdom of heaven."

Jesus told His disciples that God especially loves people who are as humble and small in their own eyes as children.

Jesus also added some words that were more stern and threatening than any words

He had ever spoken. He said, "Whoever receives such a child, such a humble disciple in My name receives Me. But whoever causes one of these little ones who believe in Me to sin, it would be better for him if a large millstone were hung around his neck and he were cast into the sea."

The disciples had much to forgive each other. But Jesus, who was more humble than any of them, had to extend more forgiveness than any of them.

73: Seventy-seven times

Jesus taught His disciples much in Capernaum. He taught them, for example, how they were to conduct themselves if a brother mistreated them.

The person who was mistreated must not just become angry and go around telling people about it. Instead he must go to that brother and the two of them must discuss the matter in a friendly way. If the brother repented, he should be forgiven, no matter how serious the offense was.

Peter thought about these words. "What happens if I forgive him now, and he does it to me again? If that brother keeps doing it to me, what then?"

He brought his question to Jesus. He asked, "Lord, how many times must I forgive my brother if he sins against me? As many as seven times?"

That would be asking quite a lot, thought Peter. The scribes declared that three times was enough. If it happened a fourth time, one could take revenge. But the Master was much more gentle and forgiving than the scribes. He would probably say that one should forgive *seven* times.

Peter had not understood the Master as well as he thought. Therefore he was surprised when Jesus answered, "Seven times is not enough. You must forgive seventy times seven fold." He really meant, of course, that it had nothing to do with counting. If a person were genuinely willing to forgive the wrong done him by others, how could he even *think* of counting?

A long time ago, a wicked man had sung a song of vengeance: "If Cain is avenged sevenfold, Lamech shall avenge seventy-sevenfold!" Jesus now declared that we are to *forgive* seventy times sevenfold.

The song to sing in the Kingdom of Jesus is the song of love. Just as Lamech was always ready to hate and take revenge, the disciples of Jesus must always be ready to love and forgive.

To make it clear to His disciples just how important this was, Jesus told them a parable.

Once there was a mighty eastern king, He explained. This king wanted to settle accounts with his servants. He had them all appear, one by one, to pay him what they owed.

One servant who was brought in owed the king an especially large sum. He was supposed to pay the king 10,000 talents, or millions of dollars.

This servant stood before his lord with empty hands. The king therefore decreed that the servant should be sold, with his wife, children and everything he had. At least some small part of the debt would be paid.

Trembling, the servant threw himself down before the throne and pleaded for mercy. "Lord, have patience with me, and I will pay you everything I owe."

The man could never pay back such a sum, of course, but the king was a merciful master. He was more gentle and warm-hearted than any other king, and he felt very sorry for the servant. "Arise," he said. "I have forgotten your debt completely."

The servant was overjoyed when he left the king's presence. All his cares had been lifted from his shoulders in an instant. The generosity of his master had saved him from horrible misery and suffering.

Outside the palace he met one of his fellow servants who owed *him* money. It was only a small sum, not much more than a few dollars. Still, it was a debt, and the servant had a right to his money. He grabbed the man roughly by the throat and cried out, "Pay me what you owe me!"

The man fell down at *his* feet, just as *he* had fallen down earlier before the king, trembling and begging for mercy. "Be patient with me, and I will pay you everything I owe."

What did the first servant do? The king had shown him such mercy and generosity, but now he was stern and unmerciful to the servant who owed him a small sum. He had been forgiven much, but he forgave nothing himself.

He dragged his victim across the street and had him thrown into prison. The second servant would have to labor there until his debt was paid.

Other servants of the king had seen what had happened. With disappointment in their voices, they told the king.

The king summoned the unmerciful servant and spoke angrily to him, "You wicked servant! I forgave you that enormous debt because you pleaded with me. Shouldn't you have been merciful to your fellow servant, just as I was merciful to you?"

There was no more mercy for the first servant. He had let his fellow servant plead in vain, and now he pleaded in vain himself.

The king sentenced him to heavy forced labor until his huge debt was completely paid. That day, of course, would never come. He would never get his freedom back. It was a just punishment.

When Jesus was finished telling this story, He said, "That's how My heavenly Father will treat each of you unless you forgive each other from the heart."

74: Two Samaritan responses to Jesus

It was time for the Feast of Tabernacles. This was one of the great festivals celebrated by the Jews. All the roads from Galilee to Jerusalem were crowded with joyful groups of people on their way to the holy city for the celebration. It almost seemed as if the whole country would be there.

Jesus and His disciples did not prepare to go to Jerusalem. They stayed quietly right where they were.

The brothers of Jesus—James and Joseph, Simon and Judas—couldn't figure it out. Why did Jesus want to stay in the background? Why did He remain where He was with His disciples? Didn't He want to be the Redeemer of His people? If so, He would have to go to Jerusalem; all the people were gathered there. He would have to start doing the miracles there that He had been doing in Galilee. If He demonstrated His power to all the people, they could be proud of Him. Shouldn't He be seeking honor from all the people?

That was their line of reasoning. It showed that even Jesus' own brothers didn't believe in Him. They had grown up with Him in the same house, had eaten with Him at the same table and were cared for by the same mother. Still, they did not believe in Him!

"Go away from here and travel to Judea," they said to Jesus. "Make Yourself known to the world."

Jesus shook His head. He knew how much the rabbis hated Him. Although He was not afraid of them, He did not want to give them the opportunity to kill Him before His work was finished. Calmly He said, "You go to the feast without Me. My time has not yet come." He stayed in Galilee.

Soon, when all the people going to the feast had left and the roads were quiet again, Jesus set out for Jerusalem anyway.

Jesus chose the shortest route to Jerusalem. He and His disciples descended

times, Elijah had summoned fire from heaven. The fire had consumed his enemies, who had come to take him captive. But those times were long ago. Now the Messiah Himself, the Lord of Elijah, walked through this area as He approached the land of the Samaritans.

Jesus sent a couple of His disciples ahead to a village in that half-heathen land. They were to find a place for Jesus and the disciples to stay overnight.

When the people of the village heard that Jesus was on His way to Jerusalem, they refused to receive Him. Anyone going to the feast in Jerusalem was a Jew, and the hatred between the Jews and the Samaritans was still as great as ever.

The disappointed disciples returned to

from Galilee's hill country, passed through the plain of Jezreel, and kept moving south from there. Far away, to their right, they saw the top of Mount Carmel, where Elijah had made fire come down from heaven. That time the fire had lit the sacrifice that he had prepared for the Lord. Two more

Jesus. Bitterly they reported what the Samaritans had said to them.

All the disciples were indignant—especially James and John. Their eyes blazed with wrath. They wanted vengeance on those hated Samaritans. Was there no place for the Messiah, the Lord of heaven and earth, in their town? Then no punishment was too severe for them!

They asked Jesus, "Lord, would You like us to command fire to come down from heaven and consume them?"

Jesus turned around and rebuked them. They should not allow the spirit of hatred and revenge to control them. The spirit of love was to move them instead. They were to bless those who cursed them.

Jesus calmly led the way to another village, where the people were more hospitable.

Jesus traveled farther, across the boundary of Samaria and Galilee. As they approached a small village, His name was suddenly called out. Ten lepers, keeping a proper distance, extended their arms to Him and cried out, "Jesus, Master, have mercy on us."

Jesus tested their faith. If a leper was healed, he was to go to the priests to show them and to offer sacrifices. Jesus sent them on their way as they were, without curing the leprosy. "Go and show yourselves to the priests," He said to them.

They all obeyed. While they were on their way, the miracle suddenly happened. They were healed.

Nine healthy men walked on, their hearts overflowing with joy. They would go quickly to the priests, and then home. They thought only of themselves and their own happiness.

The tenth man could go no farther when he saw that the miracle had occurred.

He thought at once of Jesus, who had healed him of his leprosy. He simply *had* to go back. He ran back to Jesus rejoicing and fell down before Him in gratitude. Worshipfully he laid his head down at Jesus' feet. He was a Samaritan!

Jesus asked, "Weren't there ten lepers who were healed? Where are the other nine? Was this foreigner, this Samaritan, the only one to return and give glory to God?"

To the Samaritan He said, "Get up and go your way. Your faith has made you well."

The man was even happier than the other nine who were also healed. The love of Jesus that filled him would purify his soul from sin, just as his body had been purified from leprosy.

75: No place to lay His head

Not many people were willing to give up absolutely everything for Jesus, to think of Him alone and give themselves completely to Him. Those who were willing to give themselves completely found a happiness that was greater than any other available on earth.

Jesus traveled through the land, followed by His twelve disciples and by many other people. Whenever they stopped to rest, He gave them instruction. He spoke in such a gripping way that they all listened breathlessly to every word.

A scribe listening to Jesus cried out enthusiastically, "Master, I'll follow You wherever You go."

Jesus could see into this man's heart. He knew that this wealthy scribe was far too attached to his house and his standard of living. Would such a man be able to give up *everything* for Jesus?

Jesus knew that he would long for his house and goods again when he found out just how poor the Savior was. Therefore He warned, "The foxes have holes, and the birds of the air have nests, but the Son of man has no place to lay His head."

Someone who wishes to follow Jesus must be willing to give up not only his household but even his family and parents.

One day Jesus saw someone who loved Him, someone who could have been a good disciple for Him. Jesus said to him, "Follow Me."

Those were the same words He had addressed to Philip, and later to Levi, the tax-collector. Both had obeyed without question. The two words were enough.

For this man, however, the two words Jesus spoke were not enough. He was perplexed and didn't know what to do. He thought of his aged father, for whom he had to care. When the old man was dead and buried, he would be free. He could follow Jesus then, but not before. He said to Jesus, "Let me go home first until my father is buried."

For Jesus' sake he should have been willing to forsake even his father. Was his faith really a living faith? Or was it dead, like the faith of so many others? If it were living, shouldn't he realize that God would care for his father since he had been called to follow God's own Son? Therefore Jesus said to him, "Let the dead bury the dead. You just go and proclaim the Kingdom of God."

Another person who came to Jesus also had only half the courage and half the faith he needed. "I will follow You, Lord, but first let me say goodbye to my family."

This man would continue to think of his family if he followed Jesus. Repeatedly he would look back in his thoughts.

A farmer who looked back while he was plowing would never manage to plow a straight furrow. A disciple of Jesus who longed for his former life would never be a proper disciple. Jesus said, "If anyone puts his hand to the plow but looks back to what is behind him, he is not fit for the Kingdom of God."

There were also people who gave their hearts wholly to the Savior and placed their lives completely in His service. Jesus appointed 70 such people to go out and work on His behalf. Earlier He had sent out His *twelve* disciples to bring the gospel to the *twelve* tribes of Israel. Now he sent out *seventy* disciples to all the villages and towns He planned to visit.

He sent them out into a world full of hatred; they were sheep among wolves. They took no purse and no money with them, but their hearts were full of faith. They were without weapons, but they were strengthened by love. He gave them power to heal the sick and commanded them to preach that the Kingdom of God was at hand.

They went about their work obediently and with great zeal. When they returned, joy shone from their eyes. Even the evil spirits had obeyed them when they mentioned Jesus' name.

Jesus said, "Do you know what should really make you happy? That your names are written in heaven."

He looked at His disciples, the 70 simple men. They were as humble and natural as children. But they knew the great secret that the wise scribes did not know. Theirs was the great happiness that God gives willingly to those that are humble in their hearts.

When Jesus thought about this, He was happy. He said, "I thank You, Father, Lord of heaven and earth, that You have hidden these things from men of wisdom and understanding and revealed them to children. Yes, Father, this is Your good pleasure."

Peacefully Jesus traveled on to Jerusalem. There men of wisdom and understanding were waiting for Him with hatred in their hearts.

76: The Feast of Tabernacles

The scent of freshly cut wood was everywhere. Swaying branches of palm trees and fig trees, of fruit trees and willows, were cut down to build huts. Those huts made of leaves and foliage stood on roofs and in open squares and even on hills outside the city. People sat together in the green huts with their children and family and friends who had come to celebrate this feast in Jerusalem.

They went to the temple to offer sacrifices in gratitude to God. God had brought them into this land and had given them houses and fields. He had blessed the crops in their fields so that the people could take in a rich harvest.

Those were the things people were thinking about at this feast. They were thinking about the rich blessings God had given His people in Canaan.

The people built their green foliage huts

or tents or tabernacles so that they would always remember the 40 year-long wilderness journey, when they had been forced to live in tents.

The Feast of Tabernacles was the greatest and most joyous of all of Israel's festivals. It was said that anyone who had never joined in this feast did not know what it was to celebrate a feast.

The decorated streets were full of happy shouts. The great temple square was full of rejoicing people. More and more people came along all the roads that led to Jerusalem. They came from east and west, from near and far. They had palm branches in their hands and joy in their hearts.

When they reached the city, they all asked about Jesus of Nazareth. Where was He? Would He be coming to the feast? His name was on every tongue in every hut.

"He is a good man," said some.

"No, He's not," said others. "He is misleading the people."

Sometimes they could argue about Him heatedly, but they had to be careful. They could not make too much noise about it because they feared the rabbis, the stern scribes and Pharisees.

The rabbis had already made their plans. If Jesus came to the feast and dared to speak to the people again, it would be the last time. He would simply have to *die*. There was no other way to put an end to the trouble He was causing. They kept their eyes open and looked all around for Him.

All of Jerusalem waited for Jesus. The first days of the festival passed, and no one saw Him.

Then, suddenly, Jesus was there at the very heart of the celebration. He stood in the outer court of the temple, surrounded by His disciples.

The crowd around Him swelled quickly.

His earnest voice rang out clearly across the temple square and echoed off the high, shining temple walls.

The news of His arrival raced through the city. People streamed toward Him from all directions.

Some people from faraway areas heard Jesus for the very first time. They were amazed, for they had never heard a scribe speak in such a beautiful, stirring way.

People from Jerusalem were no less amazed. They knew about the wicked plans of the rabbis who wanted to murder Jesus. They stood listening to Him. They let Jesus speak without interruption and said nothing back to Him. Could it be that they realized that Jesus was really the Christ, the Messiah promised by God?

Not even the rabbis knew what to do. Something mysterious, something wonderful, was happening. The rabbis had been so sure of themselves and so confident about their plan. They had promised each other firmly: "As soon as He shows Himself, we'll arrest Him." But their confidence and firmness disappeared now that Jesus actually stood before them. Their hatred had not grown any less, but no one dared to step forward to touch Jesus.

Jesus' time had not yet come. No one understood that secret. Because of that divine secret, Jesus felt safe in the midst of those murderers all watching Him carefully.

77: Fountains of blessing

All the people were celebrating the Feast of Tabernacles in Jerusalem. Jesus stood in the temple every day, and taught the people. The people listened silently and were deeply moved. Many believed in Him.

"When the Christ comes, will He do more miracles than this man is now doing?" they asked. A sigh and a happy murmur spread through the crowd, "The Christ! The Messiah! Surely this man is the Messiah!"

These words soon reached the Pharisees. So far they had done nothing to Jesus during this festival, but they could restrain themselves no longer. They simply *had* to put an end to the power of this man from Nazareth. They called the temple servants and sent them over to Jesus. "Grab Him," they said, "and bring Him here as your prisoner."

A strong company of armed men walked over to the temple square. The rabbis would soon have rest again. Their hour of revenge had come.

It was the last day of the Feast of Tabernacles, the great day on which the joy reached its climax. On the earlier days of the feast, there had been a solemn ceremony. Priests came from the temple with a golden pitcher and walked through the streets to a spring outside the city, known as *Siloam.* They filled the pitcher with clear water there and brought the water back to the temple in a procession.

Trumpets were sounded when they got back. Psalms were sung in the outer courts. In the midst of the jubilant crowd, the pitcher was brought to the altar.

A silver basin stood on the ground in front of the altar. A priest waited by the basin. He then called out, "With joy we draw water from the wells of salvation!"

He took the pitcher from the priests and poured the water into the basin. From the basin it flowed to the ground on the mountain where the temple was built. It was said that the water flowed right through the earth to the valley of the brook of Kidron. The water flowed out of a rock, just as water had once flowed from a rock in the wilderness when Moses gave the command.

The scene at the altar reminded the rejoicing people of that event. Some were also reminded of the vision of the prophet Ezekiel. He saw a river spring from a rock in the mountain on which the temple was built. That river, the river of life, turned the area around the Dead Sea into a fertile plain and irrigated the whole world.

This ceremony did *not* take place on the eighth day of the feast. It was a day of rest, just like the first day.

On the eighth day someone stood up. It was the One Ezekiel had longed for, the One in whom Ezekiel's prophecies would be fulfilled. The Messiah would turn the well of salvation in Jerusalem into a river of blessing that would stream across the entire earth.

He stood in the outer court, and His voice could be heard clearly by all. "If anyone is thirsty, let him come to Me and drink. If anyone believes in Me, rivers of living water will flow outward from within him!"

By this "living water" He meant the Holy Spirit. All who believed in Jesus would receive the Spirit. All who had the Spirit of God within them would become fountains of blessing.

The people listened breathlessly. Even the temple servants sent by the Pharisees to arrest Jesus listened to Him. When they heard His words, they completely forgot the command their masters had given them.

They returned to their masters, lost in their earnest, deep thoughts. How much they were moved was clearly shown in their eyes.

The rabbis were amazed. "Why didn't you take Him back with you?" they asked.

The servants sighed, "Never have we heard a person speak the way this man speaks!"

The rabbis screamed back, "Have you been led astray too? How could you fall for His words? Has any one of the rulers or Pharisees ever believed in Him?" They cursed the servants.

One man among the rabbis gently opposed the others. He tried to get them to think carefully about what they were doing.

That man was a Pharisee himself. He was one of the leading Pharisees. It was Nicodemus, who had once come to talk to Jesus at night.

He said, "Are you sure you are acting within the law? Does our law condemn someone without having heard him and without finding out what he is doing?"

The others did not want to listen to Nicodemus. "Listen to him!" they scoffed. "Are you perhaps from Galilee also? No prophet has ever come from Galilee! Look it up on your own if you don't believe us."

They went home furious. Their hearts were full of hatred and bitterness. That was how the Feast of Tabernacles, the most joyous of all feasts, ended for them.

Jesus went to the Mount of Olives. That peaceful summer night He was alone with His Father.

78: The light of the world

The Feast of Tabernacles was over. The huts were taken down, and the people began to go home. Dried-out branches lay along the streets.

It was early morning. A group of scribes and Pharisees walked across the temple square, dragging a woman with them. The woman walked among all those important men with her head bowed.

The men's eyes gleamed with wicked joy because they had made a clever plan involving this woman. They dragged her into the outer court of the temple and pushed her roughly to the place where Jesus stood preaching. Then they let the frightened woman go and formed a circle around her so that she couldn't escape.

There she stood among the scribes and Pharisees and other people who crowded around to see what was going on. Many eyes stared at her harshly, full of contempt.

She was a sinful woman who had left her husband for another man. The Pharisees explained this without any compassion. All the people listened intently. Then they asked Jesus a cunning question, "Teacher, in the law of Moses it is commanded that a woman who commits adultery is to be stoned. But what do *You* say should be done?"

They waited eagerly for His answer. They really didn't care about the woman at all; they were indifferent to her sin. Otherwise they would have brought her directly to the judges. They really cared only about the answers Jesus would give.

They had dragged the woman here to lure Jesus into a trap. It was a very clever trap, and they did not see how He would escape. If He said, "Don't stone her," they would cry out, "He disobeys the law!" If He answered, "Stone her, just as Moses commanded," they would say, "That's the man who pretends to be so merciful to sinners!"

Jesus did not answer immediately. Everyone waited breathlessly. Silently Jesus bent over and began to write with His finger on the dusty temple floor.

The Pharisees became impatient. "Well,

Teacher, what do You say?" Wouldn't He even dignify their question with a reply?

Jesus stood up. He looked deeply into their eyes. He saw right through them; they could feel that He knew everything about them. He said, "Whichever of you is without sin, let him cast the first stone at her."

Then He bent over and started writing on the floor again. What was He writing? Was He writing words that only the rabbis understood, words that reminded them about their sins?

An old, gray man, the oldest Pharisee in the circle around Jesus, turned and walked away silently. Another followed. One by one every Pharisee slipped away. They had come to put Jesus to shame, but *they* were put to shame instead.

Finally Jesus was alone with the woman. She stood still as if she were waiting to hear the sentence pronounced. There she stood in the middle of all the footsteps in the dusty temple floor.

Jesus stood up and said to her, "Woman, where are they? Is there anyone here to condemn you?"

She stammered, "No one, sir." That was a miracle to her, for she knew that she was guilty as charged.

The man who now stood before her could certainly throw the first stone at her, for *He* was without sin. Instead He said, "I do not condemn you either. Go your way and sin no more."

Jesus had come into the world to save sinners. He had come to let the light of God's love shine.

That same day He carried on with the work for which the Father had sent Him into the world. He stood by the treasury in the women's court. That was the busiest place in the temple. The people congregated there.

On the last day of the feast, many lights had burned there. The crowd had gathered around two large standards, each with four lamps. The people, carrying their torches, had celebrated until late into the night, bathed in a sea of light. That was their way of remembering how the column of fire had led the people in the wilderness and shed light on their path.

But now the lamps had been put out. The torches burned no more. The feast was over. That night darkness would be there again.

Jesus, who could lead the people better than any column of fire, stood there. Jesus wanted to bring them to a land that was much better than Canaan. "*I* am the light of the world," He said. "Anyone who follows Me will never walk in darkness but will have the light of life."

The rabbis came to Jesus again to argue

with Him. They hated Him more than ever, because He had put them to shame. They didn't even pretend to be pious, for they knew that He wasn't fooled. They showed themselves in all their hatred and sin.

They knew they were sinners, but they were not sorry for their sin. They knew Jesus, but they did not believe in Him. They stood before Him with clenched fists and eyes blazing with wrath. When they finally saw they could not defeat Him in debate, they began to pick up stones. They were going to stone Him instead!

But Jesus walked away from the temple calmly. He walked right between them with royal majesty. The raging rabbis shrank back as He walked toward them, and their arms fell to their sides. No one reached out to seize Him, and no one threw a stone at Him.

79: Born blind

The man sat by the gate of the temple begging, just as he had for years. The people knew him; they knew he had been born blind.

He always sat in the same place. When people came along, he stretched out his hand and stared right into the bright light of the sun with his blind eyes, begging for alms. He even stayed at his post when it rained. People often walked right past him without seeing him, for they had become used to him.

He sat there as a forgotten man. He heard bits of conversations as people entering the temple walked by. A certain name had often come to his ears in recent days. Everyone was talking about Jesus, about the things He said and the miracles He performed. They said that He had healed many sick people. He had even made blind people see again! But surely He had never healed someone who was *born* blind. Such a thing had never happened. Never had the eyes of someone born blind been healed.

No, there was no hope for him to be healed. If Jesus came by, He might not even notice him. Jesus must have passed by the gate sometime during the Feast of Tabernacles. That would mean that the blind man had even heard His footsteps, and perhaps His voice. But Jesus had walked right by.

The blind man was convinced that he could never be healed. Despised, he would sit there all his life, begging for bread. He would be a helpless creature until the day of his death.

The blind man heard footsteps again. A large group was coming out of the temple toward him. The people stopped near him. The blind man heard a voice ask, "Rabbi, who sinned to cause blindness in this man—the man himself, or his parents?"

That was a question the blind man had often heard people ask. People sometimes asked this question aloud as they walked past him. They seemed to think he was *deaf* as well as blind. They did not seem to realize that the question caused the blind man a lot of pain. Either he or his parents must have committed some great sin, they thought. Otherwise God would not have punished the poor man so severely. That's why everyone despised the man.

Listen! What was that?

The blind man heard words more kind and merciful than any he had ever heard before. A friendly voice said, "Neither this man nor his parents sinned to cause the blindness. The man is blind so that the works of God may be displayed in his life."

The kind voice continued, "We must work while it is still day, for the night is coming in which no one can work. As long as I am in the world, I am the light of the world."

The light of the world? Who was this man, that he could describe himself as the light of the world?

"It must be Jesus!" the blind man said to himself, deeply moved.

Suddenly he felt a hand laid gently on his head. A finger was smearing something over his eyes. Jesus had moistened some mud with spit and was putting it on the man's eyes. He said to the blind man, "Go and wash in the pool of Siloam."

The blind man stood up, trembling with hope. He had never heard of someone who was born blind being healed. Still, because it was Jesus who told him, he obeyed.

He hurried away along the temple walls.

He found his way through the streets, for he knew them by feel. He came to the pool of Siloam and kneeled down next to it. He scooped up water with his hands and washed the mud out of his eyes.

What happened then was so overwhelming that his joy was almost too much for him: he could *see!* He saw the water, and the blue sky reflected in the water. He stood up, and his freshly opened eyes looked on the golden glory of the sun. He saw the trees with their bright green crowns, and he saw people walking around. He looked everywhere, delighted and amazed. He looked at everything in that beautiful world that had opened before him. He was so happy that he didn't know what to do.

He went back into the city dancing and rejoicing. He saw the houses shining in the light. He saw the play of sun and shadow on the ground. He went home and saw his mother, whom he had never seen before and knew only from her voice and her hands. Now he saw her for the first time, and found her beautiful. The whole world looked beautiful. A *new life* lay open before him, for he had become a *new man.*

80: The man called Jesus

A man who had been blind all his life was healed of his blindness simply by washing in the pool of Siloam. Yet it was Jesus who put mud over his eyes and told him to go to the pool.

The blind man's parents could hardly believe the change in him. They could hardly believe their son now walked freely and boldly through the streets. No one who remembered him from before could believe it.

The neighbors asked in amazement, "Isn't he the one who used to sit begging by the temple?"

Some said, "Yes, he's the one." But others argued, "No, that can't be. It must be someone else."

He stood before them, looked at them with shining eyes, and said, "Yes, I am the one."

"How is it that your eyes are now opened?" the people asked him in amazement.

He answered, "The man called Jesus spread some mud over my eyes and said to me, 'Go and wash in the pool of Siloam.' I did as He said, and after I washed I could see."

The *man* called Jesus! Those were the words he used. He had not yet had a chance to think about Jesus. He had spent all his time looking around and enjoying himself. He was still overcome by the miracle.

The miracle was too much for his neighbors. They didn't know what to do or say. They had to ask other people who were wiser than they were how this was possible. Therefore they brought the man in a great procession to the Pharisees.

The Pharisees asked the blind man why he could now see. He told them the same story: "He put mud over my eyes, and then I washed, and now I can see." That was his whole story.

There was another side to his story that he had not mentioned, but the Pharisees thought of it at once. All this had happened on the sabbath! Some of them spoke up angrily and said, "This Jesus is a great sinner, for He does not keep the sabbath!" Others said, "If He is a sinner, how can He perform such miracles?" They argued about this for a long time, but they could not agree.

The man born blind stood by silently. He was thinking. When they finally asked him what *he* thought about Jesus, he said resolutely, "He is a prophet."

By now he was convinced that Jesus was not an ordinary human being. When his eyes were blind to the light, so was his heart. But now the light was also starting to flood his heart.

The wise rabbis would not agree that Jesus was a prophet. They were almost *forced* to believe that He had performed this great miracle, but they really didn't want to. They would much rather believe that Jesus was a *deceiver*.

A thought suddenly occurred to them: the man had never been blind! It was a hoax!

They summoned the man's parents and asked, "Is this really your son. Was he *born* blind? How is it that he can see now?"

The two old people trembled before the stern Pharisees. In their fear they said only, "We know that he is our son and that he was born blind. We don't know how it's possible for him to see now. He is of age. Why don't you ask him yourselves?"

The parents did not dare to say a good word about Jesus, because they knew how angry that would make the rabbis. The rabbis had decided that anyone who dared to say that Jesus was the Christ would be severely punished. He would be expelled from the synagogue.

That was why the parents hesitated and told the Pharisees to question their son directly.

They left quickly. They were happy that they didn't have to face the Pharisees any longer.

81: Disciples of Moses

The Pharisees were angry. People had come to them with a story about a man who was born blind and was healed by Jesus—on a sabbath. They finally concluded the story was a hoax, but they got nowhere with the parents.

They decided to call the blind man again. They had no good grounds for denying the miracle. Yet, they wanted to make sure that the man did not go about the city telling people what Jesus had done.

"Listen to us," they told him. "You must tell people that it was *God* who healed you. We know that this Jesus is a great sinner."

The man did not like what he heard. He could hear hatred for Jesus in the rabbis' words and that made him sad. Why should he waste any more time talking to these men? Outside the sun was shining; there was the beautiful world he wanted to see and enjoy.

He decided to be finished with these rabbis as quickly as possible. He said, "I don't know if Jesus is a sinner. All I know is that I was blind before, but now I can see."

The Pharisees were not about to let him off so easily. They began asking him more questions. "What was it that He did when He healed you? *How* did He open your eyes?"

The man's patience was at an end. "I told you that already," he said. "Why do you want to hear the whole story over again?"

In his impatience and his dislike of the rabbis, he went too far. He started to joke about the whole business. "Why this great interest in Jesus?" he asked. "Are you thinking about becoming His disciples too?"

That was the worst thing he could

possibly say. Enraged, they jumped up and began to yell at him. "*You* are one of His disciples!" they screamed. "But *we* are disciples of Moses. We know that Moses was a servant of God, but as for Jesus, we don't know where He comes from."

Now the man finally dared to stand up for Jesus. As the rabbis said more against Jesus, the man began to love Him more. He said, "Isn't that remarkable? You claim you don't know where Jesus comes from, although He has opened my eyes."

Then he spoke more earnestly to them. "Jesus is no sinner!" he said bravely. "He is doing God's will. Otherwise He would never have been able to perform such a great miracle. Never before have we heard of anyone who was able to open the eyes of the blind."

The rabbis attacked the man again. "How dare you lecture us?" they screamed. "You were born blind because of your sins!"

They grabbed him and threw him angrily into the street. He would never again be allowed in the synagogue. He was cast out, scorned, despised. So many outcasts followed Jesus!

Jesus heard that the rabbis had thrown the man out, and He went to find him. The man saw someone standing before him whom he did not know, a friendly man with kind, gentle eyes. The stranger asked him, "Do you believe in the Son of man?"

He recognized the voice immediately! He could have picked it out from a thousand other voices. It was the voice of Jesus, the one who had healed him!

Trembling with joy, he asked, "Who is He, Lord, that I may believe in Him?"

Jesus said, "You have now seen Him. He is the one who is speaking to you."

The man kneeled down before Jesus and stammered, "I believe, Lord!"

Jesus had not only opened the man's eyes. He had also opened his heart. The happiness that now was in his heart would never be taken away from him.

82: The good shepherd

The sheepfold stands out in the open field under the stars. The dense eastern night is dark and still. Four walls made of stones piled on top of each other and topped with thorny branches form the sheepfold. Within the fold the flock is asleep on the dry sand. They are pressed closely together; the sheep are separated from the goats.

A small opening in the wall serves as a doorway. There is no door to swing shut and block the opening. The shepherd himself lies on guard before this doorway. The watchful shepherd shuts off the sheepfold with his own body. He forms a living door that allows no stranger to enter the sheepfold.

He raises his head to listen carefully whenever he hears an unusual sound. If a thief or a beast of prey tries to climb over the wall into the sheepfold, the shepherd will sense it at once. A heavy club, a cudgel, is fastened to his wrist with a belt. It lies ready in his grip as a fearsome weapon.

The flock is asleep; all the animals feel safe. The dark figure of the shepherd who watches over them is at the door.

When it is morning and the sun is out, the shepherd rises and calls the sheep. He calls each one by the name he has given it.

The sheep hear his voice and obey. They push and press against each other as they file past the shepherd and leave the sheepfold. They wait outside the fold for the whole flock to gather.

All the sheep fix their gaze on the shepherd. Their ears perk up when they hear his voice. Wherever he goes, they follow, for they know his voice.

The sheep would not follow if a stranger called them. They would be afraid of the stranger and would run away from him.

Just as a father cares for his children, the good shepherd cares for his sheep. He walks ahead of them and finds the safest paths along the dangerous ravines in the hill country. He leads them into green pastures. Later, when they are tired and thirsty, he leads them to water. He lets them rest in the shade when the sun burns high in the sky. He binds their wounds when they become tangled in thorns. If a little lamb cannot walk with the other sheep, the shepherd carries it. The lamb snuggles up against him contentedly.

The shepherd watches over his sheep all day and cares for them lovingly. If a sheep wanders from the fold, he chases it back with a warning rock fired from his deadly accurate sling. If a beast of prey tries to steal an animal from the flock, the shepherd attacks it with his cudgel and rescues the poor sheep. He is prepared to lay down his life for the sheep, if he must.

The good shepherd leads his sheep through all dangers and brings them back in the evening to the sheepfold. He stands by the opening and stretches out his staff. The sheep go in one by one, passing under the shepherd's staff. He counts them and does not rest until he knows they are all safely in the fold. Only when there is nothing more for him to do does he stretch his weary body out before the doorway to sleep. His cudgel is always ready for unexpected visitors. Once more he forms a living door behind which the sheep are safe.

Jesus spoke to the people about the shepherd's work. They all knew how that went in the fields around Jerusalem. They also understood that Jesus was telling them a parable, a story with a lesson. They did not know what the lesson was.

Then He declared, "I tell you the truth, I am the door for the sheep. I am the good shepherd. The good shepherd lays down His life for the sheep."

The disciples must have understood these words. They were always safe with Jesus, regardless of dangers all around them. He had led them and cared for them like a shepherd, with love and patience.

The disciples also knew that the scribes

and Pharisees were false shepherds who sought only their own honor and advantage. The sheep in Jesus' flock had not listened to them. When Jesus came, they recognized the voice of the good shepherd and followed Him.

The disciples would better understand Jesus' words about the good shepherd after He had given His life for them. Then the flock would grow much bigger. From all lands and nations people would come to Jesus when they heard His voice.

He told them about this in advance. He said, "I have other sheep that are not in this fold. I must lead them also. They will listen to My voice, and they shall all be *one* flock with *one* shepherd."

83: The good Samaritan

Jesus was preaching again, surrounded by people. He talked about the glory of God's Kingdom and the great happiness of all those who with their whole hearts wished to serve God.

A scribe stepped forward and interrupted Jesus. He had watched jealously how intently the people listened to this carpenter's son.

"I'll ask Him a couple of tough questions," he thought. "If He can't answer them, He'll look like a fool in front of all the people. If He gives the wrong answer, I'll accuse Him of being a false teacher."

He asked, "Teacher, what must I do to inherit eternal life?"

Jesus looked at the man. He recognized the slyness in those proud eyes. He saw contempt in the smile that formed on that proud mouth. He understood the man's wicked plan.

Gently and patiently Jesus answered, "Surely you know! What is written in the law? What do you read there?"

The scribe answered quickly, as if reciting memory work: "You shall love the Lord your God with all your heart and with all your soul and with all your strength and with all your mind, and you shall love your neighbor as yourself."

Jesus nodded approvingly. "You have answered correctly," He said. "Do this, and you will live." Then He turned His attention to the people again.

The proud man stood ashamed and embarrassed, like a schoolboy before his teacher. He quickly raised another question so that he wouldn't look so foolish. "Who is my neighbor?" he asked.

Jesus then told this learned man a story to show him who his neighbor was. He told the story of the good Samaritan.

A man was traveling from Jerusalem to Jericho. He moved along a lonely, dangerous road between bare, gray hills. Suddenly, he was attacked by a band of robbers who had been hiding in the hills. They beat him, threw him down, stripped off his clothes, took everything he had, and left him on the road half dead.

After the poor man lay there for a while, too weak to move, he heard someone coming. He struggled to lift his aching head and saw that it was a priest. The priest was coming from Jerusalem, where he had been offering sacrifices in the temple and praying for the people. This pious man would surely have mercy on him!

The priest stood still and looked. He saw the poor man and heard his moans. But the sacrifices and prayers in Jerusalem had not brought about a change in his heart. He thought only of himself and his own safety. What a dangerous road this was! *He* could also easily be attacked by those robbers. He could not afford to stop; he had to keep going. If *he* also fell victim to the robbers, the damage would be twice as great.

That was how the priest reasoned as he hurried by the man on the far side of the road. He may have prayed for the man as he walked past, but he did not *help* him. His footsteps died away in the distance.

It was still again. The poor man could hear a raven crowing in the distance. He was alone in the burning sun with his fear and the pain of his wounds.

Then he heard more footsteps approaching. This time it was a Levite, another servant of God. Like the priest, he had been engaged in pious work in God's house in Jerusalem. Now, on his way home, he saw this poor man lying by the side of the road.

Like the priest, the Levite quickly walked past the man. He, too, knew how to justify this to himself. Wasn't his own life worth much more than the life of this unknown man? Moreover, there were no witnesses. No one had seen him ignore the poor man.

The wounded man lying on the road thought that he would surely die. If the priest and the Levite were not willing to help him, where could he look for deliverance?

Then he heard footsteps for the third time. The person approaching was a Samaritan traveling outside his own land. He came riding on his donkey.

The Samaritan was really his enemy, for the Jews and Samaritans had hated each other for centuries. Each group took delight in the misfortunes of the other. Jews and Samaritans scorned each other whenever they could. The man simply hoped that his enemy would pass by quietly without tormenting him.

The donkey stopped. Footsteps approached. A gentle hand worked its way under the wounded head. When the man looked up in amazement, he saw a pair of eyes full of compassion. Then he knew he would be saved.

The Samaritan simply could not go on when he saw the wounded man lying there. The sight of suffering made him forget everything else. He washed the man's wounds with pure wine and put some oil on them to ease the pain. Then he helped the poor man onto his donkey and walked alongside to prop him up.

Slowly the two moved down the dangerous road together. The Samaritan brought him to an inn and made sure that he would be cared for properly there. The next morning he called the innkeeper, gave him two silver coins, and said, "Take care of this man. If there are any more costs, I will pay you when I return."

When Jesus was finally finished with this story, He looked at the man who had asked who his neighbor was. Jesus asked, "Which of these three, do you suppose, was a neighbor to the man who fell among thieves?"

The proud Jews, who hated Samaritans, had to answer, "The one who had mercy on him."

Jesus said to him, "Go and do likewise."

This proud man seemed to know just what he had to do to enter heaven: love God above all else and his neighbor as himself. But he had never put this into practice. The beautiful answer he had given Jesus was just a string of words for him.

"Go and do likewise."

If only he would truly do his best to love his neighbor! Then he would find out what a petty, cruel person he really was. At that point he would be closer to heaven than ever before!

84: Mary and Martha

Bethany and Jerusalem were built on opposite sides of the Mount of Olives. Jerusalem, with its marble palaces and its temple with a golden roof, was on the west. It was a shining city on the hill. Bethany didn't impress many people. It was hidden between the hills along the road that led to Jericho.

Jesus was shown more love in little Bethany than in the great city of Jerusalem. He enjoyed more peace in little Bethany than in the great city of Jerusalem, which was known as the city of peace.

In Bethany Jesus found some true friends. When He preached in Jerusalem and suffered the hatred of the Jews, he would leave by the East Gate. He would go through the Valley of Jehoshaphat, across the brook Kidron, and along the path up the Mount of Olives. He would pass the Garden of Gethsemane, which lay on one of the slopes. It was a familiar place, for He sometimes went there to be alone and to pray to His Father. Then He would reach the top of the Mount of Olives, which would give Him a good view of much of the land. From there it took only a few minutes to reach Bethany.

Martha would be waiting at the door to welcome Jesus. Mary, her eyes shining with delight, would be happy to see Him too. Lazarus always received Jesus heartily.

The Master was always welcome in the home of these three friendly people. The two sisters and a brother had continued to live as a family after the death of their parents. They had enough money and had many friends among the leading Jews. But their best friend was Jesus. They were happiest when He was with them.

One day Jesus came to their house and sat down. Mary immediately sat at His feet to listen to Him. She showed her love for Him by sitting by Him quietly, eager to hear every word He said.

Martha showed her love in a different way. She was an ambitious woman who thought it was important to always be busy. When Jesus came to visit, there was a lot of work to be done. Nothing was too good for this special guest.

Martha cooked and baked. She kept an eye on the fire and set the table. She paced back and forth anxiously. She heard a few of Jesus' words now and then, but before they sank in properly they were chased away by her cares. She became more and more nervous; she was afraid she would never get all the work done.

She had to do all the work alone, for Mary with shining eyes continued to sit at Jesus' feet. Mary didn't seem to notice how busy Martha was.

Martha sighed as she thought of Mary sitting at Jesus' feet. Reproachfully she looked at her sister. She bustled past Mary to try to draw her attention. Soon she was feeling sorry for herself.

"How can the Master approve of what Mary is doing?" she asked herself, disappointed. "Surely He can see that I'm left doing all the work alone."

Martha began to look more and more cross and harried. Finally she couldn't remain silent any longer. She grumbled, "Master, doesn't it matter to You that my sister lets me do all the work by myself? Tell her to help me!"

Jesus shook His head. He knew Martha well. He knew that she loved Him just as much as Mary did, and that she was doing all that work out of love for Him. But she had to learn that Jesus had not come to

them just to be served a lot of delicious food. He had come to bring them happiness through His Word.

Martha had fussed too much. She did it out of love, but also to be praised. Her work and her concern about the food had occupied her completely. She had almost no time to listen to Jesus. She had even grumbled to Him!

Jesus addressed her in a friendly way, "Martha, Martha, you are worried and concerned about many things, but there is really only one thing that is important. Mary has chosen that and it will not be taken away from her."

Mary and Martha, the two sisters from Bethany, both loved Jesus. Each served Him in her own way. In the midst of the difficulties Jesus faced, the love of these two women was a great comfort to Him.

85: The rich fool

Jesus was preaching by the Jordan, at the same spot where John the Baptist had started baptizing. He was surrounded by His disciples and a great crowd of people. His name was known through the entire region, and many believed in Him.

"John did not perform miracles," they said to each other, "but everything John said of this man is true." They looked up to Jesus in great respect. His words made a deep impression on them.

A man who lived in the area noticed this. He decided to profit from the respect Jesus enjoyed. His brother had received an inheritance, and he felt he should have part of it. But his brother refused to share the inheritance with him.

"If only Jesus would help me!" the man

thought. "Jesus is a great prophet. If He says the inheritance must be divided between us, my brother will not dare to refuse."

He made his way through the people with an injured look on his face and said, "Master, tell my brother to divide the inheritance with me."

Jesus had not come to earth to be used for such purposes. He answered, "Who appointed Me a judge between you two?" As all the people watched and listened, He admonished the man for his selfishness. He showed them that even a lot of money was no guarantee of a peaceful life. To make sure they would never forget this, He told them the parable of the rich fool.

Once there was a rich man who owned a great deal of land. One year his harvest was so large that he hardly knew what to do with it. He could not put it all away in his barns. He looked around, proud and satisfied, and wondered what to do next.

He looked at his grain and his fruit, but he did not look up to heaven. He was not grateful and he did not think of the Giver of all these good gifts. All his life he had thought of himself. He had worked and saved to become rich. Now he was rich, and he no longer had to work. He could simply enjoy life.

Finally he said, "I know what I'll do. I'll tear down my barns and build bigger ones. I'll store all my grain and all my goods there. I will say to my soul, 'My soul you have enough good things stored up to last you for many years. Take it easy, eat, drink, and be merry.'"

My soul—that's what he said. He had forgotten that his soul really belonged to God.

God said to him, "You fool! Tonight your soul is required of you. Now who will get all those good things you have stored up for yourself?"

The man had saved a lot of money, but it did him no good. Others would enjoy his money. His life of sweating and saving had been foolish and useless. The soul that had gone hungry all his life could no longer be saved. It was too late. No amount of money could help now.

The man thought he was *rich*, but he was really very *poor*.

Jesus added a closing comment. He said, "That's what happens to those who try to store up good things for themselves and are not rich in God."

86: A daughter of Abraham

It was a quiet sabbath morning. An old woman shuffled down the street, laboring to put one foot down properly in front of the other. The poor woman's back was so badly bent that she faced straight down and could not see where she was walking. Still, she *had* to make her way to the synagogue to hear the law and the prophets, to be comforted by God and to glorify Him. She was a pious woman, a true daughter of Abraham, the father of all believers.

Painfully she turned her head about to see if she was going the right way. She recognized the route from the stones in the streets, and the doorsteps. She couldn't see any higher; she couldn't see the blue sky at all.

She had been bent over for eighteen years. Because of an evil spirit, some horrible disease had bent her back, and she couldn't straighten up at all. Her body was as rigid as if she were bound by unbreakable bonds.

Satan had made an attack on her body, and now he used force to keep her bent over, facing the earth. In her great need, her soul had not forgotten God in heaven above. She was still close to the Lord.

As she dragged herself through the streets, she hardly looked like a human being. Small and bent over, she stumbled into the synagogue between the other worshipers who had upright, healthy bodies. She groped for a place in the section reserved for women. Carefully, with great difficulty, she worked her way onto a bench. She sat there bent over as if she were looking for something on the floor.

She could not see the lectern at the front. Her eyes could focus only on her feet and the floor. Still, she listened intently, for her heart was open to the Word of God.

This sabbath had begun like so many others for her, but it brought her a great blessing that she had never dared to expect.

Jesus was in the synagogue that day, and He was teaching the people. He had seen her when she came stumbling in. He could not bear the sight of a human being in torment at satan's hand.

The woman heard Him say, "Woman, you are set free from your infirmity." Then she felt hands with an amazing healing power on her sick body. A surge of energy flowed through her.

The bonds that had held her in their grip for years were finally broken. She could stand straight again! For the first time in many, many years, she could stand straight up in the synagogue and look around. She was overcome with happiness. She saw her deliverer, and the love in His eyes.

The woman rejoiced. She expressed her great gratitude and glorified God.

The people in the synagogue were so moved that they all remained silent.

Yet, one man finally dared to say

something. This great miracle had not made much of an impression on him. His hard heart was full of conceit and hatred for Jesus. This man was the ruler of the synagogue.

On a normal sabbath, the people in the synagogue looked up to this man in awe. Now the people had forgotten him, although he was really in charge. All the people looked at Jesus, who did as He pleased without asking the ruler of the synagogue for permission.

The people were eager to listen to Jesus, who had broken sabbath laws. Jesus had healed a person on the sabbath, and that was strictly forbidden by the rabbis. Jesus *worked* on the sabbath.

The furious ruler of the synagogue stood before the people. He really wanted to admonish Jesus, but he didn't dare. Therefore he directed his words of reproach to the people instead.

"There are six days for working," he cried out indignantly. "So come and be healed on one of the other days. Don't come on the sabbath."

That was unfair, because the woman had not come to the synagogue to be healed. She had come to worship God. Still, the people remained silent. They always remained silent, for fear of the rabbis.

Jesus answered with a stern rebuke: "You hypocrite! Which of you does not untie his ox or his donkey from the stall on the sabbath to lead him away and let him drink? Why shouldn't this woman, a daughter of Abraham who has been bound by satan for 18 years, be set free on the sabbath?"

These words made a deep impression even on the conceited ruler of the synagogue. It was true, he, too, looked after his animals on the sabbath. Was a person worth less than an animal?

The ruler of the synagogue was ashamed and turned away. But the people rejoiced at the glorious things that happened whenever Jesus was around.

87: The last shall be first

One sabbath day, a leading Pharisee served a dinner at his house for several guests. He was an important man, and his guests were important people, scribes and Pharisees, like himself.

The guests were received with the proper ceremonies. They washed their hands often, just as the rabbis prescribed. Then they were led into the banquet room and assigned to their place at the table.

The oldest and richest guests sat closest to the host. The guests eyed each other suspiciously. Is *he* richer and more important than I am? Don't I deserve more honor than he? If a guest did not come to the feast, someone else would quickly take his place. Sometimes that was a higher place than he was entitled to.

Poor people were not invited. The host would have been foolish to invite them. They could never afford to invite him back. To invite poor people to the meal was to throw money away.

Jesus of Nazareth was the only exception. At this time, Jesus was in Perea, where this Pharisee lived. Jesus was preaching and performing miracles. A great crowd followed Him around and worshiped Him.

Jesus was almost the poorest person around, but the Pharisee had a special purpose in inviting Him. He had invited Jesus to a feast on the *sabbath* because he wanted to lay a trap for Him.

A man with a swollen body also lived in Perea. He was suffering from dropsy. When the meal was underway, this sick man came inside and stood before Jesus. Jesus saw the man. He also noted how carefully the guests were watching. At once He realized what was going on. They were wondering if He would dare to break the sabbath rules laid down by the scribes.

Jesus wanted to give an answer to the question no one dared to ask aloud. Calmly He said, "Is it lawful to heal on the sabbath or not?"

No one said a word. Before anyone realized, the miracle had taken place. The man was healed.

Then Jesus said, "If one of you has a son or an ox that falls into a pit on the sabbath, wouldn't you pull him out at once?"

They didn't know what to answer, for they knew the truth. They were willing to violate those strict sabbath laws to save their property.

The wicked plan had failed. The scribes and Pharisees did not dare say anything to Jesus about what He had just done.

As the meal went on, it became apparent that Jesus did have something to say to them. "When someone invites you to a wedding feast," He said, "do not take the place of honor for yourself. Maybe someone more important than you was also invited. The host would then have to say to you, 'Give this person your seat.' To your shame, you would be assigned a lower place.

"When you are invited to a feast, take the lowest place of all. The host might well say to you, 'Friend, move up to a better place.' You will be honored before all the guests. Everyone who exalts himself will be humbled, and whoever humbles himself will be exalted."

Again the guests were silent. They realized that Jesus could see right through them.

88: The great banquet

Jesus was having dinner at the home of an important Pharisee. Other important Pharisees and scribes were also present.

Jesus wanted to teach His host a lesson. The host was holding this dinner for carefully calculated reasons. Jesus wanted to show him how much better it would be for him to act out of *love*. He said, "If you hold a dinner again, don't invite your friends and family and rich neighbors. They can invite you back and repay you. Invite beggars and blind people and lame people and deformed people. That will make you much happier. They have no way of repaying you. *God* will reward you for it in His Kingdom."

The host said nothing, but one of the guests began to speak. He said to Jesus, "Yes, blessed are those who join the feast of the Kingdom of God."

That sounded very pious, but the man was really no better than the others. He did not yearn for blessing, for he did not come to God in humility and obedience. For almost three years the Savior had traveled through the land, inviting people to enter God's Kingdom. The rich people and the leaders kept saying "no."

Therefore Jesus told this man the parable of the great banquet. That parable was an earnest warning for him and for all the other guests.

One day a man made arrangements for a banquet and invited many guests. When the hour for the banquet arrived and the tables stood ready, he sent his servant to all the invited guests with a message: "Come, for everything is ready."

The guests began to make excuses. The first said, "I have just bought a field, and now I must go and see it. Please excuse me, for I cannot come." That was not a good excuse, for he could have looked at the field later.

Another said, "I have just bought five yoke of oxen, and I must try them." That wasn't a good excuse either. The proper time to try oxen is *before* you buy them.

A third said, "I have just married a wife, therefore, I cannot come." That one didn't care about the host either; otherwise he would have kept his word.

The servant came back and told his master what the people had said. The table was heavily laden with the choicest food, but the banquet room was still empty.

The master became angry and said to the servant, "Go quickly into the streets and alleys of the town. Bring in the poor, the crippled, the blind, and the lame."

The servant obeyed. They came, surprised and delighted, but they did not fill the great banquet hall. The servant went to his master and said, "We did as you commanded, but there is still place left over."

The master said, "Then go into the roads and lanes outside the city and call the foreigners and the wanderers. If they don't dare to come pull them along with you. Force them to come in, so that my house will be full."

That was the story Jesus told to the scribes and Pharisees. Did they understand who the host in the story was? Did they understand that the despised sinners and tax-collectors, and even the Gentiles, would go into the Kingdom of God before them?

Jesus made one more statement. His voice was stern and powerful as it resounded in the house of this important Pharisee. He said, "I tell you, not one of those men who were invited will get a taste of My banquet."

"*My* banquet!" Jesus said.

The Pharisee thought *he* was the host, for he had invited poor Jesus to his table. It turned out that the poor guest was really the great heavenly Host.

89: Lost and found

Jesus was traveling through Perea, the area east of the Jordan. Wherever He went, a great crowd of people followed Him.

Whenever He sat down to rest, they sat down around Him to listen to His words. His words had awakened them from their lives of sin. They had made the greedy tax-collectors forget their money. They had made sinners yearn for a purer, better life and for forgiveness of their sins.

People surrounded Him every day, tax-collectors and sinners, poor lost people. They opened their homes to Him and invited Him to eat with them.

Jesus would be friendly to even the greatest sinners. There was a deep love for sinners in His heart.

The scribes and Pharisees grumbled about this; they simply couldn't understand it. Every sabbath day they preached that one should despise and avoid sinners. Sinners were people who wandered away from God, and God despised them too.

The scribes and Pharisees would often point disdainfully at Jesus and scoff, "*He receives sinners and even eats with them.*" Jesus therefore told them three parables to teach them that He was sent by God to seek and save the lost. He told them the parable of the lost sheep, the parable of the lost coin, and the parable of the prodigal son.

These three parables were strikingly similar and belonged together. Each one made the same point—God's great love for sinful man.

Once there was a shepherd who had 100 sheep, Jesus explained. One day when he was out in the field with them, he realized that one of the sheep had become lost on the way to the pasture. That sheep had disobeyed and had not listened to the shepherd. Foolish and stubborn, it had gone its own way.

As time passed, it wandered farther from the rest of the flock. Soon it was wandering around in the hills, surrounded by dangers and bleating anxiously.

It was the sheep's fault. Didn't it deserve to be torn apart by wild animals?

That was not how the shepherd saw it. He did not say, "I have a lot of sheep anyway. It doesn't matter if I lose one disobedient one." No. He thought about the lost sheep more than the 99 who were safe with the rest of the flock.

He loved that sheep because it belonged to his flock. He would not rest until he had found it and brought it safely back. He left the other sheep in the field and quickly retraced the path they had taken earlier that day. He looked everywhere and he called for the sheep. Sadly he wandered along the narrow paths in the hill country. He even went into the deep ravines, risking his life. He was tired, but he would not think of resting. He could think only of the sheep. He would look until he had found it.

And he did find it! Joyfully he lifted the sheep up on his shoulders and carried it back to the flock. When he went home that evening, he was still overwhelmed with joy. He called his neighbors and friends together and said, "Rejoice with me! I am so happy, for I have found the sheep that was lost!"

That was the story of the lost sheep. When Jesus finished it, He added, "I tell you, that's the kind of joy there is in heaven over a single sinner who repents. There is more joy over him than over 99 righteous people who do not need to repent."

Jesus told another story. There was once a woman who had a necklace of ten shining coins. She had received the necklace from her family as a wedding gift, and she wore it around her neck every day.

One day, when she was at work in her house, she noticed that one of the ten coins was missing. What a shock! She simply *had* to find that coin. Until she found that coin, the beautiful necklace was spoiled for her.

Quickly she lit a lamp, for there was very little daylight in her house. Carefully she searched every area where she had been that day. She took a broom and swept all the dust together, first in her own living quarters and then where the animals were kept. She was heart-broken by the loss of the coin.

Finally she caught sight of something shiny under all the dust and rubbish, and heard a tinkle on the floor as she swept. It was the missing coin!

Gratefully the woman seized the coin. She didn't care that the coin was tarnished and dirty from being on the floor. She polished it on her clothes until it shone like the others. Then she ran over to her neighbors quickly and cried out, "Rejoice with me! I have found the coin that was lost."

That story was the parable of the lost coin. When Jesus was finished telling it, He said once more, "I tell you, that's the kind of joy there is in heaven over a single sinner who repents."

Jesus was not finished with His parables yet. He still wanted to tell the parable of the prodigal son. It was really the most beautiful of the three, because the father's love for his lost son was even greater than the shepherd's love for the lost sheep and the woman's love for the lost coin.

90: The prodigal son

A father had two sons, and he loved them both. His most fervent wish was to see both of them happy.

The older son seemed happy enough as he worked on his father's land. He didn't show his father much love, but he also didn't cause him any pain. He was a calm, sensible young man who did not make a strong impression on people.

The younger son was entirely different. He was not satisfied with the quiet life in his father's house, and he did not work willingly. His thoughts were not on his work. His thoughts wandered far away, exploring the wide world and foreign lands. Those lands were no doubt much more beautiful and pleasant than his own. He could surely be happy in one of those lands.

He longed to be able to travel and enjoy life fully. He envied the birds, for they could fly wherever they wanted.

At home he felt like a prisoner. His life was monotonous, and he began to hate it more and more. He could not properly return his father's love. In fact, he was hardly aware of that love.

Later, when his father died, he would be free. Then he would receive one third of everything his father owned, and his older brother, who was the first-born, would receive two thirds. When that happened, life would finally become exciting for him. More and more, the boy longed for the day when he would be free.

Why should he have to wait so long for that day? Why couldn't he ask for his share of the inheritance right now?

One day he found the courage to take the matter up with his father. He said, "Father, give me my share of the property."

The father knew his son well, and the request did not surprise him. Still, it frightened him and made him sad. He knew that his son would not find happiness in the wide world. But he did not try to hold him back, for he knew that the boy wouldn't believe anything he said. Instead he would feel even more like a prisoner and would begin to hate his father.

Sorrowfully, the father gave in. He divided his property between his two sons.

The boy would have to learn his lesson through misfortune and shame. That was the only way he would find out that his father was wiser than he was.

Soon the younger son set out on a journey to a faraway land. He took all his money with him. He didn't give a single thought to the sorrow he was causing his father; he was blind to his father's love. He thought only of his own pleasure and of all the beautiful things he would see. He left as a happy and excited young man. He was rich and dressed in beautiful clothes. Off he went in search of happiness.

The father followed him with his eyes, until he could no longer see his son through his tears. Even then, his heart went with the boy.

The son made it to the land of his dreams, where he found all the glorious things for which he had yearned. He enjoyed all of them, for they could all be bought with money.

Wherever he went, people bowed before him and gave him a hearty welcome. They gave him such a warm welcome, it almost seemed that they had been expecting him. He made many friends and gave them expensive gifts. His life became one long, continuous feast, for he denied himself nothing. He lived extravagantly. Every morning brought new enjoyment; each day brought new happiness.

Happiness? It was not real happiness. There was a quiet unrest in the boy's heart. No amount of celebration and enjoyment could dispel that unrest.

That unrest, that uneasiness, grew daily. Sometimes he seemed to hear the voice of his father giving him a stern warning. He did not want to listen. Instead he tried to ignore the unrest, for he was finally free.

The boy's life became a trance, a dream from which he never wanted to awake. He kept foolishly wasting his money, as if he were deliberately throwing it away.

Finally all his money was gone. He shook his purse, but only a few small coins, some fluff, and a bit of dust fell out.

It was finally time to wake up. The dream was over. His friends came and found out that all the money was gone, and they disappeared, one by one. No one volunteered to help him; no one offered him comfort. There was nothing left of that friendship; those friends had only been after his money.

The boy was left alone. People no longer bowed before him. They wanted nothing to do with him, now that he had no money.

He wandered through the foreign land where he lived and sold his last possessions to buy bread. He sold his costly garments. He sold the golden ring that his father had given him, as a symbol of his freedom. That it was a gift from his father did not matter. He didn't want to think about his father.

Bread was scarce and expensive at that time, for there was a great famine in the land. The boy had to go hungry.

Because he did not want to starve to death, he had to give up his precious freedom. After much pleading, a citizen of that land hired him, and gave him the lowliest work there was. He sent the boy out to the fields to watch over the pigs.

The free son who had gone into the world to find his happiness was now a herdsman looking after pigs.

If his father knew . . . . But no, he didn't even want to think about his father. He still didn't want to admit that his father was right. Stubbornly he clung to his pride and independence. He sat in the field with the pigs. He was hungry because his master did not give him enough to eat.

He watched as the pigs wallowed in the mud. He watched as the pigs greedily devoured the bean pods he brought them. He was so hungry that he felt like filling his own belly with the pigs' food. No one looked after him the way he looked after the pigs.

The world seemed very cruel. He had been foolish enough to think that he would find happiness out in that world!

Finally he came to his senses and took a careful look at himself. He was skinny, unhappy, and clothed in miserable rags.

The truth frightened him. He thought to himself, "My father's hired hands have more than enough food, and here I sit, starving."

He thought back to his life at home with his father. He had lived like a *prince*, but now he was no better than a *slave*. Finally he admitted to himself how foolish he had been.

In his mind's eye he saw himself leaving home. He saw the sorrow and disappointment which he had ignored, written on his father's face. He began to yearn for the love which he had not appreciated then. He finally understood how much he had sinned and how deeply he had grieved his father.

Suddenly he knew that he could not stay where he was. He *had* to go back to his father. He would not go back to ask for his father's love. He had no right to that love. He would ask for *forgiveness*, and for a chance to earn his bread. He could not be a son, but he was willing to be a hired hand. He would promise to work hard. If only his father would hire him, he would be saved from the misery he now lived in.

The boy said to himself, "I shall arise and go to my father and say to him, 'Father, I have sinned against heaven and against you. I am no longer worthy to be called your son. Please make me like one of your hired men.'"

He set out for home.

91: The fattened calf

The prodigal son was on his way home. He had gone to his father one day and demanded his share of the inheritance, for he was fed up with life at home. He wanted to go to a faraway land and live a life of luxury.

His father let him go, and he wasted all his money on wild living. He wound up as a hired hand looking after pigs in a field. Then he realized how foolish he had been,

and he set out for home. He did not deserve to be received as a son again. He would ask his father to make him like a hired hand.

The boy had left home full of high hopes and expectations. It was a joyous journey. The journey back home was as sad and difficult as the journey away from home had been exciting. He had left home a rich and important young man. He returned as a poor, miserable wanderer, recognized by no one.

When he finally saw his father's house in the distance, his courage failed him. When he saw those familiar surroundings, he realized just how wicked he had been.

He did not dare go any farther. He stayed near his father's house, but he kept his distance.

But the father had already seen him coming and had recognized him. That poor, filthy wanderer was *his* son. His heart overflowed with love and compassion, and he ran toward him with outstretched arms. He threw his arms around the boy and kissed him.

The son stammered, "Father, I have sinned against heaven and against you. I am no longer worthy to be called your son."

The father cried out in delight to his servants, "Bring out the best robe and put it on him. Put a ring on his finger and shoes on his feet. Then kill the fattened calf, and we'll have a celebration, because my son was dead and is alive again! He was lost, but now he is found!"

A little later the son sat next to his father. He was washed, and he wore beautiful clothes. A ring sparkled on his finger.

Gratefully the son stroked his father's aged hands. He rested his head against his father and felt like crying with joy. He was actually being received back as a son.

Finally, he realized where he could find

the happiness that he had traveled all over the world to seek. Happiness was at home with his father, whose faithful heart was filled with love for him.

The older son was at work in the field, just as he always was. He had forgotten about his brother; that seemed best to him. Now the land, the home and the property were all reserved for him.

"I have always done my work faithfully," he thought. "I'm careful about what I do, and no one can say anything against me."

He was satisfied as he headed home after the day's work in the field. When he reached the house he saw a sight that filled him with amazement. He heard music and happy voices, and he saw people dancing.

He called one of the servants and asked what was going on. The servant said, "Your brother has come home. Your father has killed the fattened calf because he is so happy to have him back safe and sound."

Your *brother?* Did he still have a brother? Suddenly he began to hate that fool who had come back. Why had his father let him in the door? He should have kicked him off the property. "That's what *I* would have done!" thought the older brother.

He didn't even consider going inside to join the festivities. *He* would not sit down next to that sinner. He was much too angry to take part in any celebration.

The father found out and came outside to talk to him, hoping to coax him inside. He hated to miss either of his sons.

The older son said to him, "Look! I have served you faithfully for years without ever disobeying your orders. You never gave me even a young goat so I could celebrate with my friends. Now this son of yours comes back after squandering your property on wild living and evil companions, and you kill the fattened calf for him!"

The father said, "My son, you are always with me, and everything I have is yours. Be happy and celebrate with us, for your brother was dead and is alive! He was lost, and is found!"

92: Stewardship

Once there was a man with a great deal of money. He had property, servants, houses, stables, and livestock. A steward managed it all for him. He supervised the servants, paid the wages, and collected rent for the properties. Everything the master had was entrusted to this steward.

The steward was a dishonest man who served his master poorly and wasted his master's property. When the master discovered this, he said angrily, "What's this that I hear about you? Get ready to render account of what you've done with my money and property. I cannot have you as my steward any longer."

Things were looking dark for the steward. Soon he would be standing on the street without money and without work.

What could he do? He was not strong enough to dig ditches, and he was ashamed to beg.

He got out the wax tablets that showed how much everyone owed his master. He picked out one tablet; it showed that one of the debtors owed 100 barrels of oil as rent for an olive grove. The letters in the soft wax could be easily wiped out or changed.

He was still the steward, so he could do with his master's goods as he saw fit. He seized his opportunity to make some friends quickly. Soon, he would be alone in the street without work or money. He would need friends willing to open their door to him and help him.

He summoned the first debtor and asked, "How much do you owe my master?"

The man knew it well, for the debt constantly worried him. "One hundred barrels of oil," he said unhappily.

The steward smiled and said, "Here is your bill. Sit down quickly and change it to 50 barrels of oil."

The debtor did what he was told and went away feeling grateful. He would not forget how the steward had helped him.

A second debtor was summoned. The steward asked, "How much do you owe?"

"One hundred sacks of wheat," came the answer. This debtor was just as grateful as the first one when the steward allowed him to change it to 80 sacks of wheat.

When all the debtors were called in and had their debts reduced, the steward could await the future feeling secure.

The master, meanwhile, had found out what the wicked steward was doing, so he fired him immediately. Still, he had to admit that the dishonest man had acted very cleverly, and he praised him for this.

Jesus told this story to the great crowd of disciples who followed Him. Jesus wanted to hold up the steward as an example to them, although he was dishonest and selfish. Jesus wanted His listeners to learn that people are only *stewards* over the goods that God as Lord of the entire world entrusts to them. God is the real owner. People are only allowed to manage property and goods on His behalf.

People often wrongly think that *they* are the real owners. But they are only stewards for a little while. Then they have to appear before their Master to render account of what they have done with His money and His goods. Those who remember that it is *God's* money, and those who help people on earth with that money will be praised in heaven. For all eternity they will have nothing to worry about.

Jesus said, "I tell you, use worldly wealth to gain friends for yourselves, so that when it is gone, you will be welcomed into eternal dwellings."

93: Riches and poverty

Jesus had told His disciples the parable of the dishonest steward. He wanted to remind them that they were also stewards, managing what God has given them. The

Pharisees scoffed at Him when they heard this parable. Most of them were wealthy and selfish. Their money made them feel secure.

That security had been shaken; Jesus' words had made them feel uneasy. To build up their courage again, they said, "It's easy for Him to talk, for he doesn't have a cent to His name."

Then Jesus told another parable, especially for them. He wanted to make clear to them what would happen if they did not repent.

Once there was a very rich man, He explained. He lived in a beautiful house and wore fine linen and rich purple, as if he were a king.

At his door lay a beggar waiting for the crumbs that fell from his table. Those crumbs might be thrown to him. He lay there day after day, wrapped in filthy rags. He was sick, miserable, and covered with sores.

The rich man had many friends, who were as rich and well known as he was. The beggar had no friends, but the dogs in the streets came and licked his sores.

The rich man's name is not important. He was like many other people who never think about God. They live as if this life on earth will go on forever.

The poor man's name was *Lazarus*, which means "God is my helper." The name almost seemed a joke, because of the poor man's plight.

The rich man and the poor man knew each other well. Whenever the rich man went out his door, he would see the poor man lying there. Then he would feel even richer and more important.

What is high and exalted in the eyes of men, however, is sometimes disgusting in God's eyes. What people look down on of-ten brings God delight. God knows our hearts.

One day the poor man was found dead by the rich man's door. He was not even given a proper burial. His unclean body was dragged away quietly to a hidden spot outside the city.

Angels carried Lazarus' soul to heaven. Lazarus was given a place of honor close to Abraham. God was his helper after all!

The rich man also died. His body was embalmed, and he was buried with great ceremony in a costly grave. But *he* found himself in hell. There was nothing left of his earthly happiness.

Darkness surrounded him. He was tormented with sorrow and regret for how he had lived. Remorse burned like a fire within him.

He could see light far away. In that light he caught sight of Abraham. Lazarus, the beggar who used to lay by his door, was with Abraham.

The rich man thought that Lazarus owed him something. He did not realize that life on earth was less real than what he was experiencing now. *He* was far from God, first on earth, and now here. But Lazarus was close to God.

The rich man was really poor, and Lazarus was rich. On earth no one was able to see that, but here it was obvious.

The unhappy man cried out, "Father Abraham, have mercy on me and send Lazarus to dip the end of his finger in some water and cool my tongue."

Abraham answered, "Son, remember how you received only good things during your life on earth, and Lazarus only evil? Now *he* is receiving comfort, and *you* are suffering. Moreover, there is a great gulf between us which no one can cross.

Then the man realized how foolish he

had been to love money. His money was now completely useless to him. He thought of his brothers, who were living just as he had lived. He asked Abraham to send Lazarus to the earth to warn them.

Abraham answered, "They have the books of Moses and the prophets. Let them listen to them."

The man replied, "No, father Abraham. If someone were to rise from the dead and go to them, they would repent."

But Abraham said, "If they do not listen to Moses and the prophets, they will not be convinced even if someone comes to them from the dead."

94: The death of Lazarus

Two women sat by a bed. On the bed lay a man locked in a struggle with death. The two women were Mary and Martha of Bethany; the man was their only brother, Lazarus. Sickness had seized him in the midst of his work. The calm happiness of this little family was suddenly shattered by the horrible fear that Lazarus would die.

The doctors didn't know what to do. Mary and Martha prayed fervently for their brother's recovery, but God didn't seem to hear those prayers.

The two sisters and their brother had been very happy. They lived together in love, and enjoyed everyone's esteem and affection. Lately, since Jesus was their friend and sometimes stayed in their house, that happiness had grown even greater.

If only Jesus was nearby! His wonderful power could heal the illness in an instant and take away all their cares. He would have been happy to do so, for He loved Mary and Martha and their brother

Lazarus. But He had not been in Bethany for a long time. Because of the hatred of the Jews, He had left Judea. Now He was somewhere east of the Jordan, at least a day's journey away.

Jesus probably didn't even know what was happening in Bethany. He probably didn't know how much His friends there yearned for Him, they reasoned. But someone must tell Him, the sisters decided. Only He could save Lazarus. Therefore they sent someone to find Him and give Him a message: "Lord, the one You love is sick."

The two sisters waited and hoped. They looked after their brother and whispered to him that *Jesus* was coming. In their deep sorrow and fear, that name was their only comfort. If only Lazarus could hold out until Jesus arrived in Bethany!

The messenger raced to the land east of the Jordan and found Jesus busy in the midst of His disciples. He bowed before Jesus and gave Him the message: "Lord, the one You love is sick."

There was no fear and worry in Jesus' eyes when He heard that message. Calmly he answered, "It is not a sickness unto death but a sickness that will glorify God so that the Son of God may be glorified through it."

That was good news! The messenger set out for Bethany at once to bring this good news to the sisters. It was *not* a sickness unto death! How happy Mary and Martha would be when they heard that!

When the messenger neared Bethany and hurried toward the house, people looked at him sadly. Why? And why was Martha's house full of mourners?

Haltingly he passed on his message: "The Master says, 'This sickness is not a sickness unto death but a sickness that will glorify God.'"

Not a sickness unto death? The sisters had never received a stranger, more mysterious message. Lazarus was *already* dead. That day his body was wrapped in linens and cloths and carried to a still, dark grave. Lazarus was in a cave. The opening was sealed by a great stone.

Not a sickness unto death? Could the Master have made a mistake? That was impossible, for He was the Son of God!

The sisters were surrounded by sympathetic friends. The message from Jesus, which was intended to comfort them, became a riddle.

"If the Master had been here, Lazarus would not have died," sighed one.

"Yes," sobbed the other. "It would not have happened."

They were sure of it. But that was no comfort.

When Jesus heard that Lazarus was sick, He stayed two more days in the place where He was. Calmly, as if nothing serious had happened, He went ahead with His work. On the third day He said to His disciples, "Let's go to Judea again."

This suggestion frightened them. They knew how much the leading Jews in Jerusalem hated Jesus. Their Master's life would not be safe there for a moment.

"Master," they said, looking worried, "just a little while ago the Jews wanted to stone You. Now You want to go to them again?"

Jesus explained that He would not die before His work was completed. Until His hour came, no one would be able to harm Him. Then He said, "Lazarus, our friend, has fallen asleep. I must go to wake him."

"Lord," they said, "if he is sleeping, he will get better." They thought to themselves, "Then the Master will not have to make this dangerous journey."

But Jesus was speaking of Lazarus' death. For Him the death of a child of God was only a deep sleep. Only someone who lived in sin, far from God, could be spoken of as dead. In fact, such a person was already dead before he breathed his last breath.

The disciples did not understand this. Jesus finally said to them, "Lazarus is dead. For your sakes I am glad I was not there, so that you may believe. Now let us go to him."

The disciples knew that they could not hold Jesus back. Thomas, the most pessimistic disciple stepped forward first to follow the Master. Thomas had given up hope that this journey would turn out well. He thought the Master would be seized and put to death by His enemies, the rabbis.

Thomas did not want to desert Jesus. "Let's go with the Master and die with Him," he said somberly.

A quiet, despondent group of disciples followed Jesus to Judea.

95: Lazarus raised from the dead

Jesus was in no hurry as he traveled to Bethany to help His friend Lazarus. By the time He arrived, Lazarus had been in the grave for four days.

Mary and Martha's pain and sorrow had not subsided at all. All their friends, including some leading Jews from Jerusalem, had come to comfort them with words of kindness and love.

But what good would *words* do in the face of their great loss?

Suddenly people came running to tell them that *Jesus* was almost in Bethany. When Martha heard that, she stood up and went to meet Him. Mary stayed in the house, overcome by her pain.

Martha went out of the village to meet Jesus, the one person who could have saved her brother if He had not arrived too late. When she saw Him, she sobbed, "Lord, if You had been here, my brother would not have died." While she said this and looked at Jesus, a ray of hope shone through her disappointment. She added haltingly, "But even now I know that God will give You whatever You ask of Him."

Jesus said calmly, "Your brother will rise again."

Rise again? Of course! That was not new to Martha. On the last day, all who loved God will rise from their graves. Therefore she answered, "I know that he will rise again in the resurrection of the last day."

Jesus did not mean that. He said, "*I am the resurrection and the life. Whoever believes in Me will live, even if he dies; and whoever lives and believes in Me will never die. Do you believe this?*"

Although Martha did not fully understand those glorious words, she nodded. She believed it, because Jesus said it. Therefore she answered, "Yes, Lord, I believe that You are the Christ, the Son of God, the one who was to come into the world."

She hurried back to call her sister Mary. Mary should be with Jesus too. Only with Jesus was there comfort for them. She whispered in her ear, "The Teacher is here and He is calling you."

Mary stood up at once and went out of the room. The people who were with her saw her leave. They said to each other, "She must be going to the grave to weep there. Come, let's not leave her alone." They got up and followed her.

When they got outside the village, they saw that Mary had fallen down at Jesus' feet, overcome with grief. They heard her sob and cry, "Lord, if *You* had been here, my brother would not have died."

That sounded so full of despair that tears came to the eyes of the onlookers. Jesus saw the sorrow of all those crying people. More than any of them, He felt the horror of death, which also threatened Him. He was touched and deeply moved by the world's misery.

"Where have you laid him?" He asked.

They answered, "Come and see, Lord." And they led Him to the grave.

Jesus wept. The people whispered to each other, "See how He loved Lazarus!"

Some of them asked, "If He was able to open the eyes of the blind, couldn't He have kept Lazarus from dying?" Mary and Martha had often asked each other that same question.

Lazarus' grave shone in the sun. The whitewashed rock had a large stone rolled in front of the opening. With Jesus at its head, the procession stopped in front of the grave. Death was just as unmerciful as the rock was hard. Who could possibly break the power of death?

Jesus said, "Take the stone away."

Martha shrank back at the thought. "Lord," she said fearfully, "there will be a bad odor, for this is already the fourth day."

She forgot that Jesus had given this command. She looked first at the grave and then at Jesus.

Jesus said to her quietly, "Haven't I told you that if you believe, you will see the glory of God?"

The stone was rolled away, although no one understood why Jesus would ask such a thing. The people stared into a black space.

Jesus was not weeping anymore. Only *He* realized that death did not rule in that dark cave.

Lazarus was only lying there sleeping. His soul came back into his body as Jesus uttered a silent prayer. Then Jesus looked upwards and said, "Father, I thank You for hearing Me. I know that You always hear My prayers. But I have said this for the sake of the people standing around Me, so that they may believe that You have sent Me."

After saying this, Jesus cried out with a loud voice, "Lazarus, come out."

Soft noises came from the depths of the cave. A white figure slowly emerged, and stood at the entrance to the cave. The people, trembling with fear, saw that it was Lazarus. He had obeyed Jesus' command and had risen from the grave.

Hindered by the strips of linen in which his hands and feet were wrapped, the white figure stumbled ahead. Even his face was still covered with a cloth.

No bystander stepped forward to help Lazarus. Then Jesus said, "Release him from those grave clothes and let him go."

Soon Lazarus was on his way home, walking between his two sisters. There was great amazement in his eyes. He walked like someone who had just awaked from a very deep sleep.

He walked between Mary and Martha, who could not keep their eyes off him. They could hardly believe that their brother had really been restored to them.

His sickness was not meant to lead to death after all. It was intended to glorify God. Many Jews who had seen this miracle believed in Jesus.

96: An unexpected prophecy

Jesus was back in Judea. Against His disciples' wishes, He had come to Judea when He heard that His friend Lazarus lay ill in Bethany.

Lazarus was dead by the time Jesus got there. He had been in his grave for four days. Yet, Jesus called him and he came forth, amazing all who were present.

Some Jews came to believe in Jesus after this miracle. Others still wouldn't believe. They went to Jerusalem and told the Pharisees what Jesus had done. The high priests and Pharisees quickly called a meeting of the Sanhedrin, the highest legal body of the Jews. That distinguished body then discussed anxiously what they should do next.

"What must we do?" they asked. "This man does so many signs! If we leave Him alone, all the people will believe in Him and make Him king. They will rebel against the Romans, and the Romans will punish us severely."

They would surely lose their power if they let Jesus do as He pleased. How could they stop Him? They had already tried to find a reason to put Him to death but they had failed. They looked at each other helplessly.

Then Caiaphas, the high priest, stood up. His face was twisted with hatred. Were they still wondering what reason they could use? Jesus would have to *die* with or without a reason! What difference did it make if Jesus were guilty or innocent? He screamed, "All of you know nothing! Can't you see that it is better that one man die for the people than that the whole nation be lost?"

Just as godless Balaam was once used by God against his will, so the tongue of Caiaphas had been directed to speak the Word of God. Caiaphas had spoken the truth. Jesus would have to die for the people. He would die for the Jews and for all the people in the world—regardless of when and where they lived—who believed in Him. Jesus would die for the great people of God.

Jesus knew He would not die at an assassin's hand. He knew that the rabbis were watching for an opportunity to kill Him. Therefore He withdrew with His disciples to Ephraim, a quiet little town in northern Judea.

He spent the last peaceful days of His life on earth there, in the company of His disciples. Soon the One who had raised Lazarus from the dead would have to bear the pain of death Himself. Jesus would indeed die for the people, as Caiaphas had said in His unexpected prophecy.

97: The persistent widow

One day Jesus wanted to teach His disciples to persist in prayer and not to falter. They should never give up hope that God would hear their prayer. He made this point through the parable of the persistent widow and the unrighteous judge.

Once there was a judge, He said, who did not fear God or care about people. Whenever two rich people came to him to have a dispute settled, he would rule in favor of the one who could offer the bigger gift. If a poor person came with a complaint, the judge wouldn't listen to him. He sought only his own advantage and sympathized with no one.

In his city lived a widow who had suffered a great injustice. Someone had robbed her of her property, and she had nothing to live from. She went to the judge with her problem and pleaded with him, "Grant me justice against my adversary!"

The judge saw how poor she was and turned away from her in contempt. He had more important things to worry about.

The widow went home disappointed. The next day she went back to the judge and pleaded with him again, "Sir, help me! Grant me justice against my adversary!" Again she was chased away. The judge didn't care about her problem.

She came to him on the third day, and also on the fourth. She gave him no rest. Every day she appeared before the judge, and he heard her complaint: "Sir, grant me justice!" He snarled and cursed at her, but she kept coming back to him with her plea. She followed him on the street wherever he went and cried out for help. When he woke up in the morning, she was already standing before his door. Her outcry was the first thing he heard each day. And when the judge opened his chamber each day, she was the first to come in.

The judge had no peace or rest. Wherever he went he met the woman.

Day after day she followed him with her plea, "Sir, grant me justice against my adversary."

Finally it was too much for him. He said to himself, "Although I don't fear God or care about any human being, yet because this widow keeps bothering me, I will grant her justice, otherwise she may eventually wear me out with her pleading."

When Jesus had told this story, He said, "Listen to what the unrighteous judge said. Will God not grant justice to His chosen ones who cry to Him day and night? Will He keep putting them off? I tell you, He will quickly grant them justice."

98: The Pharisee and the tax-collector

Two men went to the temple to pray. One was a Pharisee, the other a tax-collector.

The Pharisee walked up the steps slowly, with his head high and a proud smile on his face. He was at home in the temple. If anyone had a right to come here and appear before God, it was he. He was more pious and religious than anyone else.

The Pharisee strictly observed all the laws of Moses and more laws besides. In the law it was written that the people were to fast once a year, when the great Day of Atonement came. *He* fasted twice a week on Monday and Thursday. He made sure that everyone knew how pious and righteous he was.

In the law it was written that the people were to bring one tenth of their income to the priests. The Pharisee made sure that he gave one tenth of even the smallest plants in his garden. Yes, he was a holy man; he believed he was the best of all men.

The tax-collector looked embarrassed as he slipped into the temple and stole a glance at the people around him. The Pharisee looked down on the tax-collector with great contempt. What was that sinner doing in this holy building? Did he think that God would want to listen to *him*?

The Pharisee walked proudly through the outer court in his beautiful long cloak. He walked right up to the Holy Place.

He stood erect before God and raised his clean, white hands toward the heavens. He did not find it necessary to ask God anything in his prayer. He only summed up his own virtues and accomplishments.

His voice could be heard far away as he prayed, "O God, I thank You that I am not like other people—robbers, unrighteous men, adulterers." Then, with a contemptuous gesture toward the tax-collector, he went on, "And I thank You that I am not like this tax-collector. I fast twice a week and give You one tenth of *all* my income."

Far away, in a quiet corner of the temple, stood the tax-collector. He felt so un-

turned to Him in humility. "Whoever exalts himself will be humbled," He said, "and whoever humbles himself will be exalted."

99: The rich young ruler

A young man was on his way to see Jesus. He wore expensive clothes. Everyone who knew him greeted him politely, for he was already the ruler in his synagogue. He kept all the commandments faithfully, as the Pharisees taught. No one could have done so more faithfully than he.

Everyone thought that this young man must be very happy. What more could he want? He lacked nothing. He was rich and did not need to worry about anything. If *he* were not happy, how could anyone possibly be happy?

Still, the young man was so uneasy that he couldn't sleep at times. His money and his importance did not help him. Not even his piety brought him comfort. There was a great desire in his heart to be closer to God, and he did not know how to achieve that.

Therefore the young man set out to find Jesus, whom he greatly admired. Jesus was a great prophet. Perhaps He could tell the young man what he had forgotten to do.

When he saw Jesus coming down the road, he walked up to Him and fell down before Him humbly on his knees. "Good teacher," he asked, "what must I do to inherit eternal life?"

He addressed Jesus as "Good teacher." That was the same name the rabbis used for Moses, who had given Israel the law. The rich young ruler didn't understand that someone stood before him who was even greater than Moses, someone who was truly good and without sin.

worthy that he did not dare raise his eyes to heaven. "I am the most wicked of all men," he thought, full of sorrow.

When he could no longer hold it in, he beat his breast and sobbed, "O God, be merciful to me, a sinner."

Suddenly he felt as if some invisible hand had lifted a heavy burden from his shoulders. A feeling of freedom coursed through his body. It was the grace of God for which he had prayed.

God had forgiven this man his sins and received him in love as a lost son.

When he left the temple, he was a different man. He was no longer a wandering sinner but a child of God. A new life lay ahead of him.

The Pharisee left the temple just as he had entered. He asked nothing of God, and he had received nothing. He was still the same proud, unrepentant man who did not know the meaning of true happiness.

Jesus told this parable to some proud people. These people looked down on others because they believed themselves to be righteous. He wanted to warn them that God would be gracious to them only if they

But that was exactly the point he would have to understand clearly if Jesus were to help him. He had to realize that the Son of God was addressing him.

Jesus asked him, "Why do you call Me good? No one is good except God alone."

Then He tested the young man and said to him, "If you want to enter life, keep the commandments."

The young man asked, "Which ones?"

Jesus mentioned a few for him: "You shall not kill; you shall not commit adultery; you shall not steal; you shall not give false testimony; honor your father and your mother, and love your neighbor as yourself."

The young man said, "I have observed all those commandments from my youth."

He meant it sincerely, and he really had done his best. He had an upright desire for God in his heart. Jesus could see that. Jesus loved the young man, but He knew that his wealth was keeping him from serving God with his whole heart.

"Where do I fall short?" the young man asked.

"There is one thing you lack," Jesus answered. "If you wish to be perfect, go and sell all that you have and give it to the poor, and you will have treasure in heaven. Then come and follow Me."

The answer surprised the young man. He shook his head sadly, for he was very rich. What Jesus asked of him was too high a price to pay.

He turned away disappointed and went back to his money. Jesus said sadly, "How difficult it is for the rich to enter the Kingdom of God!" When His disciples stared at Him in amazement, He said once more, "Children, how difficult it is to enter the Kingdom of God! It is easier for a camel to go through the eye of a needle than for a rich man to enter the Kingdom of God."

This confused the disciples even more. "Who, then, can be saved?" they asked.

Jesus looked at them and said, "With people it is impossible, but not with God. With God all things are possible."

Then the disciples finally understood. God can even make rich people feel small and humble, so that they no longer attach any importance to their money.

The rich young ruler was gone, but Peter could not forget him. "We are different," he thought to himself. "When the Master called us, we didn't hesitate. Will there be treasure for us?"

Therefore Peter asked Jesus, "We have given up everything to follow You! What will there be for us?"

Jesus' answer went far beyond the disciples' hopes. The Savior said, "I tell you the truth, everyone who has given up home or brothers or sisters or father or mother or wife or children or fields for Me and the gospel will receive one hundred times as much and will also inherit eternal life. But," Jesus added with a warning, "many who are first will be last, and many who are last will be first."

100: The workers in the vineyard

Jesus had told His disciples once more that many who were last would be first, while many who were first would be last. These words still sounded strange to the disciples. How could the first be last?

Jesus then told them a parable to help them understand. He said that the Kingdom of heaven is like a landowner who went out early in the morning to hire some workers for his vineyard. He agreed with these workers that they would be paid one denarius for the day's work and sent them into the field. They picked the heavy, ripe clusters of grapes and dragged them to a wine press which had been carved from rock in the middle of the field. There the grapes were pressed. The juice flowed through the opening in the bottom of the press and was caught in tubs.

The harvest was great, and there were not enough workers. Therefore the master went out again around nine o'clock in the morning to look for more workers. He found some men standing at the labor market. The landowner said, "Go into the vineyard too, and I will pay you what is fair." They set off at once to help with the great work.

The morning passed and the sun climbed high in the sky. Now it was burning from the south. A hot east wind scorched the vineyard.

The workers endured the heat without complaint, for they were happy to have work. The master saw that there still weren't enough workers. Therefore he hired more men at twelve o'clock, and still more at three. He did not tell them how much they would be earning, but he did promise them that their wages would be fair.

Even at *five* o'clock in the afternoon the master went to the labor market, where he found more workers. He asked them, "Why are you standing here all day doing nothing?"

"Because no one has hired us," they answered sadly.

The master said, "You go into the vineyard too." By then the sun was low in the sky. The coolness of the evening was creeping across the land, and the work was much more bearable.

When darkness fell the men stopped. The master of the vineyard said to his overseers, "Call the workers and pay them their wages."

The last workers hired were the first ones called. They had worked for only a little while, but they each received one denarius. They went home happy.

The same thing happened to the workers who had come at three, at twelve, and at nine. They all received one denarius, the wage for a full day's work. It was more than they expected.

Finally it was the first workers' turn. They had worked hard from early morning. Tired and sweaty, they stood before their master and believed that they would receive more than the others. But they, too, received one denarius.

This made them grumble about the

workers who had come later. Those workers had received too much. They said, "Those who came last worked for only one hour, but you gave them the same pay that you gave us, who endured the burden of the work and the heat of the day."

Their mood was spoiled by their envy. They had been the most important workers, but now they were the least important.

The master said to them, "Friends, I am not doing you an injustice. Didn't you agree that you would work for one denarius? Take the money and go. I want to give the workers who came last the same pay as you. Am I not allowed to do as I please with my money? Don't be envious because I was generous to the others."

When Jesus was finished with this parable, He said once more, "The last shall be first, and the first last." In the Kingdom of heaven, things would go just as they had gone in the vineyard.

In the great vineyard of the Lord, many workers are busy. More are coming all the time to join in the work.

The disciples were first to be called by their Lord. But if they thought this gave them the right to look down in pride on other workers, they would soon become the least in the Kingdom.

Only those who wish to serve the Lord in humility can be good workers in His Kingdom.

101: Let the children come to Me

Women walked down the road with small children in their arms. They led other children by the hand. These women were looking for Jesus. They wanted to go to Jesus with their children.

The women had seen the miracles Jesus performed and heard His words. They

knew how much He loved people, and they knew about His power. He had healed the crippled and the blind, given comfort to those who mourn, and brought sinners back to God. All who were touched by His hands were healed, regardless of their sickness. Wherever Jesus went, blessings flowed.

The mothers wanted their children to share in those blessings. The children were still small and did not understand much. But it would be wonderful if Jesus laid His hands on their heads! If *He* would only look at them, they might never forget His shining, holy eyes. If Jesus, the one who lived so close to God, would pray for them, God would surely be gracious to them.

When the mothers found Jesus, He had just argued with the Pharisees about marriage and other difficult topics, and had given His disciples further instruction.

The disciples didn't want to let the women through to the Master. They couldn't understand what the mothers wanted. Children don't belong with Jesus, they thought. Children don't count for much. What would the Master want with children? Could *children* understand His words? Could *they* be His servants and fight for His Kingdom? No, the Kingdom was not for children.

The disciples rebuked the mothers for wanting to bother Jesus with their foolish plan. They wanted to send the mothers and children away.

When Jesus saw the women, unhappy and deeply disappointed, He was angry at His disciples. He said, "Let the children come to Me and do not hinder them, for the Kingdom of God belongs to such as these."

Then He called the children over to Him. They may never have seen Him before, but they came to Him at once when they heard His voice. Not one child was afraid of Him. They crowded around Him. He put them on His lap and talked to them in a friendly way. They were still small, but they under-stood that Jesus loved them.

They looked at Him with bright eyes. Even the babies in His arms laughed. They trusted Jesus and laid their little hands in His without hesitation.

Jesus did not only *touch* the children, as the mothers hoped He would. He also put His arms around them and pressed them to Himself. After that He blessed them.

The mothers watched with tears of joy in their eyes. They were deeply moved. The disciples were amazed. In their shame they didn't say a word.

Jesus then said to them, "I tell you the truth, anyone who does not receive the Kingdom of God like a child will never en-ter it." Then the disciples realized again that they still had a great deal to learn.

Jesus was not looking for wise and learned people or for big, strong people who were proud of their power. Those who felt that they were small and unimportant, those who were as humble and full of faith as the children who came to Him—*they* would be His true disciples.

102: Back to Jerusalem

It was almost time for the Passover feast again. A great number of people began to make their way along all the roads leading to Jerusalem. They would celebrate the holy feast of deliverance there just as they did every year.

Jesus and His disciples were among the travelers on the road that led to Jerusalem by way of Jericho. Jesus walked before them resolutely. The disciples followed, somber and still.

They were surprised when they discovered that their Master wanted to go to Judea. Had He forgotten how the rabbis there watched His every move? Only a few weeks before He had withdrawn to the quietness of Ephraim, where He would be safe from the rabbis' hatred. Now He went openly to His enemies in the midst of all these people traveling to Jerusalem to celebrate the Passover feast. The disciples did not under-stand, and they followed fearfully.

The Savior had not forgotten how the priests and scribes hated Him. He knew that this would be His last journey to Jerusalem.

His hour had come, and He calmly went to meet it. Out of love for His people, He *wanted* to suffer. He even wanted to *die* for His people. He had come to earth to bear the punishment that *they* had earned.

At this Passover feast *He* would be the Passover lamb. That was how He would deliver the people from their guilt and make them right with God. When He would arise from the grave on the third day, death and satan would be conquered.

His disciples didn't know that yet. He had already told them twice, but they didn't seem to understand. They still hoped that He would become king, chase out the Romans and live in a beautiful palace in Jerusalem. Surely they should have realized by now that things would go much dif-ferently from what they originally ex-pected.

Jesus took the twelve aside. For the third time He talked to them about the suffering that awaited Him. Earnestly He said, "We are going to Jerusalem. The Son of man will be delivered into the hands of the chief priests and Pharisees, who will condemn Him to death. They will turn Him over to the Gentiles. He will be mocked, insulted, whipped, and put to death. But on the third day He will arise."

The disciples listened in amazement and still did not understand. They simply couldn't believe that He really meant it. If Jesus knew in advance that all this was planned for Him in Jerusalem, surely He would never go there! He must have something else in mind. Perhaps He was telling them a parable. The *Messiah* was to die? No, that was impossible! He was to become *King!*

The disciples and their Master joined one of the great caravans traveling to Jerusalem from Galilee. They noticed how happy the people were when they saw Jesus. With shining eyes they pointed to Him and with excitement they surrounded Him.

The disciples heard what the people were whispering. "Why is He going openly to the feast?" people asked. "That hasn't happened in a long time. Is He finally going to fulfill our wish and accept the crown?"

Happily they nudged each other and smiled. "Of course! *Now* it will finally happen. This is a very good time for it. All His followers from the entire land will be together at the Passover feast. The whole nation will be there."

When the disciples heard all this, their fears disappeared. Their hearts began to beat fast in joyful expectation. Why had they been afraid when they saw that their Master was on the way to Jerusalem? Wasn't He now marching on His enemies openly to defeat them all?

Insulted? Mocked? Whipped? Put to death? Of course Jesus meant something else when He said those things! The disciples would never allow the enemy waiting in Jerusalem to put their Lord to death. They would fight for Jesus until the last enemy was chased away. Then Jesus' Kingdom would finally come!

That was how the disciples thought as they walked with Jesus to Jerusalem. But Jesus knew it was not to be.

103: Service and a ransom

Among all the people traveling with Jesus as He went back to Jerusalem for the last time walked Salome. She was the mother of James and John and the sister of Mary, the mother of Jesus. She had joined the people as they whispered excitedly about Jesus becoming king in Jerusalem. In her thoughts she already saw Jesus sitting on David's throne in a beautiful palace in Jerusalem. She wondered who His most important servants would be.

The answer seemed simple: the twelve disciples, including her two sons. "If only my sons were granted the most important place of all!" thought Salome. "If only my sons were allowed to sit closest to King Jesus."

They had a rightful claim to this honor, she thought. They had been with Jesus from the very beginning and were even related to Him!

She whispered about this with James and John. "I'll go ask Him," she said. "Come along."

When the caravan stopped to rest, the three of them approached Jesus. They bowed before Him respectfully.

Jesus asked, "What is it you want?"

Salome answered, "Lord, let my two sons have the most important place in Your Kingdom."

"Yes, Master," begged James and John. "Allow one of us to sit on Your right side and the other on Your left when You come into Your glory."

Jesus had to be very patient with His disciples. He had already told them so often not to seek the highest place for themselves. Repeatedly He had explained that His Kingdom was the Kingdom of *heaven*, and that He would suffer much before that Kingdom came. Hadn't they understood at all what a bitter cup of suffering He would have to drink?

If they had understood that, they would not have come with their request. Therefore Jesus said, "You do not know what you are asking. Can you drink the cup of suffering that I shall drink?"

Without hesitation they answered, "Yes, we can." They thought His suffering would only be a short but violent struggle against His earthly enemies. That struggle would end quickly in a glorious victory for Jesus. They would gladly join such a struggle. They were courageous men.

Jesus saw that they were sincere. Only *He* knew what the two would suffer later as His apostles. James would be beheaded in Jerusalem, and John would be imprisoned for a long time. Still, they should not ask for the most important place. One day the Father in heaven would assign them places in His Kingdom.

When the other ten disciples heard what James and John had asked, they were very angry at the brothers. But Jesus called them and restored harmony.

He taught them that, in His Kingdom, things would be just opposite to what they are in the world. Whoever is great and important in the world likes to boss people around and make them serve him. "That's not the way it should be among you," said Jesus. "Whoever of you wishes to be great must serve others. Whoever of you wishes to

be first will be the slave of all the others."

His own life was an example of true humility. He said, "The Son of man did not come to be served but to serve, and to give His life as a ransom for many."

They traveled farther down the road. The crowd grew more and more excited as time passed. They were getting closer and closer to Jerusalem.

Death—not a worldly kingdom—awaited Jesus in Jerusalem. Still, He did not hesitate. Jesus wanted to serve others and give His life as a ransom for many.

104: Bartimaeus

The son of Timaeus sat by the side of the road. He sat there every day and begged. He was blind.

His name was Bartimaeus. He lived in Jericho, the city of palm trees and roses, the pleasure garden of Palestine. Every morning, as he was brought from his home to the place where he begged, he smelled the fragrant flowers. All day long he would listen to the wind in the distant palm trees.

Whenever someone came toward him, he could tell from the footsteps if it was a man or a woman. When the person passed, he could tell from the scent if it was an important man whose head was anointed with oil, or a simple farmer who had worked all day in a field. His other senses had become very sharp during the years he had lived in darkness. But what good did that do? He remained a beggar, for he could not work.

If only he could see, he would not be an outcast. People would no longer regard him as someone suffering a curse. They would not regard him as someone whom God had punished with blindness because of his

many sins. If only God would give him
back the light of his eyes!

It was possible, he knew. In the last few
years many blind were made to see. Not
long ago in Jerusalem, a man born blind
had been made to see again. Great miracles
had occurred since Jesus started traveling
through the land.

Bartimaeus knew that Jesus was the
Messiah. He was the Son of David, who
would establish the Kingdom again.

Jesus must have passed through Jericho
more than once. He was from Galilee, from
little Nazareth. That's why He was called
Jesus of Nazareth. Whenever He traveled
from Galilee to Jerusalem, He would have
to go through Jericho. He had passed
through without Bartimaeus realizing it.

Again the helpless blind man sat by the
side of the road and listened to the footsteps
of the people passing by. The roads were
crowded, for many people were on their
way to Jerusalem to celebrate the Passover
feast.

Now there was a very large group passing
by. Bartimaeus could feel the ground tremble under hundreds of feet. The shouts from
excited voices came closer. Why did the
people crowd each other so much? They
filled the whole street and almost stepped
on Bartimaeus.

"What is this?" cried the blind man.
"What's going on?"

A couple of people on the road answered,
"Jesus of Nazareth is passing through."

That startled the blind man and shook
him up. He thought that, perhaps, this
might be the day on which he would be
healed.

He trembled with joy and excitement. At
the same time he was afraid that this opportunity might pass him by.

He began to cry out in a husky voice full

of emotion, "Jesus, Son of David, have
mercy on me!"

The people near him became angry. "Be
quiet," they told him. "Stop that shouting."

Others cut in, "Be still, you beggar. Do
you suppose that Jesus has time for you
now? He's going to Jerusalem to become
king."

Bartimaeus would not be silenced. Let
them try to be blind once and beg for bread
at the side of the road!

This was his chance, and he was not
about to let it slip by. He cried out still
louder, "Jesus, Son of David, have mercy
on me!"

In all the noise of voices and feet that echoed off the walls of the houses, Jesus heard the trembling voice that cried out to Him. He felt the poor man's plight very keenly. He could sense the yearning in the blind man's heart. He stopped where He was and ordered the blind man to be brought to Him.

Many people then crowded around the blind man and cried out, "Take courage and stand up. He's calling you."

Bartimaeus was so happy that his legs could hardly support him. He cast aside his cloak, which was hindering him, and stumbled toward Jesus. Helpful hands guided him.

When he reached Jesus, Jesus asked him, "What do you want Me to do?"

Bartimaeus stammered, "Lord, I want to see."

Jesus answered, "Your faith has saved you. Go, and you will be able to see."

At that very moment light entered his eyes and shone even into his soul.

He saw the sky, the trees and the people. He also saw Jesus, who had delivered him. He threw up his hands in delight. He rejoiced and thanked God for being gracious to him, an outcast.

The procession, with Jesus in the middle, traveled on toward Jerusalem. Bartimaeus went along, without his cloak and the mat he used to sit on. He only desired to be close to his Deliverer.

105: Zacchaeus

Someone else in Jericho longed for Jesus. He was not a beggar. He was a rich man who lived in a beautiful house. Still, that man was looked down on just as much as the blind man—or even more—for he was hated throughout the whole city.

The people spat on the steps and the door whenever they passed his house in the darkness. They turned their heads when they met him in the street and cursed him in silence. He was a tax-collector.

In fact, he was the chief tax-collector for Jericho, a prosperous trading center. His name was Zacchaeus, and he had become rich quickly. With his servants' help, he stopped the caravans that came from the east loaded with all kinds of goods to be traded. He demanded his portion as tribute to be paid to the Romans.

His customs office was at the city gate. No one could bring in goods without paying him an import tax. Much of the money paid in taxes disappeared into Zacchaeus's own pockets. That is how he became richer and richer.

Yet, all that money did not make Zacchaeus happy. His house with its costly carpets and decorations brought him no real satisfaction. Zacchaeus was very lonely and unhappy, for he suffered the hatred and contempt of his fellow citizens. They called him a traitor because he, a Jew, was serving the Romans, the oppressors of the Jews. They also called him a thief and a sinner.

Zacchaeus felt very sinful, and he thought that God must be looking down on him in contempt too. That bothered him most of all, for in his heart there was a great yearning for God. He would gladly have given up all his wealth if God would take him back in grace. Would God want to bother with such a man as Zacchaeus?

Then Zacchaeus heard about Jesus. Jesus did not despise tax-collectors. People even scorned Him by calling Him a friend of tax-collectors and sinners. One of His disciples had been a tax-collector.

A tiny bit of hope was born in Zacchaeus's despairing heart. Perhaps his life wouldn't be a complete loss after all. Perhaps there was still hope for him.

The more Zacchaeus thought about it, the more he yearned to talk to Jesus and pour out his heart before Him.

When Jesus came to Jericho, Zacchaeus was determined to see Him. All he really wanted was just to *see* Jesus. His lonely life had made him suspicious. He feared that the rumors about Jesus' kindness might be exaggerated. If Zacchaeus *saw* Him, he would know if the reports he had heard were true. Then He could go to Jesus if he wished.

Zacchaeus stood in his beautiful cloak. He was waiting along the side of the road that Jesus would take on His way through the city.

Zacchaeus was afraid he would see nothing. In front of him was a large crowd of people waiting to see Jesus. Zacchaeus was short; even if he stood on his toes he would see only heads and shoulders. Naturally, no one moved aside for him.

Jesus was approaching. Some people near Zacchaeus had already caught sight of Him.

Zacchaeus moved farther along the road to try to find an opening in the crowd, but the road was heavily lined wherever he went. All of Jericho had turned out to see Jesus.

Zacchaeus was suddenly afraid that he wouldn't see Jesus after all. Just then he spotted a wild fig tree. He cast aside all thought of dignity, ran over to it, and climbed it. It was an easy tree to climb, for it had branches almost to the ground.

Zacchaeus climbed the tree easily, although he was no longer a boy. Soon he sat panting on a strong, thick branch. He

was high above the people. He pressed some leaves aside so that he could see what was happening in the street. People laughed at him and made fun of him, but he ignored them. He was *determined* to see Jesus.

A great procession approached slowly. Then Zacchaeus saw the one he had longed for so much. He saw Jesus' form and face. He saw the gentle, kind eyes of Jesus, who was now looking up into the fig tree.

Then Zacchaeus received the greatest surprise in his entire life. Jesus stood right where He was and said very simply to Zacchaeus, as if He had known him for years, "Zacchaeus, come down from the tree at once. I must stay at your house today."

"*My* house?" thought Zacchaeus. He was confused. "Would Jesus come to *my* house, where no Jew would ever set foot?"

Jesus stood there waiting. He meant it!

"Yes, Lord, I'm coming," stammered Zacchaeus. Hastily he scrambled down from the tree. Respectfully he walked next to Jesus through the crowd of people. In his heart he was rejoicing. "*He*, the one on whom Israel fixes its hopes, is willing to spend the night at my house. There may be deliverance for me. God will surely want to hear me."

With great joy he received Jesus in his house.

The crowd outside Zacchaeus's house could not figure out why Jesus would go into this house. This was the house of a tax-collector, a swindler who betrayed his own people. He could have gone to houses of pious Jews! Indignantly they mumbled, "He has gone into the house of a sinful man to be his guest."

Zacchaeus knew perfectly well how sinful he was. Jesus had come into his house and was seated on the expensive couch to rest in the middle of luxurious surroundings. Now, Zacchaeus was even more aware of his sins. Every penny he had ever taken by unrighteous means accused him of wrongdoing. He *had* to make it clear to Jesus that he wanted to begin a different life. He wanted a new life, and he was willing to sacrifice anything for God.

Suddenly this small, dignified man stood up before Jesus. He looked at Him respectfully and said, "Look, I will give half of my possessions to the poor. Any money I have taken from people unjustly I will repay fourfold."

Jesus was delighted, for He could see faith in Zacchaeus's eyes and hear it in his voice. He said, "Today salvation has come to this house, for this man, too, is a son of Abraham. The Son of man has come to seek and save what was lost."

Just as the prodigal son in the parable sat next to his father, so Zacchaeus sat next to Jesus at the table. He enjoyed the happiness that no one could ever take away from him. Even if the people despised him, God had accepted him in love.

106: Hosanna!

Jesus had spent the sabbath with His friends in Bethany. It was the last sabbath before His death, but only Jesus realized this.

The people thought that Jesus was about to become king. The great caravan from Galilee with which Jesus had traveled through Jericho had gone on ahead to Jerusalem. It brought the news that Jesus was on the way.

Soon Jesus' name was on every tongue. The people looked forward to seeing Him. When He did not appear in the temple the next day, the people streamed out of the city and went to Bethany.

They did not go there only to see Jesus; they also wanted to see Lazarus, whom Jesus had raised from the dead. People who had come from all over the country for the Passover feast had heard about this miracle from the people of Jerusalem. It became a busy sabbath in Bethany, busier than any sabbath before it.

The chief priests and scribes were beside themselves with rage. The leaders had decreed that, if anyone knew where Jesus was, he should go to the rabbis at once and inform them. The rabbis would then arrest Jesus and put Him to death. Yet, all the people were looking forward to being with Jesus. The people revered Jesus now and paid no attention to their leaders.

The people were all running after Jesus, and they also wanted to see Lazarus. "We should put Lazarus to death too," the rabbis hissed. "As long as he is alive, the people will be reminded of Jesus."

But they didn't dare. They were afraid of the people. The sabbath before the Passover caused them a great deal of anger.

Now it was Sunday, the first working day of the new week in Israel. On that day the Jewish leaders would have even more to anger them.

Jesus was on His way from Bethany to Jerusalem with His disciples and a great crowd of people. Along the way lay Bethphage, a small village on the side of the Mount of Olives.

As Jesus approached this village, He sent two of His disciples ahead with a strange command. He said to them, "Go to the village ahead of you. As you enter it, you will see a colt on which no one has ever ridden tied up. Untie the colt and bring it here. If someone asks you, 'Why are you untying the colt?' say to him, 'The Lord needs it.'"

When the disciples heard that, a suspicion began to swell in their hearts, and their eyes began to shine.

Everything fell into place just as Jesus said it would. They came into the village, and there they saw a colt tied to the door of a house.

The disciples walked into the yard and silently untied the colt. A few men who were standing nearby—probably the owners of the colt—walked up to them and asked, "Why are you untying the colt?"

"The Lord needs it," the disciples said. The men nodded and let the colt go. That single sentence was enough for them.

The two disciples returned to their Master with that young, almost full-grown animal for Him to ride on. Suddenly the people realized what was about to happen. The excitement that had glowed in their hearts for days now broke out into open rejoicing. A shout of triumph erupted. Now they understood! They were on their way to Jerusalem, and this time Jesus would enter the city as a king! He would march into His capital in triumph. The great day for which they had hoped so long had finally come. Now it appeared that Jesus was willing to become their king after all. He would deliver them from all their enemies!

A few disciples had already laid their cloaks across the donkey's back to form a saddle. With hearts beating wildly, they helped their king climb in the saddle. That young animal that had never been mounted before did not refuse to bear this holy burden. Calmly and patiently the donkey walked along in the midst of the swirl of people. A great multitude of people surrounded Jesus and rejoiced as they accompanied Him to the city.

The farther they went, the greater the crowd became. The news that Jesus was coming had raced ahead to Jerusalem. More and more people came from the city to welcome Him.

"This is the one who called Lazarus from the grave," some people shouted in delight.

"Blessed is He!" the crowd chanted. "Blessed is the one who comes in the name of the Lord!"

They reached out toward Him in ecstasy. They tore their cloaks off and spread them out before Him on the road. He entered the city upon a carpet of clothing. They also laid down palm branches that they cut off the trees hastily. Others swayed along with

great green branches, signs of peace and victory. They danced along ahead of the procession.

"Hosanna to the Son of David! Blessed is the one who comes in the name of the Lord! Hosanna to the highest heaven!"

When they reached the highest point in the road they saw the city lying ahead of them, white and shining on the hills. Their excitement reached an even higher pitch. There lay the city of the Great King, still ruled and oppressed by the Romans. Here came the King, the Son of David, who would bring new power to the city and would rule in glory within her walls.

Thousands of people burst out in rejoicing. The sound resounded through the hills. "Blessed is the King, who comes in the name of the Lord! Hosanna!"

Some Pharisees stood by the side of the road. They were pale and upset and angry. They were desperate for they realized that they were powerless against Jesus. They could do nothing against Him if He wanted to stop them. They said to each other, "We can see with our own eyes that we won't get anywhere against Him. The whole world is running after Him."

Other Pharisees cried out indignantly, "How does He dare let the people call Him the *Son of David* and their king? This will lead to a rebellion!"

They pressed their way through the disciples and cried out to Him, "Teacher, rebuke Your disciples!"

But Jesus rode on calmly, for He really was their King. All these things *had* to happen. The prophets long ago had foretold it. Therefore Jesus answered, "I tell you, if these people kept quiet, the very stones would cry out."

In the midst of all this rejoicing, Jesus rode down the mountain into the Valley of Kidron. He was almost in Jerusalem.

107: Disappointed disciples

Jesus was on His way into Jerusalem, surrounded by a cheering, jubilant crowd. People hailed Him as the Son of David and threw down clothing to form a carpet for His donkey to walk on. Jesus was being received as a king!

He was indeed a King, but a different sort of king from what the people were expecting. He was not a fighter or a conquerer on a fiery war-horse. He was a gentle King, a Prince of Peace.

An earthly king would have been proud and happy during such a triumphant journey. Jesus was sad.

While thousands rejoiced, He rode through the valley and looked ahead to the high, proud walls of Jerusalem and the beautiful temple. His eyes were filled with tears.

The people around Him thought only of the moment. They lived wholly in their beautiful dream of a new, powerful kingdom that might be set up that day.

Jesus knew more as He looked into the future. He knew that the people who had come rejoicing to meet Him that day would reject Him later in the week. Farther in the future, some 40 years on, He saw the frightening punishment that would strike the city on account of that rejection. He knew that enemies would besiege the city and destroy it, not leaving one stone on the other. Unspeakable agony would come over His people.

Jesus wept. "O Jerusalem!" He said sadly. "If only you knew today what would bring you peace! But now it is hidden from your eyes." That day of entry in the midst of a jubilant crowd was also a day of suffering for the Lord.

The people did not understand this. The people entered the city shouting and rejoicing, like a river that could not be stopped. Soon they had the whole city in an uproar. All the houses in Jerusalem were empty. "Who is that?" cried the foreigners who saw Him riding through the streets.

"That's the prophet, Jesus of Nazareth in Galilee," the people shouted in response. They crowded around Jesus full of hope.

Now He would surely gather His followers and march with them against the Roman garrison.

He rode to the temple and dismounted there. He went into the outer court. Surely He would start giving His orders from there. The people would follow those orders courageously and resolutely.

The people streamed into the temple. Their hearts pounded. In their feverish excitement they prayed silently, "O King, speak to us now! Call us to battle. Our souls are without fear if God will be our commander. King Jesus, lead us in this holy war!"

Then a great disappointment came. Jesus was silent. He didn't say a word. He walked around the temple and saw everything that was going on, but He gave no command. With a single word from Him all those excited people would have become His faithful servants. They were willing to lay down their lives for Him. He resisted the temptation and remained silent.

Finally the excitement and passion began to subside. People began to slip away one by one. Those who held on to their hopes to the very end watched Jesus. But He remained silent in the midst of all His disappointed disciples. Then Jesus went out of the city and back to Bethany.

The road between Jerusalem and Bethany was calm in the evening twilight. No hosanna resounded between the hills. The palm branches on the ground were the only reminders of the day's excitement.

The disciples were somber as they walked behind their master. It had all been in vain. Why had Jesus let this great opportunity slip by?

They sighed. They still did not understand that Jesus did not want to establish a kingdom by force. He wanted to establish the eternal Kingdom of peace.

Only later, when Jesus ascended to heaven, would they think of these events again. The prophet Zechariah had already foreseen these events when he wrote, "Behold, your king comes to you, gentle and riding on a donkey, on a colt, the foal of a donkey."

Later the disciples did not understand how they could ever have been so blind!

108: The barren fig tree

Jesus spent two more days in the temple. They were long, difficult days for Him. He said a great deal to His disciples and the people. He also said a great deal to the chief priests and scribes.

In those days the rabbis and the people had their last chance to repent, but they didn't. They thought there was no need for them to repent. They certainly seemed pious and religious, especially during those days. They were bringing great sacrifices to the temple.

All those sacrifices were lies, for their hearts were without love and faith. All their pious talk was empty and fruitless. The people of Israel looked like the barren fig tree that Jesus had cursed.

The fig tree grew near the road that led from Bethany to Jerusalem. Because it was spring, the other fig trees were practically bare. But between the swelling buds there were already small, green fruits that promised rich harvest. That's how the fig tree develops: the fruits come before the leaves. Here and there on a bare branch an old, ripe fig from the previous season still hung. Those old figs were still good to eat.

But that one tree stood proudly at the side of the road displaying a beautiful spread of shining green leaves.

That tree looked much better and more fruitful than the others. Perhaps a treasure of ripe figs from the last harvest could still be found under its leaves.

Jesus walked over to the tree. He had left Bethany very early that Monday morning and had not eaten yet. But there were no figs on the tree. There were neither ripe figs from the previous year nor small, developing figs that would ripen in the season ahead. That beautiful display of leaves was misleading, for the tree was barren.

When Jesus saw that, He spoke to the tree as if it were a person. He said aloud, so that His disciples could hear Him, "May no one ever eat fruit from you again." He was hungry as He went to the city, where His work awaited Him.

He went into His Father's house, the temple. He had cleansed it three years before because it had been made into a house of commerce and trade. The money-changers sat there behind their tables. Merchants stood around with doves and various animals for sale.

With the same holy wrath that He had shown the other time, Jesus drove them all out of the temple. Again they all bowed to His power. He said, "It is written, 'My house shall be called a house of prayer, but you are turning it into a den of robbers.' "

No one contradicted Jesus. The merchants fled, the scribes stood biting back their wrath, and the people watched in amazement.

The eyes of the people shone as they observed Jesus in action. He was powerful and angry and bold as only a king could be. That was the Jesus they loved to watch!

That same day they also saw another Jesus, a gentle Jesus who was full of mercy. Blind and crippled people came to Him in the temple, and He healed them all. They came to Him moaning and went away rejoicing. The children who were in the temple rejoiced with them. They loved Jesus, who was so kind and friendly to them. They shouted what they had heard the grown-ups shouting the day before: "Hosanna to the Son of David!"

That was too much for the chief priests and scribes. They did not want to go through the same uproar that had seized the city the day before. Therefore they quickly forced their way through the crowd and pushed the children to the side. They cried out indignantly, "Do You hear what the children are saying?"

"Yes," Jesus answered calmly. "Have you never read, 'Out of the mouths of children and infants You have brought forth praise'?"

They had no answer, so they backed off. Yes, they had certainly read that text. One of the psalms of David stated that even the smallest children were to praise God. But who did Jesus think He was, daring to use those words in this setting? Was He trying to put Himself on the same level as God?

"How does He dare!" the scribes murmured. "The blasphemer!" Again they busied themselves with plans to put Him to death.

If they dared, they would strike Him down right where He stood. But Jesus preached in the temple all day, unafraid. His enemies did not dare harm Him there. They were afraid of the people, who breathlessly listened to Jesus.

Later that day Jesus returned to Bethany. He was tired. He spent the night there.

Early the next morning, Jesus and the disciples were on their way to Jerusalem again. Peter suddenly cried out in amazement, "Master, look at the fig tree You cursed yesterday. It has withered."

The other disciples also saw it. Then Jesus taught them that they would be able to do even greater miracles if their faith were strong enough. When they went to God in prayer, they had to make sure that their hearts were free of any evil thoughts, hatred, and resentment. If they did not doubt that the Father in heaven would hear them, but believed firmly that whatever they asked Him for would surely come to pass, then their prayer would be granted. All that they desired *in faith* they would surely receive.

As the disciples walked toward the city, they kept looking back at the tree in amazement. It no longer stood showing off its leaves, as it had done the day before. It stood revealed for what it really was, a useless tree, dead and dry from the roots up. That tree would soon be cleared away.

That tree was a symbol, a visual reminder of the horrible punishment in store for Israel.

109: Two sons

On Tuesday of that week, Jesus set foot in the temple for the last time. Only *He* knew that.

The chief priests and scribes, filled with hatred and wicked plans, followed Him around all day. They went up to Him repeatedly to argue with Him and ask Him tricky questions.

Their cunning was no match for Jesus' divine wisdom. Never did Jesus speak to them so sternly and openly about their sins as on that last day.

He was hardly in the temple, and they were there already. They were still seething about the events of the day before, when Jesus had driven the money-changers and merchants out of the temple. He had acted as if He were Lord and Master there.

"Who gave You the right to carry on here in such a way?" they asked, challenging Him.

Jesus did not answer this question. Once before they had sent a delegation to John the Baptist. He had told them that Jesus was the Son of God. The Son of God was Lord and Master in God's house. If they had believed John, that question would not have been necessary.

Therefore Jesus said, "I will ask you a question, and if you can give Me the answer, I will answer you. Tell Me: was John the Baptist a prophet, or was he a lying deceiver? Was his baptism from heaven or from men?"

This simple question threw the rabbis into confusion. They thought to themselves, "If we say that it was from heaven, He will ask, 'Why didn't you believe him?' But if we say that his baptism was from men, the people will stone us. They are convinced that John was a prophet."

Finally they stammered, "We don't know."

Jesus responded, "Then I won't tell you who gave Me the right to do these things."

Jesus did not really want to throw the

scribes into confusion. He really wanted to show them their sins. They acted as if they respected God, but in their hearts they were stubborn and wicked. The sinners and tax-collectors were better than they were, for they had repented and turned away from their sinful life.

To bring out this difference, Jesus told the scribes the parable of the two sons.

There was once a man with two sons. The man went to the older son and said to him, "Son, today you are to work in the vineyard."

The son gave his father an insolent answer: "I will not!" When his father left him, the son felt sorry for what he had said. He went to work in the vineyard anyway, because he loved his father.

The father went to the younger son and said, "Son, today you are to work in the vineyard."

The son gave a respectful answer: "I shall go, Father."

But he did no such thing! His answer was a lie, and his respect was false. In his heart there was no love and obedience.

When Jesus was finished telling this story, He asked the scribes, "What do you think? Which of the two sons did the will of his father?"

"The first one, of course," they answered unsuspectingly.

Then they received a shock. Jesus pointed a finger at them sternly and said, "I tell you the truth, the tax-collectors and sinners will enter the Kingdom of God before *you*. John the Baptist showed you the way of righteousness, but you did not believe him. But the tax-collectors and sinners believed him. Although you knew that, you still did not repent and believe."

All the people watched and listened as Jesus addressed them sternly. The eyes of the rabbis were filled with hatred and anger. Repent? They were ready to murder Him right then and there!

110: The wicked tenants

The rabbis were questioning Jesus in the temple. They were enraged by His answers. He told them that tax-collectors and sinners would enter the Kingdom of God before they would.

Again Jesus showed them that He could see right through them. This time He used the parable of the wicked tenants.

There was once a master who owned a beautiful vineyard, He told them. First he planted the finest vines on a sunny hillside. Then he built a high stone wall around the vineyard to keep out robbers and foxes. He even erected a watchtower so that someone could stand guard and see if danger threatened. He also dug a winepress in the middle of the vineyard. There the juice could be pressed from the grapes. He spared no expense or effort to make everything beautiful and useful.

Then he rented the vineyard to tenants. For a long time he was gone on a journey to a foreign land.

When harvest time came, he sent a servant to receive a portion of the harvest as rent. The tenants were wicked, ungrateful men. They had reaped a rich harvest, and they wanted to keep it for themselves. They acted as if the vineyard were their own property. They made fun of the servant, beat him up, and sent him away empty-handed.

The master sent another servant to them, but they gave him even worse treatment.

The good master was patient with the

wicked tenants. He sent more servants, thinking to himself, "Surely they will come to their senses. They will give me the part of the harvest that they owe me as rent."

Again he was disappointed. All the servants were roughly treated by the tenants. Not one came back with the rent.

At last the master sent his own son to the vineyard. It was his only son, whom he loved greatly. He thought to himself, "Surely they will respect my son."

One of the tenants standing up in the watchtower saw him coming and told the others. They said, "He is the heir! Come, let us kill him, and then the inheritance will be ours." They seized the master's son, threw him out of the vineyard, and killed him.

When Jesus reached this point in the story, He looked at the scribes and asked, "When the owner of the vineyard comes, what will he do with those tenants?"

They heard Jesus pronounce judgment upon them with this question. *They* were the tenants who wanted to be the boss themselves and did not honor their master. Israel was the beautiful vineyard that God had allowed them to rent. They had acted as if they themselves were the owners. When God sent prophets to them, they persecuted and killed them. Now they devised plans to put His only beloved Son to death. Just like the wicked tenants in the parable, they wanted to be masters forever.

Did they still not understand? Or were they trying not to understand? Jesus had asked them what the owner of the vineyard would do. Shamelessly they answered, "He will make those wicked men die a horrible death and will then give the vineyard to others."

Jesus spoke some stern words in response: "Therefore I tell you that the Kingdom of God will be taken away from you. It will be given to a people who will produce fruits."

That statement finally frightened them. Would *they* no longer be God's people? "Never!" they cried indignantly.

Jesus then reminded them about a psalm that was sung in those days of the Passover feast. "The stone that the builders have rejected has become the cornerstone. This is the Lord's doing, and it is wonderful in our eyes."

A prophet had sung those words to make the people realize what would happen when the Messiah came. They, the chief priests and scribes, were the builders about to reject the Messiah. He was a stumbling block to them. God would make Him King over all who believed in Him. He would rule over the new people of God that He would gather from all the lands of the world.

When the rabbis heard those words, they walked away. They were white with anger at Jesus for daring to say those things. But His great display of wisdom also made them

afraid. Deep in their hearts they knew that He was indeed the Son of their Master. A voice in their hearts whispered to them, "Go to Him and kneel before Him. Confess that Jesus is the Christ!"

But they silenced that voice. They would *not* go to Jesus. They did not *dare*. They were afraid that other rabbis would despise them and expel them from the synagogue.

Those rabbis cared very deeply about the honor paid them by men. They cared more about that honor than about the honor of God. What poor, foolish men those scribes were!

111: Offerings and taxes

Jesus did not encounter only hatred and unbelief on this last day in the temple. There were also some truly pious people in Israel.

He was seated opposite the box in which the offerings were received. He watched the people bring their offerings when they entered the temple. The rich people threw a lot of money into the box. The clink of large coins could be heard whenever these people extended their hands above the box.

A poor widow came along. She was alone in the world, and had no one to look after her. The Pharisees and scribes oppressed the widows in Israel. Often widows' possessions would find their way into their greedy hands.

Despite all her cares, this woman had not become bitter and had not forgotten the Lord. She went into the temple and put her small gift in the offering box. Her gift was only two small copper coins, hardly worth more than a penny. Jesus knew that this was all she had. Her trust in God was great.

She did not know what she would have to live on from then on.

He called His disciples to Him and said, "I tell you the truth, this poor widow has brought a bigger offering than any of the others. The others all gave gifts from their surplus. She, despite her poverty, gave all that she had to live on."

That was one of the very few joyful events on that day. Meanwhile, the Pharisees and scribes got together to figure out how they could humiliate Jesus. They did not dare kill Him, for they were afraid of the people. Therefore they tried once more to trap Him with one of their clever questions.

This time they came up with a cunning plan indeed. They didn't go to Jesus themselves, for that would immediately have aroused His suspicion. Instead they sent their disciples.

Those disciples acted as if they greatly revered and admired Jesus. They said to Him, "Teacher, we know that You are a man of integrity. You speak the truth always and are not swayed by men. Indeed, You pay no attention to what or who they are. Tell us, then, is it right to pay taxes to Caesar or not?"

They hoped He would say, "No, strictly speaking, it is not right." That was the opinion of many in Israel. They argued that it was sinful for God's people to turn over all that treasure to a heathen emperor.

If Jesus joined this view, they could tell the Romans that He was a rebel. If He said that it was all right to pay taxes, the people would despise Him.

Jesus saw through their trickery. He replied, "Why are you trying to trap Me, you hypocrites? Show Me the coin used for paying taxes."

They brought Him a Roman coin with the image of the emperor stamped upon it. Jesus asked, "Whose portrait is this? And whose inscription?"

"Caesar's," they replied.

Then Jesus taught them that they could both be good servants of God and faithful subjects of the emperor. Didn't God Himself give the emperor power over the Jewish people? "Give to Caesar what is Caesar's, and to God what is God's," He said.

Silent and ashamed, the people who raised the question went back to their masters. Their wicked plan had failed.

112: Woe to you!

Jesus was teaching in the temple for the last time. The scribes and Pharisees had sent some people to Him with a tricky question, but they had failed to trap Him.

One scribe present wanted to try a different approach. He went to Jesus and asked politely, "Teacher, what is the greatest commandment in the law?"

He knew that the Pharisees divided the commandments into greater and lesser, more important and less important. He hoped that Jesus would give a careless answer. Then He would be ridiculed before the people.

What a fool! Who would know the law better than Jesus, the only person who ever fully kept the law?

Jesus said to him, "You shall love the Lord your God with all your heart and with all your soul and with all your mind. This is the first and greatest commandment. And the second is like it: love your neighbor as you love yourself. All the law and the prophets depend on these two commandments."

When the scribe heard this answer, his cunning and his ugly plans vanished. In genuine reverence he cried out, "Teacher, You're right! To love God above all else and your neighbor as yourself is best of all. That means much more than burnt offerings and sacrifices."

Jesus rejoiced that this man could be so upright in his answer. He said to him, "You are not far from the Kingdom of God." Then no one dared to ask Him anything else.

When everyone was finally silent, Jesus addressed some stern words to the people. He exposed the sins of the scribes and Pharisees.

They were the last words He addressed to a large group of people. He had been patient for a long time and had given the people time to repent. They had closed their hearts to Him. They had fought against Him, slandered Him, and pursued Him throughout the land with devilish hatred.

Now His time of preaching was drawing to a close. He said straight out what no one had dared to say before. All the people could hear it. His voice echoed off the walls. He was a stern and righteous judge as He pronounced judgment.

"The scribes and the Pharisees have taken Moses' seat," said Jesus. "Do all that they *tell* you, but do not do what they *do*. They do not keep their own rules. They make heavy burdens and lay them on the people's shoulders. They are not willing to lift a finger to move those burdens.

"Woe to you, scribes and Pharisees. You are hypocrites. You devour the houses of widows and make a show of praying long prayers. Your punishment will be great.

"Woe to you, scribes and Pharisees. You are hypocrites. You give tithes of your spices—mint and dill and cummin—but you neglect justice and mercy and faithfulness. You tell people to do this and not to do that. You blind guides! You strain a fly out of your drink but you swallow a camel!

"Woe to you, scribes and Pharisees. You are hypocrites. You clean the outside of your cup and your dish, but within, you are full of greed and self-indulgence. You blind Pharisees! Clean the inside of the cup first. Then the outside will also be clean.

"Woe to you, scribes and Pharisees! You are hypocrites. You are like whitewashed tombs that are beautiful on the outside but are full of dead men's bones and impurity. Outwardly you look righteous to people. Inside you are full of hypocrisy and contempt for the law. You brood of vipers! How will you ever escape the condemnation of hell?"

Jesus said many more things in holy wrath. The people listened, trembling. When He was finished, a deep stillness covered the temple square. People hardly dared to draw a breath. Jesus' cries of "Woe to you!" still seemed to echo off the shining walls.

Jesus had often stood in that very place calling the people to Himself because there was peace and security only with Him. He thought about this and His mind was full of sadness. "Jerusalem, Jerusalem!" He said. "You kill the prophets and stone those who are sent to you. How often I would have liked to gather your children as a hen gathers her chicks under her wing, but you refused!"

113: Children of the light

For three years Jesus had preached to His own people, but they had turned their backs on Him. Now, on His last day of preaching in the temple, something wonderful happened, which brought Him great joy.

There were Greeks at this Passover feast in Jerusalem. They were people of heathen origin who loved the God of Israel. They had heard so much about Jesus that they also yearned for Him. They said to Philip, one of the disciples, "We would like to see Jesus."

Philip and Andrew together went to Jesus with this request. When Jesus heard it and saw the Greeks, there was great joy in His heart. He knew that even if Israel rejected Him, others would believe in Him. His Kingdom would spread across the entire earth.

First death and the grave would come. First He would bear the punishment for sin and thereby make sinners right with God. His death would bear rich fruit.

Jesus spoke about this in a parable. He said, "I tell you the truth, unless a kernel of wheat falls in the ground and dies, it remains only a single seed. If it dies, it brings forth much fruit."

When Jesus thought of His great suffering and death which were near, His soul was filled with anxiety. He raised His eyes to heaven. His soul sought His Father, who had sent Him to save the world. Could He now ask that He be spared this horrible suffering?

He did not make this request. He thought of the world, which He loved. He thought of His Father, whose name was to be glorified in all the earth.

As these thoughts filled His mind, Jesus spoke a prayer. His voice, quiet but clear, could be heard in the temple square. "Now My heart is troubled. What shall I say? Father, shall I ask to be delivered of this hour? But it was for this reason that I came to this hour. Father, glorify Your name!"

There was a deep silence. In that stillness a voice from heaven said, "I have glorified it, and I will glorify it again." That was the Father's answer.

Those who loved Jesus heard these words clearly. Those who did not believe were unable to understand God's voice. They stood staring at the sky in amazement.

"Listen to that thunder!" some of them cried in fear.

Others said, "An angel has spoken to Him."

Jesus said, "That voice was for your benefit, not Mine."

The sunlight was fading. As Jesus prepared to leave, He issued one last warning to the people. "You will have the light with you only a little while longer," He said. "Believe in the light as long as it is light, so that you will be children of light."

Did they understand that the Light of the world was leaving them at that moment?

114: Jerusalem's destruction

Evening settled upon Jerusalem. The sun sank behind the hills of Judea. In its fading golden light walked Jesus with His disciples. They went out the city gate and down the road that led to the Mount of Olives. They walked earnestly and silently, following their shadows as they took the rising path.

It looked as if Jesus could not yet put Jerusalem behind Him. He sat down on the slope of the Mount of Olives surrounded by His disciples. At their feet lay the city in all its glory, still clearly visible in the last rays of the setting sun. There was a purple sheen over many of the roofs and a reddish gleam on the walls in the dying light.

It looked like a heavenly city of gold. Beyond Jerusalem glowed the evening sky in bright colors. It seemed as if heaven's gateway had been opened.

On that beautiful, peaceful spring evening, Jesus and His disciples talked about the future. First they talked about the fate awaiting the beautiful city of Jerusalem.

Earlier, as they were leaving the temple, one of the disciples had expressed wonder at the beauty of the building. Jesus had looked at the temple with the same sorrow He had felt when He had entered the city two days before. He had answered, "Do you see these great buildings? Not one stone will be left upon another. It will all be broken down."

Now, in the twilight, Jesus taught His disciples more about the city's coming destruction. He gave them a careful warning. When great armies would surround Jerusalem, they were to flee to the hills. At that point nothing could be done to save the city.

God would allow Jerusalem to fall and be taken by enemy soldiers. The city would be destroyed, and the people would be scattered across the entire earth. That would be Israel's punishment for rejecting the Messiah.

Jesus also talked about the glorious work that awaited the disciples. Soon they would be sent out into the world as heralds, bringing the good news of God's love and mercy.

It would not be easy! They would suffer much and be disappointed often. They would be hated and persecuted for Jesus' sake. They would be deceived by their friends and betrayed and thrown into prison.

But there was no reason for them to be afraid. In all those trials, Jesus would watch over them. He would lead them and strengthen them through His Spirit.

When they appeared before kings and governors, they would not need to worry about what they should say. They wouldn't have to think about it in advance. Jesus Himself would give them wisdom that no opponent could possibly refute.

The church of Christ would grow and expand in an amazing way until it filled the entire earth. After the gospel had been proclaimed to all people, the end would come.

115: Ready for Christ's return

Jesus and His disciples were seated on a slope of the Mount of Olives. He told them about the great day when He would return on the clouds to judge the world.

Many great signs would appear before His return. The sun would be darkened and the moon would not shine. The stars would fall from the sky, and all the powers of the heavens would be shaken.

People all over the earth would be overcome with fear. Then they would see the Son of man come on the clouds. Those who loved Jesus would have nothing to fear. They could raise their heads in joy, for Jesus' coming would mean their deliverance.

When would that day come? The disciples were eager to know. Jesus said,

"No one knows the day and the hour, not even the angels in heaven or the Son of man. Only the Father knows."

That day would surely come. The disciples could count on it. "Heaven and earth will pass away," said Jesus, "but My words will never pass away."

Many people would put all thoughts of Jesus' return out of their minds. They would live in their sins as people did in the days of Noah. The faith in their hearts would go to sleep and die. They would not expect the great day of Jesus' return. It would be a *horrible* day for them!

Fortunately, the light of faith would continue to shine in many other hearts. Sometimes it would be small and weak, and almost go out. But the Holy Spirit would watch over it and keep it burning.

The Spirit of Jesus is the oil that keeps the lamp of faith burning. Those whose lamps were still burning when Jesus came again would go with Him into heaven's banquet room.

To teach His disciples this, Jesus told them the story of ten bridesmaids.

Ten young women waited by the side of the road one dark evening. They wore their most beautiful clothes. Each one carried an oil lamp attached to a wooden stand.

They waited with their flickering lamps in their hands.

They peered down the road, but saw nothing. It was still and dark, and they were all alone. No one approached.

A great wedding feast was to be celebrated that night. The bridegroom had passed that spot earlier in the evening on his way to pick up his bride from her father's house. Now that it was dark, he would surely come back this way soon with his bride. A festive procession would move to the bridegroom's house, where the two

would live. In that house a great feast lay ready for the bride and groom and their guests.

The ten young women waited impatiently. When the joyful procession of the bride and the bridegroom and their friends passed, they would join the others. They were also friends of the bride. They were invited to join the feast that would go on for days.

Why did the bridegroom delay so long? Ten pairs of eyes peered down the road. Night had fallen, and the procession still had not come.

The bridesmaids were tired of waiting. They became drowsy. One by one they sat down by the road. Still the bridegroom did not appear. Then, one by one, they fell asleep.

Ten silent figures dressed in white sat in the dark night. Among them burned ten weak flames in ten lamps. The flames became steadily smaller, for the oil in the lamps was almost gone.

The ten bridesmaids slept till midnight. Suddenly they heard voices, "The bridegroom is coming! Come out to meet him!" There came the festive procession with music, singing, joyful voices, and lamps held high.

The bridesmaids were startled. Hastily they rubbed their eyes and got up. They reached for their lamps. No one was allowed into the wedding feast without a burning lamp. Every guest present had to help make the feast nice and bright.

The lamps had almost gone out. Then it became apparent that five bridesmaids were *wise*, while the other five were *foolish*.

The foolish ones had not prepared properly for the feast. They had been too easily satisfied that everything was in or-

der. They had not taken along extra oil to refill their lamps.

The five wise ones had been more careful. They loved the bride and bridegroom and had taken great care not to disappoint them. Quickly they refilled their lamps so that they shone brightly again in the darkness.

The five foolish bridesmaids were embarrassed and ashamed as they watched. "Give us some of your oil," they said, "for our lamps are going out."

But there was not enough oil for all of them. The five bridesmaids could not offer any oil, but they did offer some advice. "Go to the people who sell oil and buy some," they said.

The five foolish bridesmaids hurried away in the darkness. The five wise ones danced off to join the procession.

The door of the banquet room was wide open. It was not closed until the last person in the procession was inside.

When the wedding feast began, the five foolish bridesmaids were still buying oil for their lamps.

A little later they came. Although they had done nothing to honor the bridegroom, they knocked on the door and cried out, "Sir, open the door for us." They knocked and begged in vain.

The bridegroom said, "Truly, I tell you, I do not know you. You do not belong among our friends. All our friends were with us in the procession when we went inside."

The five wise bridesmaids joined the glorious feast in the beautifully lighted banquet room. The five foolish ones stayed outside in the darkness.

When Jesus was finished telling this

story, He said, "Keep watch, therefore, since you know neither the day nor the hour."

116: The parable of the talents

Jesus did not want His disciples to think that they should sit and wait for His return without doing anything, like the bridesmaids waiting by the roadside. Those who truly loved Jesus and yearned for His coming would ask themselves every day what they could do for Him. They would do their best for Him and try to expand His Kingdom.

Some people would accomplish more than others, for not all were equally clever and strong and capable. Some had received more talents and gifts from God than others. But no one could say, "There is nothing I can do for Jesus."

Every person has received some gift or talent from Him. Each one must work with the gifts God has given him. Anyone who does will be praised by God and invited to enter the Father's house. But anyone who is lazy and evil, who thinks only of his own desires and enjoyment, is a useless servant. He will not enter the Father's house.

To make this clear to His disciples, Jesus told them yet another story. He told them the parable of the talents.

A master was about to take a long journey to a faraway land. Before he left, he called his servants and gave each one a sum of money to work with.

The master knew his servants well. He knew who was the most capable and could take the greatest responsibility. That servant received five talents. A second servant received two talents, and a third servant received one. No servant was left out; they all had something. A single talent was quite a sum of money. It was more than a thousand dollars.

The master set out on his journey, and the servants were left with their talents. The one who had received five talents went right to work with them. He bought and sold and traveled and traded and planned and calculated. As a result, he made quite a profit.

The servant who received two talents also got busy right away. He did not manage to make as much profit as the first servant, but he also did his best. The money entrusted to him increased.

The servant who had received one talent did nothing with it. He decided to take it easy. He was angry and jealous of the other servants, who had received more than he.

"Why should I work with my talent?" he thought to himself. "I might make money, but I might also lose some. What would my master say? I'll put the money away in a safe place. That way I can be sure I won't lose it."

He dug a hole in the ground and hid his master's money. It would be safe there. He did not care that he had been disobedient. He would take it easy until his master came back. He hoped the master would stay away a long, long time.

The master did stay away for a long time. When he returned, he summoned his servants to find out what they had done with his money.

The first servant said, "Master, you entrusted five talents to me. I have used them to earn five more."

The master said to him, "Well done, you good and faithful servant! You have been faithful when you looked after only a few things. Now I will put you in charge of many things. Come and share your master's joy at the feast."

The second servant was next. He said, "Master, you entrusted two talents to me. I used them to earn two more."

The master also said to this servant, "Well done, you good and faithful servant! Because you have been faithful when you looked after only a little, I will place you in charge of much. Come in and share your master's joy at the feast."

It was time for the third servant to speak. He knew he had done wrong, but he did not want to admit it. He tried to put the blame on his master, by telling him a lie. He said, "Master, I knew that you are a hard man, reaping where you do not sow and harvesting where you do not scatter seed. I was afraid that I would lose that talent, so I hid it in the earth. Here is your money; you can have it all back. Now you have nothing to complain about."

The master saw through this lie. He answered, "You wicked, lazy servant! If you knew that I reap where I don't sow, why didn't you lend out my money? That way I could at least have collected interest on it."

Then he said to his other servants, "Take the talent away from him and give it to the one who has ten talents. Everyone who has will be given more and will enjoy an abundance. But whoever has nothing, even the little he has will be taken away from him. Throw that useless servant into prison."

117: The day of judgment

On the great day when Jesus returns, He will judge the living and the dead. How can those who love Him serve Him best as they wait for His coming?

They do not all have to engage in trade, like the servants in the parable of the talents. What can they do instead with all the gifts and powers God has given them?

They must all live by faith. They must try to love God above all else and their neighbors as themselves.

They should follow the glorious example set by Jesus while He was on earth. Jesus could never ignore a poor person, an oppressed person, or a sorrowing person. Whenever He came upon someone in need, He reached out to him, full of compassion.

He told His disciples to do the same. If they are true disciples, the love of Christ will *drive* them to acts of mercy. It will be clear from their deeds who belongs to the great congregation of the children of God, the congregation which will enter heaven someday.

When Jesus comes in glory, He will seat Himself on a throne. All people of the earth will then be gathered before Him.

He will divide them into two groups, just as a shepherd divides the sheep from the goats when they come to the sheepfold in the evening. Those who loved Him will be on His right hand, and those who hated Him will be on His left.

He will say to those on His right, "Come, you blessed of My Father. Inherit the Kingdom that has been prepared for you from the foundation of the world. I was hungry, and you gave Me food. I was thirsty, and you gave Me something to drink. I was a stranger, and you invited Me in. I was naked, and you gave Me clothes. I was sick, and you visited Me. I was in prison, and you came to Me."

Those on His right will not understand why they are worthy of such great honor. In amazement they will say, "Lord, when did we see You hungry and feed You, or thirsty and give You something to drink? When did we see You a stranger and invite You in, or naked and clothe You? When did we see You sick or in prison and come to You?"

The King will answer them, "Truly, I say to you, if you did these things to the least of My brothers, you did them for Me!"

He will say to those on His left, "Go away from Me, you who are cursed. I was hungry, and you gave Me nothing to eat. I was thirsty, and you gave Me nothing to drink. I was a stranger, and you did not invite Me in. I was naked, and you did not clothe Me. I was sick and in prison, and you did not visit Me."

They will answer Him, "Lord, that's not true. When did we see You hungry, or thirsty, or a stranger, or naked, or sick, or in prison, and fail to serve Your needs? We never saw You."

He will answer them, "Truly, I say to you, if you did not do these things for the least of My brothers, you did not do them for Me."

Those on His left will be condemned to eternal punishment, but the righteous will receive eternal life.

When Jesus was finished talking to His disciples on the slope of the Mount of Olives, He stood up. Darkness had settled on them; it was nighttime. The moon, almost full, hovered behind them over the Mount of Olives and cast its light on the dark city.

Jesus said just a few more words, that sounded very sad after all He had said before. "As you know, the Passover is two days away. The Son of man will then be handed over to be crucified."

Jesus turned around and led His disciples to Bethany.

118: Anointed for the grave

It was Wednesday evening, the last evening before the Passover. Important gatherings were held on opposite sides of the Mount of Olives. One gathering was held in Jerusalem and one in Bethany.

Both were held for the sake of Jesus. One was dominated by *hatred* of Jesus, and the other by *love*.

The Sanhedrin met in Jerusalem, in the high priest Caiaphas' house. All the prominent, well-dressed Jews who were members of this high council, including chief priests, scribes and elders sat in a great chamber. They talked once more about how they could trap Jesus and put Him to death.

They would have to go about it in a cunning way, for the people were very excited. There would surely be an uproar if they knew what was going on. Therefore Jesus could not be arrested during the Passover feast. A few days afterward, when Jerusalem was almost empty again, they would have a good opportunity to seize Jesus. Then they would finally have Him in their power.

Their eyes gleamed in triumph at the thought. They discussed their plan until late in the evening.

In Bethany Jesus sat peacefully in His friend Simon's house. Simon had once been healed of leprosy by Jesus. People still called him *Simon the leper*.

A meal had been prepared for Jesus and His disciples in Simon's house. Jesus' other friends from Bethany were also there. Even Lazarus, who had been dead and four days in the grave, was among them. He was strong and healthy and his happy eyes focused on Jesus.

Martha was there too. Naturally, she could not sit still. She walked back and forth serving the guests and keeping busy. This time she did it quietly and calmly. Her face shone with gratitude as she looked at Jesus, who had restored the happiness in her home.

Jesus saw only love and warmth as He looked at His upright friends gathered in Simon's house.

One person was missing. Where was Mary, the sister of Martha? She did not arrive until after the meal had begun. Quietly and earnestly she stood by the door. There was great sorrow in her eyes.

Mary sensed something that none of the others was even thinking about. This would be the last evening that Jesus was in their midst. She had sat at His feet so often listening quietly and had perhaps loved Him more than any of the others. She had understood something of the great mystery. She sensed that Jesus was to die at the Passover feast.

When she realized what was going to happen, she decided to show Him her deep love and devotion once more. She bought a jar of the most expensive perfumed oil she could find. It was an alabaster jar with a narrow neck. One must pour out this expensive oil very carefully, drop by drop, making sure not to waste any.

But that was not how Mary wished to use the oil. Hadn't a *stream* of blessing come into her life through the one who now lay before her?

Without hesitating, she snapped off the neck of the bottle as she stood by Jesus. She let the costly perfumed oil pour out onto His head. Weeping, she knelt down at His feet and anointed them too, drying them with her hair.

Everyone could see how much anguish she felt and how deeply she revered Jesus. Everyone could smell the exquisite scent that filled the house. Not everyone understood why Mary did it. Only those who loved Jesus as much as she did could understand.

Judas Iscariot, one of the disciples, didn't understand at all. Judas thought of the money Mary must have paid for the oil. Money was his idol. From the beautiful scent and the alabaster jar, he figured out that it must be the most expensive oil that money can buy. All that money was wasted.

It pained Judas to think of all the money that had been wasted in just a few minutes. He almost wished he had torn the jar of oil from Mary's hands.

He grumbled, "Why all this waste? The oil could have been sold for more than a year's wages. Then we could have given the money to the poor."

Judas was not concerned about the poor. He wanted the money in his own hands. He would have received it, because he looked after the money for the disciples. He often stole from the money entrusted to him, because he was a thief.

The other disciples did not know that yet. They thought that there was something to what Judas said. They, also, didn't understand Mary's action.

The oil was worth 300 silver coins, which was more than a year's wages for a laborer. It was really too much. The other disciples agreed with Judas. Frowns covered their faces.

But there was only love and joy in Jesus' eyes as He looked at Mary. He knew Mary's heart. He was delighted that someone understood what suffering He was to face and had tried to make it more bearable for Him.

He said to the others, "Leave her alone. Why are you bothering her? What she has done for Me is something very beautiful. You always have the poor with you, and you can help them whenever you wish, but you will not always have Me. Mary has done what she could; she has anointed My body for the grave. Truly, I say to you, wherever the gospel is preached throughout the world, people will remember what she has done, and will tell others about it."

119: The price of a slave

Because Jesus was to die in a few days, Mary anointed Him with a costly oil. The disciples had grumbled about the money this gesture cost, but Jesus had silenced them. The disciples bowed their heads in shame.

One of the twelve stood up and walked into the night. That disciple did not belong among Jesus' friends. He sensed this himself, for he no longer wished to honor and love Jesus.

"Anointed for the grave?" he asked himself bitterly. "Is that really how things will end, with Jesus in the grave? What am I doing with His disciples? What am I waiting for? Does He think I'll serve Him for nothing?"

Resolutely he walked toward Jerusalem. He would go to that gathering in Jerusalem, where Jesus' enemies were plotting against Him.

He really belonged there. Judas was a traitor!

Judas had finally reached the point where he could be unfaithful to his Master and turn his back on Him. Money was the most important thing of all to Judas.

Earlier his attitude toward Jesus was one of passionate admiration. He believed that Jesus was the Messiah, and he saw Jesus as his golden opportunity. If Jesus were to become king and rule over Israel, then he, Judas, would be one of His leading officials; Judas would become rich and powerful. He was happy to look after the money. Perhaps later he would be in charge of the king's treasury. His greedy fingers now fondled coins. One day he might be surrounded by gold and precious stones.

Whenever Judas thought about this, his eyes shone with anticipation. Jesus' *words* usually passed him by. Repentance, conversion, and forgiveness of sins were all secondary to Judas. He was after power, honor and wealth! That was why he followed Jesus, and that was what he was waiting for.

He had trembled with joy after Jesus had miraculously fed all those people by the Sea of Galilee. The excited people had wanted to proclaim his Master their king. He had been bitterly disappointed and had cursed, when Jesus had refused to go along. The next day, when people had begun to forsake Jesus and He had sadly asked His disciples, "Aren't you going to forsake Me too?" Judas had stayed with Jesus. He had not yet given up hope.

Since that day he had gradually lost hope. The waiting had become more and more of a burden. That was why Judas had begun to steal some of the money entrusted to him. At least he would get something out of the time he had spent with Jesus.

Then came that unforgettable Sunday, just three days ago. How excited Judas had been as he had shouted, "Hosanna! Blessed is the one who comes . . . !" How disappointed he had been when that effort, too, had failed.

Afterward he had begun to think again about the somber words he had heard from

Jesus on a number of occasions: ". . . to be delivered into the hands . . . to be put to death . . . to be crucified."

Now Jesus had said it again. He was to be *buried*, and Mary was anointing Him for the grave.

This time Judas believed it, and the last flicker of hope within him died. There was nothing left in his heart to bind him to Jesus, for he did not love Jesus. Only anger and resentment lived in his heart. All that time spent following Jesus had been wasted!

He had thought he was following the Messiah. Could this man really be the Messiah? Why would He let such fine opportunities slip by and start talking about dying instead?

Judas did not believe in Jesus anymore. Jesus was a fool, a deceiver. The Pharisees who hated Him so intensely were right after all. Judas was ready to vent his wrath on Jesus.

At that moment satan whispered a horrible plan in Judas's ear. It was a devilish plan that would still allow him to make some money from his association with Jesus. Judas would betray Jesus. He would sell Jesus to His enemies like some animal sold for slaughter.

Judas knew just where to go. His hatred showed him the way. That was why he set out for Jerusalem that night after leaving Simon's house in Bethany.

He was admitted to the meeting of the rabbis and looked at them with troubled eyes. "What will you give me?" he asked them. "I will deliver Him into your hands."

At first the rabbis didn't quite trust him. Soon they saw that he really meant it, that his heart was full of a wicked joy.

"Without an uproar?" they asked.

"The people won't even know about it,"

said Judas. "I'll wait for just the right moment."

They said they would give him 30 pieces of silver if he could deliver as promised. That was the price one paid for a slave in those days. It was hardly an immense sum.

It was also the price that the prophet Zechariah had mentioned. None of those wise scribes and rabbis stopped to consider that. They were eager to get on with the plan.

They counted the money before Judas's greedy eyes. He saw the gleam of the coins and heard their clink. Judas decided that he would not rest until he kept his part of the bargain and the money was his. He slipped away again into the darkness. He had sold God's Son for the price of a slave.

He rejoined the other disciples and acted as if nothing had happened. He waited for his chance.

Poor foolish Judas! Didn't he realize that Jesus knew exactly what he was up to?

Mary and Judas had both been busy that night. They were both close to Jesus, and they both knew that He was to die.

Mary wanted to *honor* Him one last time, for her heart was full of love. Judas *betrayed* Jesus, for his heart was overflowing with hatred.

120: Preparing for the Passover

It was Thursday. That evening the Jews would eat the Passover meal. Through that celebration they would remember their deliverance from slavery in Egypt centuries before.

Jesus summoned Peter and John. He said to them, "Go and make preparations for us to eat the Passover."

"What place do You have in mind?" they asked.

Judas listened closely. If he knew the place, he could perhaps have Jesus arrested there without anyone knowing what was happening. The people of Jerusalem would be indoors eating the Passover meal!

Jesus knew what Judas was thinking. He would not let Himself be arrested that evening. He wanted to celebrate the Passover with His disciples, undisturbed, for the last time. He made sure Judas would not know in advance where the Passover meal was to be held.

Jesus said to the two disciples, "When you come into the city, you will meet a man carrying a jug of water. Follow him into the house he enters and say to the owner of the house, 'The Master wants to know what room He can use to eat the Passover with His disciples.' He will show you a large upper room fully supplied. Get things ready for us to eat the Passover meal there."

Peter and John went away with this amazing set of instructions. Everything worked out just as their Master had said it would. They met the man carrying the jar of water. They talked to the owner in the house he entered, who must have been a friend or admirer of Jesus. He showed them the most beautiful room in his house, a large upper room where they could be alone and undisturbed.

The two disciples went about their work eagerly. They slaughtered the Passover lamb in the temple. The lamb had been selected four days earlier, and it was free from blemishes and broken bones. Then they joined the crowd in the outer court to offer the lamb's fat on the altar of burnt offering. They took the meat with them to be cooked and prepared for the Passover meal.

They also made sure there was hard, unleavened bread and bitter herbs. The herbs would remind them of their bitter slavery in Egypt. They placed a sauce in which the bread would be dipped on the table. Finally, they added some red wine with a pleasant scent.

They prepared the couches. They placed a washbasin and a pail of water to wash the feet of the guests by the door.

When all the preparations were completed, they only had to wait for Jesus and the other disciples.

121: Jesus sets an example

Evening fell in Jerusalem. The stars began to shine. From the temple a pure note was sounded three times as a signal. It was the long, drawn-out sound of the silver trumpets, and it carried far across the city and the surrounding area. "Come, everything is ready. Come and eat the Passover meal. The day is over and the hour of the feast has arrived."

Jesus and ten of His disciples walked through the streets in the twilight. They reached the house where Peter and John were waiting and climbed the stairs to the upper room. They went inside and greeted the two waiting disciples.

The disciples congregated near the door as if waiting for something. They stole uneasy glances at each other. The water was ready and so was the washcloth. There was no servant to wash their feet, as they had expected there would be. Who would be the servant? Who was willing to humble himself and kneel before the Master and the other disciples to wash the dust from their feet?

No one stepped forward to volunteer. No one was willing to bend over the basin and do the lowly work of a slave. Finally they shuffled to their places at the table without having their feet washed. Each disciple whispered to his neighbor, suggesting which of the twelve should have taken the lowly job.

Jesus sat in their midst. He thought about how this would be the last Passover He would celebrate on earth. He and His disciples would remember how the blood of the lamb had protected the people of God from death. But the next day *He* would become the true Passover lamb, and die for the sins of the world.

Jesus was deeply moved as He picked up the cup, blessed it, and passed it to His disciples. He looked at them and said, "I have a burning desire to eat this Passover with you before I undergo My suffering. I tell you that I will surely eat nothing more until the Kingdom of God has come."

Did the disciples hear those moving words properly? The whispering at the table did not stop. The disciples were still arguing about their status in relation to each other. That same old question had always divided them. That question had so often caused their Master disappointment.

Then something very unusual happened which they never forgot. It brought a sudden end to their whispering and arguing.

Jesus stood up and silently walked to the door. He took off His outer garment. He took a cloth that hung by the basin and tied it around Himself like an apron. He poured water into the basin, kneeled over like a slave in front of a disciple and began to wash his feet. He dried them with the apron.

The room was deathly still. The startled disciples looked in amazement as their Master did a slave's work. Each disciple had disdained that work. The Messiah, the Son of God, the King of heaven and earth, was willing to be regarded as the least of them all. Was it right for Him to humiliate Himself so much? Could the disciples permit this?

"No," thought Peter, red with shame when he saw Jesus kneeling before him. He pulled his dusty, sweaty feet back. He almost screamed as he said, "Lord, are *You* now going to wash *my* feet?"

Jesus looked at him calmly and answered, "Right now you do not understand what I am doing. Later you will understand."

Jesus was right: Peter didn't understand it at all. It did not occur to him that Jesus wanted to cleanse his *heart* as well as his *feet*. Deeply ashamed, he cried out, "You shall *never* wash my feet."

Jesus said earnestly, "If I do not wash you, you can have no more fellowship with Me."

Peter had to give in. No more fellowship with Jesus? He answered, "Lord, not only my feet but also my hands and my head!"

That wasn't necessary. Each disciple had taken a bath before coming to this feast. Only their feet, which had walked along the dusty road, needed washing.

Therefore Jesus said, "A person who has had a bath needs to wash only his feet, for his whole body is clean." Then He added, "You are clean, but not every one of you."

Jesus knew which disciple would betray Him. He had washed Judas's feet, but Judas's *heart* remained closed to Him. That was why Jesus said, "You are not all clean."

When Jesus had put on His outer garment again, He took His place at the table and said to the disciples, "Do you understand what I have done? You call Me *Master* and *Lord*, and rightly so, for that's what I am. If I, your Lord and Master, have washed your feet, shouldn't you wash each other's feet? I have given you an example. You must do just as I have done."

The disciples were silent. They hardly dared to raise their eyes to Jesus.

"Master, Master!" they thought. "Do You really love us that much? How often we have hurt You and disappointed You with our pride!"

122: A traitor among the disciples

The disciples were ashamed. When no one stepped forward to wash all those dusty feet, Jesus finally did it Himself.

One man among the disciples did not feel sorry and repentant at all. He sat among the others at the table. He put his lips to the cup from which His Master had drunk. He took the bread and ate some of the lamb. He dipped the bread in the sauce, just as his Master did. But his thoughts were busy with a horrible plan. He was about to betray Jesus.

Jesus knew what was in his mind and could bear it no longer. As He ate this holy meal with His disciples, Judas's thoughts made Him deeply unhappy.

His voice was full of pain when He said,

"Truly, truly, I say to you, one of you will betray Me."

This threw an awful scare into the disciples. One of *them* was to betray Him?

They looked at each other with dismay in their eyes. Who would be capable of something so horrible?

"Am *I* the one?" each one thought. "Could *I* ever do such a thing? No, surely He means someone else!"

Sadly the disciples said to Jesus, one by one, "Surely You don't mean *me*, Master! Please say that I am not the one."

Jesus answered simply, "The one who will betray Me dipped his bread in the same dish I used to dip My bread. The Son of man will depart, just as it is written. But woe to the man by whom the Son of man is betrayed. It would be much better for that man if he had never been born."

The disciples looked at each other despairingly, still trying to figure out to whom Jesus was referring. Peter, seeing that John was sitting closest to Jesus, signaled him to ask Jesus who it was.

John understood at once. He leaned over to Jesus and whispered, "Lord, who is it?"

Jesus took a piece of bread in His hand and answered softly, "The one to whom I give this piece of bread after I dip it in the sauce." He spoke so softly that only John heard Him.

At that moment Judas bent over the table and said, "Surely You don't mean *me*, Rabbi!"

Jesus dipped the bread in the sauce and gave it to Judas. Looking into the eyes of His faithless disciple, He answered, "You have said it." He said this very softly.

This, too, was not heard by the other disciples. But John heard it. Now he knew who the traitor was. He looked at Judas in dismay, but he did not doubt for a moment that Judas was the one. Judas's eyes were filled with hatred and rage as he took the bread Jesus offered him. It seemed as if satan had taken possession of Judas.

Jesus looked at Judas and said to him earnestly, "What you are about to do, do quickly."

No other disciple understood what Jesus meant by this. Judas looked after the money, and therefore some of them thought that he had to buy something for the meal. Perhaps he had to bring something to the poor.

They watched as Judas stood up and went to the door. His figure was outlined briefly against the dark night sky. Then he closed the door behind him.

The traitor was on his way to carry out his horrible assignment.

123: The Lord's supper

Jesus and His disciples were seated together at the table. The meal was almost over. It was Jesus' last supper with His disciples.

The end of Jesus' life on earth and the end of God's covenant with Israel was near. The Jews could no longer be God's people if they killed the promised Messiah.

A new day was dawning. There would be a *new* people of God living on the earth, a people that bore the name of Christ.

There would be no place for Israel's Passover feast among that new people of God. They would remember their deliverance from the power of sin and death rather than from Egypt's might. They would use not the blood of the lamb to help them remember but the blood of the true Lamb of God, Jesus Christ, who would surrender His life on the cross.

Jesus wanted to make sure that the new people of God never forgot how He died for them. He wanted them to realize that God was willing to forgive all their sins only because *He* had borne punishment for those sins. Therefore, on this last evening before His suffering, He instituted the Lord's supper.

The disciples must have sensed that something very special was about to happen. They could see from their Master's eyes that He was deeply moved. Carefully He took the bread in His hands and blessed it. Then He broke the bread, as a symbol of how His body would be broken for them.

He gave them each a piece of the bread and said: "Take and eat. This is My body, which is given for you. Do this in remembrance of Me."

Then He took the cup of red wine and blessed it too. He passed it around to all of them and said, "Drink of it, all of you. This cup is the new covenant in My blood, which is poured out for you and many others for the forgiveness of sins."

Silently and reverently, the disciples ate the bread and drank the wine. Although they did not quite understand what Jesus meant by all this, their hearts were full of love for Him. They knew that they would never forget this ceremony.

Since that day, the Lord's supper, the holy communion instituted by Jesus Himself, is celebrated in churches all over the world. Whenever believers see how the bread is broken, they think of how Jesus' body was broken for them. When they see the red wine poured into the cup, they are reminded that the blood of their Savior flowed for them.

When the disciples had celebrated this first Lord's supper, Jesus assured them once

again that He would *always* love them. He was to die for *their* sins too.

124: Final words to the disciples

During that last evening with Jesus, the disciples still did not understand very much. They could not believe that Jesus was going to leave them, although He told them openly He would.

What the Savior said to them that night sounded so strange! They sat around Him, thinking of how much they loved Him, but He declared that they would be unfaithful to Him.

Sadly He said, "You will all fall away on account of Me. It is written, 'I will strike the shepherd, and the sheep of the flock will be scattered.' But after I have risen, I will go ahead of you to Galilee."

They hardly heard the last couple of sentences. Fall away on account of Jesus. Forsake Him? They shook their heads firmly. That was impossible! They felt so sure of themselves, so strong and faithful in their love! They didn't realize how weak their faith was and how strong satan was. They did not know how easily they could fall if God did not protect them.

Peter felt stronger than any other disciple. He was almost angry that Jesus dared to say such things. He gave Jesus a fiery answer from his heart, "Even if all the others should fall away, I will *never* forsake You."

He did not yet know what a horrible night this would be. Peter would be attacked by satan himself.

Jesus knew what was to happen. Therefore He warned him, "Peter, Peter! Satan has asked to have you, to sift you as

wheat. But I have prayed for you so that your faith might not falter."

Even this rebuke did not restrain Peter. "Lord, I am ready to go with You into prison, and to die with You," he said. "I will give up my life for You."

The Savior shook His head sadly and asked, "Will you give up your life for Me? Truly, I say to you, even before the rooster crows twice, you will deny Me three times."

Peter and the other disciples simply didn't believe Jesus. Deny Jesus? Claim that he did not know Him and was not one of His disciples? Peter would rather die than do such a thing!

Jesus had much more to say to His disciples that evening. He was addressing some final words to them. The disciples could sense that. Their hearts were heavy with disappointment and sadness.

Jesus comforted His disciples and explained why He had to leave them. He was going to His Father's house to prepare a place for them. Later they would come to Him and stay with Him forever.

He would not leave them all alone on the earth. He promised to pray to the Father to send the Holy Spirit into their hearts. The Spirit would comfort them and lead them and always stay with them. He would help them understand all that now seemed mysterious to them.

125: The vine and the branches

It was time for Jesus and His disciples to leave the table. The meal was over. Still, Jesus was not ready to take leave of His disciples. He wanted to say a few things first.

He deeply desired that the disciples

would always give Him the central place in their hearts, just as He always had a place for them in His heart. He wanted them to be one with Him, just as a leaf is one with the tree and a branch is one with the vine.

This time His words did not include Judas, for Judas was not with them. Judas *appeared* to belong to Jesus, but he was not really bound to Him with cords of love. Therefore Judas was cut off like a withered, wild branch that bore no fruit. The eleven remaining disciples would not be cut off like Judas.

Jesus addressed them now with a beautiful comparison, "I am the true vine, and My Father is the gardener. He takes away every branch of Mine that bears no fruit. He trims every one that does bear fruit so that it will bear even more fruit. Abide in Me, just as I abide in you. The branch can bear no fruit by itself if it does not remain in the vine. You can do nothing if you do not abide in Me. I am the vine, and you are the branches. Anyone who abides in Me and I in him bears much fruit. Without Me you can do nothing."

Then Jesus talked about the love that was supposed to bind all of His disciples together and bind all of them to Him. He said, "People will know whether you are My disciples or not, if you love one another."

When Jesus was finished speaking to His disciples, He raised His eyes to heaven and led them in prayer. The high priest in Israel bore the names of the twelve tribes on his heart when he went into the Holy of Holies. Jesus, the true High Priest, bore all the people of God in His heart as He went to God's throne.

Jesus prayed for Himself and for His work. He prayed for His disciples. He prayed for all who would later come to believe in Him through the disciples' preaching. He was now about to die for millions of people, so that they could be with Him forever.

His voice was reverent and full of trust: "Father, it is My wish that where I go, those who are with Me, whom You have given Me, may also go to see My glory. You have given Me that glory, for You loved Me even before the foundation of the world."

As Jesus prayed that beautiful high priestly prayer, He did not forget a single one of us.

Then Jesus and His disciples sang a song of praise together. Their trembling voices, husky with emotion, were led by the powerful, pure voice of their Master.

The cup was passed around once more. Then Jesus led His disciples out of the room, down the stairway, and into the dark night. His disciples surrounded Him, uneasy and concerned, looking anxiously in all directions. The moon was high in the sky, and the houses cast black shadows.

Jesus walked through the shadows. By the light of the moon, He went out the city gate, across the bridge over the brook Kidron, and along the path to the Mount of Olives. On the mountain slope was Gethsemane, an olive grove where Jesus often sought silence to pray.

Jesus went to Gethsemane. His hour was now very near.

126: Gethsemane

Jesus and His disciples had come to Gethsemane, an olive grove on the slope of the Mount of Olives. It was a silent, lonely spot, in the middle of the night. The cool night wind swished through the trees. The moonlight played on the crooked, knobby tree trunks. The stars shone brightly in the dark sky.

Jesus and His twelve disciples had often come to this quiet garden on mild nights. This time only eleven disciples were with Him. The twelfth one would be there soon too, because he knew where Jesus would surely go.

Jesus left eight of His disciples in the outer part of the garden and said to them, "Sit down here while I go on ahead to pray. He took Peter, James and John with Him farther into the dark garden.

Then something very strange happened. No human being will ever understand it. Jesus, who had always led His disciples calmly and securely, seemed to suddenly lose courage. A great sadness came into His heart, and a frightful anxiety took hold of Him. His voice was filled with emotion as He said, "My soul is overwhelmed with sorrow to the point of death. Stay here and keep watch with Me."

It was not just the fear of suffering and dying that made Him speak these words. He had often spoken without trembling of the suffering awaiting Him. He had even mentioned it earlier that night.

There was something else bothering Him, something mysterious, much more horrible than the physical suffering awaiting Him. He Himself was surprised at the horrible pain He suddenly felt.

That pain was caused by the burden of our sins, the sins of the entire world, which God now placed on Jesus' shoulders. Jesus, who had never done wrong, suddenly felt God's wrath resting upon Him. That wrath of God was directed at all of man's wickedness. Jesus had chosen to bear the punishment for that wickedness, and now He felt the pain that His decision involved.

He was so horribly afraid and anxious that sweat broke out all over Him. He trembled, and then He collapsed. His soul seemed to be ripped open by fear.

Jesus went farther into the garden, about a stone's throw from His disciples. Then He sank to the earth to pray. In His great hour of need, only prayer could help Him. This time He did not raise His eyes to heaven, as He usually did. He bent over with His face to the ground and wrung His hands together.

Finally He could no longer hold it in. He cried out, "My Father, if it is possible, may this cup be taken from Me." But He added quickly, "Still, not *My* will but *Yours* be done."

No one on earth ever suffered so much as Jesus did during that horrible hour. No one could offer Him comfort.

He stood up after His prayer and went to the three disciples, who were to keep watch with Him. How He yearned for their friendship, for a word of love that would strengthen Him.

Even that was denied Him. The three disciples lay wrapped in their cloaks on the spot where He had left them. They were fast asleep. Even Peter slept. The sadness of that final evening with Jesus had exhausted them.

Peter, despite his brave words about never forsaking his Master, had let Jesus down.

Jesus woke them up. Sadly He said, "Peter, are you asleep? Couldn't you keep watch with Me for even one hour? Watch and pray that you will not fall into temptation. The spirit is willing, but the flesh is weak."

Startled, they raised their heads. They did not know what to say to Jesus. Their eyes were heavy, and their hearts were sad.

They tried to answer Him; they tried to pray.

The disciples wanted to keep watch and pray with Jesus, but their heads sank to their arms, and soon they fell asleep again. As long as they slept, they were not tormented by their great sadness.

Jesus had to continue His great struggle alone. The darkness of night filled His soul. The loneliness that surrounded Him was infinite. The pangs of death held Him in their grip; the anguish of hell attacked Him.

Jesus kneeled on the ground again. So great was His fear that sweat, like drops of blood, fell from His face.

Still, not one rebellious word passed from His lips. His voice was respectful and obedient as He said, "My Father, if this cup cannot be taken away without Me drinking it, so be it. May Your will be done."

Again Jesus found His disciples asleep when He turned to them for comfort. They did not grant the last favor He ever asked of them.

Still hungering for their comfort, He went back to the place where He prayed. For the third time He prayed the same prayer to God.

He surrendered Himself entirely to the Father. He wanted what the Father wanted. Therefore He prayed once more, "Your will be done."

Then an angel, a messenger sent by the heavenly Father, descended to be with Him. That angel could comfort Him more than any human being. After that Jesus felt strengthened and refreshed. A deep joy filled His heart. Despite whatever might happen, He would not waver for a moment. He would let Himself be led as a lamb to the slaughter, and no complaint would come from His lips.

Jesus fought His greatest battle in the garden of Gethsemane. He emerged victorious through His obedience unto death.

He went back to His disciples again, but this time He did not need their comfort. He said to them, "Go right ahead and get some rest. The hour is now very near when the Son of man will be delivered into the hands of sinners."

When He saw that they were awake anyway, He pointed to some lights flickering in the distance. People with torches were looking around in the darkness. "Arise," He said. "Let's go. The one who is to betray Me has arrived."

127: Betrayed with a kiss

The stillness in the garden of Gethsemane was broken by the sound of many feet and voices. With torches swaying in the darkness, a band of dark figures moved between the trees and approached Jesus.

Judas Iscariot was with them. He had come to carry out his horrible mission. He knew that Jesus would go to Gethsemane after the meal with His disciples. In the middle of the night he had gone to the chief priests and scribes to tell them that they now had their opportunity to arrest Jesus without stirring up the people.

Hastily they called some armed servants together and summoned the temple guard. Was that group large enough? What if the disciples put up a fight and ran to get help? Many Galileans had pitched their tents close to Gethsemane. They had accompanied Jesus on His triumphant journey to Jerusalem.

The arresting party would have to be strong. They quickly sent a message to Pilate, the governor, to ask for a company of Roman soldiers to help them arrest a dangerous rebel.

The Jewish servants, the Roman soldiers with their captain, and some of the chief priests marched together into Gethsemane. It was a strong band of men armed with swords and clubs.

How would the servants and soldiers know which man to arrest? How would they know Jesus in the darkness of night?

Judas solved the problem for them. "I'll act as if I'm still His friend," he told them. "I'll go ahead of you, as if I've come to warn Him. I'll greet Him with a kiss. The one I walk up to and kiss is the one you are to arrest."

The traitor knew the garden well, for he had often been there with Jesus. When he saw Jesus standing before His disciples, he hurried over to Him as if he was happy to see Him.

"Greetings, Rabbi!" he said, and he kissed Him.

That was the most cruel kiss anyone on earth has ever received. It must have burned into Jesus' face. His soul must have been filled with loathing at this treachery.

He asked Judas simply, "Are you betraying the Son of man with a kiss?"

Judas shrank back in confusion. He hid among the servants and soldiers who arrived on the scene with their swaying torches.

The soldiers stood there looking. They did not know what to do next. Judas had gone too far ahead of them, and they had not seen him kiss Jesus. Which of those men were they supposed to arrest?

Then someone stepped forward. He stood clearly outlined in the light of the moon and asked calmly, "Whom do you seek?"

"Jesus of Nazareth," they shouted.

The man standing before them said, "I am Jesus."

Those simple words had an amazing, mysterious power. The armed men and Judas all shrank back. They stumbled and fell to the ground.

When they got back on their feet, they saw that Jesus was still standing at the very same spot. They were anxious and frightened as they looked at Him. They realized that they were powerless before Him.

He asked them again, "Whom do you seek?"

"Jesus of Nazareth," they stammered.

Jesus replied, "I already told you that I am the one you are looking for. Therefore let these men go." He pointed to His disciples, who stood behind Him, trembling with fear and anger.

He was thinking only of them, for He wanted them to be spared. He would go along with the soldiers without a struggle.

The soldiers finally stepped forward and took hold of Jesus.

128: Peter takes up the sword

The disciples watched the scene in the garden of Gethsemane without doing anything. They said nothing when Judas kissed Jesus, and they watched as the soldiers fell back in fear.

But when the soldiers finally stepped forward to seize Jesus, the disciples rushed forward indignantly. "Master," they cried out, "shall we attack them with the sword?"

Peter did not wait for an answer. He rushed to get in front of Jesus with a sword flashing in his hand. In his despair he swung at the soldiers. He didn't know how

to handle a sword properly; he had never done it before.

Peter's sword just missed one servant's head. The man felt a searing pain and put his hand to his head. His right ear was gone!

The whole band of screaming soldiers was about to attack the disciples. It looked as if their Master's effort to protect them would be in vain, and they would be captured anyway.

But Jesus could protect them even in this situation. He stepped before the soldiers like a king and held them back with a single gesture. Then He turned to Peter and said, "Put your sword away, for all who live by the sword will die by the sword. Did you think that I could not pray to My Father and have Him send more than twelve legions of angels to be at My side instantly? Should I not drink this cup that the Father has placed before Me? Then how would the Scriptures be fulfilled when they say that all these things must take place?"

Peter was ashamed. He retreated into the darkness.

Jesus walked over to the wounded servant, touched the man's ear, and healed him. The man's name was Malchus; he was a servant of the high priest. Malchus was the last person on earth to be healed by the touch of Jesus' hands. Malchus had been sent out to do evil, but Jesus showed him mercy.

Right after this miracle, the soldiers seized Jesus again and tied His hands together. The chief priests watched, feeling satisfied at last.

Jesus said to them, "Am I a robber, that you have come out with swords and clubs to capture Me? When I was in your midst in the temple every day, you did not arrest Me. This is your hour, the hour that belongs to the powers of darkness."

The chief priests and soldiers said nothing in return. Some soldiers started to lead Him away. Other soldiers looked around for the disciples.

The disciples forsook Jesus. They did not try to follow Him. Instead they fled in all directions into the darkness.

The soldiers saw only one person left in the garden, someone dressed in a long white sheet. They grabbed him. He was a young man.

The young man tore away from them and left the sheet in their hands. He fled naked into the darkness.

The young man was not one of the disciples. It may have been John Mark of Jerusalem. Whoever it was had heard of what was going on, quickly wrapped a sheet around himself, and followed the soldiers to the garden of Gethsemane.

Everything had taken place just as Jesus had predicted. The disciples had forsaken Him. He was taken down the dark road that led through the valley of Kidron to the city. He was a prisoner.

129: Questioned by Annas

The palace of the high priest was quiet that night. It was the night of the Passover. The streets were deserted. The moon beamed brightly on the sleeping city.

Quietly, some servants came through the gate of the great house. They spread quickly through Jerusalem and knocked on the doors of the leading Jews who were members of the Sanhedrin. They woke them up and told them they should meet at once in the house of Caiaphas.

From all directions, elders and scribes in their long, beautiful robes hurried over to the high priest's house. They knocked on the door, and a servant girl let them in. They hurried to the spacious inner court. A fire was burning in the darkness for the armed servants to warm themselves. They walked on and entered one of the large rooms that had been added to the mansion.

There Caiaphas, the high priest and the chairman of the Sanhedrin, greeted them. His eyes were shining with wicked delight as he told them that Jesus had finally been arrested. Soon He would be led into the room, and they would condemn Him to death. They all knew that in advance. They were determined that He was to die whether or not He was guilty. They needed only an accusation to bring against Him.

The punishment was already decided— death. Now they need only find a crime to go with it.

First Annas, the father-in-law of Caiaphas, would question Jesus. Annas would conduct a preliminary hearing until the Sanhedrin was ready to begin meeting.

Annas was old and gray, but he was just as powerful and cunning as Caiaphas. He had served as high priest in the past, but the

Romans had removed him from office. His sons took over from him, and then the office passed to Caiaphas, his son-in-law. But Annas was still referred to as the high priest.

He sat in a room on one side of the inner court. Jesus stood bound before him, between the servants who had brought Him in.

Annas looked at Jesus in pride and contempt. He asked Jesus all sorts of tricky questions about His disciples and His teaching. He hoped that Jesus would give a careless answer.

But his cunning did not get him anywhere against Jesus. Although Jesus had been betrayed by one of His disciples, He would never betray them. He also refused to say anything about His teaching. Why was Annas asking about that? Surely Annas knew what Jesus had taught. Jesus did not say things in secret.

He answered boldly, "I have spoken freely and openly to the world. I taught constantly in the synagogues and the temple, where all the Jews gather, and I taught nothing in secret. Why do you ask Me these questions? Ask those who heard Me when I taught. They can tell you what I said."

Annas didn't know what to answer, for he felt that Jesus could see right through him. A servant, eager to help, went up to Jesus and slapped Him in the face. "Is that any way to answer the high priest?" he shouted indignantly.

That was the first blow Jesus received. He turned to the servant calmly, with earnestness rather than wrath in His eyes. He said gently, "If I said something wrong, then tell Me what I said that was wrong. If it was good, why do you strike Me?"

The mean servant looked down at the floor in shame. Annas sensed that he would get nowhere against Jesus' wisdom. Angrily

he sent Jesus across the inner court to the judgment hall of Caiaphas.

130: False accusations

Israel's judges sat in a great semi-circle. They had been called together in the middle of the night for this urgent meeting.

In the flickering light of the torches and lamps, they hid their wicked joy and delight behind false earnestness.

The cruel, callous armed servants were also in the room. Outside the room the witnesses waited. They were eager for the reward they would receive when they said all sorts of bad things about Jesus.

Among all those godless people stood the Son of God, innocent but bound like a criminal. He faced them all like a king. He was calm. His eyes did not seek the floor although leering, contemptuous looks met Him from all sides. It almost seemed as if *He* were to judge all those well-dressed murderers.

How could they accuse Him? They all knew that He had done nothing wrong. Therefore they produced men who would lie if they were paid for it.

Many witnesses were called. The judges hoped that two witnesses would make the very same accusation. The law required that. Only if there were two witnesses to back up a certain accusation could an accused person be found guilty.

As more witnesses were called, the judges became desperate, for the witnesses contradicted each other. Jesus listened to their slander in silence. He did not have to make any effort to defend Himself.

At last two witnesses told basically the

same story. "He spoke scornfully in the holy temple," they testified. "He said, 'I will break down God's temple, and within three days I will build it up again'!"

Suddenly the judges had hope, for that was a very serious charge. The temple was the holy house of the Lord. Anyone who spoke scornfully of it offended God and was guilty of sacrilege. That sin could be punished only by death.

Caiaphas, the high priest, leered at his prisoner in triumph. What would Jesus say in response to this charge?

Caiaphas knew perfectly well that Jesus had never made that foolish statement. If Caiaphas questioned these false witnesses, it would soon become clear that they had twisted Jesus' words. But let Jesus prove that He had *not* said it.

Jesus was silent. He would not defend Himself against such an unworthy accusation. Three years earlier He had indeed referred to His body as a temple of the Holy Spirit. He had said that His *body* would be broken and raised up again after three days. That very day His body would indeed be broken. On the third day His body would rise from the grave.

When Jesus remained silent, Caiaphas began to tremble with anger and impatience. He stood up and shouted, "Don't You have anything to say? What are these men accusing You of?"

Jesus fixed His eyes calmly on Caiaphas. He was waiting for a question that was bound to be asked eventually. By remaining silent, He forced Caiaphas to ask that question. It was Caiaphas's last hope. He said, "I charge You under oath by the living God: tell us if You are the Christ, the Son of God."

At last Jesus answered. In the deep stillness that filled the room after this question, His powerful voice resounded clearly: "I am indeed the Christ. You shall see the Son of man seated at the right hand of Power and coming on the clouds of heaven."

Caiaphas jumped up at once and acted outraged by this answer. With both hands he reached for the top part of the beautiful, sky-blue priest's robe he was wearing. He tore it in false rage as a sign that he was greatly offended. That robe was never supposed to be torn.

"He has blasphemed God!" he cried out in mock rage. "Why do we want witnesses? You have heard the blasphemy with your own ears. What is your verdict?"

The excited judges jumped up and screamed together, "He deserves to die!"

They crowded around the man they had condemned to death. He stood, innocent, with His head high. All the hatred in those well-dressed murderers was now unleashed. Grinding their teeth, they milled around Him, pouring scorn on Him, mocking Him, spitting in His face, hitting Him with their fists.

The servants joined in. They covered Jesus' head with a filthy rag and began to beat Him. Scornfully, they said, "Aren't You the Christ, who knows everything? Prophesy to us, Christ; who hit You?" They thought of many more ways to plague Him and hurt Him and humiliate Him.

Still, no lightning struck the high priest's palace, to destroy Jesus' tormentors. The angels did not come down from heaven to rescue their Lord. God was silent.

The Son of God was silent too. He suffered, and bore all the abuse without complaining. As the blood began to flow down His face, only thoughts of love went through His mind. He thought of all those who would be redeemed through His suffering.

The punishment that brings us peace was laid upon Him. Through the lashes He received, we are healed.

The light of the torches faded. The first pale light of the new day came into the room.

131: Peter's denial

When Jesus was bound in the garden of Gethsemane, Peter, like the other disciples, fled into the darkness. He found a hiding spot and stayed there. He watched the swaying torches as the band of soldiers led Jesus out of the garden toward Jerusalem.

Jesus had given in as willingly as a lamb. He let Himself be dragged by the godless rabbis of Jerusalem, who had so long yearned to have Him in their power.

Peter moved ahead in the darkness from one hiding place to another. He reached the gateway of the garden and watched as the band of soldiers descended into the valley of the Kidron. He sneaked along behind them, staying just off the road. He did not know why. He could do nothing to help; he wasn't even allowed to fight for his Master. He still wanted to be with Jesus. The love in his heart urged him on. His heart was crying out in despair; "Why, Master? Why? You could have commanded the angels to come to Your aid!"

Peter did not know what to do with that riddle. He had trusted in Jesus. He had expected a glorious future with the Messiah. But now it was falling apart. This was the end.

Could it be that the rabbis were right when they said that Jesus was a deceiver? No, that couldn't be. Jesus was the Messiah! Despite his despair, Peter believed that with his whole heart.

He didn't understand how all these events were possible. It was the darkest night in his life. With a pounding heart he followed the band of soldiers. He was full of fear and full of compassion for Jesus.

Suddenly, not far away, he caught sight of another figure moving in the same direction in the same cautious, fearful way. When the moon broke through the clouds, he saw that it was John.

John was not able to abandon the Master completely either. Together they whispered excitedly about the horrible event that had just taken place. They slipped into Jerusalem and walked in the shadows of the houses until they reached Caiaphas's house. The procession had already passed through the gate when they got there.

John had been to this house before, and the servant girl at the gate recognized him. He went inside, but Peter did not dare follow. He stayed outside.

This John realized when he was in the inner court. He went back, talked to the servant girl at the gate, and brought Peter inside.

Peter did not feel comfortable there. Wouldn't it have been better to stay outside than to run the risk of mingling with the enemy? Fear ran through his body whenever anyone looked at him. He glanced around for a place to stay out of the way.

In the middle of the inner court, the high priest's servants were sitting around a fire warming themselves. Peter sat down among them and put out his hands to be warmed by the fire. That way it would appear that he was a servant and did not belong with Jesus.

From where he was seated, he could see his Master standing silent and bound in a second story room. Despair swept over him whenever he looked at Jesus. He sat silent among the servants, with a heart full of hatred and fear.

It was cold, and the fire drew the people together. The servant girl at the gate came over to the fire. She had already been suspicious of Peter when she let him in. As the flickering firelight fell on his sorrowful face, she took a hard look at him. Suddenly she said, "Aren't you one of this man's disciples?"

Peter was terrified. His heart was pounding, and his throat was dry. But he recovered and said in an indifferent tone, "Not me. I don't know what you mean." The servant girl was not sure of herself, so she went away without saying anything else.

Peter didn't feel safe there anymore. He would be throwing his life away if anyone recognized him. Therefore, a few minutes later, he walked toward the gate. A rooster crowed somewhere in the neighborhood. Peter heard it, but he paid no attention. He was thinking only of his safety.

A group of people stood talking by the gate. The servant girl was among them. When she saw Peter again, she said to the others, "That man was with Jesus of Nazareth."

Another servant girl looked at Peter and said, "That's right. You belong with Him."

Peter snarled gruffly, "I tell you, it's not so. I don't even know this Jesus."

Now his fear was still greater. He couldn't leave right away, for that would only arouse suspicion. The servant girl in charge of the gate might not let him out.

He pretended to be pacing back and forth to keep warm, but inside he was burning with fear. Finally he went back to the fire and sat down among the yawning servants who were talking in low tones.

He sat there for about an hour, keeping an eye on Jesus as the trial progressed. He was too far away to understand what was being said. But when he saw how his Master was mocked and beaten, he understood what was happening. He had to bite his lip to hold back his anger and tears.

Suddenly a voice spoke up by the fire and frightened him again: "Aren't you one of His disciples?"

"No, not me," he answered. "I don't even know the man." He sensed that all eyes were fixed upon him. The men around the fire were suddenly very interested in him.

"I can tell from the way you talk," said one of them. "You're a Galilean."

A servant took a look at Peter. He was a relative of Malchus, the man whose ear Peter had cut off. In a threatening tone he asked Peter, "Didn't I see you in the garden?"

Peter turned white with fear as he thought of what he had done in the garden. His short sword hung at his side under his cloak. It was still stained with Malchus's blood.

Peter began to curse. He swore that he did not know Jesus, that he had never seen Him, that they could put Him to death right then and there if it were not so . . . .

Peter's horrible words were interrupted by a rooster crowing loudly. Peter's voice trailed off. It was as if he had awakened from a sinful stupor, a horrible, wicked dream.

He looked at Jesus in dismay. Jesus turned around at exactly that moment and looked at Peter. Peter could feel Jesus' eyes looking deep into his. He could feel those eyes penetrating deep into his heart. In his mind he heard Jesus saying, "Truly, I say to you, even before the rooster crows twice, you will deny Me three times."

Suddenly, what the servants thought no

longer mattered to Peter. Whether he lived or died did not matter to him. He turned away, sobbing. If he had not felt so hopelessly wicked, he would have run right into the room where Jesus was. He would have made his way through the men mocking Jesus and thrown himself down at the Master's feet. But he did not feel worthy to ever come near the Master again.

Peter staggered away in the darkness. He went out the gate. When he was alone, he cried bitterly. He felt that he was surely the most wicked of all men. His heart was consumed by sorrow for his sin. Never did he love his Master so much as now.

His tears were a prayer. Deep in his heart lived the faith that the Savior still loved him and would one day forgive him for his horrible unfaithfulness.

132: Blood money

Judas Iscariot lacked something that Peter had. Judas lacked the faith that God's mercy is greater than the most horrible sin imaginable.

Like Peter, Judas felt sorry for what he had done. When he saw that Jesus was condemned, the money he had received seemed to point a finger of accusation at him. Only then did he fully realize what he had done. *He* would be responsible for Jesus' death.

This guilt was a heavy burden on Judas's soul. He wanted to be released of that burden, and he would gladly have bought Jesus back if that were possible. He didn't care about the money now that his heart was filled with remorse. Even if Jesus were not the Messiah, He was a kind and innocent person. There was no reason for Him to die.

Judas could not shake off the idea that he was really Jesus' murderer.

In the early twilight he hurried over to the temple. The priests were busy making preparations for the morning sacrifice. He stormed inside, his face twisted and his eyes frantic. He held out the money with trembling hands and screamed, "I have sinned; I have betrayed innocent blood."

It was a raucous scream in the temple. It was the scream of a man who had reached the end of the line.

The priests looked at Judas with cruel, cunning grins. "What do we care?" they said. "That's your problem."

It did not matter to the priests that a human soul was lost. They had their prey in their power; they would not let Him go for all the money in the world.

They didn't even want to take back the money Judas offered them. He threw the silver coins on the temple floor and hurried away.

Judas's last hope had been crushed. The sky was reddening in the east, but his soul was black as night. He felt like a cursed man who could never be redeemed. His guilt would always be shackled to him. Never again would he have rest. The question would always pursue him: "Judas, did you betray the Son of man with a kiss?"

Judas had fallen into satan's power. He did not believe in love and forgiveness. Only his guilt and the curse he would have to live under seemed real to him.

Judas did not have the courage to go on living. He went to a lonely place and put an end to his sinful life.

How blind he was! Did Judas think he could atone for one murder with another?

While Judas's body lay outside Jerusalem, broken on the rocks, the priests met and discussed in pious tones what they should do with the 30 pieces of silver. They had picked up the coins from the floor, but they did not want to put them in the offering box. To have blood money in the holy treasury would have been a great sin!

After talking for a long time, they decided to use the money to buy a field. They bought an almost worthless piece of ground full of pits and hollows where a potter had dug out some clay. They used that field as a burial ground for foreigners.

That field was called *akeldama*, that is, *field of blood*.

133: What is truth?

It was still early in the morning when Jesus was led out of the high priest's palace. His face was covered with bruises and scratches. The high priest's servants dragged Him down the quiet streets to Pilate's hall of justice.

The rabbis followed unhappily. They would gladly have killed Jesus themselves, but they were under Roman rule. Any death sentence had to be approved by the Roman governor and carried out by the Roman soldiers.

The procession hurried along. It was important that Jesus be in the hands of the Romans before people started to appear on the streets. Even if the people created an uproar, it would be too late then to save the troublemaker from Nazareth.

The rabbis and their servants entered the square in front of the Roman headquarters. They stopped by the steps. It was the time of the Passover, and that meant they must not enter a Gentile's home. If they did, they would defile themselves, for there would surely be yeast in that house. They were not afraid to defile themselves with the blood of an innocent man, but they stayed away from a tiny bit of yeast.

Jesus was led up the steps by some Roman soldiers. Pilate came outside to listen to what the Jews had to say.

They stood facing each other: the leaders of the Jews, and Pontius Pilate, the most important Roman in the country. They had always hated each other. Pilate let his power be felt whenever he had the chance. He also secretly lined his pockets with the Jews' money. The Jews baited Pilate whenever they got a chance and had defied him more than once.

On this particular morning the Jews were very polite and friendly to Pilate. They needed his help to get rid of Jesus, whom they hated more than Pilate.

When Pilate asked what crime Jesus was guilty of, the Jews acted righteous. "If He weren't an evildoer," they said, "we would not bring Him to you."

They thought that the governor would be satisfied with this answer, but they had a bitter disappointment. Pilate took a look at Jesus and could not believe that this silent, calm man had done anything for which He deserved to die. "*You* take Him," he said, "and judge Him in accordance with *your* law."

That was not what the Jews had in mind. "He must die!" they cried out.

"Why?" asked the governor.

Indeed, why? Because He had blasphemed God and said that He was the Christ, the Son of God? That was really what the Jews had condemned Him for. Would Pilate care if Jesus claimed to be God's Son? He would most likely laugh, for he was a pagan. Pilate probably didn't believe in God at all.

"He is a dangerous man," they said. "He misleads the people by telling them not to pay taxes to the emperor. He says that He is the Christ, the King!"

Jesus stood and listened to all of this without saying a word. He was not going to defend Himself against such accusations. Pilate sensed that the accusation could not possibly be true. If Jesus really had tried to cause an uproar among the people, the Jews would have honored Him for it!

Pilate was curious. He looked at Jesus. "Don't You hear all these things that they are saying against You?" he asked.

Jesus did not answer, and that made Pilate even more curious. He went into the hall of justice and had Jesus brought inside. He wanted to know more about this strange, gentle man who stood so calmly that He really did seem to be a king.

Pilate asked Him, "Are you the king of the Jews?"

Jesus looked at him and said, "My Kingdom is not of this world. If My Kingdom were of this world, My servants would have fought to keep Me from falling into the hands of the Jews."

When he heard that answer, Pilate was certain that Jesus was not a rebel. He knew that the Romans had nothing to fear from Jesus. "So You are a king?" he said to Jesus.

"Yes," answered Jesus, "I am a king. For this I was born, and for this I came into this world, to testify to the truth. Everyone who loves the truth listens to My voice."

Pilate did not know what Jesus was talking about. The truth? What did Jesus mean by that? The wise men in Rome said that no one was able to know the truth. Perhaps there was no truth at all in this world. Pilate was not a believer; he doubted everything.

He shrugged his shoulders. With a look of hopelessness, he said to Jesus, "What is truth?"

Pilate went outside again where the Jews were eagerly waiting to hear something. "I find no crime in this man," he told them.

134: Jesus before Herod

The rabbis were indignant. They had brought Jesus to Pilate, telling him that Jesus was a troublemaker who deserved to die. But Pilate now told them that Jesus was not guilty of any wrongdoing.

"Not guilty?" they shouted back at him. "He has the people in an uproar, from Galilee all the way to Jerusalem!"

Pilate did not reply, but he did note how excited and angry the Jews were. In his heart he was somewhat afraid of them. His duty was to let Jesus go, for he had declared Him innocent. What were the Jews saying? Galilee?

"Is this man a Galilean?" he asked. A clever idea suddenly came to him. He thought of a way to free himself of this ticklish matter without angering the Jews.

Pilate was governor only over Judea. King Herod ruled Galilee. Herod happened to be in Jerusalem for the Passover season.

Let Herod take responsibility for making this difficult judgment. He was welcome to it. Pilate and Herod had been enemies for years. It would look as if he were being very polite to Herod.

He gave Jesus back to the Jews and sent them over to Herod. He sighed with relief when he saw them hurry out the gate. He felt satisfied as he went back into his house.

Herod was happy when he saw Jesus coming, for he had often hoped to see Him. Repeatedly he had heard of Jesus' wonders, and a secret fear had taken root in him. His conscience still tormented him for murdering John the Baptist. He was superstitious. He feared that Jesus might be John the Baptist back from the grave, looking for revenge on his murderer.

When he finally saw Jesus, this foolish fear vanished at once. The pale, tired man who stood silent and bound before him was not a fearsome figure. Was He really the wonder-worker that people talked about so much? If so, Herod wanted to see Him perform His tricks.

Jesus would no doubt be happy to oblige. A prisoner would do anything to gain his freedom.

He asked Jesus to do some tricks, but he received no answer. He asked Jesus questions, but Jesus remained silent. Jesus said nothing in response to the grave accusations made by the chief priests and scribes.

Herod was disappointed and finally gave up. He still wanted to get some enjoyment out of this matter, so he began to mock Jesus and bait Him. By now he was not afraid of Jesus. His soldiers joined the fun.

"He wants to be a king?" asked Herod, laughing in contempt. "Well then, let's put Him in some royal robes." He had a beautiful garment thrown over Jesus' shoulders. Perhaps it was a robe that he used to wear himself.

Jesus did not shake off the robe. There was no anger in His eyes. He let people do all these things to Him and showed amazing patience. Herod never once heard Jesus' voice.

Herod sent Jesus back to Pilate in that shining robe. That showed what he thought of Jesus. He was pleased that the governor had recognized him by sending Jesus to him. It made him forget how much he hated Pilate. Herod wanted to be polite too.

That day Pilate and Herod became friends.

135: Crucify Him!

The sunshine was warming the streets by the time Jesus was led through the city again. From all the streets and alleys people came running. They cried out in amazement when they saw that Jesus was a prisoner. The man they had listened to breathlessly in the temple, the man who had dared to lash out at the scribes and Pharisees, that man was now a prisoner. He was in the rabbis' hands. Were the rabbis more powerful than Jesus after all?

Shouts of fear and excitement rang through the streets. More and more people joined the procession. An excited crowd swirled around Jesus. The large, jubilant procession moved through the city toward the hall of justice.

Pilate heard the noise in the square in front of his residence. When he looked outside, his face darkened. Would he have to look into those wonderfully pure, innocent eyes again? Would he have to listen to the screaming of the hated Jews? He was afraid of those eyes, but he was also afraid of the rebellious Jews. How they could carry on when they were worked up!

But *Pilate* was the governor, after all. He, not the stubborn rabbis, was in charge. He pressed his lips together resolutely and stood tall as he stepped outside. He tried to look proud as he signaled the chief priests and Jewish leaders to come forward. There was determination in his voice as he addressed them: "You have brought this man to me as someone who is misleading the people. I examined Him in your presence and was not able to find anything wrong with Him. Neither did Herod find anything, for he has sent Him back. This man has done nothing to deserve death. Therefore I will have Him whipped and then release Him."

There was an enraged outcry from the Jews. It grew louder and wilder. Had they gone through all the trouble of capturing and trying Jesus only to have Him released? No, Jesus must die!

Pilate was frightened when he saw how determined the Jews were. His courage and resolution began to waver. After all, he had to be careful in how he dealt with those excited Jews. He did not want to spark a riot.

Suddenly a clever plan came to his mind. It was customary to let one prisoner free each year during the Passover. The people were allowed to choose. The prisoner was shown grace because of the festival in the city.

Pilate knew that there was a notorious robber in prison. That robber had killed someone during an uprising. His name was Barabbas. What if Pilate were to present Jesus and Barabbas for the people to choose between? Pilate knew that the people revered Jesus. Only the chief priests, who had Him arrested, hated and despised Him. The people would surely choose to have Jesus freed.

Pilate had Barabbas brought from prison and placed next to Jesus. He turned to the people, doing his best to act friendly and generous.

"You have the custom that one prisoner is released at the time of the Passover," he said. "Who should be released, Barabbas or Jesus, the one who is called Christ? Do you want me to release the King of the Jews for you?"

There was silence among the people. Only the excited whispering of the rabbis could be heard. The people looked at Barabbas and Jesus in surprise.

Pilate smiled. He did not doubt which prisoner they would choose.

At that moment a servant hurried over to Pilate and gave him a note from his wife. Pilate turned away to read the note. Why would his wife disturb him while he was trying this case?

Pilate read the note. Jesus, meanwhile, stood on display before the people next to Barabbas. The Son of God was placed on the same level as the murderer.

The rabbis moved among the people and urged them to vote for Barabbas. Barabbas was a brave man who had fought against the Romans. What had Jesus done? If He were a hero, why had He let Himself be taken prisoner so easily?

The people looked at Jesus and nodded. They had thought He would become their king and would free the people from Roman rule. But He had not. Perhaps He was afraid. How could they have assumed that He was the Messiah!

Pilate had not seen how much the priests stirred up the people. He was engrossed in his wife's note, for she had some amazing things to say about Jesus. She knew that soldiers had been sent out the evening before to take Him prisoner. Now she wrote, "Don't get involved in the case of this righteous man. I have suffered a great deal today in a dream on account of Him."

It was Pilate's final warning. Did Pilate need that warning? In just a few minutes he would be able to free Jesus.

Pilate turned to the people with a smile. "Well, which of the two would you like me to release?"

From a thousand mouths came the answer, "Away with Him! Release Barabbas!"

The smile vanished from Pilate's face. "Then what must I do with Jesus, who is called Christ?" he asked, deeply disappointed.

"Crucify Him! Crucify Him!" shouted the people.

"What has He done wrong?" Pilate cried out in despair. "He is innocent!"

His words were drowned in the people's shouts and screams. "Crucify Him! Crucify Him!" That commotion echoed between the walls and was heard throughout the city. A wild, excited mob milled about in the square before Pilate.

Pilate turned pale, and his soldiers clutched their spears uneasily. Only one person stayed completely calm. He looked down at the screaming people without losing any of His composure. Because of Him all of this was happening.

Those same people had shouted, "Hosanna to the Son of David!" only a few days before. Now they were screaming for His blood.

They had brought the sick, the cripples and the children to Jesus. Jesus had never turned them away. Now they were driving Him to the cross.

He had loved them so much. He still loved them with all His soul. That was why He suffered in silence. Through that suffering a great blessing would come to them. The unfaithfulness of those blinded people, this horrible ingratitude caused Him the greatest anguish just then.

"Crucify Him! Crucify Him!" The people pressed forward up to the Roman buildings. The soldiers watched the governor impatiently, waiting for an order to beat back the rebellious mob. Pilate gave no such order.

He let Barabbas go. Barabbas leaped into the crowd with a wild, happy shout and was greeted joyously. Pilate turned Jesus over to the soldiers to be whipped.

136: Jesus' humiliation

Who could ever describe Jesus' suffering on that horrible day? They took Him into the hall of justice, tore off His clothes, and tied Him. Then they whipped Him. Unmerciful lashes rained down on His bare back.

No cry came to Jesus' lips. Silently He withstood the cutting pain that He did not deserve. Many deserved to be punished, but He wanted to bear the punishment for them.

The Lord let the unrighteousness of us all fall upon Jesus. He was beaten and abused, but He suffered it all willingly and did not open His mouth.

Who can possibly understand the depth of the humiliation and scorn Jesus faced?

Pilate's men were not satisfied with whipping Jesus. They took a purple cloak, which had been used by a soldier, and threw it over His shoulders.

"There is His royal robe," they scoffed. "Didn't He say He was a king?"

They made Him a crown of thorns and pressed it on His head. "There is His crown," they laughed.

They shoved a cane into His right hand.

"That's His scepter," they said, laughing.

They played a cruel game with Him. They walked up to Him one by one as if they were approaching the throne of a mighty ruler. They bowed and kneeled before Him and scoffed at Him. "Greetings, King of the Jews!" Their scornful laughter echoed through the hall of justice.

Suddenly they decided they had had enough of that game. They showed only contempt for this man who let them abuse Him without saying a word. They struck Him with their fists. They took the cane out of His hands and hit Him on the head with it. The crown of thorns worked its way into His flesh. They spit in His face to get Him to curse them, as other victims always did.

Suddenly their frenzy was halted. They stood at attention as the governor walked in.

Pilate saw Jesus standing there, bleeding from many wounds. He was pale and exhausted. Pilate could see from Jesus' costume that the soldiers had been mocking Him. He did not rebuke them.

Pilate had not defended Jesus out of love or mercy. He had done so out of a sense of justice, and because he was annoyed with the Jews. Even then he still thought he could save Jesus.

The unruly mob outside had demanded Jesus' life. They wanted to see His blood. Fine, they would see it. Maybe then they would be satisfied.

He walked out of the hall of justice and said to the people, "Look, I will bring Him out before you so you will know that I find no guilt in Him."

Jesus was brought outside with His crown of thorns and His purple garment. There He stood—the one on whom the people had fixed their hopes. Had they really thought that *He* could save them? Now they despised Him. They wanted nothing to do with that sort of messiah. A suffering Christ was not what they had in mind.

Pilate said, "Behold the man."

There was no mercy in their hearts. Their hearts were filled with hatred and loathing. Again they screamed, "Crucify Him! Crucify Him!"

Pilate saw that he had made another mistake in his guess of how the people would react. But he was not yet ready to give in.

"Take Him and crucify Him yourselves," he said to them, "for I find no crime in Him."

Pilate knew perfectly well that the Jews would not crucify Jesus themselves. That was not within their rights. They didn't want to do it themselves either. Again they demanded that the governor and the Roman authorities sentence Jesus to death on the cross.

Finally they named the real reason why they had condemned Him. "We have a law," they said. "According to that law He must die, for He called Himself God's Son."

When Pilate heard that, he decided he would question Jesus once more. He wanted to find out what this charge meant.

137: Pilate's verdict

Pilate and Jesus faced each other again. The King of heaven and earth faced the governor who ruled in the name of the Roman emperor.

Pilate groped for words. What did it mean that Jesus was supposed to be God's Son? Where was Jesus born, and who were His ancestors? "Where do You come from?" the governor asked.

Jesus gave him no answer.

Pilate became irritated and impatient. "Don't You want to speak to me? Don't You know that I have the power to release You and the power to have You crucified?"

Jesus looked at him earnestly and said, "You would have no power over Me if it had not been given to you from above. Therefore the one who handed Me over into your hands is guilty of a greater sin."

At that moment Pilate decided again to let Jesus go. This man could not be put to death. If Pilate chose, he could have the square cleared by his soldiers. After all, he was governor. It was about time for him to show who was boss.

He went back to the Jews and gave them his decision. They screamed threats at him, "If you let this man go, you are not a friend of the emperor! Anyone who proclaims himself king is stirring up rebellion against the emperor!"

Pilate's heart beat fast with fear. If the rabbis brought accusations about him to the emperor, he would not be allowed to remain governor. His life would be in danger. Tiberius, the emperor, was a cruel and suspicious man, and Pilate's conscience was not clear. Would he have to risk his life to save Jesus? That sacrifice was too great.

Pilate was downcast. All his cleverness, his delays, his halfway measures had done him no good. He lacked the true courage of an honest man.

If he had to give up this struggle, he wanted to show the people that he did not wish to bear the responsibility for Jesus' death.

He had a bowl of water brought out so that he could wash his hands in front of the people. "I am innocent of His blood," he said. "You will have to take responsibility."

The people were so completely blinded by their excitement that they shouted, "Fine! Let us take the blame! His blood be on us and on our children!"

Forty years later, those words were fulfilled when Jerusalem was destroyed.

Pilate had Jesus brought to the judgment seat. It was an open, elevated area in front of the fortress. The open side led down to the street and was paved with smooth tiles. Therefore the place was known as "The Stone Pavement."

Pilate said to the Jews, mockingly, "Behold *your* king!"

They cried out, "Away with Him! Away with Him! Crucify Him! Crucify Him!"

Pilate asked, "May I crucify your King?"

The Jews' hatred of the Romans was nothing compared to their frightening hatred of Jesus. "We have no king but Caesar," they shouted.

Pilate finally delivered his verdict. He condemned the innocent one to death.

Pilate had washed his hands to show that

he was innocent. All the water in the ocean could never wash away the great guilt in his soul.

The soldiers took Jesus away. They took off His purple robe and gave Him His own clothes. They led Him away to be crucified.

138: The way of suffering

It was almost nine o'clock in the morning when Jesus was led toward the hill known as Golgotha to be crucified. The morning sacrifice was being offered in the temple, but Jesus was on His way to offer the greatest sacrifice the world has ever known.

They put the cross on His shoulder and He dragged it along, panting. Behind Him came two robbers, condemned to death, also dragging their crosses. Roman soldiers drove them on; a captain led the way on horseback. The sorry procession plodded ahead through the narrow streets along hedges of curious people straining to get a good look.

For the people of Jerusalem, it was a day of joy. They were celebrating the feast of deliverance. But the three who were condemned to death could look forward only to a long period of torment followed by death.

Not one of all the thousands who were watching understood. No one knew that through the death of this one man, now despised and mocked, the true feast of deliverance would be prepared for them.

The procession moved on; the three condemned men carried their crosses.

Jesus had already suffered much. He had been tested severely the night before in the garden of Gethsemane. He was exhausted from the hearings before Annas and Caiaphas and Pilate and Herod. He had

been whipped and beaten by the servants and soldiers. Still, He plodded along, drawing on His last reserves of strength. His clothes stuck to His bleeding body. His knees were knocking. He sweated profusely. He took a few more stumbling steps, and then fell beneath His burden.

At once the soldiers seized a man from among the many who were watching, a man who was on his way into the city from the countryside. They made him follow Jesus and carry His cross.

As the procession moved toward the place of execution, this man walked in Jesus' footsteps with a cross on his shoulder, as if he were one of the condemned men.

The man who lightened Jesus' load that day was from a city in North Africa. His name was Simon the Cyrene, and he will never be forgotten.

Only later did Simon find out whose cross he had carried. His sons Alexander and Rufus came to love Jesus. They were among the very first Christians in Rome, where there was a church.

Jesus did not experience only mockery and contempt on that painful journey. Among the people who walked with Him were some women from Jerusalem, who wept out loud and moaned.

Jesus did not answer those who mocked Him, but He did address these women. Even then He was not thinking of Himself. He thought only of the people He loved and of the city that rejected Him, the city that would be subjected to utter agony.

He turned and cried out sadly, "Daughters of Jerusalem, do not weep for Me, but weep for yourselves and for your children. There will be days when people will say to the mountains, 'Fall upon us,' and to the hills, 'Cover us.'"

His soul was still filled with compassion, even when He was about to collapse because of His suffering.

Slowly the sorry procession shuffled through the city gate toward a small, bare hill. That strangely-shaped hill lay shining in the sun like a bleached skull at the intersection of two roads.

That hill was the place of execution. It was known as *the place of the skull* or *Golgotha*.

The way of sorrows was almost at an end. The last and most horrible suffering of all was about to begin.

139: The King of the Jews

No one on earth will ever be able to fully understand the love of Jesus. No one will ever be able to understand how He could willingly go through that horrible suffering for *sinners*.

The crosses were set up, each one with its end in a hole in the ground. Silently Jesus watched. Then His clothing was removed; He had only a loincloth left. Jesus suffered this in silence.

A soldier approached Him with a full cup and offered it to Him.

Jesus reached out for it eagerly, for He was tormented by a burning thirst. As soon as He put it to His lips, He pulled back and handed it to the soldier again. It was a mixture of wine and myrrh, a drink that dulled the senses and lightened the pain. Jesus was determined to drink the bitter cup of His suffering to the last drop. He wanted to suffer for His people with a clear mind.

How could people stand on that hill and watch this horrible punishment? His body was lifted against the cross. There was a wobbly support for His feet near the bottom. His hands, which had so often been opened in blessing, were now opened to have nails driven through them. His feet, which had never rested while there was a place to go to help someone, were nailed to the cross. Blood ran down the cross.

Then, in that intense pain, Jesus made His voice heard. What came from His mouth was not a curse but a prayer for the men who were nailing Him to the cross: "Father, forgive them, for they know not what they do."

No one knows if those rough soldiers heard and understood Jesus' words. They were already busy with the two robbers. One was crucified to Jesus' left, and the other to His right. Above each of the condemned men they put a small sign on which they wrote an accusation.

The sign above Jesus' head was in three

languages—Greek, Latin and Hebrew. The sign said: "Jesus of Nazareth, the King of the Jews."

Those words were written at Pilate's orders. It was a final cruel joke on the people who had proven too strong for him.

The chief priests understood the joke. They raced to the hall of justice and said to the governor indignantly, "Don't write: 'The King of the Jews.' Write: 'He *claimed* to be the King of the Jews.' "

Pilate answered, "What I have written, I have written." He did not let the Jews take away this last bit of revenge.

There hung the King of the Jews, the Redeemer, the one for whom the people had yearned for centuries. Now they had let Him be crucified.

The King of heaven and earth, the Son of God, hung there as a cursed man. Through His freely chosen suffering, He did penance for the sin of the world.

The soldiers did not understand this miracle. They sat by the cross and divided His clothes, for He wouldn't need them anymore. There were four soldiers, and each one got something. One got a turban, and the others got His belt, His outer garment and His sandals.

Only His undergarment was left. It was a costly piece of clothing woven of one piece of cloth, without a seam. They said to each other, "Let's not divide it into pieces. Let's cast lots instead to see who gets it."

While Jesus suffered His terrible pain, the soldiers sat at the foot of the cross throwing dice to see who would get His undergarment. This fulfilled a prophecy that had come from David a thousand years before: "They divide my garments among them, and cast lots for my clothing."

The sun moved steadily toward the south and burned down on Jesus' wounded body.

His heart pounded. A fiery fever streamed through His veins.

How could people mock such agonizing suffering? Satan must have come into their hearts that horrible day.

People who passed by slandered Him and cried out, "So You were going to break down the temple and build it up again in three days? Save Yourself if You can, and come down from the cross!"

The chief priests and scribes stood before the cross and made fun of Jesus to humiliate Him further: "He saved others, but He cannot save Himself. If He is truly Israel's King, let Him come down from the cross. Then we will believe in Him. He says He has put His trust in God. Let *God* deliver Him if He takes pleasure in Him. Didn't He say He was God's Son?"

No human being would have put up with such humiliation and scorn if he had Jesus' power. A single word from Jesus would have been enough to destroy them all. Yet, He remained silent. He had not come to destroy people but to save them.

The soldiers made the suffering even worse for Him. They saw that He was thirsty and held before Him vinegar—a sour but refreshing soldier's wine. They continued to taunt Him: "If You are the King of the Jews, then save Yourself."

Jesus suffered all this in silence.

140: Compassion in a time of torment

The robbers, the two men who were crucified next to Jesus, did not remain silent. Painfully they turned their heads to look at Jesus, who was being mocked and scorned so much. If Jesus was the Christ, surely deliverance was still possible for them! They laughed bitterly and cried out in scorn, "Aren't You the Christ? Then save Yourself and us!"

One of the robbers had hardly uttered these words when he stopped to think. What caused this sudden change? Had he seen something in Jesus' eyes? Was it Jesus' prayer for His enemies? Was it something he had once heard Jesus say?

His soul was suddenly filled with reverence. While the other robber went on mocking Jesus, faith was born in his heart. He believed that the suffering man next to him really was the Messiah.

He could no longer stand to listen to the other robber's mockery. He turned to him and asked, "Don't you fear God, now that you have received this sentence? *We* deserve this punishment, for we are only being repaid for what we did. This man has done nothing wrong."

While his head was turned to the side, he pleaded with Jesus reverently. "Jesus, remember me when You come into Your Kingdom."

A holy joy shone in Jesus' eyes, for this sinner could still be saved. He gave the murderer a comforting look and said to him, "Truly, I say to you, today you will be with Me in Paradise."

Never before had the man been filled with such a deep peace.

Jesus continued to show love and compassion to the very end. Even while He was on the cross, His deepest desire was to help others and comfort them.

With burning eyes He looked down at the people gathered on Golgotha. His gaze rested on a small group of weeping people.

In the distance He saw the women who had followed Him from Galilee. Mary of Magdalene, a faithful disciple whom He

had once released from seven evil spirits, was there. Mary the wife of Clopas, who had served Him in love, and Salome, the mother of James and John were also there. His own mother Mary was in the group as well. She stood weeping by her son's cross. To see Him suffering such agony was just like being pierced by a sword. The prophecy of aged Simeon was fulfilled.

His mother's despair and anguish caused Jesus even more pain than His wounds. Jesus saw John standing close to Mary. John would be able to look after her better than anyone else and comfort her with his faith.

Looking at His mother, Jesus said, "Woman, behold your son."

Then He said to His disciple, "Behold your mother."

They understood at once what He meant. From then on they belonged together. That day John took Jesus' mother into his house and treated her as his own mother.

141: Why have You forsaken Me?

The hours crept by slowly as Jesus hung on the cross. The sun was high in the sky and beamed down almost directly on the heads of the crucified men. Their breathing grew more and more labored.

The One who had taken away so much pain suffered this intense agony Himself. The One who had healed so many wounds hung there tormented by wounds. The One who had made the lame walk couldn't move. The One who had given life to the dead would now die, defenseless. The One who had lived a life of overflowing love was mocked and scorned in His hour of deepest agony.

Suddenly the scoffers were silenced. They all looked up at the sky. The noonday sun, which had beamed down on them so brightly, became as red and distant as an evening sun.

It seemed as if the sun was about to disappear over some invisible horizon, withdrawing from the sinful earth. A threatening darkness moved in. A black veil settled over the earth.

In that darkness Jesus hung on the cross and endured His last struggle. It was a struggle like the one in Gethsemane, oppressive and frightening. But in Gethsemane there was still light; there were still friends nearby. In Gethsemane He could kneel and wring His hands and bow before God. An angel had even come from heaven to comfort and strengthen Him.

But now Jesus hung between heaven and earth like a condemned figure suffering a curse. He wanted to reach out toward heaven, but He couldn't. He yearned for light, but there was none. There was only thirst and fever—the anguish of death and unremitting pain. There was darkness and emptiness around Him and in His soul. Never before had He felt forsaken.

Jesus cried out to the Lord, but the Lord was not there. God had turned away from Him. In unspeakable loneliness, Jesus bore the burden of God's wrath, God's anger at the sin of the world.

That boundless, unfathomable suffering lasted three hours. Jesus' agony was so horrible that He cried out with a loud voice, "Eli, Eli, lama sabachthani?" "My God, My God, why have You forsaken Me?"

That cry was heard in heaven. The darkness retreated and the sun came back. The light of God's presence also came back and filled Jesus' heart. God's wrath was stilled. He looked down upon His Son in love again.

Jesus knew that His battle was over. He had won through His complete submission.

He wanted to cry out in jubilation, but He was too weak. He was now very close to death. Hardly a sound would come from His parched lips.

He moaned, "I thirst."

The rabbis, who had heard His cry in the darkness, now had enough courage to mock Him again. Someone attached a sponge to a stick and dipped it in sour wine. When the sponge was held to His lips, the rabbis cried out, "Stop it. He cried out to Elijah. Let's see if Elijah will come and save Him."

But the man was more merciful than the rabbis. He wanted to give Jesus something to drink.

Jesus then had just enough strength to cry out in a loud voice, "It is finished!"

Now He felt no more anguish and pain. The great work that the Father in heaven had given Him was finally finished. Death could come and claim Him. In death the Father would take care of Him. Jesus was ready to entrust Himself to the Father.

He said, "Father, into Your hands I commit My spirit." His head sank to His chest. He was dead.

When the King of heaven and earth died, the ground trembled and rocks split. Graves were opened, and the dead arose.

The captain who stood watching Jesus saw how He died. He said, "Truly, this man was the Son of God. This man was righteous."

The people on Golgotha, the mockers and the godless, were deadly afraid. They beat their breasts in fear. In despair they fled to the city.

Priests in the temple were offering the

evening sacrifice. The beautiful curtain that separated the Holy of Holies from the rest of the temple suddenly tore from top to bottom. Only the high priest was allowed in the Holy of Holies—once a year, on the great Day of Atonement. Now, with the curtain torn in two, the Holy of Holies was open to all.

There was no longer a separation between God and man. The priests and sacrifices were no longer needed. The great High Priest had offered the final, all-sufficient sacrifice. Atonement had been made for the sin of the world, and heaven was open to all.

This was the most glorious news the world had ever known.

142: The burial of Jesus

It was almost evening. The shadows cast by the crosses on Golgotha grew longer and longer. The sun was just above the horizon and cast a tender light on the bodies of the condemned men.

The lifeless body of Jesus hung on the cross, still and white. Next to Him two robbers still struggled with their pain.

The soldiers began to take down the bodies of the crucified men to burn them in a lonely place. The Jews had asked this of Pilate because the sabbath was approaching. The bodies could not be left hanging when the sun was down. Otherwise the land would be defiled and the sabbath violated.

Those rabbis were so pious! They knew the law so well! The sooner Jesus' body disappeared into ashes and smoke, the happier they would be. Then no one would think of Him again. Perhaps even they would be able to forget about Him.

The soldiers went about their horrible work without showing any emotion. They saw that the robbers were still alive, so they broke their legs with a heavy hammer to make them die faster.

Jesus' body was not struck as it hung on the cross, for the soldiers could see that He was already dead. One of them, still doubtful, stuck a spear into His side. Water and blood came out at once. Then they were sure He was dead, and they did not break His bones. An age-old prophecy of David was fulfilled, "No bone of His was broken."

While the soldiers were busy by the crosses in the reddish evening light, two prominent men came up the hill in a great hurry, followed by their servants. They were rabbis from Jerusalem. The two were even members of the Sanhedrin. But they had not joined the dignified circle of rabbis who condemned Jesus the night before. They had not joined because they loved Jesus in their hearts.

But they hadn't done anything to defend Jesus either. They were fearful disciples with little faith, and they had never dared to admit that they believed in Jesus. Day after day they had denied Him, for fear of the other Jews. Now, after Jesus' death, they showed their respect and their faith.

One of them, Joseph of Arimathea, had summoned all his courage to go to Pilate and ask for the body of Jesus. The governor sent for the captain, who told him that Jesus was already dead. The request was granted.

The other rabbi was Nicodemus, who had come to Jesus once during the night. He had heard some amazing, wonderful words: "Just as Moses lifted up the serpent in the wilderness, so the Son of man must be lifted up, so that whoever believes in Him will have eternal life."

Now he had seen for himself what Jesus meant, for the Son of man had indeed been lifted up on a wooden cross. Nicodemus's faith now overcame his fear. Together with Joseph he came to Golgotha with precious spices, about a hundred pounds of myrrh and aloes.

Carefully and reverently, the two wealthy, dignified rabbis took the torn body of Jesus down from the cross. They carried it to a garden not far from Golgotha. Mary of Magdala and some other women who had not yet been able to forsake their Master followed, weeping.

The garden belonged to Joseph of Arimathea. He had planned to be buried in that quiet garden. Therefore he had had a grave carved out for himself in the rock wall. He now gave up that grave for Jesus.

Together Joseph and Nicodemus anointed Jesus' body with sweet-scented, costly oil. They wrapped the body in pure linen and put a cloth over Jesus' face. They carried it into the cave and put it down on a bed of spices. That way it would not immediately be attacked by decay.

143: Tending Jesus' grave

Mary of Magdala and other women who had followed the procession to the burial ground watched as the body of their beloved Master was laid in His grave. The men needed all their strength to roll the heavy stone in front of the opening.

The women were still sobbing as they headed back to Jerusalem. They did not have much time left to do something for their Master, for the sabbath was at hand. Hastily they prepared some more spices and oils. They promised each other that on Sunday morning, when the sabbath was over, they would go to the grave again. They would do more for the body of Jesus than they could do now, in this short time. They could preserve the body for a long time, perhaps even for years. They would go to the grave often to weep there and think back to the days when Jesus was alive and among them on earth.

That was their only comfort. It was such a small comfort that it did nothing to lessen their pain and sorrow. In their despair they forgot—just as the disciples forgot—that Jesus was to rise again from the grave. He had told them this often.

The chief priests and Pharisees had not forgotten those statements of Jesus. They remembered that they had asked Jesus for a sign that He really was the Son of God. Jesus had answered that He would give them no other sign than the sign of the prophet Jonah. Just as Jonah was three days in the belly of the fish, so the Son of man would be three days in the heart of the earth.

If the rabbis had had their way, Jesus' body would have been burned with the bodies of the robbers. But Jesus was buried instead. Could it be that His prediction would somehow be fulfilled after all? Could it be that they were not rid of their enemy for good?

They had gathered on the sabbath to discuss this difficult question. They did not dare tell each other about their secret fear. Instead they said that the disciples might sneak over to the grave, steal the body of Jesus, and hide it somewhere. Then they would proclaim that Jesus had arisen from the grave, and the people might be foolish enough to start worshiping Him all over again.

Together they went to Pilate to ask him

to seal the grave and place a watch there for the first three days.

The governor was in no mood to do any more than was absolutely necessary for them. They got soldiers to stand guard by the grave, but if they wanted a seal, they would have to look after that themselves.

Although it was the sabbath, they went to the garden at once with the soldiers. They stretched a cord in front of the stone, sealing the grave, and attached the official seal of their high council to it. Now the grave could not be opened without breaking the seal. If anyone dared to break the seal, he would be severely punished.

The rabbis breathed a sigh of relief. They went back to the city to say their long prayers, read the Scriptures, and give alms to the poor.

In the quiet garden of Joseph of Arimathea, the soldiers stood guard by the sealed grave. But how could anyone ever stand in the way when the Prince of life decided to rise from the dead?

144: The empty tomb

It was still dark in the garden of Joseph of Arimathea, the garden where Jesus was buried. The cool night mist still hovered near the ground. The moon was low; it shone down on the helmets and spears of the soldiers.

The soldiers were keeping watch by the tomb. They were not asleep. Any Roman soldier who slept while standing guard was punished severely.

The soldiers did their duty faithfully by the sealed grave. Each one had a spear in his hand and a sword attached to his belt. No one would dare move the stone that sealed the tomb as long as *they* were on duty.

The first pale rays of morning light were breaking through in the east. A bird began to sing his shy song, shattering the almost sacred stillness.

Then, suddenly, it happened. It was as if lightning came from the sky—that's how quickly the angel descended to the garden. The earth trembled when his feet touched the ground. The garden was suddenly flooded with light.

The soldiers shrank back in fear. They watched as the heavenly figure walked over to the grave, rolled the stone away with a single shove, and sat down on the stone. His shining garments were white as snow.

The soldiers fled in fear.

Early that morning, on the first day of the week, the Sunday morning of the Passover, the great divine miracle took place in the stillness of the garden. There was no human being present to watch.

Jesus rose from the dead and left the tomb. The Prince of life could no longer be held by the bands of death.

There was no more humiliation or suffering or death in store for Him. He had fought His great fight, and His work on earth was done. Through the sacrifice of His life, He had reconciled the world with God. Now heavenly glory awaited Him.

Not one of His disciples knew what had happened. Not one of them believed that their Master would rise from the dead.

They had spent the whole sabbath together in mourning. It was the saddest day of their lives, a day of despair and deep sorrow. Now that they had lost their Master, their lives were shattered.

Among the many disciples were a few women who still had a purpose in mind. They wanted to anoint the body of Jesus again and prepare it even more for the grave.

As soon as the sun went down and the sabbath was at an end, they set out to buy more spices. And now, early on Sunday morning, they were on their way to the tomb. They did not know that the tomb had been sealed the day before and that Roman soldiers were assigned to guard it.

The sun was rising when they reached Joseph's garden. The sky shone with beautiful morning colors, the birds sang everywhere, and the earth lay gleaming in the light of a new day.

But the women saw nothing of all that glory. They walked somberly, bowed low with grief—Mary of Magdala, Mary the wife of Clopas, Salome, and Joanna the wife of Chuzas. The closer they got to the grave, the sadder they became.

Then one of them raised a question they hadn't thought of before in their sorrow: "Who will roll the stone away from the entrance to the grave?"

Indeed, who could do it? The stone was much too big and heavy for a few women to move by themselves. They did not know how to manage this, but they walked on anyway until they reached Joseph's garden.

Suddenly they stood still and stared. A great fear seized them as they stared at the rock wall shining brightly in the sun.

A dark opening stared back at them! Who had done it? Who had violated the grave in which the body of their beloved Master lay? Had the chief priests and scribes, in their terrible hatred, been unable to even leave the *body* of Jesus alone?

Mary of Magdala was convinced that the chief priests and scribes were responsible. Sobbing, she turned around and hurried back to the city. She would bring the disciples the horrible news that the body of Jesus had been taken away.

The other women walked on toward the grave, trembling. With pounding hearts they entered the shadowy cave.

Inside they saw a shining figure that looked like a young man in a long white garment. The figure was seated right by the place where the body of Jesus was supposed to be.

They bowed in fear before that figure, for they realized that it must be an angel. A happy, friendly voice asked them, "Why do you seek the living among the dead?"

When they looked up again, they saw to their surprise that there was a second angel. *Two* heavenly messengers stood before them in shining clothes. They said, "Don't be afraid. You seek Jesus, who was crucified. He is not here, for He has arisen, just as He said He would. Come, look at the place where His body lay."

Respectfully the women came nearer and looked at the empty place. "He has arisen?" They still didn't understand.

Then they heard one of the angels asking, "Don't you remember what He said to you when He was still in Galilee? He said, 'The Son of man must be delivered into the hands of sinful men and be crucified, but He will arise *on the third day.*' "

Suddenly all the sadness and doubt disappeared from their hearts, to be replaced by light and joy. They now remembered that Jesus had indeed said that. He had said He would arise on the third day. How could they ever have forgotten? In their pain and sorrow they had been blind, thinking that all was lost.

They felt deeply ashamed.

"Go now," said the angel, "and quickly tell His disciples. Tell Peter too. Tell them that He is going ahead of them to Galilee,

and that He will see them there. That, too, He told you beforehand."

They nodded. They were so happy that they couldn't even speak.

The women made their way out of the tomb and hurried away to bring others the glorious news that Jesus had risen from the grave.

145: Two responses to the resurrection

The women were hurrying back to Jerusalem with the good news that Jesus had risen from the dead.

Who was this that they suddenly saw before them on the road? His voice was so friendly and familiar. "Greetings!"

It was Jesus, their Master, who had just arisen from the dead!

They hurried over to Him, fell on their

knees, and worshiped Him. In great love they wrapped their arms around His legs and stroked the feet that had been pierced by nails.

From His mouth they heard the same message that the angels had given them: "Don't be afraid. Go and tell My brothers that they are to go to Galilee. They will see Me there."

When they looked up, He was gone. He had disappeared just as quietly and mysteriously as He had come.

Was it a dream? Had they seen Jesus in a vision?

No, it was not a dream. They had really seen Him! All the women were sure of it. They had touched His feet and heard His voice. And they had felt His holy gaze resting on them!

Now they hurried even more to get to the disciples as quickly as possible. When they found a couple of disciples, they surrounded them with their excitement and joy and told them jubilantly about the empty tomb and about the angels. The Master Himself had met them along the way!

The men stared at them in amazement and dismay. They shook their heads compassionately. "Nonsense!" they said to each other. "Foolishness! Sorrow has overwhelmed these poor women. In their overwrought state, their imagination is playing tricks on them."

Those disciples simply didn't believe it. It was too much for them to think that there could be a sudden end to all their sorrow and disappointment. The miracle that their beloved Master had risen from the dead was too much for them.

But the chief priests who had put Jesus to death did believe it when they heard the news. They trembled in deep fear.

They had hardly arrived at the temple that morning when some soldiers came up to them, trembling and white as sheets. They were the soldiers who were supposed to be guarding Jesus' grave.

Their story made a deep impression on the priests. Hastily they called their council together to consider what move to make next.

They did not doubt the soldiers' word for a moment. Still, although they believed, they did not repent. At this point they would stop at nothing.

In their fear they thought up a wicked plan to make sure that the news about Jesus' resurrection did not go any farther. They took some money from the temple treasury and put it down before the soldiers. They said, "All of this is for you. Just don't tell anyone what happened. Say that the disciples came during the night and stole Jesus' body while you were sleeping. If this report comes to the governor, we will talk to him and take care of his fears. Don't worry! Nothing will happen to you."

The soldiers accepted that deal. What did they care? Those prominent Jews who had sent them out there to stand guard were welcome to have things their own way.

The soldiers took the money. Wherever they went, they told people the story that the rabbis instructed them to use.

But it was an awkward story that made little sense. If the soldiers were asleep, how did they know that the disciples stole the body? And if they really had fallen asleep on duty, wouldn't they have paid for it with their lives?

The people who heard their story, however, did not stop to ask such questions. The story about the disciples was circulated widely among the people. To this day there are Jews who believe that the disciples stole

Jesus' body and hid it somewhere to make it appear that Jesus had risen from the grave.

146: Peter, John and Mary

Mary of Magdala had hurried back to the city quickly to bring the disciples the horrible news that Jesus' grave had been violated. She went to Peter and John in despair and cried out, "They have taken the Lord out of His tomb, and we do not know where they have laid Him."

The news came as a terrible shock to the two disciples. They set out for the garden in a great hurry, with Mary following them. They took a different route from the one that the women took to return to the city. Therefore they did not meet them on the way.

The closer they got to Joseph's garden, the more uneasy they became. They quickened their pace, and then began to run.

John was younger than Peter and reached the grave before him. He bent over and looked into the tomb. His heart was pounding.

The sun was higher now, and it was much lighter in the tomb. John could clearly see the cloths in which Jesus' body had been wrapped. He didn't know quite what to do, and so he stood at the opening of the tomb looking in.

Peter approached. He was panting, but he did not hesitate. He went right into the tomb. John followed him.

They stood together by the place where Jesus had lain. The clothes were still there. Strangely enough, the cloth that had covered Jesus' head was not lying loose with the others but had been carefully rolled up.

Would robbers first remove the cloths from the body and then take the extra time to roll up the cloth that covered the head? It didn't make sense.

Peter shook his head and did not know what to think. He was uneasy as he left the tomb and hurried back to the city. But John, who followed behind more slowly, thinking as he walked, suddenly looked up toward the sky in joy. A happy suspicion filled his heart, a suspicion that quickly became a certainty. He remembered that Jesus had said He would arise from the grave. Now he believed.

There was jubilation in his heart. "The Master's body has not been taken away," he said to himself. "The Lord has risen from the grave!" He hurried to catch up to Peter and tell him this glorious news.

Mary of Magdala stayed behind in the garden. She stood by the tomb weeping. Then she bent over to go inside.

She saw two men sitting by the grave in white clothes. One sat at the head end of the niche where Jesus' body had lain, and one at the foot end. She did not ask herself what those men were doing there. She was so upset that she couldn't even think straight.

She heard one of them ask, "Woman, why are you weeping?"

She sobbed as she answered, "Because my Lord has been taken away, and I do not know where you have laid Him."

Then she turned around and saw another man standing behind her. It was Jesus Himself, but she did not recognize Him through her tears.

Jesus said to her, "Woman, why are you weeping? Whom do you seek?"

Mary was so upset that she didn't even recognize the voice. She thought the man who asked her the question was the groundskeeper. She cried out, "Sir, if you have carried Him away, tell me where you put Him, and I'll go get Him." She turned away without even waiting for an answer.

Then Jesus spoke a single word to her. He addressed her as only He could. He said, "Mary!"

A deep thrill of joy ran through Mary's body.

"Rabboni!" she cried out. "Teacher!"

She hurried over to Him to take hold of Him so that she would never be separated from Him again. But Jesus could not stay with her the way He had stayed with His disciples earlier. He had arisen from the grave with a heavenly, glorified body, and God was expecting Him. Therefore He said to her in a friendly way, "Do not hold on to Me, for I have not yet ascended to the Father. Go to My brothers and tell them that I am going up to My Father and your Father, to My God and your God."

After these words Jesus suddenly disappeared. Full of joy, Mary hurried off to find the disciples and bring them the glorious news. "He lives!" she cried out. "I have seen Him!" She told them what He had said.

The disciples shook their heads sadly and shrugged their shoulders with a sigh. They did not believe Mary. They would have loved to believe her, but they didn't dare. What a horrible disappointment it would be if she had imagined it all!

That same day Jesus appeared to one of the eleven disciples who had been with Him from the very beginning. Which of the eleven received this great privilege? The one who regarded himself as the least and most sinful of them all, the one who asked himself in deep shame if he could even count himself one of the disciples anymore—Peter, the disciple who had denied his Master three times.

No one else was present when Peter encountered Jesus, and no one knows what words were spoken. But this much is certain: Jesus received His unfaithful disciple in love and forgave everything. Their relationship was completely restored.

When Peter went back to the other disciples and told them that he had seen the Lord, there was such joy and deep happiness written all over him that the other disciples could not doubt any longer. When *Peter* proclaimed it, they believed. Their Master had risen from the dead!

Their sadness turned into joy. They stayed together that evening in a house in Jerusalem. They could not talk enough with each other about the great miracle.

Now a fiery desire burned within them. They wanted to see Jesus too!

147: On the road to Emmaus

It was the afternoon of the day of Jesus' resurrection. Two men were walking along the road that led from Jerusalem to Emmaus, a little village a few hours away in the hill country of Judea. They were talking busily. They looked somber and discouraged. From time to time they sighed and shook their heads.

They had come from Jerusalem, where they had been with Jesus' disciples. They were disciples too. They had believed in Jesus and loved Him. They had longed for the day when all the people would revere and honor Him as their king. Instead they had seen a day when all the people *rejected* Jesus. They had thought of Jesus as ascending a *throne*, but He was nailed to a *cross* instead.

It seemed that His amazing power had

suddenly left Him. He had allowed them to make fun of Him and whip Him and crucify Him. He had made no effort to resist. He was like a lamb led to the slaughter. They had hoped He would be the lion that arose from Judah's tribe to chase away all the enemies of Israel.

Now Jesus was dead and buried. His life had ended, just as everyone's life came to an end sooner or later. No, He could not possibly be the Messiah. A prophet, perhaps, but not the Messiah.

That morning some women had reported excitedly that Jesus was alive, but who could believe it? Peter and John had gone to the tomb and found it empty. Now John, too, believed that Jesus had arisen. How was that possible?

If it was true that He had risen from the dead, He must be the Messiah, the Son of God after all. But if He was the Son of God, why had He subjected Himself to all that suffering?

They simply didn't understand it. They grappled with a terrible riddle that confused and depressed them. They simply couldn't stop talking about it and probing each other for answers. But they got nowhere, and the riddle grew more and more mysterious.

Suddenly they sensed that they were not alone. Someone had come up behind them and was now walking alongside them. They took a quick look at Him, but they didn't recognize Him. They said hello in a halfhearted, sorrowful way.

The man asked them, "What were you two talking about as you walked?"

The surprised answer came from the one named Cleopas: "What do you expect we would be talking about? Are you the only stranger in Jerusalem who doesn't know what has happened there in the past few days?"

"What do you mean?" the man asked.

His voice was so warm and friendly that they trusted Him at once and poured out their soul before Him.

"Don't you know what happened to Jesus of Nazareth?" they said. "He was a great prophet. He performed many miracles and said many wonderful things. But our chief priests and leaders delivered Him up to be condemned to death and crucified."

They sighed deeply. All their sorrow rose anew in their hearts. "We hoped He was the Messiah," they said in despair, "the one who would deliver Israel. But He has already been dead for three days."

There were tears in their eyes, but they were not ashamed.

"Some of the women in our midst have brought us alarming news. Early this morning they went to the tomb, but they did not find His body there. They came to us and said that they had seen angels who told them that Jesus is alive. A few of our friends then went to the grave and saw for themselves that the tomb was empty, but they did not see Jesus. We can't bring ourselves to believe that He has truly risen from the grave. If He is able to overcome even death, why didn't He overcome His enemies? Why did He let Himself be taken captive and beaten and whipped and mocked and put to death?"

They looked at the stranger sadly. They assumed that He would now shake His head and join them in their mood.

Instead He chided them. He did it in a friendly way, but He definitely straightened them out. He said, "How foolish you are and slow of heart! Didn't the Christ *have* to suffer all this in order to enter His glory?"

Then He began to explain the Scriptures to them. He went back to the books with

which they were raised. They were instructed from those books each sabbath, but they had almost completely forgotten them.

He talked about Moses and David and the other prophets, who had all mentioned the Messiah's suffering. He quoted Scripture passages that they had known all their lives but had never understood clearly until then. He reminded them about Isaiah's words concerning the Messiah. Isaiah had called Him a "man of sorrows."

This was Isaiah's song: "He took our sicknesses upon Himself and bore our pain. We considered Him tormented—stricken and afflicted by God. He was pierced for our transgressions and crushed for our iniquities. The punishment that brings us peace was inflicted upon Him, and through His lashes we are healed. All of us, like

sheep, have gone astray; we have all turned to go our own way. Yet the Lord laid upon Him the iniquity of us all. He was mistreated and oppressed, but He did not open His mouth. Like a lamb led to the slaughter and like a sheep that is silent before the shearers, so He did not open His mouth."

As Cleopas and his friend listened to all this, the sun seemed to rise within them to chase away all the darkness of doubt and unbelief. Now they finally understood the glorious prophecies they had listened to so often without understanding.

Jesus *had* to suffer all those things. That was how He bore the punishment for the sin of the world and reconciled people with God.

Then He was the Redeemer after all, the

Messiah. He had the power to destroy His enemies, but He did not do it. Out of love for His people and obedience to God, He submitted freely to His suffering.

When that message finally sank in, they were joyful and deeply moved. Never had they felt such complete happiness before. They would have gladly listened to that wise stranger for hours, but they had been talking for so long that they were finally in Emmaus, standing before the house of Cleopas.

The stranger seemed about to continue His journey, but the two men did not want to part with Him yet. They urged Him not to go on. "Stay with us," they said, "for it is evening. The day is almost done."

The stranger agreed and went inside with them to eat supper. Soon He was reclining at the table with them. He took the bread, asked for a blessing, broke some off, and offered it to them.

Who was this stranger who took on the role of host in the home of Cleopas? His eyes were more pure and kind than any other eyes they had ever seen. And there were nail holes in His hands!

Suddenly the eyes of the two men were opened. They trembled. "Jesus, Master!" they stammered, and they reached out toward Him.

But His place was empty. He vanished. They didn't even have a chance to kneel before Him.

Pale and deeply moved, they looked at each other and said, "How our hearts burned within us while we were on the road to Emmaus and He opened the Scriptures for us!"

148: Peace be with you!

The two men in Emmaus were too excited to eat the supper before them. Jesus had been with them!

After their holy adventure, all feelings of hunger and weariness left them. They let their meal stand and set off immediately for Jerusalem, following the same long road they had just taken to Emmaus. They *had* to go straight to the disciples to bring them the good news they had just received!

It was dark when they arrived at the house where the disciples were gathered, but there was still a light burning inside. They had to knock on the door, for the door was barred against the Jews. When they said their names, they were let in at once.

As they stood on the threshhold, before they had a chance to say a word, they were given some joyful news themselves: "The Lord is truly risen and has appeared to Peter!"

Then they told with great joy how Jesus came up to them when they were on the road to Emmaus and how they finally recognized Him when He broke bread with them. They were all as happy as lost children who had found their father at last.

Even while they were talking about these glorious things, they suddenly found someone standing in their midst. A calm voice said, "Peace be with you!"

The disciples shrank back in fear. Was it Jesus who stood before them? That was impossible. The doors were all closed and barred! Or could it be a ghost, a spirit from the realm of the dead?

But the voice they loved, the voice they could have picked out of thousands, spoke up and said, "Why are you dismayed, and why do you think such strange things? Look at My hands and My feet, and you will see that it really is Jesus who stands before you. Touch Me and see for yourselves. A spirit does not have flesh and bones, as I have."

He extended His hands to them and showed them His feet. They could clearly see the marks left by the nails. Then He rebuked them gently because they had so little faith.

They were still so happy that they could not quite believe it but continued to stare at Him in silent amazement. He said, "Do you have anything to eat here?"

They handed Him a piece of baked fish. Jesus ate some, to banish the idea that the heavenly body in which He now appeared to them did not need food. Then they finally believed and surrounded Him, full of joy, with adoration in their hearts.

It was a rare, glorious evening for the disciples. They sat at their Master's feet just as they used to do and listened to His kind, friendly voice. They could not keep their eyes from Him. But they no longer interrupted Him and did not contradict Him the way they used to do. They listened in silent reverence and adoration.

When Jesus explained the Scriptures to them, just as He had done for the two men on the road to Emmaus, they bowed their heads in deep shame. Now they finally saw how little trust they had placed in their Master and how little faith they had. They had hardly remembered His words at all.

Even so, Jesus still wanted them as His disciples. And that wasn't all: He wanted them to become His *apostles*. They were to go into the world as *His* emissaries and bring people everywhere the good news that Jesus had died for the sins of others and had arisen from the dead. To all who believed in Him, the disciples were permitted to say, "Your sins are forgiven. Heaven now stands open before you."

149: Thomas

One of the eleven disciples was not present on the glorious evening in Jerusalem when Jesus appeared to His own. That disciple was wandering in the darkness with his sorrow. He was having an even harder time than the others, for he was more deeply trapped than they were in feelings of disbelief and hopelessness. It was Thomas, who was also called *Didymus*, which means *the twin*.

Thomas was a melancholy man, someone who always said, "Don't even try it, for it won't work anyway." He always looked at the dark side of things and was the first one to insist that something would go wrong.

Earlier, when Jesus was still honored and loved, Thomas had been full of hope. At the time even he believed that Jesus' Kingdom would come.

But as soon as hatred and conflict came into the picture, Thomas's hopes began to fade. When people abandoned Jesus, he was deeply disappointed. He did not abandon Jesus himself, for he loved Him greatly. But when Jesus wanted to go back to Judea because Lazarus needed Him, Thomas was convinced that the Master would die there. Somberly he said to the others, "Let's go with Him and die with Him.'

Now Jesus was dead. What had come of all those beautiful dreams? Where was that glorious Kingdom for which they had all hoped? Thomas wished he was dead. Now that he no longer had Jesus, there was nothing left to await or hope for.

Then came that Sunday morning when the women returned from the grave excitedly telling their story. Mary of Magdala also came running back from the grave with tears in her eyes. Later Peter showed up with a beaming face. They both insisted that the Lord had risen from the dead and that they had seen Him personally.

How cruelly all the other disciples had let themselves be deceived! The problem was that they desperately wanted to believe those reports, so they did.

The same thing had happened to Thomas earlier. He desperately wanted His people to be redeemed through Jesus, and therefore He actually believed it would happen.

No, it was all a beautiful dream that Peter and the women had had, a dream they mistook for reality. Thomas would not let himself be misled. They could say whatever they wanted, but he was not about to believe it.

When they did not stop assuring him that it was really true, that they had seen Jesus and had heard His voice, he almost became angry at them because of their foolishness. He couldn't stand to look at their happy, shining faces anymore, and so he went off on his own, feeling bitter and dissatisfied.

When Thomas saw the disciples again, he was feeling even more unhappy than before. Yet they surrounded him with their excitement and joy. "Thomas," they cried, "now we have *all* seen the Lord! He came to us one evening when you were not there."

A ray of hope began to shine in Thomas's melancholy eyes, but it died at once. He shook his head. He did not believe it.

"Doubting Thomas!" they said to him. "Why must you be so stubborn! He has spoken to us and eaten with us and told us that He will send us out into the world as His apostles!"

Thomas continued to shake his head and shrug his shoulders. He was irritated by their joy. He was far too discouraged to join them in their enthusiasm; he had been deceived too often.

From now on Thomas would only believe what he saw with his own eyes. Even that wasn't enough. The other disciples claimed they had *seen* Jesus, but Thomas wanted more. Only if he could actually *touch* and *feel* would he believe. Therefore he said, "Unless I see the nail marks in His hands and put my fingers in the holes where the nails were and put my hand in His side, I will not believe." Despite what the others said, Thomas refused to believe.

Still, deep in his proud, doubting heart, Thomas envied the other disciples. If only it was true that the Lord was alive! The next day, when he was alone again, he found himself almost hoping that the Lord would appear to him too.

But the Lord did not appear. Finally Thomas could not hold out any longer on his own. The other disciples were his friends, and even if they had imagined it all, they meant well. Thomas was still bound to them with bonds of love. He belonged with the disciples, for he was one of them.

The next Sunday, a week after the resurrection, Thomas was with the other disciples. He was part of the circle again, still looking somber and disappointed, but no longer so willful and proud.

Only then did Jesus finally appear to Thomas. As long as Thoms stubbornly wandered around on his own, Jesus did not appear to him. Now, with the doors closed and locked just like the time before, Jesus was suddenly in their midst again.

Thomas saw Him and he heard His voice, "Peace be with you!"

Then Thomas found out that Jesus knew all about his doubts. The Master looked at him and said, "Come over here and look at My hands and put your finger in the holes. Stick your hand in My side and stop doubting. Just believe."

Thomas fell down at Jesus' feet in adoration and stammered, "My Lord and my God!"

Jesus then said, "Because you have seen Me, you believe. Blessed are those who have *not* seen Me but believe anyway."

150: The stranger on the shore

It was early morning. The sun rose from behind the hills by the Sea of Galilee. The mountains were shining. Slowly day was dawning on the lake.

Close to the shore bobbed a fisherman's boat, dragging a large net through the water. The oars splashed as they churned the water. The waves rippled against the bow.

There were seven men on board, all of them disciples of Jesus—Simon Peter, Thomas, Nathaneal, James and John, and two others. All night long they had been fishing. Time after time they had thrown out the heavy net. Now the gray hillsides were slowly gaining color, but they still hadn't caught anything. All their labor was in vain.

"Tell My brothers to go to Galilee. They will see Me there."

Those were the words Jesus had spoken to the women when He met them as they returned to Jerusalem from the empty grave. The angel at the grave had given the same command. And the evening before His death, Jesus had said to His disciples that He would go ahead of them to Galilee after His resurrection.

Because of this command which had come to them three times, the disciples journeyed back to the area where they had spent so much time with their Master. Now

they were waiting in Galilee, where almost every little town reminded them of their glorious past with Jesus. But Jesus had not yet come to them.

One evening Peter said, "I'm going fishing."

Six others said, "We'll go with you." All that night they toiled and hoped in vain.

That had happened to them once before, when Jesus was still with them. In the morning He had joined them in the boat in order to speak to all the people who crowded around Him on the shore. After that He went out on the lake with them, and through His miraculous power they caught so many fish that their nets were torn.

How glorious it would be if He came to them once more! How the disciples yearned for their Master!

In the early morning stillness, a voice reached them across the water. The disciples looked up and scanned the shore about 100 meters away.

Against the dark background of the hills they saw the white figure of a man. "Children," he cried out, "don't you have anything to eat?"

"No," they shouted back.

"Then cast your net on the other side of the boat, and you'll catch plenty of fish," the stranger called out.

The disciples had already done so much work that night that they didn't mind trying once more. They threw the net out over the waves on the other side of the boat, just as they were told. They rowed a little way and then pulled on the net to haul it in. Their hands held the ropes tightly and their feet were planted on the bottom of the boat, but the net was suddenly far too heavy for them. There was a tremendous splashing in the water from all the fish in the net.

Great joy and amazement flooded the disciples' hearts. John, who always thought things through before he spoke, was first to figure out who was responsible for this miracle. Delirious with delight, he said to Peter, "It's the Lord!"

The Lord! Of course! And Peter, impetuous Peter, who never thought before he spoke, immediately gathered his mantle around his legs and jumped into the lake. Quickly he waded through the water, for he wanted to be with the Master!

The others came rowing behind him, dragging the net to shore. When they reached land, they saw that a fire awaited them. Fish were being cooked for breakfast, and there was also some bread to eat.

By the fire sat Jesus. He was waiting for His weary disciples, and He had a meal ready for them.

151: Doubts about Peter

It was a happy morning for the disciples on the shore of the Sea of Galilee. Jesus said to them, "Bring the fish you caught."

Peter was again the first to jump up. He pulled the net onto the shore. He also counted the fish. There were 153 large fish—fat, shining bass and squirming carp. Even with all those fish, the net was not torn.

Later the disciples sat in a circle around the fire. They could not find words to express their joy and gratitude. The sun beamed down on the hills, the flowers released their sweet odors, and the birds sang around them. This was the most glorious rest imaginable after that tiring night on the lake. Their Master was with them and He was their host, just as in the old days. He broke bread and divided the fish with them. He blessed the food with His pierced hands.

The disciples had much to think about. Before long they would become fishers of men on the great world sea. Then their work, just like the work they had done that night, would often be difficult and tiring and seemingly fruitless. But Jesus Himself would stay close to them. If they listened to His voice, they would be richly blessed.

There were 153 fish in their net! The number of those who were brought to Jesus through their preaching would also be great.

The net hadn't even ripped under the strain. Of all the fish they had caught, not one was lost. And of all the believers who would later be gathered on the heavenly shore, not one would be lost.

Then there would be rest for the tired workers. God Himself would receive them in heaven at His table.

Fishers of men! They would also be shepherds of the flock Jesus would gather from all the nations.

But what about Peter? Would he be a shepherd too?

That morning fire of burning coals made them think of the fire that burned at the home of the high priest on the night of Jesus' trial.

Armed soldiers had warmed themselves around that fire. Nearby, Jesus had stood before His judges, bound and guarded like a criminal.

Among the servants warming themselves by the fire that night sat a man in the grip of a deadly fear. That man, a disciple of Jesus, swore, "Jesus? That one over there? I don't even know the man! I don't know what you're talking about!"

Now the happy disciples were sitting around another fire. With them was Jesus, the glorified Savior. Also sitting close to Him was the same sinful disciple who had denied Him.

Then Peter had said, "I don't know the man! I don't know what you're talking about!" But *now* Peter jumped out of the boat into the lake because he was eager to be with Jesus again.

Things had been straightened out between Jesus and Peter. On the day of His resurrection, Jesus had appeared to weak, sinful Peter before He appeared to the others. Peter knew that his sin was forgiven.

Something still stood between Peter and the other disciples. They had never talked about it openly, but they had all wondered about it. Peter had also asked himself, "Can someone who has fallen into sin so deeply as to deny Jesus openly still be His apostle?"

152: Feed My sheep

Jesus and His disciples were sitting around the fire early in the morning. The meal was over.

Suddenly Jesus asked, "Simon, son of John, do you truly love Me more than they do?"

The question frightened Peter, for he had said exactly that. How had he ever *dared* to say it? Peter felt Jesus' eyes and the eyes of the disciples fixed upon him. He bowed His head.

What could he answer? He could no longer say, "Even if all the others fall away, I will never forsake You! I will give up my life for You!" He no longer dared to talk that way. He had learned not to boast.

Neither could he say, "Lord, look at my life. I have proven how much I love You." That would have been a lie.

Peter gave a simple, modest answer, "Yes, Lord, You know that I love You."

Jesus answered, "Take care of My lambs."

It was still for a while. But Jesus asked again, "Simon, son of John, do you truly love Me?"

Peter let his head sink even farther this time. Why did Jesus have to ask that question again? Didn't He believe Peter anymore? It was Peter's own fault that no one trusted him now. Peter didn't even trust himself. But if there was one thing he was convinced of, it was that he was still strongly bound to Jesus. Therefore he could only stammer, "Yes, Lord, You know that I love You."

Jesus answered, "Watch over My sheep."

The same tense silence fell again. It was broken when Jesus asked for the third time, "Simon, son of John, do you love Me?"

Peter felt very sad that Jesus felt He had to ask this question *three times*. Now he understood: three times he had denied Jesus, and three times he would have to retract that denial. In the presence of the other disciples, he was being confronted with his sin once more.

Jesus, the Son of God, knew everything. Therefore He must have known of the love in Peter's heart. He knew of Peter's repentance and the deep desire in his heart to be a good and faithful servant of the Lord.

Peter sobbed, "Lord, You know everything. You *know* that I love you."

Jesus said to him, "Feed My sheep." Then He continued, "Truly, truly, I say to you, when you were younger, you dressed yourself and went wherever you wanted. But when you are old, you will stretch out your hands. Others will dress you and bring you where you don't want to go."

Peter understood what Jesus meant. A lot of struggle and hard work awaited him. But he was not afraid, for he would be an apostle of Jesus just like the others.

On that glorious morning, Peter openly confessed his sin and was publicly restored to his office by Jesus. Now the others could no longer doubt that Peter belonged among them. No one could reproach him for his sin. That sin was forgiven and forgotten.

Through that sin Peter had learned humility. He was closer to God than ever before, and he knew that nothing would ever be able to separate him from the love of Christ.

Not long afterward the eleven disciples gathered on a mountain designated by Jesus. The eleven, who were to become apostles, were joined by many of Jesus' other disciples from all over the country. Those other disciples had also listened to Him, and He had recognized them as His brothers.

Among them were the women who had wept at His grave. Perhaps His friends from Bethany were there too, along with Zacchaeus, Bartimaeus, Jairus, the king's official, and the others who had come into contact with Jesus' love. Some had been saved from evil spirits, and others from illness or blindness or some crippling infirmity. They all had Jesus to thank for their happiness.

More than 500 happy people had gathered to see Jesus. And Jesus did appear to them in His royal glory. Yet there were still some who doubted that the heavenly figure before them was really Jesus.

Jesus came closer to them and said, "All power in heaven and on earth has been given to Me. Go and make disciples of people from all nations, and baptize them in the name of the Father and of the Son and of the Holy Spirit. Teach them to observe all that I have commanded you. Whoever believes and is baptized will be saved. But whoever does not believe will be condemned."

Those orders were meant for the apostles. But Jesus also spoke some parting words of comfort that were meant for all who were present and also for all believers who would come after them. "Behold, I am with you always, even to the end of all things."

Then Jesus disappeared from their sight. The disciples went home, silent and filled with happiness. Never would they forget that special, holy day.

Now they could all be sure: the Lord had truly risen from the dead!

153: Ascension into heaven

Jesus stayed on the earth for 40 days after His resurrection. His Father in heaven was waiting for Him, for His work was finished.

He spent those 40 days on earth comforting and strengthening His disciples. He also wanted to give them some final instructions.

On the fortieth day after the resurrection, the hour came for Him to leave His disciples. He appeared to them for the last time in Jerusalem. He spoke to them once more about the work that would surely be coming for them soon.

They were to begin the work in Jerusalem. The city that had hated Him and crucified Him would be the first to hear the joyous message of God's love and grace. After that the apostles were to go out into the world. The world was a big place, and the work was difficult, but there was no reason for them to be afraid. God's Spirit would lead them.

They were to stay in the city until they received the Holy Spirit. Jesus Himself would send them the Spirit when He was back in heaven.

They would not remain on the earth all alone, then. The Spirit would comfort and teach them, just as Jesus had done. With the Holy Spirit living in their hearts, they would always be very close to Jesus.

They sat for the last time in the presence of their Master, and listened breathlessly to every word. Sadness filled their hearts.

For the last time they walked with Him along the familiar path that led from Jerusalem to the Mount of Olives. How often they had taken that path with Him! They thought back to that late evening six weeks earlier when they walked along that path by the light of the moon before Jesus was arrested and the disciples were scattered. At that time He was headed for *suffering* that He would have to bear all alone, but now He was headed for *glory*.

They stuck close to their Master as they went up the mountain, for they did not want to miss a single word. They surrounded Him reverently when He stood still and looked at them with eyes full of love. Then He raised His hands and blessed them.

Suddenly He was free of the earth. With His hands extended in blessing, He began to rise toward heaven. The disciples watched in adoration, deeply moved. They extended their arms toward the person they had grown to love more than anyone else on earth.

Soon a bright cloud removed Him from their sight. God's Son had gone on to His Father's house.

The sun went on shining as if nothing had happened. The houses of Jerusalem gleamed in the sunlight, and in the streets of the city life went on as usual.

The disciples could not tear themselves away from the place where they had seen their Master for the last time. They stared up into the sky and could hardly bring themselves to believe that He was gone forever.

Suddenly they heard a joyful voice addressing them: "Men of Galilee, why do you stand there and look into the sky? This Jesus who was taken up from you into heaven will return in the same manner in which you saw Him go up into heaven."

There were two men standing by the disciples, and they were dressed in white clothes. They were angels sent by Jesus, and they had a final message and greeting for the disciples.

Jesus was to *return*. He would come back on the clouds of heaven one day to judge the living and the dead.

154: Matthias

The hearts of the disciples were full of joy as they thought about the majestic way their Master had entered His Kingdom. In heaven there were angels waiting to greet Him, and God the Father gave Him a place at His right hand. There He sat enthroned as King of heaven and earth. In that Father's house with its many, many rooms, He would prepare places for His followers and take each one to Himself in time.

The disciples walked back to Jerusalem. They saw how the sun gleamed on the roof of the temple.

There stood the temple, just as if nothing had happened! But now it was no longer God's house. Sacrifices were still being offered, but that wasn't necessary anymore. The Lamb of God who takes away the sin of the world had been sacrificed at Golgotha.

The high priest would still enter the Holy of Holies on the great Day of Atonement to sprinkle blood, but the ceremony was now without meaning. The *true* High Priest had already entered God's Holy of Holies. His blood had made atonement for the world once and for all; the great reconciliation was accomplished.

In an upper room in Jerusalem, perhaps the same one in which the disciples held their last supper with their Master, Jesus' followers came together to wait and pray.

There was harmony among the 120 people in the room for they all loved Jesus. Mary, the mother of Jesus, was there, and so were His brothers.

That's right—His brothers! Jesus had even appeared to James, one of His brothers, after His resurrection. Now all His brothers believed in Him.

Even with all those people present, there was an empty place. Jesus had chosen *twelve* apostles because Israel was made up of *twelve* tribes. But Judas Iscariot was dead; he had given up his place for 30 pieces of silver.

Peter thought this over and realized that Judas's place would have to be filled. When the Holy Spirit descended, there could not be an empty place in their ranks.

Peter stood up and suggested that one of the men present be chosen as the twelfth apostle. It should be someone who had followed Jesus from the time of John the Baptist.

There were not many who qualified. Two men were nominated. One was

Joseph, who was also called *Barsabbas* and bore the last name *Justus*, which means *the righteous one*. The other candidate was *Matthias*.

They all kneeled and prayed, "Lord, You know the hearts of all men. Therefore show us which of these two You have chosen to serve as apostle."

They cast lots, and the lot fell upon Matthias. From then on Matthias occupied the place in the circle of the apostles that had once been held by Judas Iscariot. He joined the other apostles in waiting and pleading in prayer for the coming of the Comforter promised by Jesus.

155: Pentecost

Seven weeks after Jesus' resurrection there was a great harvest feast. On that day an incomprehensible miracle occurred: the Holy Spirit was poured out.

In a house near the temple, perhaps in one of the adjacent buildings, the disciples had come together. It had been ten days since the Savior ascended to heaven. All that time they had not stopped praying for the Spirit, the Comforter promised to them by Jesus.

That day their prayer was answered. The Spirit came, invisible as the wind but powerful and irresistible as a storm. The Spirit descended as a fire that purifies and lightens men's hearts.

Suddenly there was a sound in the sky, a sound that filled the whole house. It was like the sound of a tremendous gust of wind. It was a rushing, whistling sound, and yet the air remained calm. No door was blown open, and no dust swirled through the air.

The disciples saw flames descending on each other's heads—pointy flames like tongues of fire. But not a single hair on their heads was scorched.

They understood what was happening, for it had been foretold by John the Baptist when He said, "*I* am baptizing you with water, but there is someone coming who is stronger than I am. *He* will baptize you with the Holy Spirit and with fire."

What they heard and saw was not the most important thing of all. The gust of wind and the tongues of flame were only *signs*. The most important thing was happening silently and unobserved; no one present knew what was going on inside the others. Each one felt his own heart being filled with the Holy Spirit.

An unspeakable joy and a heavenly power filled all their hearts. Jubilantly they raised their hands to the heavens. They could not find words adequate to express the fullness of their joy. They began to speak in foreign languages, although many of them were simple people who had never been outside their own land. The Spirit led them and gave them wisdom. He flooded their minds and directed their tongues. In many languages they praised God!

The mysterious sound was also heard in the streets and in the temple. There was a great commotion. Soon a crowd of amazed people stood by the house from which the sound had come. Hesitantly the people went inside.

In the house they found a group of simple people, which amazed them even more. The people who went into the house were from many different lands—Persia, Mesopotamia, Asia, Egypt, Rome, Arabia. Each one heard God's praises in his own language.

They cried out, "Aren't these people

Galileans? How is it, then, that they speak to us in our own language?" They were greatly puzzled and stammered, "What do these things mean?"

Some scoffed, "They have had too much wine."

Suddenly there was silence in the room. Peter stepped forward and addressed the people.

His eyes were shining with joy. In a firm but happy way, he declared, "You Jews and all who live in Jerusalem, listen to me. We are not drunk, as you suppose, for it is only nine o'clock in the morning, which is too early for drinking. These things you see happening were foretold by the prophet Joel: 'And it shall come to pass in the last days, says God, that I will pour out My Spirit upon all flesh. Your sons and your daughters shall prophesy. And it shall be that all who call upon the name of the Lord will be saved.'"

After that he started to talk about Jesus. All the people had heard of Him, and many had seen His miracles and witnessed His suffering. They had joined the shouting before Pilate: "Crucify Him! Crucify Him!" They knew He had died and been buried.

There was nothing Peter would rather talk about than his Master. He delivered a long, fiery speech, making it clear to the people that Jesus *had* to suffer in order to bear the punishment for the people's sins. He showed from the Scriptures that Jesus could not remain in the grave but was awakened by God from the dead. He had then ascended to heaven, where He was enthroned at God's right hand.

Peter spoke with so much wisdom that all the people were amazed. They had often read the Scriptures, but only now did they understand what it all meant. Now it finally dawned on them what they had

done when they rejected Jesus. They heard Peter say, "Thus you may know assuredly that God has made Him both Lord and Christ—this Jesus whom you crucified."

The message affected them deeply. Had they crucified the Christ? Then God's wrath would rest upon them heavily. In despair they cried out, "What must we do, brothers?"

Fortunately, there was still deliverance for them. God was willing to forgive them this evil, if only they would turn to Him in repentance. Jesus had died for *them* too; the One whom they had hated loved them.

Peter said, "Repent and be baptized, every one of you, in the name of Jesus Christ, for the forgiveness of your sins."

A glorious harvest feast was celebrated that day in Jerusalem, for many people accepted Peter's words and were baptized.

When it was evening, about 3000 people had been won for Jesus. They were the first fruits in the great world harvest. That's why Pentecost turned out to be a great harvest feast.

When many of the people returned to their own land after the feast, they carried a great happiness with them in their hearts. They could not keep it to themselves. The Kingdom of heaven grew and began to spread across the earth.

156: The lame man at the temple gate

A man sat leaning against the wall by one of the temple gates. That gate was known as the Beautiful Gate because it was more beautiful than any other, decorated with bronze. The man was a beggar wrapped in miserable rags. His wretched state formed a sharp contrast with the beauty of the gate.

The men and women of Jerusalem walked past him as they went into the temple. It was three o'clock in the afternoon, the time of the evening sacrifice. Soon the priestly incense would rise from the golden altar of incense. The people would stand in the outer court and send up their prayers to God. The beggar would not go into the temple with them. In fact, he wasn't even *allowed* inside, for he was a cripple from his youth.

He was about 40 years old and had never been able to walk a step. When he was small, his mother had not taught him how to walk; his little legs were limp and powerless. When he grew a little older, he saw other boys running and playing in the streets, but he sat to the side. No one ever paid any attention to him. Now he was grown up, and the other boys were strong men who worked to earn their bread. The others all had a wife and a house and children and money, but he had nothing but his rags and his two useless legs. He had become a beggar, a despised, worthless person, a good-for-nothing.

What else could he do but beg? Early each morning he was carried over to his spot by the temple gate. More traffic passed that spot than any other. He sat there all day long holding out his hand. In the evening he was carried home again, clutching the few pennies he had managed to pick up from people who had paused by him for a moment.

It was a sad life. He had prayed for healing, but God did not heal him. He had nothing to look forward to.

One day two men came walking toward him. They were on their way into the temple. They did not look like rich people, but rich people were not the most generous ones anyway.

The lame man stuck out his hand and asked for alms. The two men stood still. Then a voice said, "Look at us."

The beggar was puzzled. People who tossed him alms usually didn't have a word to say. Could it be he would get a little more than usual this time? He looked up at the two earnest, friendly faces and sensed that something special was about to happen.

The older of the two men said calmly, "I have no silver or gold, but what I do have I will give you." In a firm voice, he issued a command: "In the name of Jesus Christ of Nazareth, walk!" He took the crippled beggar by his right hand and pulled him to his feet.

At that very moment, a wonderful power coursed through the lame man's limp muscles. His feet and ankles became firm and strong. The beggar was on his feet, and he remained standing when the man let go of him.

Trembling with amazement, he took a few steps this way, and then that. Jubilantly he cried aloud. His voice echoed across the temple square: "The Lord has performed a great miracle in me! He has given health to my lame legs!"

Peter and John, who had given this lame beggar more than any other almsgiver, went into the temple. The beggar went with them, running and jumping and praising God.

157: Arrested in the temple

The people in the temple looked surprised when a jubilant man came inside

praising God. They were shocked when they saw who it was; they could hardly believe their eyes. When they heard that Peter and John were responsible for this great miracle, they surrounded them in the outer court and stared at them in amazement and awe.

In the old days Peter would have enjoyed such attention, but not anymore. He was no longer interested in his own honor. Every time he had the chance, he talked about his Savior. God had given him an opportunity to bring the gospel to all these people, and he would not let it slip by.

He said, "Men of Israel, why do you stare at us as if we were able to make this man walk through our own strength or piety? *We* are not responsible for this but *Jesus*, whom you delivered up, whom you denied before Pilate even after Pilate judged that He should be set free. You denied the holy and righteous one and asked to have a murderer released. You killed the one who was to lead you to life.

"Yet God raised Him up from the dead. *We* can testify to that, for we have seen Him after His resurrection. Through faith in *His* name, this man whom you know and see here has been healed."

"You *denied* Him," Peter had said. Yes, that was what they had done, on the same day as Peter. Peter knew who it was that he had denied, but the crowd, stirred up by the rabbis, had not acted with the same knowledge. Would there be no forgiveness for those people? Hadn't there been forgiveness for *him*?

Peter said, "Brothers, I realize that you did not know what you were doing. Therefore repent, so that your sins may be wiped out."

He then explained the Scriptures to them. He showed from the prophets that

Jesus was the Christ and that He had suffered for the sins of the world. Peter could never say enough about the great miracle that Jesus had chosen to bear the punishment for sinful people.

At the same spot where their Master had so often preached and had once narrowly escaped stoning, the disciples now stood preaching in His name.

Just as Jesus encountered enmity, His disciples ran into opposition. The priests saw what was going on in the temple. Indignantly they went up to the captain of the temple guard and his servants. The name of Jesus was no longer supposed to be mentioned in the temple. Jesus was dead, and the people should not hear another word about that rebel. The disciples had stolen His body while the soldiers slept. What business did these two men have telling people that Jesus had risen from the dead?

The two men were arrested and put into prison. By taking a firm stand, the authorities would soon put an end to the work of these troublesome people. They wanted to hear no more about Jesus, for they had had enough trouble with Him.

There sat Peter and John in prison. They were locked up and would have to spend the night there.

This did not make them sad. They felt close to Jesus in prison. In their hearts they were thankful that they had been allowed to suffer a little for their Master, who had suffered so much for them.

Their thoughts were with the brothers and sisters of the congregation who would be gathering that night. The work of preaching would go ahead, even though Peter and John were in prison! How could the priests imagine that they could ever call that work to a halt?

The number of believers had already swelled to 5000. That meant 5000 mouths expressing joy about Jesus. Was it so serious, then, that there were two who could not join them that night?

158: The name of Jesus

The next morning the Sanhedrin met. Crafty old Annas and Caiaphas were among the clever members of that distinguished high council. They had thought that they were finished with Jesus for good. Would it now turn out that all their efforts were in vain?

They had Peter and John brought in, with the man whom they had healed. Sternly they asked, "How is it that this man can walk now? Through what power or in what name have you done this?"

Peter spoke up bravely. He stood before these powerful figures, these men who had condemned and scoffed at his Master. Suddenly he felt the inexpressible power that had come into his heart when the Holy Spirit was poured out on Pentecost flooding his soul again. Filled with the Spirit, he feared no one and even dared to throw accusations at his judges.

"It is because of the name of Jesus Christ of Nazareth that this man stands before you healed," he said. "It is because of the one whom you crucified, who was later raised from the dead by God. *He* is the stone that you, the builders, rejected. Now He has become the cornerstone. No other name has been given under heaven by which we will be saved."

The distinguished judges were filled with silent amazement. They could not understand how simple men with little education could stand before them so boldly. How could this older man address such wise, powerful words to them?

They recognized Peter and John as men who had been with Jesus. Because they saw the lame man healed and standing next to them they could say nothing against them.

They sent Peter and John out of the room. They wanted to talk the situation over and decide what to do next. It was quite a problem. How could they best approach it?

All of Jerusalem knew that a miracle had taken place. There was no denying it. At the very least, they would have to keep the disciples from preaching about Jesus. The name of Jesus would have to be forgotten as quickly as possible: it would have to be rooted out completely.

When they called Peter and John back in, they threatened them with severe punishment if they ever dared to mention Jesus' name again.

The two apostles smiled as they thought about it. Keep silent about Jesus, their Master, their Savior? They would keep talking about Him until the day of their death. Wasn't that what He had commanded them to do?

They answered, "Should we obey you rather than God? We cannot possibly stop talking about what we have seen and heard."

The judges threatened them some more, and then let them go. They would like to have punished them, but they didn't dare because of the people. The whole city was talking excitedly about the miracle that had taken place by the Beautiful Gate.

The man who had received the sign of healing was more than 40 years old. He had been lame from birth, and now he walked around just like anyone else! Wasn't that a divine miracle?

When Peter and John rejoined their friends, they told them all that had happened. They told them what the chief priests and elders had said.

This gave the church reason to rejoice, but it was also a reason for concern. Once the enmity of the Jews was awakened against the church, the Jews would not rest until their hatred had cooled. That was clear to all the disciples. But they knew where to look for help.

They kneeled down together and begged God to make them courageous and strong. They begged Him to show the people through signs and wonders what a blessing the holy name of Jesus was.

After this prayer, the ground shook beneath their feet and they were all filled with the Holy Spirit. Then they talked about the Word of God with boldness.

The Jews would never attain their goal. They had not been able to wipe Jesus out, and they would never erase His name. That name would live to all eternity.

159: The seed of selfishness

The first church of Christ, the congregation in Jerusalem, was holy in its life and great in its love. The people who belonged to this congregation lived together like brothers and sisters. They were one in heart and soul. There was no selfishness among them and no jealousy. They all loved their neighbors as much as they loved themselves.

There were many poor people in the congregation, but no one suffered need. The houses of the rich were open to the poor, who were always welcome at their tables. Earthly goods were of no value to these people anymore, now that they had found the heavenly treasure of Jesus' love.

No one said that this or that was his personal property. They had all things in common and formed one big family.

Some people sold their houses or their fields and gave the money to the apostles. That's what Joseph did. Joseph was the man whom the apostles called *Barnabas*, which means *son of comfort.*

Barnabas sold his land, brought his money to the next meeting, and laid it at the apostles' feet. He felt there was nothing else he could do; he simply *had* to give the money to God as a thank offering. The joy in his heart drove him to do it. Such joy in Christ could not be bought, no matter how great a sum of money one might offer for it.

The apostles took the money and shared it with those who were in need. In this way the first congregation lived together in love. It seemed as if heaven had descended to the earth in Jerusalem.

But satan was still prowling around, seeking to disrupt God's work. He was looking for a heart through which he could penetrate the congregation.

There was no place for satan in any heart filled with the Holy Spirit. Thus most hearts were closed to him. But finally he found a heart he could enter—the heart of Ananias. The heart of Sapphira, Ananias's wife, was also open to him.

Like the others, Ananias had come to the apostles to be baptized. However, he had not come because he was sorry for his sins. Ananias did not love Jesus; he loved only himself and his money.

Ananias observed what Barnabas and others had done, and he admired them for it. He, too, would like to be honored and respected for his generosity. What if *he* were to sell a piece of land and give all the money to the apostles? But no, that was too much for Ananias!

Then an idea came to him: he would sell his land and give *part* of the money, holding the rest back for himself. Yet, wouldn't the brothers ask him why he didn't bring *all* the money? They would still honor him, but not as much as Barnabas.

When Ananias reached this point in his thoughts, a voice in his heart suddenly whispered, "Why would anyone have to know that you were giving only *part* of the money?"

Ananias nodded happily. Of course! He would pretend that he was bringing in all the money. Secretly, he would hold part of it back. Then he would receive full honor and be known as a very generous man. It would not have to cost him all his money.

He discussed the idea with Sapphira, who told him that it was a beautiful plan. It was really a lie, but no one would be any the wiser.

They did it. They sold their land and hid part of the money they received for it. The rest of the money would be given to the apostles.

That was satan's way of sowing the seed of selfishness. He wanted to sow the lie in the midst of the truth, and weeds among the wheat. The bad seed would spread and grow and choke the good seed. Then nothing would come of the Kingdom of God.

160: God's holiness

Satan forgot one thing when he sowed the seed of selfishness. He forgot that God watches over His congregation and will not let anyone spoil His holy work.

Ananias, carrying his money, walked proudly through the room in which the believers were gathered. With a proud smile he laid the money at the apostles' feet.

He waited for the words of thanks they would surely give him. He expected to be honored and praised for making this great sacrifice.

Peter saw right through him, for God sharpened his gaze. He saw right into the sinful soul of this hypocrite and shook his head sadly. "Ananias," he said, "why has satan put it in your heart to deceive the Holy Spirit and hold back some of the money you were given for the land? You have not lied to men but to *God*!"

As soon as Ananias heard these words, he fell to the floor and breathed his last breath. God had punished him with death. The heavenly gardener cut a wild branch from the vine.

Some young men from the congregation carried the body of Ananias away and buried it. A great fear came over all because God had severely punished a sin in the congregation.

About three hours later Sapphira walked into the room. She did not know what had happened. Perhaps she expected that she would now be praised for her generosity.

As soon as she entered, silence fell. People had strange, earnest looks on their faces. She found it odd that she did not see her husband anywhere.

Peter summoned her. The money Ananias had brought still lay at his feet. Peter asked her gravely, "Tell me, is this all the money you got for the land you sold?"

He hoped Sapphira would now tell the truth. There was still time for her to repent.

But Sapphira did not look down to the floor in shame. She raised her head and looked defiantly at Peter. Who could prove that she was not speaking the truth?

"Yes," she said, "that's all of it."

Those were her last words.

Peter said to her, "How is it that you have agreed together to tempt the Spirit of the Lord? The feet of the men who buried your husband are at the door. The same men will carry you out."

At that very moment, Sapphira also fell dead at the apostles' feet. There she lay, right next to the money that meant more to her than Jesus.

Satan's plan had failed. The Lord's field was cleared of the dangerous weed.

The people outside the congregation trembled at this display of God's holiness. No hypocrites dared to enter the congregation anymore.

The believers now lived together in even greater purity and love. And they continued to grow in number.

161: A miraculous escape

As Peter walked through the streets of Jerusalem, people streamed toward him. They carried the sick out of their houses and laid them on beds and mattresses along the road so that Peter's shadow would pass over them as he walked by. There seemed to be amazing powers issuing from Peter and the other apostles.

They had asked the Lord for signs and wonders, and God had responded in a generous way. Even people from the surrounding towns and villages came to Jerusalem with their sick and possessed. All were healed.

The name of Jesus became known throughout Judea. The apostles' influence grew steadily.

Finally the high priest could not stand it any longer. He and the whole proud company of priests were filled with jealousy. They had hesitated because they feared an uproar, but finally they intervened. They sent out their servants, who locked the apostles in prison.

The heavy prison door swung shut. Armed servants were placed by the door as guards.

Finally the chief priests could feel at ease. The apostles' hated work would not continue. The leaders of Israel could not bear to have it continue for one more day.

But God in heaven did not want the great work to stand still for even a single day. That night an angel of the Lord descended to Jerusalem. He joined the apostles in prison, opened the doors for them, and led them outside. The watchmen did not even notice. They continued to stand guard over an empty prison.

The captives walked undisturbed through the city in the cool night air. The angel said to them, "Go and stand in the temple and speak words of life to the people."

When the first visitors came to the outer court of the temple in the morning, they found the apostles there, calm as ever. The apostles went about their work just as if there were no hostile priests around.

That morning the High Council met. Seventy distinguished judges solemnly took their places and looked sternly toward the door. In a moment the prisoners would be led in. The servants had already been sent out to get them.

But the servants came back without any prisoners. They acted confused. "The prisoners have fled," they cried out. "The prison was locked up and the watchmen were at their posts, but when we went inside we found that the prisoners were gone."

When the judges heard that, their courage failed them. The prisoners had fled? Through locked doors and past armed guards? Did they have magical powers? How could the Sanhedrin ever deal with this problem of Jesus' disciples?

Even before the judges had time to recover from the shock, a messenger entered the room with some news: "The men you took prisoner yesterday are standing in the temple teaching the people!"

Teaching the people? That was what the judges feared most of all! Couldn't those men somehow be forced not to talk to the people anymore? Would there never be an end to this problem of Jesus?

162: Gamaliel

The Sanhedrin sent out the captain and his men to arrest the apostles once more. They were not to use force! Rather, they were to be very careful about it. The people adored the apostles and might stone anyone who tried to harm them.

Peter and the other apostles went along without resisting. All twelve appeared calmly before the Sanhedrin. There they stood, those amazing men who could escape through locked and bolted doors.

But that was not what the high priest wanted to talk to them about. He didn't even want to think about it. In his heart he was afraid of the apostles, and so were the other members of the Sanhedrin. They robbed him of his rest by talking about Jesus and His death and His blood that was shed even though He was innocent.

"His blood be on us and our children!"

the rabbis had screamed before Pilate. Perhaps that wish would yet be fulfilled!

Caiaphas did not feel at all certain of himself, but he kept his composure and said sternly: "We expressly forbade you to teach in that name. Now you have filled Jerusalem with your teaching, and you want the blood of this person to be upon us."

"This person," he said. He did not even want to mention Jesus' name.

But it was that name that gave the apostles power. They answered calmly, "We must obey God rather than men. The God of our fathers has raised Jesus, whom you killed by hanging Him on a cross."

They said openly, "You killed Him." Then they went on to preach the gospel even to their judges. "God has elevated this Jesus to be our Leader and Savior," they said, "to give repentance to Israel and forgiveness of sins."

When the rabbis heard that, they were furious. They wanted to put all the apostles to death.

Just then one of the judges stood up. He had listened to everything calmly. His name was Gamaliel, and he was a famous Pharisee and scribe in Jerusalem. The people respected him highly.

Gamaliel asked that the apostles be sent out of the room for a few minutes. When this was done, he said to the other judges, "Men of Israel, consider well what you are to do with these men. It won't help to become angry about them. Perhaps the situation is not as serious as it looks. We've seen things like this before. Once there was a man named Theudas who seemed to think he was something special. About 400 men joined him, but he was killed and all his followers split up and fled. After him came Judas the Galilean. Many rebels went over

to his side, but he was put to death too, and his followers were scattered. Therefore I think we should leave these men alone. If this is the work of men, it will perish in time. If it is of God, we will not be able to destroy it. Then we will discover one day to our dismay that we are busy fighting against God."

These wise words calmed the judges for a while. But they still wanted to punish the apostles.

When they called the apostles back in, they had them whipped. They forbade them once more to speak in the name of Jesus. After that they let them go. This time they would surely obey, for they would remember the power of the Sanhedrin because of the pain they felt.

When the apostles were in the street again, their faces were beaming with joy. They were happy not because they were free but because they had been allowed to suffer for Jesus. They were not *ashamed* of the punishment they had received but counted it an *honor* to be mistreated for Jesus' sake.

Their Master had been whipped for *their* sakes. Now they were happy to bear the same punishment for *His* sake.

If the wise priests and scribes had understood that, they would have realized that there was no stopping the apostles' work.

163: The first deacons

The more the church in Jerusalem grew, the more work there was for the apostles to do. They not only preached but also doled out the money given by the rich to help the needy. They had to look after *all* the needy brothers and sisters, from all over the city.

The entire responsibility for that great family circle rested on their shoulders.

The double task was too much for them. There was no way they could get all their work done.

There were two kinds of Jews in Jerusalem, and both kinds were represented in the congregation: Greek Jews, or Hellenists, who had earlier lived in Greece or some other heathen land but had moved to Jerusalem, and Hebrews or Palestinian Jews, who had lived in Palestine all their lives.

Grumbling began among the Greek Jews. They complained that their widows were not being taken care of as well as the widows of the Palestinian Jews.

The apostles called a meeting of the congregation and declared that they needed some help in their work. Otherwise they would neglect the preaching in order to care for the poor properly. They proposed that the congregation choose seven wise, God-fearing men to take over the work of mercy. The proposal was accepted, and the first deacons were chosen.

Then things were back in order. Peace was restored, love began to grow again, and the work of preaching went ahead with renewed vigor.

Jesus' disciples now grew even more rapidly in number. Many of the priests halted their opposition and came to the apostles to be baptized.

Day after day the seven deacons went through the city, helping and comforting people.

One of the deacons appointed to look after the poor was Stephen. Stephen was a fiery man, full of grace and power. He not only carried out his duties zealously, he went far beyond what was expected of him. He brought food and money to the poor,

but wherever he went, he also brought the good news of God's grace. He could not stop talking about Jesus' love and power. He demonstrated that power by performing miracles and great signs, just as the apostles did.

He was one of the most courageous preachers in the congregation. The enemies of the church hated *him* most of all. Some of the rabbis began to follow him everywhere, hoping to frustrate him in his work. His former friends, Jews from Greek synagogues, attacked him harshly and argued with him every chance they got.

They were no match for Stephen's wisdom. When he showed them from the Scriptures that Jesus was indeed the Messiah, there was nothing they could say in response. When he showed them that the entire law of Moses had been fulfilled in Christ, they did not know what to say. Many times they were defeated in argument. Stephen kept warning them to repent before it was too late, before the city and the temple were destroyed. He kept reminding them about the punishment foretold by Jesus.

164: The stoning of Stephen

The more Stephen warned the rabbis and pleaded with them to repent, the more they hated him. When they realized they would never win an argument with him, they began to lay plans to overcome him in another way. They bribed some men without conscience to slander Stephen's name and get the people angry at him. Then they arrested him and brought him before the Sanhedrin.

The false witnesses accused him of

blasphemy. They twisted his words and said, "This man never stops speaking out against the law and the holy temple. We heard him say that this Jesus, the one from Nazareth, will break down the temple and change the customs that have been passed down to us by Moses."

The angry, stern eyes of the judges focused on Stephen. But Stephen stood before his enemies looking calm and happy. His face beamed with heavenly joy, just like the face of an angel. Again the high priest was uneasy because of the mysterious confidence that all these followers of Jesus seemed to enjoy. They acted as if nothing could harm them.

After all the accusations, Caiaphas asked Stephen, "Are these things true?"

Stephen fixed his shining eyes on his judges and spoke to them as no one had ever spoken to them before.

He spoke reverently about Moses and the temple, but he showed them how foolish and wrong it was for them to glorify the temple and believe that God could not speak to His people apart from the temple. Hadn't God often spoken to His children long before there was a temple? Hadn't He revealed Himself to Abraham and the other patriarchs? Hadn't He appeared to Moses in the burning bush, and hadn't the people of Israel heard His mighty voice at Mount Sinai? Then how could those proud rabbis still think that the Most High God would dwell in a temple made with hands? Hadn't Solomon himself said when the temple was dedicated that the heaven of heavens could not contain Him?

Stephen talked about earlier generations. He showed that they never wanted to believe in the deliverance God sent them in their hour of need, just as the rulers of Israel refused to believe in Jesus.

He talked about Joseph, who was sold by his own brothers but later saved them from starvation by bringing them to Egypt. He talked about Moses, who wanted to protect his people but fled when they betrayed him. Later, when he was Israel's leader, the disobedient people defied him for 40 years.

When Stephen was finished listing all these examples of unbelief, he turned his eyes on the judges in holy indignation as he applied the same accusation to them, "You stiff-necked people, you always resist the Holy Spirit, just as your fathers did! Which of the prophets did your fathers not persecute? They even killed the prophets who spoke to them about the coming of the Righteous One whom you betrayed and murdered—you who received the law as though given to you by angels and still could not keep it!"

At that point Stephen was interrupted by angry shouts from the judges. His words cut them to the quick. They gnashed their teeth in anger and rushed toward Stephen.

Stephen stood in the middle of this furious mob just as if he heard and saw nothing. He was looking up toward heaven, and his face beamed with inner joy.

He saw the glory of God, with Jesus, his Savior, standing next to God's throne, ready to receive him. God was rewarding His courageous servant by giving him this miraculous glimpse of the world that stood ready to welcome him.

What did the hatred of his judges matter to him now? He didn't even see them anymore. "Look!" he cried out in delight. "I see the heavens opened, and the Son of man standing at the right hand of God."

The Jews began to scream. They plugged their ears and rushed at him. They were acting as if they had gone out of their minds.

They dragged him out of the room,

through the small winding streets, and out of the city. There they began to stone him. The false witnesses threw the first stones.

Hastily they laid down their garments for safekeeping at the feet of a young man. That young man was named *Saul.*

Soon the first stones struck that courageous witness of Jesus. A shower of sharp stones followed. No complaint came from Stephen's lips—only a prayer. He called out, "Lord Jesus, receive my spirit."

When he had fallen to his knees and was bleeding from many wounds, he raised his eyes to heaven once more. He cried out with a loud voice, "Lord, do not hold this sin against them."

With those words on his lips, Stephen died. He had glorified Jesus in life, and he also glorified Him in death.

Stephen died praying for his enemies. He followed the example of his Master. He was the first martyr.

After his enemies had marched back to the city in triumph, his friends came to the place where his broken body lay among the blood-stained stones. Sadly they carried his body to the grave, and for a long time they mourned him.

Stephen was already with his Master. There was no pain where he was, nor was there any sorrow or enmity. Stephen was faithful unto death and received the crown of life.

165: The seed spreads

After Stephen's death, the chief priests and scribes unleashed fierce persecution against the church in Jerusalem. Their wrath had finally broken loose, and there was no holding them back. Not even wise Gamaliel could restrain them.

Saul, a young Pharisee who was a disciple of Gamaliel, was the most zealous of all in persecuting the church. He was the young man who had taken care of the witnesses' garments when Stephen was stoned. Saul had enjoyed seeing Stephen die. That was the fate all Christians deserved, he believed, for they betrayed the old faith.

Saul went through the city with the servants of the high priest and brought devastation on the congregation. He went into house after house, dragging out men and women to be imprisoned.

A storm had struck the Lord's little garden. Many beautiful plants were injured and trampled down. But that storm carried the seed of God's Word throughout the whole country. It scattered the seed in fertile places where it would bear fruit and bring new life.

Those who were scattered in all directions, throughout Judea and Samaria and far across the borders to other countries, traveled far and proclaimed the gospel wherever they went. God's Kingdom continued to expand quickly.

Philip, who was one of the six deacons left after Stephen's death, also fled Jerusalem. He wandered through the land and came to Samaria, a city the Jews despised thoroughly. But Jesus despised no one, and neither did Philip. Therefore he began to preach the gospel to the Samaritans.

The people streamed toward him. No one contradicted him and no one turned his back on him in indifference. It seemed as if they had been waiting for his joyous message, and they were united in accepting what he told them.

God helped Philip in his work and gave him the power to perform miracles. He healed the sick. When people with unclean spirits came to him, they went home purified.

Great happiness had come to the city. A new congregation was born, made up of a family circle of joyful people who knew the Savior.

166: Simon the Sorcerer

There was an amazing man living in Samaria when Philip came there to preach. Until then he had been revered by the whole city. His name was Simon, and he was a sorcerer. He admitted this openly and was proud of it.

"I'm something special," he would tell people. Then he would chant some mysterious formula and do tricks which amazed the people. They would cry out to him in delight and say, "This man has the power of God!"

When Philip came to Samaria, that was the end of Simon's fame. The humble, simple believer who never talked about himself but only about Jesus could do greater tricks than the sorcerer. When the men and women of Samaria were baptized and came to know the joy of Jesus, they were no longer interested in Simon's magic.

Simon didn't really care. He was astounded at the wonders Philip performed and kept a close eye on him every day. He listened to Philip carefully. Although he didn't understand much, the seed of faith began to grow in his heart. It was only a small seed and a weak faith, but it was there. Simon, too, was baptized, along with the other people of Samaria.

Still, Simon could not give up his old profession. The miracles Philip performed attracted him more than the words he spoke. Whenever Philip healed a sick person or a cripple by faith in Jesus, Simon was right there watching. Every time he was amazed by the mysterious power Philip possessed.

The news that Samaria had accepted the Word of God went through the entire land. It also reached the apostles, who were still in Jerusalem, faithfully keeping watch at their dangerous post.

They could hardly believe that the half-heathen Samaritans would accept the good news. Therefore they sent Peter and John to look into the matter.

How happy these two apostles were when they saw for themselves that the reports about Samaria were not exaggerated. At once they began to help Philip with his glorious work. At a meeting of the congregation, they prayed to God to pour out His Holy Spirit in Samaria, too, just as He had done in Jerusalem on Pentecost. After that prayer, when the Samaritan believers came forward and the apostles laid their hands on their heads, their hearts, too, were filled with the Holy Spirit.

Simon was watching again. He was amazed. But God's Word was still a closed book to him. He thought that Peter and John themselves had the power to pour out the Holy Spirit. He thought it was some sort of magic that one might learn.

Finally his original heathen nature came to the fore again, and he was gripped by a great desire to learn the new magic. Was there some special magic formula one had to learn? Simon wanted to do it too!

He called the apostles aside. When he was alone with them, he offered them money and said, "Let me have that power too, so that if I lay my hands on someone, he will receive the Holy Spirit."

He shrank back at once when he saw the anger that flared up in Peter's eyes. Peter was shocked at that superstition. He admonished Simon sternly.

"May your money perish with you!" he said. "Did you really believe you could obtain this gift of God with *money*? Your heart is not right before God. Repent of your wickedness and ask the Lord to forgive your sin. I can see that you are caught up in unrighteousness."

Simon trembled with fear. At once he was sorry; he had made his foolish request out of ignorance. He begged the apostles to pray for him so that God would not punish him for his sin. He still believed that they had some sort of special power and that *their* prayer was much more likely to be heard than his.

Confusion reigned in Simon's heart, but faith was also at work. If he would only study the Scriptures with great humility and devotion, the light of Jesus would drive all darkness from his heart.

167: Philip and the Ethiopian

Peter and John could not stay in Samaria for long. They went back to Jerusalem, preaching the gospel in the Samaritan villages they passed through.

Philip also left. An angel of the Lord said

to him, "Arise and go to the lonely road that leads from Jerusalem toward Gaza."

That was all the angel said, but for Philip it was enough. He set out on his journey and did not rest until he reached the road that wound its way through the dry, lonely hill country of Judea. Then he stretched out at the side of the road and waited for God to tell him what work he was to do there.

Soon he saw a caravan coming down the sunny road from Jerusalem. Dark-skinned armed horsemen led the way. Slaves followed, walking next to heavily-laden camels.

In the middle of the procession rode a powerful lord in a beautiful chariot. The man in the chariot was dressed in exquisite clothes. He sat bent over a scroll and was not paying any attention to the countryside around him. He was completely absorbed in what he was reading.

As Philip watched this scene, a voice inside him said, "Step forward and approach the chariot."

Philip obeyed this command of the Holy Spirit and silently walked alongside the chariot. The traveler didn't even notice him. He was reading aloud. Philip heard him say, "Like a sheep led to the slaughter and like a lamb that is silent before the shearer, so He opened not His mouth."

The man sighed and shook his head. Then he sat there thinking about what he had read. It appeared that he simply didn't understand it.

Philip recognized those familiar, beloved words from the prophecy of Isaiah. Suddenly he understood why God had sent him here. "Do you understand what you are reading?" he asked.

The figure in the chariot looked up in surprise. Only now did he notice the stranger. He looked into those two wise, friendly eyes and trusted Philip at once.

"How can I understand," he answered sadly, "if I have no one to show me the way?" He invited Philip to step up into the chariot and ride with him.

Philip accepted the invitation. He sat down next to the traveler.

The traveler came from Ethiopia or Abyssinia. He was one of the leading officials of Candace, the queen of the Ethiopians. He was in charge of her treasury. In his faraway African homeland, he had heard about the powerful God of the Jews. He had made the difficult, dangerous journey to Jerusalem to worship that God in His own temple. That was where he had bought the book he was reading. It was a Greek translation of Isaiah's prophecies. With Philip beside him, he reread the passage he found so difficult: "Like a sheep led to the slaughter and like a lamb that is silent before the shearer, so He opened not His mouth."

He looked at Philip and asked, "About whom does the prophet say this—about himself or someone else?"

Philip could see that this man greatly desired to know God better. He explained what Isaiah meant by these words. He told the Ethiopian about Jesus and His suffering, His love for sinners, His resurrection, and His ascension into heaven. He talked about faith in the name of Jesus, who can make anyone happy, regardless of the nation he belongs to. He explained to the Ethiopian about repentance and baptism.

While Philip was talking, the dark eyes of the high official began to shine. He saw that his long, tiring journey was not in vain. Now he finally found what he had sought in vain in the temple among the proud scribes in Jerusalem.

This simple, wise man had shown him the path to everlasting happiness. Jesus had also come to earth for *him*, an Ethiopian! While he was serving at his queen's court back in Ethiopia, where he hardly thought about God, Jesus had died for *him*!

The black official was deeply moved as he turned this over in his mind. Suddenly he cried out, "Look, there's some water! Is there any reason why I cannot be baptized now?"

Philip answered, "If you believe with your whole heart, you may receive baptism."

The official said reverently, "I believe that Jesus Christ is the Son of God."

That was enough. Anyone who believed that had already found the path to heaven.

The chariot stopped. The black man and the white man went into the water together. There, in a lonesome region of Judea, the official was baptized in the name of Jesus.

He was deeply moved when he came out of the water. He looked around for Philip, but Philip was nowhere to be seen. The Spirit of the Lord had suddenly taken him away.

The official was alone with his servants
again, but he didn't mind. He went his way
with joy in his heart. He carried with him a
treasure he would not trade for all of his
queen's wealth.

In Ashdod Philip continued his work.
From there he went on to preach the gospel
in all the cities, until he came to Caesarea.
There, in the city by the sea, where the
palace of the governor stood, he settled
down. He continued to bring the good news
to everyone whose heart was open to
receive it.

168: Saul of Tarsus

When a farmer in the ancient Near East
plowed his field, he would drive the oxen
ahead with a long stick that had iron points
on the end. If one of the oxen did not want
to listen to the master's voice and stubbornly tried to kick the plow to pieces, the
master would hold out this long stick and
let the animal kick backwards against the
sharp points, which were known as
"pricks." The angrier the animal became,
the more it would hurt itself. Finally the
message would get through, and the animal
would obey its master.

Any human being who lives in rebellion
against God is like a foolish, stubbon ox
kicking against the pricks. His rebellion will
not change God's will; all he manages to do
is to make himself unhappy.

Saul, who persecuted the congregation in
Jerusalem, kicked against the pricks for a
long time, although he did not realize what
he was doing. He thought it was his *duty* to
oppose and harrass the disciples of Jesus of
Nazareth.

He was tormented repeatedly by a painful sense of unrest as he went about this
work, but he would say to himself, "I have
not yet done my best." Then he would rage
even more furiously against the believers.
The result was that he would feel still more
unhappy.

Saul was born in Tarsus, a beautiful
Roman city in the southeast part of Asia
Minor. His father was a Jew of the tribe of
Benjamin, the same tribe from which King
Saul was born. That may be part of the
reason why he called his son Saul. But as a
Roman citizen, he also had to give his
children a non-Jewish name. Hence Saul
was also called *Paul*.

Saul grew up in a heathen city, but he
received a strict upbringing and training in
the ancient doctrines of the Jews. His father
was a very pious man, a Pharisee. From his
father Saul heard stories from the Scriptures and learned the laws of Moses. His
father also taught him to work with his
hands. He learned to make tents out of
goat's hair. Tent-making was an important
industry in Tarsus.

Saul was not destined to spend his life
working with his hands. He was to become
a scribe, and therefore he was sent to
Jerusalem while he was still a young man.
In the holy city he sat at the feet of
Gamaliel, eager to acquire wisdom.

Saul was the most zealous of all the
students and went far beyond the others in
his work. Great was his faith in the laws of
Moses, and also in his forefathers and his
nation. His trust in the rabbis was unboun-
ded. He became a strong, fiery Pharisee, a
zealot when it came to the law. He believed
his people could only be saved by keeping
the law faithfully.

Saul may even have seen Jesus during his
days as a student in Jerusalem or heard Him
speak. But he did not believe in Jesus. Saul

was convinced that Jesus was an enemy of the Jewish people and the greatest deceiver that ever lived.

When the disciples later began to spread the teaching about Jesus, Saul quickly became their chief opponent. He was present when Stephen was stoned and he approved, for Stephen had accused Saul's teachers of breaking the law. He had called them traitors and murderers!

From the day of Stephen's stoning, Saul knew what he would live for. The name of Jesus had to be wiped from the earth. He, Saul of Tarsus, would bring this about. Surely God would bless him for it.

169: The road to Damascus

Saul had deliberately chosen a horrible mission in life, and in time he grew increasingly extreme and angry. But when he saw how calm his victims remained in prison and when he remembered the shining eyes of the dying Stephen, doubts arose in his heart. It was as if a voice was saying to him, "Saul, stop it! After all, they are children of God. You are fighting against God Himself, Saul. Jesus was the Messiah."

But Saul did not want to listen to that voice. He was convinced that it was not the voice of his conscience. It was unbelief to think such thoughts.

Then he would throw himself even more fiercely into the battle against the disciples in order to silence that voice once and for all. He had them whipped in the synagogues until they cried out for mercy or slandered the name of Jesus in their great fear or succumbed to the torment. He breathed threats and slaughter and became like a wild animal that throws itself at its prey. There was no rest for him while there were still Christians to harrass and torment.

Saul heard at one point that a new congregation had arisen in Damascus. He wanted to destroy that congregation too. He went to the high priest to ask permission.The high priest was happy to let him go ahead, and he praised Saul for his zeal. He gave him letters of introduction to the rulers of the synagogue in Damascus. They would surely be willing to help him.

Soon Saul set out in a great hurry, accompanied by some soldiers. It was a long journey, but that didn't matter to him. He thought only about finding Christians in Damascus and bringing them back, bound, to Jerusalem.

That journey of five or six days along quiet, lonely roads must have seemed terribly long to Saul. As he moved along somberly at the head of the party, he was tormented more than ever by the painful thoughts that bothered him often, but he pressed on. He was determined to keep working until the name of Jesus of Nazareth was rooted out from the earth.

He approached Damascus in the middle of the day. The sun was high in the sky. It was the hour when caravans usually rested, but Saul saw the great white city with its green trees and bushes just before him, and so he drove the soldiers on. He wanted to get started with his horrible work as soon as possible, so that he could silence that voice in his heart.

Just then a great miracle occurred, a miracle that put an end to Saul's fury and rage in an instant.

When warnings and rebukes didn't help, Christ Himself took hold of this man who was galloping ahead like a blinded horse and brought him to a standstill.

Suddenly a great light from heaven surrounded Saul and his men. That light was so bright that the sun seemed pale by comparison. Saul and his men quickly covered their eyes with their hands. They all fell to the ground and hid their heads in their arms.

As he lay on the ground in great fear, Saul heard a voice asking him, "Saul, Saul, why are you persecuting Me?"

Whose voice was that? Saul did not know, and he did not dare look up. He could only stammer, "Who are you, Lord?"

He heard a frightening, shattering answer. "I am *Jesus*, whom you are persecuting. It is very hard for you to keep kicking against the pricks."

Saul trembled. He could do nothing but bow deeply and whisper reverently, "Lord, what must I do?"

The voice answered, "Arise and go into the city. There you will be told what you are to do."

Saul was still trembling when he stood up. Although his eyes were open, he could see nothing. He groped around in his darkness. The light of heaven had made him blind.

His men were amazed as they watched him. They went to him and took hold of him. They did not understand what had happened. They had heard a voice, but they had not understood a word that was said. Frightened at the strange misfortune that had struck their leader, they led him to the city. There they brought him to the home of a man named Judas, who was probably one of the leading Jews in the city.

Saul had set out for Damascus as a cruel, powerful man bent on persecuting the church, but he arrived there helpless and blind.

170: God's chosen instrument

Saul of Tarsus was trapped in a world of darkness. The man of force and violence was a broken man. The fiery battler for God and His service found out that he had been fighting *against* God.

People brought him food and drink, but he would not touch it. For three days he ate and drank nothing. As he thought about Jesus, the Messiah, whom he had persecuted, his soul was torn with anguish. He thought about the Scriptures and what they said about the Messiah. Because he had always known the Scriptures so well, Saul simply couldn't understand how he could have been blind for so long.

While he sat there as a blind man, his eyes were finally opened. Again he saw Stephen with his shining face, and again he heard him pray for his enemies as the blood streamed from his wounds. He saw all the others whom he had tormented and murdered, and he heard their cries.

Finally he had to cry out himself in his horrible anguish, "O God, be gracious to me, a sinner!"

Then it seemed as if a comforting hand was laid on his head and the darkness was swept away from his eyes. He saw a man standing before him, and somehow he knew that the man's name was Ananias. But at once there was darkness around him again. It was only a beautiful vision, nothing more. Perhaps it was also a message from heaven that there was still hope for him.

There really was a man in Damascus whose name was Ananias. He was highly respected and was a faithful disciple of Jesus.

Ananias did not yet know what had hap-

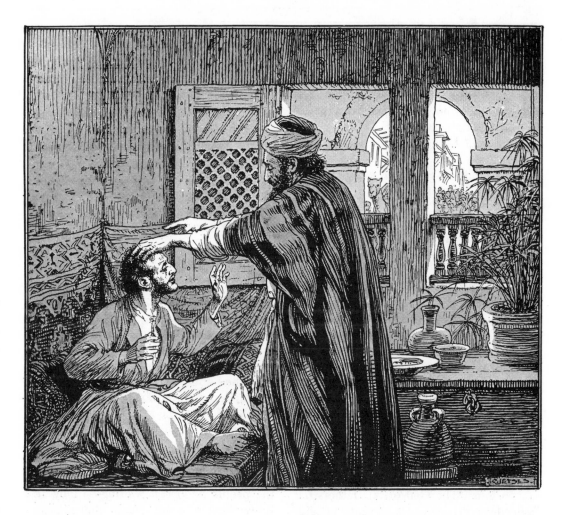

pened to Saul. The members of the church in Damascus had heard that he was coming. They knew that there was a frightening time ahead for them.

On the third day after Saul's arrival in Damascus, Ananias heard the voice of the Lord addressing him: "Ananias!"

"Here I am, Lord," he replied.

The Lord said to him, "Arise and go to Straight Street and ask at the house of Judas for a man from Tarsus named Saul. Saul is praying. In his prayer he has had a vision of a man named Ananias who came to him and laid his hands on him so that he could see."

This frightened Ananias. He could hardly believe his ears. Saul was a man to flee from. Now Ananias was being told to go *to* that horrible enemy of the Christians.

Ananias was puzzled. "Lord," he replied, "I have heard a great deal about this man and all the evil he has done to the saints in Jerusalem. Now he has authority from the chief priests to come to Damascus and take away as prisoners all who call upon the name of the Lord."

But the Lord said to Ananias: "Go, for Saul is My chosen instrument to make My name known among the Gentiles and their kings and also among the people of Israel. I shall show him how much he must suffer for the sake of My name."

Could *Saul* be a chosen servant of the Lord? Could *Saul* be a preacher of the gospel? Could Saul be a *brother* rather than an enemy? Ananias could hardly believe it.

But Ananias did as he was told and went to the house where Saul was staying. There sat Saul, blind and bowed low and hopelessly depressed. As soon as Ananias saw him, he could forgive the man all he had done wrong. Tenderly he laid his hands on Saul's head and said, "Brother Saul, I have been sent to you by the Lord—Jesus, who appeared to you on the road. He wants you to see again and be filled with the Holy Spirit."

At that very moment it seemed as if scales fell from Saul's eyes. He could see again. He saw the man who had addressed him as a brother, and he recognized him from his vision. Great joy filled his soul.

Ananias also told him what the Lord had said to him. "The God of our fathers has destined you to become His servant," he said. "You may testify before Him. Just as your own eyes were opened, so you may open the eyes of the Gentiles. You will bring them out of darkness into the light. You will release them from the power of satan and bring them to God so that they may receive forgiveness for their sins."

But Saul sat there without saying a word. Gratitude overwhelmed him, and he could not speak. Ananias finally said, "What are you waiting for? Arise and be baptized in the name of the Lord, so that your sins will be washed away."

Saul was transformed from an *enemy* of Jesus into a *disciple*. He was baptized, and a new life lay open before him. Now he knew what work awaited him. Just as he had tried to tear people away from Jesus in the past, he would lead people *to* Jesus in the future.

He would be just as fierce a fighter as always. No, he would fight even more courageously. Now there was no doubt and hesitation in his soul. Now, at last, he had rest.

171: Friends and enemies

Saul would become Jesus' apostle. To prepare himself for this great task, he would live in solitude for a while, just as John the Baptist had done. For a long time he wandered around in Arabia to be alone with God. Then he returned to Damascus and was soon preaching with great power in the synagogues.

He cried out to the Jews that Jesus was the Son of God, the Redeemer for whom the people had been waiting so long. He threw them into confusion by showing from the Scriptures that Jesus was indeed the Christ. They all stared at him in fear and said, "Isn't that the man who persecuted all the people in Jerusalem who called upon this name? Didn't he come to Damascus with the express purpose of taking such people prisoner and turning them over to the chief priests?"

It was no longer the same Saul who addressed them. Through God's grace, he had become a new man. There was nothing the second Saul wanted more than to repair the damage done by the first Saul.

Of course the damage could never be fully undone. Stephen could not be restored to the land of the living. Much of the other damage Saul had done to the followers of Jesus was also beyond repair.

Saul was never able to forget the damage he had caused. For the rest of his life, his persecution of the church of Christ caused him great pain.

Saul did not stay in Damascus long, for his life was in great danger there. The Jews hated him after his conversion and began making plans to kill him. Day and night the city gates were watched so that he would not be able to escape. His friends, the disciples of Jesus, hid him in a house in the city wall and lowered him down the wall by night in a basket. That way he got out of the city unnoticed and escaped the wrath of the chief priests. He then returned to Jerusalem as a fugitive.

Three years had passed since Saul had left Jerusalem with a band of soldiers. He had set out from the city bent on persecution, but he came back as a victim of persecution himself.

Saul was all alone in Jerusalem. The scribes and Pharisees, his former friends, were now his most bitter enemies. And his former enemies, Jesus' disciples, avoided him because they could not believe that he had really become a follower of Jesus. They had suffered too much cruel persecution at his hands to be able to shed their fears and suspicions.

Saul tried to visit them in their homes, but they locked their doors to him. They did not trust him. They thought that his conversion was a trick. They thought that he was trying to get inside the congregation in order to betray Jesus' followers.

Finally one man had compassion on Saul—Barnabas, the man who had sold his field some years before. The name the apostles had given him meant *son of comfort*.

Barnabas believed Saul's story and took him to the house where Peter was staying. He told Peter about the amazing way in which Jesus had turned Saul around. He explained that Saul had already been preaching the gospel in Damascus. Peter then laid his suspicions aside. He took Saul into his house and put him in contact with the leaders of the congregation in Jerusalem.

Saul stayed with Peter for fifteen days, but he could not sit still for long. Although there was great hatred against him, he began to preach in the Greek synagogue to the same Jews among whom Stephen had labored. They hated him fiercely and quickly began making plans to kill him. Saul knew what they were up to, but he went ahead with his work anyway.

Jesus did not want His courageous servant to die for Him so soon. When Saul was in the temple to pray, He spoke to him and told him to leave the city at once.

This was a very difficult command for Saul, but he obeyed. Quickly he set out on a journey. Some of the brothers went along to Caesarea. From there he went by ship to Tarsus, the city of his birth. He would wait in Tarsus until the Master needed him.

172: Peter's tour

After Saul's conversion there were some peaceful years for the churches of Judea, Galilee and Samaria. The church grew in strength and walked in the fear of the Lord. With the help of the Holy Spirit, the church also grew in numbers.

During this peaceful time, Peter toured the land. He walked through the Lord's fields like a gardener and rejoiced in the growth he found. Wherever he went he was greeted with joy.

One day he arrived in Lydda, a place on the road that leads from Jerusalem to the sea. In this town in the fruitful plain of Sharon, he found a man named Aeneas, who was lame and had been bedridden for eight years. Some years earlier, before Aeneas had heard of Jesus, he had been a strong, healthy man who could go wherever he wanted. Now he was helpless; now others had to do things for him as he lay quietly waiting for his death.

When Peter saw the man lying there, he remembered that Jesus was the great Physician who could heal all diseases. Jesus was just as powerful in heaven as He had been when He walked on earth.

Peter realized there was no reason why this man should remain bedridden any longer. He said to him, "Aeneas, Jesus Christ has healed you. Get up and make your bed."

At once the man stood up, amazed and overjoyed that he was again as strong and healthy as before. He walked through Lydda and the fruitful fields of Sharon. All who saw him saw the power and love of Jesus. The inhabitants of Lydda and Sharon then turned to the Lord.

Not far from Lydda lay Joppa, a large city by the sea. In Joppa, too, there was a church. But there was great sadness in that church.

In Joppa lived a woman who was an angel of goodness. Her name was Tabitha (Dorcas in Greek), and she was a disciple of Jesus. She knew that Jesus loved her, and this realization made her show her love in turn to everyone she met. Every poor person in the church in Joppa knew her. Every widow in that church had some clothes that had been made for her by Tabitha.

Suddenly Tabitha became sick and died. As she lay dead in an upper room, still dressed in the clothes in which she died, it became clear just how much good she had done on earth in her quiet way. From all around poor people came to see her one more time. They wept as they looked at that beloved face. They were so disconsolate that they could barely tear themselves away from her.

The followers of Jesus heard that Peter was in Lydda, only three hours away. They quickly sent two men over there to ask Peter to come to Joppa without delay. Perhaps Peter could bring them some comfort.

Peter came at once. He was led into the upper room, where he was surrounded by people in mourning. They all wanted to tell him about the many things the dead woman had done for them. The widows, with tears rolling down their faces, showed him the skirts and cloaks Tabitha had made.

Peter was sad too. He saw the good woman on her deathbed. Her name meant *gazelle*, but that name did not seem to fit the cold, stiff body that would soon have to be buried. Why did *she* have to die, this woman who was almost indispensable? Wasn't the Lord of death and life also *her* Master?

Suddenly a great and wonderful hunch sprang up within Peter. Why had the Lord led him to this place? Wasn't it so that He could do something great for those who believed in His holy name?

Peter sent the mourners outside. When he was alone with the dead woman and God, he kneeled down and prayed. Once he was finished praying, he knew the Lord wanted to use him in an amazing way to glorify His name. He stood erect, turned to the dead body, and said: "Tabitha, arise!"

The woman opened her eyes and looked at Peter in amazement. Life had returned to her cold body. She sat up, just as if she was waking up from a deep sleep. Peter took her hand and helped her to her feet. He called the widows and the other mourners back in, and they were speechless with fear and joy when they saw Tabitha standing before them alive again.

The news about this great miracle spread throughout Joppa. Wherever it went, new miracles occurred. Many who were dead in sins now came to new life in faith.

Peter quickly understood what fruitful work he could do in Joppa. He stayed there for a while at the home of Simon, who was a tanner.

173: Cornelius

About eight hours north of Joppa, on the coast of the Mediterranean Sea, lay the port city of Caesarea. This city was named after the caesar, the emperor in Rome. It was a Roman city in a Jewish land. It had heathen temples and idols and also a great amphitheater for sports events and festivals.

The governor's palace stood in Caesarea, and he spent most of the year there. Caesarea was also the place where the most Roman soldiers were stationed. Those soldiers had to maintain order for the Romans in the land of the Jews.

Cornelius was one of the soldiers stationed in Caesarea. He was a brave officer and a centurion in the Italian Regiment. He was not like the other Romans. The Romans looked down on the Jews and made fun of their worship, but Cornelius loved the Jews. He had seen about half of the known world while serving the emperor, but he was happiest among the Jews. He had read their Scriptures and come to know their God. Gradually he realized that the idolatry of the pagans was foolishness.

Cornelius told his servants and friends and everyone in his household about this mighty God. They, too, grew to love Him. In Caesarea, then, a God-fearing Roman lived in the midst of the pagan idol-worshipers.

The Jews knew the family of Cornelius and had great regard for him. The poor people in Caesarea knew Cornelius too, for when they came to his door seeking alms, they were never turned away.

God knew Cornelius. He knew this man desired to know Him more fully and to serve Him more faithfully. There were days when Cornelius would not eat or drink at all. He would devote all his time to God in prayer and fasting.

One day, at about three o'clock in the afternoon, Cornelius was on his knees in prayer. Suddenly he heard a friendly voice say to him, "Cornelius!"

When he looked up, he saw an angel standing by him. This frightened the courageous man of war. He stared at the shining heavenly figure in fear.

"What is it, Lord?" he stammered.

The angel said, "God has heard your prayers and seen the alms you give. Send some men to Joppa to present an invitation to a man named Simon, who is also known as Peter. He is a guest of another man named Simon, a tanner whose house is by the sea."

As soon as the angel was gone, Cornelius summoned two of his servants and a pious soldier who was one of his guards. He explained everything to them and sent them off in a great hurry to Joppa.

It was almost evening when they left. They would have to stop somewhere for the night. They did not reach Joppa until the next day.

174: Clean and unclean

Peter was climbing the stairs that led to the flat roof of the house where he was staying. He would pray on the roof, where it was peaceful. There was no other sound to be heard than the sound of the sea, and there nothing to be seen toward the horizon but the shining blue water.

In the house below, a meal was being prepared. As Peter kneeled to pray, he felt hunger pangs. When his eyes were closed, he saw something amazing. It was as if heaven had been opened. A great sheet was being lowered by its four corners. On that sheet were all sorts of animals—four-footed beasts, creeping animals, clean and unclean animals, and many kinds of birds. Peter heard a voice: "Arise, Peter. Kill and eat."

Peter shook his head resolutely. He knew that God's voice was speaking to him, but he refused anyway. On the sheet were unclean animals, animals that no Jew was allowed to eat. The clean animals were also defiled, for they had been in contact with the unclean ones. Surely God could not demand that Peter break the law! Therefore he said, "No, Lord, for I have never eaten anything impure or unclean."

The heavenly voice answered sternly, in a tone of voice that Peter would not quickly forget, "Do not call something impure when God has made it clean."

The sheet descended once more, and Peter refused again. He also refused when the sheet descended for a third time. He did not understand the Lord's strange command. Then the sheet was pulled up, heaven was closed, and Peter found himself alone on his knees, praying on the roof. The sheet had come to him in a dream, an amazing vision.

The voice continued to resound in his heart. He knew that God wanted to teach him something through this vision. Had Moses' law lost its power? Did God want to abolish the distinction between the Jews and the Gentiles? He had given those laws to His people Himself so that they would always know that they were a holy people! He had surrounded His people with a wall of holy laws to keep them separate from other nations. Did God now mean to break down that wall?

Peter had forgotten his hunger. He was lost in thought. While he was still pondering the vision, he heard someone knocking on the door below. The man at the door was asking for Peter, but Peter didn't hear him. He was still thinking about the vision, but he could find no answer to the problem it posed.

Then a voice in his heart said to him, "There are two men below looking for you. Arise and go downstairs. Don't be afraid to go along with them, for I have sent them."

It was the voice of the Holy Spirit. Peter obeyed at once and went downstairs. He saw some Romans in the courtyard. He went up to them and said, "I am the man you are looking for. What is the reason for your coming?"

They said to him, "We have come on behalf of Cornelius, a centurion in Caesarea. He is a righteous man and a worshiper of God. A holy angel told him to invite you to his house. He wants to listen to what you have to say."

Peter was amazed. A Roman centurion? A Gentile from the godless city of Caesarea? Was Peter, a Jew, supposed to enter the impure house of such a man? Was that what God wished him to do?

He wanted to shake his head again, just as he had done in the vision. He wanted to say, "Surely You don't mean it, Lord!" But then he remembered the stern voice that said, "Do not call something impure when God has made it clean."

Suddenly he understood the amazing vision. It was a divine lesson meant to remind him that God's joyous message was not only for Israel but also for the Gentiles. It was *Peter's* obligation to bring that message to the Gentiles.

Peter did not hesitate any longer. He invited the men inside and showed them hospitality.

The next day he went with them along the coast back to Caesarea. Some of the brothers from Joppa accompanied him.

175: Israel and the nations

Cornelius was waiting eagerly for the arrival of his special guest. He had invited his family and his best friends to be present for the occasion. He knew that Peter's coming would mean something special in his life, and he wanted others to share it.

When Peter arrived at the gate, Cornelius hurried out to meet him. There was the famous apostle, an ambassador of the Lord! Cornelius felt such great respect for Peter that he fell on his knees.

But Peter said, "Arise, for I am only a man." He pulled Cornelius to his feet and went inside to talk with him. Without any hesitation, he stepped over the threshold of this Gentile home, even though this was sternly forbidden by the rabbis. He was following *God's* orders. When he went inside and saw all the men and women assembled there, he realized what glorious work awaited him.

He did not call them unclean anymore, for he knew that he was no better than they were. They were creatures of God for whom Jesus had died, just as He died for the Jews.

Peter asked for what purpose Cornelius had invited him. Cornelius replied by telling him about the angel and the wondrous message. Peter then began to preach the gospel to all the people assembled there.

He talked about Jesus and His work on earth, which they had all heard something about at one time or another. The people listened expectantly. He also talked about Jesus' death and resurrection.

He wanted to tell them much more, but God interrupted as he was talking about the forgiveness of sins and the name of Jesus. The Holy Spirit came upon all the people listening to Peter. In all sorts of languages, they stood up and praised God for His love. It was just like Pentecost in Jerusalem.

The six brothers from Joppa were amazed that the gift of the Holy Spirit had been poured out over these Gentiles. But Peter cried out in delight, "Is there any reason why these people cannot be baptized with water?"

Baptized they were—all of them. Those were glorious days in Caesarea.

They were together as brothers and sisters. There was no longer any distinction between Jew and Gentile, slave and free man, oppressor and victim. They were all one in Christ.

When Peter returned to Jerusalem, the other apostles and the brothers of the congregation there had already heard about the events in Caesarea. They were disturbed that Peter had gone into the house of a Gentile and eaten with Gentiles.

Jesus had often said to His disciples that they were to go into the world to preach the gospel to *all* nations, all the way to the end of the earth. It appeared as if that had been forgotten. The apostles still saw Israel as the holy people of God, who had to be kept separate from the impure Gentiles through a wall of laws. They did not understand that those laws about purification were no longer in effect now that Jesus had purified the whole world through His death.

Peter himself could hardly understand it. Therefore he was not angry when the brothers reproached him. Calmly he told them about everything that had happened, first on the roof in Joppa and later in Caesarea. He said, "God Himself sent me there and poured out the Holy Spirit on all those people. How could I possibly oppose God in such a matter?"

Then they all understood that God had broken down the wall between Israel and the nations. Now they shared one Lord, one faith, one baptism, one Father over them all. Now Jews and Gentiles were all brothers.

How much greater and richer their work had become! It was an immense field that God was asking them to work in!

176: Peter in prison

A man lay sleeping in a dark cell. He was between two soldiers and was bound to both of them with chains.

There were more soldiers standing guard before the door of the cell. Beyond the cell door was an iron gate locked with heavy bars.

The prisoner was being heavily guarded because he had escaped once before in the middle of the night without anyone realizing it. That was ten years earlier, when he was locked up with eleven of his friends. When he made his escape, there were guards on duty and the gate was barred. That was why extra precautions had to be taken now.

It might have been safer yet to put the man to death at once. That could not be done because he had been taken prisoner during the Feast of Unleavened Bread—the Passover. That sacred feast could not be disturbed by an execution. The Jews felt strongly about this.

Now the Feast of Unleavened Bread was over. In the morning the prisoner would be tried and put to death. He would simply have to die, and he knew it himself. Even so, he slept soundly and peacefully, as if there were no danger threatening him, as if he had a long, happy life ahead of him.

This man was even more dangerous than his captors realized, for not even death could harm him. He was a child of God, and his name was *Peter*!

Another time of severe persecution had begun for the churches in Palestine. Herod Agrippa was now king over the whole land of the Jews. He was a grandson of the Herod who had murdered the babies in Bethlehem and a nephew of Herod Antipas, who murdered John the Baptist.

This third Herod was no better than the other two. He was a great hypocrite. When he was in Caesarea surrounded by Roman soldiers and officials, he celebrated the pagan feasts and never gave God a thought.

But when he was in Jerusalem, he went to the temple and acted pious and offered great sacrifices to God in order to win honor from the Jews. To win even more favor with the Jews, he began to persecute the disciples of Jesus.

Herod did not concern himself with human life or justice or such matters. He thought only about his own advantage.

He had James, the brother of John, put to death with the sword. When that happened, one of the sons of Salome was baptized with the baptism of Jesus and received the place in the Kingdom set aside for him by the Lord.

The church mourned the apostle's death, but the leading Jews laughed about it and praised Herod for it.

This encouraged the king, so he took Peter prisoner. He had him arrested during the Passover week. He then gave orders that four groups of guardsmen, each made up of four soldiers, were to take turns watching over him.

Escape was out of the question for Peter, for there were two heavy chains and three barred gates to contend with, to say nothing of the armed guards. Surely that would hold the simple Galilean fisherman. There seemed to be no way for Peter to be delivered from Herod's power.

Yet, there were people busy doing what they could to free him. There was a house in Jerusalem where men and women had been busy all night on his behalf. They were on their knees in prayer. All night long they prayed for Peter. That was the only thing they could do for him.

177: Peter's farewell

As Peter lay sleeping in his prison cell, chained to two armed guards, an angel of the Lord suddenly appeared in the prison. His shining presence shed light all around him.

The angel nudged Peter to wake him up. "Get up quickly," he said.

Peter obeyed, still half asleep. He did not realize what was going on. The chains fell from his wrists.

The angel said, "Put on your clothes and sandals."

Peter obeyed, but it was as if he was watching from a distance. It simply did not seem real. Then the angel said, "Wrap yourself in your cloak and follow me."

Peter obeyed. He followed like a sleepwalker. "It's a dream," he thought to himself.

Peter watched himself walking out the cell door and past the guards, who did not hold him back. When he reached the outer gate with the angel, he also saw guards posted there, but they did not seize him. In a dream anything is possible!

Then they came to an iron gate that led to the city. The gate swung open by itself. They walked along together for about a block, and then Peter suddenly found himself alone.

He stood still and raised his hands to his head. He was dizzy with confusion. Where was he? The cool night wind caressed him. The full Passover moon smiled down upon him from the dark sky. Could it be true? Or was it all a dream?

Peter broke the silence of the night and began to speak aloud. He said to himself, "Now I know for sure that the Lord sent His angel and snatched me from Herod's hand.

He saved me from the fate the Jews all had in mind for me."

To Peter it was glorious that he was allowed to live a while longer and work for Jesus. But even more glorious than his freedom, more glorious than life itself was the faithful concern of God shown in that amazing deliverance.

Calmly Peter considered what he should do. He could not stay in the city, for as soon as his escape was discovered, soldiers would be out looking for him. Before he left, however, he wanted to go to his friends to say goodbye.

"I'll go to Mary's house," thought Peter. The brothers and sisters often gathered in the home of Mary, the mother of John Mark.

Soon he was standing at the outer door of the house. His knock was a hollow sound in the stillness of the night.

Inside the house the followers of Jesus were still on their knees in prayer. The knock frightened them. Had the soldiers of Herod come to take them prisoner?

A servant girl named Rhoda was sent to the door to see who it was. When she recognized Peter's voice, she was so happy that she forgot to open the outer door. Instead she ran back to the others and cried out that Peter was waiting outside. It really was Peter!

All that night those men and women had been praying for Peter's release. Yet, now that God answered their prayer in such a speedy and glorious way, they did not dare believe it was true.

"You're out of your mind!" they told

Rhoda. But the girl continued to insist it was true.

"It's his angel," they said then. Peter continued to knock. When they finally opened the door to let him in, they saw him standing there looking just as healthy and happy as if he were coming in from a walk in the cool evening air.

Rejoicing and thanking God, they surrounded him eagerly. They peppered him with questions.

With a wave of the hand Peter instructed them to be silent. Then he told them how the Lord had delivered him from prison.

"But now I must flee," he said. "Tell James, the brother of the Lord, what happened, and tell the others too."

That same night Peter hurried away. He was a fugitive, but he had a powerful protector.

178: Herod Agrippa

When day dawned, there was a great uproar in the prison. The two soldiers in Peter's cell woke up with chains on their wrists, but the place between them was empty.

What had happened to Peter? How could he possibly have disappeared without a trace?

When Herod heard that Peter had escaped, he was beside himself with rage. He sent out his men to look for Peter all over the city, but their efforts were in vain. He questioned the guards carefully, but it did no good. He did not get his prisoner back.

He finally vented his wrath by executing the guards instead of Peter. Then he went back to Caesarea, where joyous feasts and games awaited him. His quiet fear at the miraculous disappearance of the apostle would not soon go away.

There was not much time left for Herod to enjoy his sinful way of life. He had shed the blood of God's children, which is precious in God's eyes. Before he had the chance to persecute the church any more, he was struck by God's wrath.

One day a great feast was held in the huge amphitheater in Caesarea. Thousands of people were present. Herod Agrippa sat proudly on his throne. Before him were emissaries from Tyre and Sidon, bowing low.

The emissaries brought lavish gifts to the king to thank him for not making war on them, as he had intended to. The men of Tyre and Sidon were very happy about this, for they were not warriors by nature. They were merchants and they bought their grain in Herod's land. Herod was enjoying himself greatly, for now all the people could see how much he was honored and feared.

Herod stood up and addressed the men of Sidon and Tyre. The sunlight reflected off his beautiful garment, which included silver threads in its weave. His voice resounded over the heads of the thousands of people assembled in the amphitheater. When he was finished speaking, the people all cried out to him enthusiastically, "The voice of a god and not a man!"

All of this happened in Caesarea, where Cornelius had once kneeled before Peter. Peter had rejected the honors offered him, but Herod delighted in being honored as if he were a god. He thanked the people with a gracious smile.

Then his face suddenly turned somber. He doubled over in pain. An angel of the Lord had come down unseen and struck the king.

When an angel came to Peter, it was to deliver him from prison. But to Herod the angel brought a horrible disease. Herod had gone wrong by failing to honor God. He was consumed by worms and died in intense pain after a few days.

That was the end of the king who had unleashed such cruel persecution on the church. It was also the end of his kingdom. The kingdom was divided after his death. But the Kingdom of God, the Kingdom he had tried to destroy, continued to grow.

179: Barnabas and Paul

It had been eight years since Saul's return to Tarsus, the town of his birth. Jesus had sent him out of Jerusalem, where his life was in danger. The Jews had refused to listen to Saul. "Go away now," Jesus told Saul. "I shall send you far away to the Gentiles."

All the years since then, Saul had waited for his Master to call him.

The waiting was very hard on him. But Saul knew that the Savior would not forget about him. His faith did not forsake him. Every day his desire to become an apostle of Jesus grew.

One day Saul saw a familiar figure approaching. Who was that man with the friendly eyes and outstretched arms?

"Barnabas!" he cried out in delight as he hurried toward him. It really was Barnabas, his friend. Barnabas was the one who had felt sorry for Saul in Jerusalem years before; he was the only one who trusted Saul at the time.

It was a glorious reunion for Saul after all those years of isolation in Tarsus. The message Barnabas brought was even more

glorious. It was the message Saul had awaited for a long time: Saul was being called to the work that Jesus had in mind for him.

Barnabas had come from Antioch, the capital city of Syria. Antioch was a great city of trade between Tarsus and Palestine. In the year that Stephen was stoned, certain refugees had fled to Antioch. Saul himself had driven them there. They had told the Gentiles in Antioch about the Lord Jesus. God blessed their work richly, and a large church arose in that city.

When the apostles in Jerusalem heard about the events in Antioch, they sent Barnabas to labor there. The work was too much for him alone. Therefore Barnabas turned to Saul for help. Saul would be a better choice than one of the apostles in Jerusalem, for he had grown up in a Gentile city.

There was nothing Saul wanted more. Quickly he went back with Barnabas, leaving his city, his family, his home, and his possessions behind. Everything that one might regard as gain he counted as loss for Christ's sake.

Saul and Barnabas worked side by side for a whole year in Antioch. They met the congregation and taught the people. The number of believers kept growing. It was in Antioch that the believers were first called *Christians*.

After a year, Saul and Barnabas made a journey together to Jerusalem. There was a great famine in the land at the time. Agabus, a prophet in Antioch had foretold it.

The believers in Judea were suffering as a result of the famine. Because of the great love in their hearts, the brothers there had sold their houses and fields and had given the money to the poor. Now they were in need themselves. In Antioch a collection was held for their relief. Barnabas and Saul brought the money to Jerusalem and presented it to the leaders of the congregation there.

This happened in the year of great persecution by Herod Agrippa. In those frightening days, the love of the brothers in Antioch was a rich comfort to the church in Jerusalem. Bearing thanks from the Christians in Judea, Barnabas and Saul set out for Antioch again.

They had come as a twosome, but there were three of them on the trip back. Accompanying them was John Mark, the son of Mary, who was a cousin of Barnabas. Mark was allowed to help Saul and Barnabas with their glorious but difficult work.

Something very beautiful happened back in Antioch. Jesus spoke through the Holy Spirit to the prophets and teachers of the congregation. He declared that Barnabas

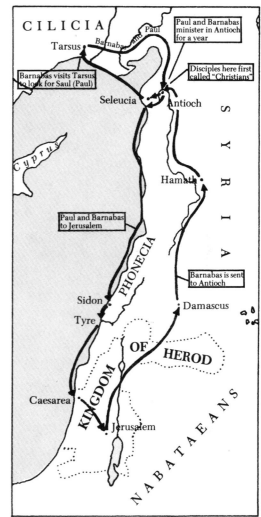

THE MISSION ACTIVITY OF BARNABAS AND SAUL.

and Saul were to be set aside for work among the Gentiles.

It was not easy for the congregation to give up Saul and Barnabas. But because no sacrifice made for Jesus is too great, they obeyed at once.

First they prayed with Saul and Barnabas. Then they wished them God's blessing and said goodbye to them. John Mark went along as their helper.

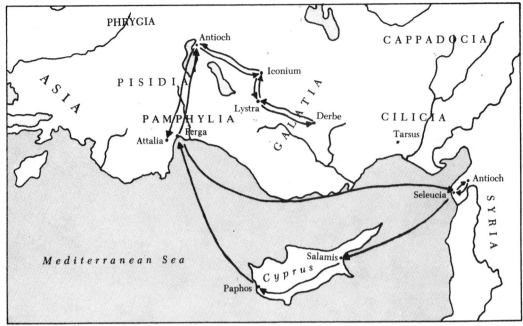

THE FIRST MISSIONARY JOURNEY OF PAUL.

Off went Saul and Barnabas into the wide, wide world. They could not possibly lose their way, for the Spirit of God had sent them out and would lead them.

The great Roman empire lay open before them. From then on Saul was known by his Roman name, *Paul*, which means *the little one*.

His zeal and his faith were great. Great, too, was his gratitude. Now, at last, he could begin the work to which the Savior had called him ten years before.

180: Cyprus

From Antioch Paul and Barnabas followed the river to the coast of the Mediterranean Sea. This brought them to Seleucia, a port city.

Far across the sea they could see some land. It was a large island—Cyprus, the birthplace of Barnabas, the land of copper mines. They set sail for this island.

They arrived in Salamis, a great city of trade. There they proclaimed the Word of God in the Jewish synagogues. There were thousands of Jews in Cyprus.

They worked their way across the entire island, from east to west. They passed through some beautiful hill country, with woods of slender, swaying cypresses. They wound up at Paphos, where the Roman governor had his residence.

The governor was Sergius Paulus. He was a sensible, friendly man. He had heard about the God of the Jews and did his best to learn more about Him. But he listened to the wrong teacher.

There was a certain Jew in Cyprus who *knew* God but did not *love* Him. He was a wicked man, a false prophet. He told people he was *Elymas*, that is, a magician, a sorcerer. He tried to become rich by means of all sorts of strange arts and tricks.

His name was Bar-Jesus—son of Jesus. He was not a true child of Jesus Christ. He opposed Paul and Barnabas with all his might.

The governor had heard of their coming, and he had his servants summon them, for he wanted to hear God's Word. He wanted to hear what they had been preaching in the city.

When they reached the palace, Bar-Jesus was there too. He stood next to the governor with a proud smile on his face. When *they* began talking about Jesus, *he* contradicted them and tried to make fun of them. He wanted to keep the governor from believing. He realized that if the governor became a Christian, there would be no place for Bar-Jesus and his magic.

Paul and Barnabas showed a great deal of patience with this godless man. Yet, it was impossible for them to bring the gospel as long as he kept interrupting.

A holy indignation flared up in Paul. He looked at the sorcerer with eyes burning with anger and said, "You son of the devil, full of all manner of deceit and evil! You enemy of all righteousness! Will you never stop perverting the right ways of the Lord? Behold, the hand of the Lord is against you. You will be blind for a while and will not see the sun."

Suddenly the proud smile disappeared from the face of Bar-Jesus. There he stood—frightened, trembling, blinking. He saw nothing; darkness had come over him. He groped around and looked for someone to lead him by the hand. Finally some servants took pity on him.

All his learning and magical tricks now did Bar-Jesus no good, for they could not give him back his sight.

Perhaps God would restore his sight in time. It was not Paul who had stricken him with this punishment. Paul had only spoken the words that the Holy Spirit had given him to say. The blindness that struck Bar-Jesus was a divine punishment that might still bring salvation to his blinded soul. Many years before, Paul had learned to pray while he was blind.

Sergius Paulus, the governor, was touched by the power of Jesus and became a Christian. When Paul and his companions traveled farther, they left a happy man behind them.

181: Antioch of Pisidia

At Paphos Paul and Barnabas climbed in a boat and sailed to the coast of Asia Minor. They traveled inland until they came to Perga, a city in a hot, swampy plain.

Paul and Barnabas did not stay there long. They wanted to go farther inland. But John Mark did not go with them. Was he afraid of the dangers in the desolate, lonely hill country, or was he homesick?

Mark simply gave up at that point and returned to Jerusalem alone. But the other two did not let danger or exhaustion hold them back. They pressed on into mountainous country. For days they walked along almost impassable paths and skirted deep ravines. Far below them raged mountain rivers. That lonely area was inhabited only by half-civilized raiders. Paul and Barnabas arrived safely at their destination—Antioch, a fortified city on a plateau. Antioch was a stronghold on the great Roman military highway that cut through Asia Minor from east to west. This city, in the area known as Pisidia, had the same name as the city from which the two had been sent out.

On the sabbath day they entered the synagogue and preached the gospel to the Jews and the God-fearing Gentiles who worshiped with them. The people in the synagogue listened carefully and were amazed at what they heard—especially the Gentiles. They even asked Paul and Barnabas to talk about Jesus again on the following sabbath.

Many people followed the two preachers to the house where they were staying. There, too, Paul and Barnabas talked to them.

During the week, the people who had heard about Jesus passed the word on to others. When the sabbath came, almost the whole city was present to hear the Word of God.

That day it became clear that the Jews of Antioch, too, would reject Jesus. When they saw all those excited people listening to Paul and Barnabas, they were filled with jealousy. They could not stand the thought of all the influence that the two men were gaining. A Messiah who came for Gentiles as well as Jews could not be the true Messiah, according to them.

Therefore they did everything in their power to oppose Paul and Barnabas. They contradicted them and slandered them.

Paul and Barnabas stood up to those proud Jews and said, "It is necessary that the Word of God be preached to you first. Now that you reject it and do not consider yourselves worthy of eternal life, we will turn to the Gentiles. God has commanded us to be a light to the Gentiles."

When the Gentiles heard that, they rejoiced. All who were destined for eternal life believed, and the Word of the Lord spread throughout the land. Soon there was a church in Antioch, a circle of happy people that grew daily.

The hatred and enmity of the Jews also grew daily. The Jews incited important women in the city against the two preachers. They also brought accusations of all sorts against them to the city council. They even managed to have Paul and Barnabas banned from the city.

The church was left without teachers and was surrounded by enemies. But the new Christians did not mourn or give up hope. On the contrary, they were filled with joy, for God sent them the Holy Spirit. The Spirit would lead them and help them remain faithful. This was even more important than having an apostle in their midst.

Paul and Barnabas did not mourn either when they were expelled from Antioch. Their Master had foretold that they would be scorned and persecuted for His sake. They shook the dust from their feet as a judgment against the Jews and set out for another city.

This time they went east down the great highway. In a few days they came to Iconium. There they preached for a long time. A great many came to faith during their stay in Iconium.

Here, too, the Jews hated the apostles and opposed them. The Jews fought against them so fiercely that Paul and Barnabas fled to avoid being stoned. By the time they moved on, there was a church in Iconium.

182: Lystra and Derbe

Paul and Barnabas traveled from Iconium to Lystra, a small heathen city in the hill country. The weary preachers found a statue of Zeus or Jupiter, the supreme god of the Greeks, in front of the city gate.

They preached the gospel in the streets and the market. Here, too, people repented and became disciples of Jesus.

There was a man in Lystra who had been lame in both legs since he was born. This man sat listening to Paul breathlessly and never took his eyes off him. For the first time in his life he was hearing about Jesus—about His love and power and about the miracles He performed. His eyes shone with joy and hope.

Paul looked at the man carefully. He could tell that the man had the faith needed to find healing. Therefore he interrupted his own sermon and suddenly said to him, "Stand upright on your feet."

The man obeyed! He did not hesitate for a moment. He stood straight up and started walking back and forth, even though he had never walked a step in his life!

The people broke out in joyful praise and cried out to each other, "The gods have come down to us in human form." Barnabas, they decided, was Zeus, and Paul was Hermes, his messenger and helper, for Paul was the one who did the talking. But Paul and Barnabas did not understand what the people were saying. The people were talking to each other, but in their local language, not in Greek.

Soon a heathen priest arrived. His helpers brought oxen with garlands, but Paul and Barnabas still did not understand.

When they finally figured out that the people intended to offer sacrifices, they were horrified. They tore their clothes in mourning, interrupted the people in their activity, and cried out, "What in the world are you doing? We are only frail human beings, just as you are. What we are telling you is that you must turn away from these useless practices to the living God who made heaven and earth."

They needed all their eloquence to restrain those pagans. The people were so enthusiastic about Paul and Barnabas that they wanted to offer them a sacrifice right then and there.

Finally they gave up, reluctantly. They were deeply disappointed. They wanted so much to believe that some gods from heaven had descended to be in their midst!

The Jews from Antioch and Iconium made use of this feeling of disappointment. With evil intentions in their hearts, they had followed the two preachers. In this city they suddenly seized on their opportunity: they stirred up the people against Paul and Barnabas.

It worked all too well. Together with a band of pagans, the Jews attacked Paul. They stoned him and dragged his bleeding body out of the city. They threw his body down among the rocks, believing he was dead.

But when they were satisfied and went away, some Christians in Lystra came out to the spot where the apostle's wounded body lay. When Paul opened his eyes, he was among friends. God had preserved him in a miraculous way. He was even able to get to his feet and go back into the city with them. The next day he went on with Barnabas to Derbe, just as if nothing had happened.

In Derbe, a mountain town even smaller than Lystra, they worked quietly for a while. Their work was richly blessed.

Paul was met with great love by the Christians there. After all the hatred and enmity he had encountered, that must have been a rich comfort for him.

He was close to his birthplace of Tarsus again, and the brothers in the Syrian city of Antioch were not far away. But Paul was not thinking of himself. Neither was Barnabas.

They traveled back along a much longer and more difficult route than the one they had taken to get there. They wanted to visit the young congregation they had established. They wanted to strengthen the believers and urge them to cling to the faith even in the face of the persecution that would probably come.

Bravely they went back to Lystra, where Paul had been stoned. They also went back to Iconium, the city from which they had fled, and to Antioch, the city from which they were banned.

In all those churches they appointed elders to lead the congregations and give instruction. With prayer and fasting they committed those churches to the Lord. Then they descended from the hill country and went on to Perga, where they also preached. From there they returned to Antioch of Syria by boat.

It was a happy day when they were safely reunited with the brothers in Antioch. It was time for a well-deserved holiday. God had gloriously opened the door of faith for many, many Gentiles.

183: Disagreements

Paul and Barnabas did not get much chance to rest. Shortly after their return, the congregation at Antioch sent them to Jerusalem, along with some other brothers. There they were to discuss a few things with the apostles and elders.

Some difficulties had arisen in Antioch. Certain Jewish Christians from Judea looked down on the Gentile Christians, believing themselves to be better and more pious. *They* were the children of God's people, the Jewish people. *They* faithfully observed Moses' laws, believing that anyone who did not observe those laws could never enter heaven.

This matter was discussed at a meeting of the apostles in Jerusalem. When differences of opinion were expressed, Peter addressed all the people present. Peter had earlier looked down on the Gentiles as unclean people. He had learned that they are God's children just as he was, once God purifies their hearts through faith.

In this meeting Peter made it clear that God does not recognize any division between Jewish and Gentile believers. Therefore no one else was to do so either.

James, the brother of the Lord, spoke in Peter's support. After that the apostles wrote a letter to the church in Antioch. They said that the Gentile believers were not required to bear the heavy yoke that no Jew had been able to bear. All that was required of them was that they lead pure, holy lives.

When this letter was read aloud in Antioch, the congregation rejoiced. Now they all knew it: only through faith are we saved, only through the grace of Jesus Christ. It does not matter whether or not you are a member of God's chosen nation, the Jews.

Paul stayed in Antioch for a while, preaching and teaching. There was no rest for him anymore. His heart was with the brothers and sisters in the young churches established during his missionary tour. Therefore he suggested to Barnabas that they make another journey together.

Barnabas again wanted to take his nephew, John Mark, but Paul was opposed to this suggestion. Mark had deserted them the last time just when the journey became dangerous. That was before the work had begun. Anyone who traveled with Paul had to be fearless in the face of danger and willing to go through the fire for Jesus. Paul was not prepared to give Mark another chance.

Barnabas, the son of comfort, who hated to disappoint anyone, did not want to leave his nephew behind. Paul was firm, and so was Barnabas. Finally the two parted company, both of them embittered. They had loved each other as brothers and had gone through a great deal of pain and suffering together. Yet, they went their separate ways.

Barnabas took Mark with him and set out for Cyprus, the land of his birth. Paul found a new travel companion in Silas, a faithful disciple of Jesus. Silas was a prophet who had come to Antioch with Paul after the meeting in Jerusalem.

Later the trouble between Paul and Barnabas was cleared up completely. In his letters Paul writes about Mark with great appreciation, saying that Mark was a great help to him (Col. 4:10; II Tim. 4:11).

Wherever the love of Jesus is present, there is no place for continuing bitterness.

184: On to Macedonia

Paul, the fiery preacher who had little patience with doubt and hesitation, set out courageously into the world again. He was a battler, a world conqueror, a soldier for Jesus.

The Word of God was his sword, and faith was the shield he used to repel all satan's attacks. Truth was his girdle, and the righteousness of Christ was the helmet that allowed him to feel safe. His burning wish to bring the gospel to all people made his feet feel light.

Accompanied by Silas, Paul headed north through the dark forests of Syria. Then they turned west, passing through dangerous mountain passes.

Soon they arrived in Derbe, where the people had shown Paul great love. He was greeted with great joy.

They also went to Lystra, where Paul had been left for dead outside the city after he was stoned. That time Lystra had almost taken away one of God's servants, but now it produced a servant for the Lord. There was a young man named Timothy living in Lystra. He was the son of a Jewish woman and a Greek man. Timothy loved the Lord very much.

His grandmother, a pious woman named Lois, had told him about God. His mother Eunice, who was also a believer, had taught him to serve Jesus. Lois gave her permission gladly when Paul asked if he could take Timothy along on his travels.

Paul, Silas and Timothy traveled on together. They went from one place to another.

It became clear that God was charting their course. They wanted to go west, to the great commercial center of Ephesus, but the Holy Spirit hindered them. Then they went north, hoping to preach the gospel in Bithynia, but the Spirit of Jesus would not permit that either.

Paul and his travel companions did not understand it, but they submitted obediently to God's will. They traveled through all of Asia Minor until they came to Troas. They could go no farther, for Troas was on the seacoast. On the far side of the sea lay Europe, that mighty heathen continent.

Alexander the Great had landed at Troas when he set out to conquer much of the world's territory. Troas was also the location of the ruins of Troy, that strong city of Achilles.

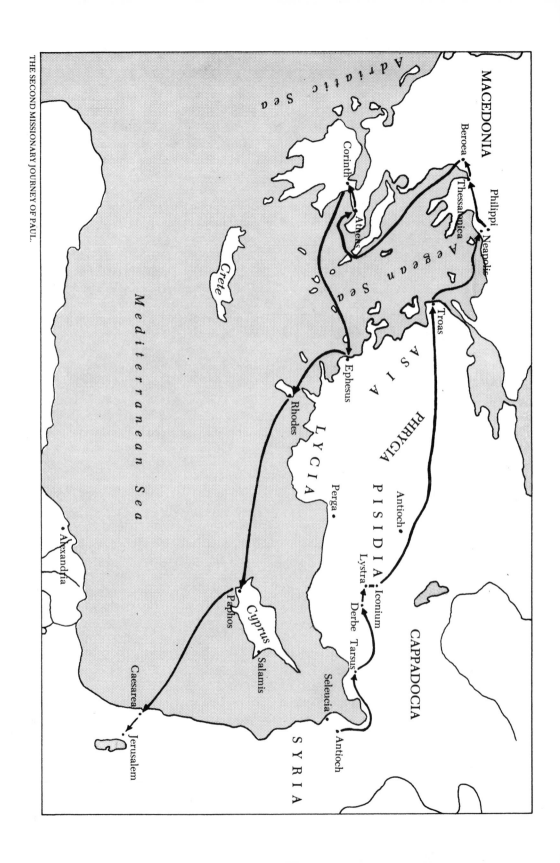

Now three emissaries of the Prince of Peace stood in Troas. Although that Prince was bent on conquering the entire world, His emissaries did not know where to go.

That night Paul had an amazing dream. He was standing on the coast looking at the land beyond the sea, the land of Macedonia, where Europe began. He saw a man with arms outstretched toward him. The man was crying out, "Come over to Macedonia and help us!"

When Paul told his companions about this dream, they finally understood why God had led them there. That morning they went to the harbor and got into a boat sailing for Macedonia.

Now there was a fourth member of their party. Luke, a physician who loved the Lord and had become Paul's faithful friend, joined them. Luke and Paul remained fast friends right to the end.

The ship had a strong wind at its back and moved quickly through the water. Seldom had Paul and his friends made such rapid progress on a journey. In only two days the ship entered the harbor of Neapolis, where the four travelers disembarked. They went immediately to Philippi, the most important city in Macedonia.

Philippi was a Roman colony with very few Jews. It didn't even have a synagogue. But there was a place of prayer just outside the city, an enclosed area by the river.

Paul and his companions went there on the sabbath. They found only a few women there, and they preached the gospel to them.

Among them was a Gentile woman named Lydia from the city of Thyatira. She was a seller of purple cloth. This woman listened especially carefully, for she revered the God of Israel. The Lord opened her heart so that it was filled with joy and gratitude when she heard the wondrous message of Jesus' love for sinners.

Lydia believed and was baptized, along with all who were in her household. Then she invited Paul and his companions to stay at her house.

Paul wanted to decline the invitation, for he did not wish to be a burden on anyone. He preferred to earn his keep with his own hands. But Lydia urged him, saying, "If you really believe that I am faithful to the Lord, come and stay at my house."

Paul and his companions could no longer refuse. From that time on, the shining purple garments were not the most beautiful thing that issued from Lydia's house. More beautiful by far was the joyous message that Jesus washes us whiter than snow, even if our sins are like scarlet or as dark as the deepest purple.

The conversion of Lydia's household was only a beginning. In time that household became the very first church on the continent of Europe.

185: Servants of the Most High God

An amazing woman walked through the city with a strange look in her eyes. She wandered around freely and did not hurt anyone, but it was clear to all who watched her that she was not like other people.

This woman had no power over her own thoughts, for an evil spirit had taken possession of her. She was the slave of a couple of men in Philippi and was free in neither body nor soul. Her masters did not bring any accusations against her. In fact, they were happy about her misfortune, for they used her as a soothsayer. People came to her to find out about their future.

The spirit that controlled her gave her the words to say. Her masters would then pocket the money that superstitious people paid for her services. In this way the poor woman brought in quite a bit of money for her masters, who became rich through her misery.

As this poor woman walked through the streets one day, she saw four men approaching. They were earnest men with friendly, calm eyes. They were the four emissaries of Jesus—Paul, Silas, Luke, and Timothy. The people of Philippi did not know who the four men were, but the woman knew. She stood still and watched them.

She began to follow Paul and his companions, crying out, "These men are servants of the Most High God. They are here to proclaim the way of salvation!" The evil spirit within her made her shout these words.

After that the woman followed Paul and his companions every day as they walked through the city. She fixed those strange eyes of hers on them and shouted her message aloud.

The evil spirit was trying to thwart Jesus' work in Philippi. Paul understood this. For days he patiently put up with the woman's outcry, but at last it distressed him so much that he felt he *had* to do something.

He did not rebuke the slave, for it was not the poor woman's fault. He rebuked the evil spirit, saying, "In the name of Jesus Christ, I command you to come out of her."

At that moment the woman was healed. Her eyes returned to normal and became just as calm as anyone else's eyes. There was great joy in those eyes now, for the woman had been delivered from her horrible slavery.

Yet, she was still a slave to her masters.

When they found out what had happened to her, they were not happy about it, for they did not care about the woman's happiness. When they realized that she could no longer make money foretelling the future, they became very angry.

They summoned all their friends and went out to seize Paul and Silas. They took them to the market to confront the Roman authorities. They did not say anything about the slave, for Paul and Silas could hardly be punished for healing the poor woman. Instead they brought all kinds of evil accusations against them.

"These men have thrown our city into an uproar," they declared. "They are Jews and are teaching the people wicked things."

That was the worst accusation possible, for there was nothing the authorities feared so much as an uproar among the people. The Jews were hated and had even been banned from Rome by the emperor.

An angry crowd began to gather at the marketplace. The leaders tore the clothes from Paul and Silas and had them bound to a pole. They didn't even want to listen to what the two men had to say; no hearing was needed. Instead they would whip them. The cutting lash seared the air and produced ugly welts on the backs of the two men.

It was frightful punishment. After many lashes the two men were dragged away to prison. The jailer was given strict instructions to watch over them carefully.

He locked them up in the innermost cell, a dark, damp chamber from which they could not possibly escape. Then he put their feet in stocks, a heavy wooden beam with holes into which their ankles just fit.

The door of the cell slammed shut. The heavy bars were put in place. There was no more work possible for Paul and Silas. It looked as if satan might win a victory in Philippi.

186: The Philippian jailer

It was completely dark in the cell. Paul and Silas could see nothing, but they felt burning pains in their backs. Their clothes were matted to their skin by their blood. Their ankles were trapped in the heavy stocks, and their wrists had chains on them.

Paul and Silas knew for whose sake they had to suffer all this. They thought about Jesus, their Master, who had suffered infinitely more for them. They raised their eyes in the darkness and prayed that *His* eyes would see them in their dark cell.

Their hearts were filled with peace and joy. Right then, in the middle of the night, they began singing a psalm of praise to God, who had chosen them as worthy of such suffering. The two powerful male voices resounded through the dark hallways and cells. Other prisoners raised their heads in surprise and listened breathlessly.

The song almost seemed magic, for the walls began to shake. The walls trembled on their foundations; they tottered, and then tore wide open under the force of an earthquake. All the doors sprang from their hinges and stood open. Through a divine miracle, all the chains shook free. Nothing held the prisoners back.

The jailer was also awakened. By the light of the stars he could see the doors standing open. He assumed that all the prisoners had escaped. A deathly fear gripped him! Surely all was lost for him. He would receive some horrible punishment for failing to prevent the escape. He became so afraid that he drew his sword to kill himself in his despair.

Just then Paul cried out, "Do yourself no harm, for we are all here."

The jailer could hardly believe it. He took a light and went into the prison.

He was trembling when he fell down before Paul and Silas. He led them outside where they would be safe from collapsing walls and ceilings. His fear and awe were so great that he did not know what to do. How could he possibly escape heavenly punishment for imprisoning and harming these men? Hadn't the slave woman cried out that these men were proclaiming the way of salvation?

He stammered, "Men, what must I do to be saved?"

They replied, "Put your trust in the Lord Jesus Christ, and you will be saved—you and your house."

Right then and there, in the middle of the night, in the inner court of the prison, Paul and Silas preached the gospel to the jailer and his household. Seldom had anyone listened to them so carefully.

God opened the hearts of these people. That same night they believed and were baptized. The jailer took Paul and Silas to his house and washed their wounds to ease the pain. Then he set the table for them and placed food and drink before them. He rejoiced that he and his whole household had come to believe in God.

When it was day, the leaders sent their servants to the prison with a message. It may be that the earthquake had also shaken them up. In any event, they now realized that the accusations made against Paul and Silas were false.

The servants told the jailer that he could free the two men. The jailer brought the news to Paul. "You're free!" he cried out. "Go your way and leave this place in peace."

Paul shook his head resolutely. The rulers of the city had subjected Paul and Silas to unjust treatment. Now they would find out that they could not simply do as they pleased with the two men.

The lesson was also important for the believers in Philippi, for Lydia and others who might be subject to persecution soon. Paul said, "Although we are Roman citizens, we were whipped in public without a hearing and then put in prison. Do they now suppose we'll go away quietly? Not on your life! Let them come and escort us out of the city!"

When the leaders heard that, they were frightened. Were those two Jews Roman citizens? To chain a Roman citizen was a serious offense, and to whip him was a crime that could be punished with death!

Trembling with fear, the rulers hurried to the prison. They offered very polite apologies and asked humbly if the two men would be so kind as to leave the city.

Paul and Silas did so. Before they left, they said goodbye to Lydia and the other Christians. And they left Luke, the physician, in Philippi to lead the young congregation. Paul, Silas and Timothy then traveled on into the wide, wide world.

187: On to Athens

Paul was wandering through Athens, the world-famous capital city of Greece, the city of artists and philosophers.

He was alone. Silas and Timothy had accompanied him from Philippi to Thessalonica, a great commercial center in Macedonia. Their labors there had met with great reward, especially among the Gentiles.

It had been a difficult time. They had worked day and night to earn their keep, for they did not want to be a burden on anyone. Often they did not have enough to eat.

Fortunately, the congregation in Philippi had twice sent money to Paul. Paul never forgot the love that the Philippian Christians manifested in that deed.

Courageously they had gone on with the work, and in time there arose a large church in Thessalonica. But there were also Jews who worked against Paul and tried to thwart everything he did in Thessalonica. Their enmity became so fierce that Paul had fled during the night with his friends.

The three had then gone to Beroea, a city at the foot of Mount Olympus. There they had preached in the synagogue of the Jews.

The Jews of Beroea were not like the Jews of Thessalonica. They were quite willing to accept the Word of God. Many Jews and Gentiles believed.

When the Thessalonian Jews found out that Paul was preaching the Word of God in Beroea, they had gone there to stir up the people and alarm them. The believers then decided that Paul should leave at once. Some of the brothers had accompanied him to the seashore and had gone on to Athens with him. But Silas and Timothy stayed behind in Beroea to continue the work there.

Now that Paul was in Athens, he missed Silas and Timothy. He told the brothers who were going back to Beroea that his two companions were to join him in Athens as soon as possible. But their work came first. As long as the church in Beroea needed them, Paul was willing to be on his own.

Paul wandered through Athens and gazed on the indescribable beauty of the city. He admired the beautiful houses of the rich with their luxurious gardens, the marble temples high on the hills, the theaters, the baths, and the beautiful buildings with their exquisite carved figures.

Paul wandered among all these treasures of art and wisdom, and no one paid any attention to him. Yet the treasure he bore with him was of much greater value than all the wealth around him.

As he walked through the city along streets and across squares, he saw that Athens was full of idols. Zeus and Hermes, Aphrodite and Apollo—they all had their images and altars. Towering high over all of them, on the Acropolis, the highest hill, stood a huge bronze image of Athena, the goddess of wisdom and the protector of the city.

The Athenians must have been afraid that they had somehow overlooked one of the gods. Because the wrath of that god would then surely be aroused, they had erected an altar without an image. The inscription on the altar read: "To an unknown god."

188: Foolishness to the Greeks

Paul felt very sorry for the Athenians when he came upon the altar dedicated to an unknown god. The Athenians were known the world over for their wisdom, but they did not possess the wisdom that comes from God. What good would all their beauty and wealth do if they did not possess true happiness? What the Athenians needed was the message of Jesus' love!

Paul could not keep silent about that message any longer. His heart burned with a desire to bring the gospel to the heathen city of Athens. He had already preached in the synagogue. Now he went to the marketplace and stood there talking about Jesus day after day.

Athens was not first of all a commercial center. Therefore there was not much buying and selling going on at the marketplace. It was a calm, peaceful square in the middle of the city. People came there more often with wisdom to offer than with goods to sell. All who had something to say to the people and all who didn't know what to do with their time came to the market square. The philosophers came there with their disciples too. They all surrounded Paul, for his words were beginning to draw their attention.

There stood the Epicureans with their round faces. They taught that a man should enjoy life as much as possible, for death is the end of everything. "Eat, drink, and be merry, for tomorrow we die."

The Stoics were there too, with their cold, proud eyes. They taught that, to be happy, a man should elevate himself above all joy and pain. It was best to have a heart of stone, for there was no merciful god. One had to be prepared to accept whatever came in life.

All those people listened to Paul, but they did not show much faith. "What is this wise guy trying to tell us?" some of them asked scornfully.

Others said, "He seems to be a preacher of foreign gods."

They took Paul up some high marble steps to a great square at the top of a hill. That square was known as the Areopagus. There they asked him to explain his new teaching to them.

They did not make this request out of an earnest desire for the truth. Their request came not from faith but from curiosity. All they were really interested in was hearing something new.

Paul then preached the gospel to all those curious people. He struck a calm, simple pose as he stood in the middle of that great marble plain and said to all those beautifully clothed Athenians, "Men of Athens, I can tell from looking around your city that, in every way, you show great respect for the gods. When I walked through your city and looked at your objects of worship, I even found an altar with the inscription: 'to an unknown god.' Now then, I will tell you about this God whom you do not know but worship anyway."

Paul then talked about the Lord of heaven and earth, who created the world. He did not offend the Greeks who listened to him. Instead he talked as if he were one of them.

Although Paul addressed the men of Athens in a friendly way, he made it clear that it was foolish and sinful to serve idols. Their own poets had already declared that man is of divine lineage and is created in God's image. How, then, could they suppose that man was an image of gold or silver or stone made by human hands? He warned them that they should repent because they would all be judged justly one day by a man whom God had awakened from the dead.

He wanted to say much more about that man—his Savior Jesus—but when he began to talk about the resurrection of the dead, he was interrupted. The Greeks began to mock him. "What nonsense!" they cried. "How could anyone rise from the dead?" They felt they were too wise and rational to believe such a thing.

But there were others who hoped they would be able to listen to Paul more often. Some of them believed and stayed close to Paul. Among them was one of the leading judges.

To the Jews the gospel was an offense, and to the Greeks it was foolishness. Yet, those who believed received eternal joy through the gospel.

189: The church in Corinth

Paul did not stay in Athens for long. He traveled farther through Greece on his own and came to Corinth.

Corinth was one of the biggest ports in the world, a city of more than half a million people. It was a horrible, godless city, famous for the wicked life led by the people there. Paul wanted to tell those people about Jesus, who was crucified for sinners. He decided to bring the gospel there in a very simple way, not in a long, beautiful speech, as he had in Athens.

First Paul had to see to his own support. He picked up his old trade of tent-making and began to work with his hands. Soon he found some friends in Corinth. Among them were a Jewish man and his wife. They had just come from Italy because Claudius, the emperor, had decreed that all Jews were to leave Rome.

The man's name was Aquila, and his good wife was Priscilla. They were tent-makers, just as Paul was. In that large, strange city, the three tent-makers lived together in one household. They worked together every day and talked about their Master often.

When the sabbath came, their workshop was closed. On the sabbath they always went to the synagogue. Through Paul's preaching many Jews and Greeks came to believe.

It was a glorious day for Paul when Silas and Timothy rejoined him. They had a lot of good news for him, but also something sad. The church in Thessalonica was being persecuted and was having a hard time. When Paul heard that, he immediately wrote a letter to the Thessalonians. In that letter he offered them comfort and gave them some good advice.

Now that Silas and Timothy were with him again, Paul stopped making tents. He devoted himself completely to his preaching, with even greater zeal and joy.

When it became impossible for him to preach in the synagogue because of the opposition of the Jews, he began preaching in a house right next to the synagogue. It was the house of Justus, a man who feared God. From then on the congregation gathered in that house to listen to Paul's words.

Before long something beautiful happened: Crispus, the ruler of the synagogue, came to believe in the Lord and joined the congregation worshiping in the home of Justus. Naturally, he was deposed as ruler of the synagogue, but he did not mind suffering loss for Christ's sake.

From then on this Jewish leader sat among the Gentiles of Corinth. He sat among the dock workers and merchant women and all sorts of people who had earlier led sinful lives. All these people praised the Lord together.

Crispus preached too, for he could not remain silent about his happiness. Many who heard him believed and were baptized.

It was a glorious time in Corinth! The opposition and hatred from the synagogue did not damage the new church.

God spoke to Paul in the night: "Do not be afraid. Speak, and do not be silent. Because *I* am with you, no one will harm you. Many people in this city belong to Me." It soon became clear that the Lord would not forget this promise.

190: Back to Antioch

In time there was a new governor in Corinth. The Jews who watched Paul's every move saw their opportunity and seized it, turning against him as one man. They brought him before the new governor and said, "This man is trying to persuade people to worship God in an unlawful way."

But Gallio—that was the governor's name—looked down at them proudly and didn't even want to listen to them. He was a Stoic, a brother of the great philosopher Seneca, and he despised those troublesome Jews with all their mysterious laws.

Paul did not feel that it was necessary to defend himself. Gallio said, "If you Jews came to me about some specific misdeed committed by this man, I would listen to you. But if it's some dispute about *your* law, you'd better settle it yourselves. I don't want to be a judge over such things." Then he sent them away from his seat of judgment.

Meanwhile, many Greeks had come to listen to the accusation. They hated the Jews and attacked them. They seized Sosthenes, the new ruler of the synagogue, and beat him right before the governor's eyes. Gallio watched with a proud smile on his face. It didn't concern him in the least.

In Corinth, then, the opposition of the Jews came to nothing. The congregation was safe from their hatred.

Paul stayed in Corinth for a year and a half. During that time he wrote a second letter to the Thessalonians, and he probably also wrote his letter to the Galatians. Galatia was the area in which Derbe and Lystra lay, the area in which Timothy had grown up.

Finally Paul said farewell to the congregation in Corinth. He boarded a ship for the journey home, and Priscilla and Aquila went with him.

The ship stopped in Ephesus for a while, so Paul spent a few days in that city. That was how he reached the city that he had hoped to visit earlier in his journey. He even found time to preach in the synagogue there, and the Jews begged him to stay longer. But he did not stay, for that was impossible. "If it is God's will, I will return," he said as he departed.

Aquila and Priscilla stayed in Ephesus, where they continued their work as tent-makers and preached the gospel. But Paul sailed away and landed safely in Caesarea.

Paul had been away for three years. There was great joy among the believers in Antioch when they found Paul in their midst again. He had left an even greater trail of love and happiness behind him than on his first tour as a missionary.

191: The church in Ephesus

It was very quiet in the synagogue in Ephesus. A learned rabbi who had just arrived in the city stood before the congregation. He spoke in such a beautiful and fiery way that the people in the synagogue listened attentively.

The rabbi's name was Apollos, and he was born in Alexandria. He had studied there and knew the Scriptures well. He had heard of Jesus and His teaching while he was in Alexandria, and he believed that

Jesus was the Messiah. But he did not know anything about the suffering, death and resurrection of Jesus. The joyous message of salvation had not yet reached Alexandria.

Apollos knew of no other baptism than the baptism of John. He was just as fiery as John. He cried out to the people to repent before Jesus came as the great judge of Israel. Apollos was a powerful speaker, and the Jews of the synagogue listened to him in awe.

When the worship service was over, the rabbi found a man and a woman standing before him, two simple people who had heard him speak in the synagogue. They were tent-makers. The man's name was Aquila, and the woman with him was his wife—Priscilla. They asked politely if Apollos would be willing to come to their house and discuss his sermon with them.

The learned rabbi was not too proud to go with them to their home. No doubt he thought that these two simple people wanted to learn more from him. But when he sat down in their home, he found out quickly that *they* proposed to teach *him*. They knew much more about Jesus than he did, and they told him everything they had heard from Paul.

Apollos listened in silent wonder. Slowly his eyes began to shine with joy. It was the most beautiful day of his life, for that day he got to know God better. These simple tent-makers had taught him more than all his learned teachers.

After that Apollos was an even more fiery and powerful preacher. When his new friends told him about Corinth and all the work to be done there, he went to Corinth himself. By God's grace, Apollos's work in Corinth greatly benefited the believers there. He battled the Jews tirelessly in public and showed from the Scriptures that Jesus was the Christ.

Not long after Apollos left Ephesus, Paul arrived there. He had not forgotten his promise. After resting for only a few months in Antioch, he had set out with a few friends and traveled across Asia Minor to Ephesus.

Paul's coming signaled the beginning of a great time in Ephesus. Through the work of Aquila and Priscilla, there was already a small congregation in the city. The congregation now began to gain new members in all parts of that heathen city.

God put extraordinary powers into Paul's hands. He healed the sick in the name of Jesus and drove out evil spirits. When he laid his hands on the believers, they were filled with the Holy Spirit.

Paul had an amazing power of healing. When handkerchiefs and aprons used by Paul in his work were laid on the sick, their illnesses disappeared. This became known throughout Ephesus, and the name of Jesus was glorified. More and more people came to Paul for help. They confessed their sins, repented, and became disciples of Jesus.

Others, who possessed books of evil with magic formulas and devilish tricks, brought those books to Paul. Paul had them burned in the presence of all the people. Paul burned a great pile of these evil books, valued at about 50,000 pieces of silver. The people did not feel any poorer, for they had found true happiness in Jesus.

It was during this time that Paul wrote his first letter to the congregation in Corinth. He had heard that there were difficulties there. He had received a letter from the congregation with all sorts of questions to which he had to give answers.

In his letter he rebuked the Corinthians for their quarrels and the wicked lives they had begun to lead. But he also spoke to them out of the great love a father manifests when he rebukes his children. Paul certainly knew what love was. In the thirteenth chapter of this letter, he wrote a song about love—one of the most beautiful songs ever written.

For three years Paul stayed in Ephesus. In the daytime he made tents and thereby earned a living for himself and his friends.

He wanted nothing more than his daily bread. He had no desire for wealth, and he did not want silver, gold or beautiful clothes. His wealth was Christ. All the time he could spare from making tents he devoted to Christ's service.

Day and night people could see him going through the city. Although there was a great deal of hatred, the congregation continued to grow. From Ephesus the gospel spread across the province of Asia.

192: Artemis of the Ephesians

Many people in Ephesus had accepted the gospel of Jesus. Were any of them still thinking about the goddess Artemis, whom they had served before turning to Christ?

The temple of Artemis, which stood just outside Ephesus, was one of the seven wonders of the world. It was a beautiful building with over a hundred marble pillars. Inside stood a wooden image of Artemis. The priests maintained that this image had fallen from heaven. The temple and the image were known far and wide. Thousands of pilgrims came every year to worship Artemis. Eagerly they bought small silver replicas of the temple made by the silversmiths of Ephesus, or small images of Artemis, or pins with her name inscribed on them.

Now that the people of Ephesus were listening to Paul, sales of these items began to fall off. All who kneeled before God knew that the service of Artemis was sinful foolishness.

Demetrius, the silversmith, was worried. The money used to come streaming into his hands, but now it came in tiny drops. And he knew the reason why! He was determined not to let his fine source of income slip away from him.

He summoned the other silversmiths and their helpers and stirred them up with angry words: "That Paul is leading more and more people astray, not only in Ephesus but in the entire area. He says that the gods made with hands are not gods at all. If we don't watch it, our line of work will become worthless. The temple of the great goddess Artemis will no longer be important. Artemis will lose the splendor that wins worship and honor for her throughout the province of Asia and the entire world."

These fiery words excited his listeners. They jumped to their feet and shouted, "Great is Artemis of the Ephesians!" They spilled out into the street as an angry mob, shouting about the honor of Artemis.

People streamed toward them from all parts of the city. The result was great confusion. Many screaming people stormed to the theater outside the city, dragging Gaius and Aristarchus, two friends of Paul, with them.

When Paul heard what was going on, he realized that the people were really angry at *him*. But he was not afraid for his life. He wanted to plunge into the mob of angry people, but his disciples held him back. Even some of the leading Roman officials in the area, who liked Paul, warned him not to go to the theater.

Meanwhile, the confusion grew greater and greater. The people were pressed tightly together and all shouted at the same time. Few of them even knew what all the excitement was about.

The Jews that were there became afraid. They did not support Artemis either, and they feared that *they* would be blamed for the decline in the sales of the images and temple replicas. Therefore the Jews shoved one of their number to the fore—a man named Alexander. Alexander would have to speak up in defense of the Jews.

But Alexander did not get a chance to say anything. He motioned for silence, but when the people realized that he was a Jew, they began to shout, "Great is Artemis of the Ephesians!"

This cry echoed through the theater and across the city, time after time: "Great is Artemis of the Ephesians!"

That was the cry of Demetrius and his followers, a cry they kept up for two hours, until they were almost out of breath and their throats were raw.

Then one of the city officals saw his chance to calm the people down. He was the town clerk, a clever and cunning man.

He addressed the people calmly: "Men of Ephesus, is there anyone in the world who does not know that Ephesus is the guardian of the great temple of Artemis and that the image of this goddess fell directly from heaven? Since this is beyond dispute, why don't you calm down? There's no need to do anything rash. These two men you have brought here are not temple robbers. They have not slandered our goddess. What you did was dangerous. If Demetrius and the other silversmiths have anything against these men, let them make an accusation before the judges. If any of you have anything else in mind, a decision must be made at a lawful gathering of the people. But if you continue what you're now doing, we run the risk of being accused of creating an uproar. Then the Romans will come and punish our city."

Those were sobering words. The people were afraid and dispersed quietly. Soon there was rest in Ephesus again.

God had preserved the congregation and would continue to protect His people. And, Paul, who had intended for a long time to move on, did not want to delay his departure. Aquila and Priscilla were not in Ephesus anymore. They had returned to Rome when it became safe for the Jews there again.

Paul yearned to follow them to the great world-city in the heart of the powerful Roman empire. He wanted to preach the gospel there. But he also wanted to go to Macedonia, and then to Jerusalem. He summoned the disciples in Ephesus and spoke some encouraging words to them. Then he said farewell and set off once more.

193: Paul in Troas

The third missionary tour Paul undertook was the greatest journey he ever made. He went from Ephesus to Troas, where he had had the wonderful dream calling him over to the continent of Europe. From there he went by sea to Philippi. He saw Lydia again, and the Philippian jailer. He spent some happy days in Macedonia.

The most wonderful thing of all was that he received some good news about Corinth while he was in Philippi. Paul had been very concerned. Now he heard that his letter had indeed saddened the believers in Corinth, but it was a sadness that fit in with God's purpose for them.

Free of his worries at last, Paul wanted to hurry to Corinth at once, but he couldn't. There was still a great deal for him to do in Macedonia. Therefore he wrote the church in Corinth another letter, a letter of joy and gratitude. He sent Titus, his co-worker, to Corinth to deliver the letter.

MACEDONIA

Corinth

Athens

Thessalonica

Philippi

Aegean Sea

Crete

Troas

ASIA

Cos

Ephesus

Miletus

Colossae

PHRYGIA

Rhodes

Mediterranean Sea

Patara

LYCIA

GALATIA

Iconium

Alexandria

Cyprus

Paphos

Tarsus

CAPPADOCIA

Caesarea

Antioch

Tyre

Ptolemais

Jerusalem

SYRIA

Not long after that, Paul went to Corinth himself, where he received a warm, loving welcome. He loved this congregation, for it was his problem child.

He stayed in Corinth for three months. During this period he wrote a letter to the church in Rome, which met in the home of Priscilla and Aquila. The priceless letter Paul wrote to the Roman church has been preserved for us, along with most of his other letters. This letter provided comfort and instruction not only for the believers in Rome but for Christians after them all over the world.

In Corinth Paul did not escape the enmity of the Jews either. He wanted to travel from Corinth to Athens, where he would board a ship for his own land. He heard that the Jews planned to attack him on this journey. Therefore he went back along the same route he had just followed, taking Timothy and some other friends with him. Once more he was in Philippi, where he and the congregation celebrated Easter to remember deliverance from sin through Jesus' death and resurrection. When Paul traveled across the sea to Troas, Luke the physician went with him.

When Paul had been in Troas for seven days, the congregation held a meeting with him. It was a Sunday evening. Paul was going to speak and say goodbye to the church in Troas.

All the men and women were gathered in a large room on the third floor of a house. They celebrated the Lord's supper together, and then Paul began his address. He had a great deal to say to his friends, and he did not pay much attention to the time. When it was past midnight, he still wasn't finished talking.

A young man named Eutychus was at that meeting. His name meant *the happy one.*

Eutychus became tired and sleepy. The air was stuffy in the crowded room, for many flickering lights were burning. Therefore Eutychus sat on the windowsill, where he would be cooled and refreshed by the night breezes. There, on the windowsill, without anyone noticing, he fell asleep.

Before anyone saw what was happening, Eutychus fell out the window. People immediately raced down the stairs to help him, but they found the young man lying dead on the stones of the courtyard.

While the people stood around the body wailing and crying, Paul came down. He stretched out over the lifeless body and put his arms around Eutychus. He prayed and then he said suddenly, "Don't be alarmed, for there is life in him."

Paul went to the room on the third floor again and sat down to eat just as if nothing had happened. He talked to the congregation until the early morning light came through the window.

Before Paul left, Eutychus was brought inside, alive and well. The congregation was especially encouraged when Paul continued his journey that Monday morning.

194: Farewell to Ephesus

After that tiring, sleepless night in Troas, Paul walked alone to Assos. The path led through great, wild oak forests. It was spring. The trees were budding, the first flowers were raising their heads, and the birds were singing everywhere along that lonesome road.

Paul had a lot to think about. In Assos his friends would be waiting for him aboard a ship. He would travel with them to Jerusalem to celebrate Pentecost there. A voice in his heart told him that there was more than joy and festivity awaiting him in Jerusalem: he would have to suffer there. It was the voice of the Holy Spirit. Paul had already heard that sad message a number of times.

It didn't even cross his mind to change his travel plans. His life was not his own but belonged to Jesus. Now that the Master was calling him to Jerusalem, he was determined to go, even if it cost him his life.

Everything around Paul spoke of freedom and life. But Paul would face imprisonment, and perhaps even death. If that was indeed what God had in mind for Paul, Paul could accept it.

From Assos he sailed south with his friends, along the rocky coast of Asia Minor and past many green islands in the sunny, shining sea. In the distance he could see Ephesus, where he had worked for so long. The ship did not stop there, which was just as well from Paul's point of view. He felt there was no time to lose. He was in a hurry because he wanted to be in Jerusalem by Pentecost if possible.

Yet he did not want to bypass his friends altogether, for his heart yearned for them. For a few days the ship stayed in Miletus, the next harbor. Paul quickly sent a message to the elders at Ephesus, asking them to come and see him in Miletus.

They did so gladly. In a moving address Paul then said goodbye to them, telling them that he would never see them again. He also told them that God was calling him to Jerusalem, where chains and affliction awaited him. He warned them that the church in Ephesus would undergo persecution. False teachers would arise in their midst, teaching false doctrines to make the believers desert the faith. He urged them to remain faithful shepherds, looking after the flock of Jesus with zeal and love.

He told them to work just as he had worked, and to think of the words of Jesus: "It is better to give than to receive."

When Paul had said this, he kneeled to pray with them, and they kneeled with him with tears in their eyes. They were very sad because he said he would never see them again. They wept as they embraced him and kissed him. They could hardly tear themselves away from him. But they *had* to bid Paul farewell, for it was God's will. Together they accompanied him to the ship.

195: On to Jerusalem

The rest of Paul's journey to Jerusalem went exceptionally well. Within two days the ship sailed along the coast of Asia Minor to Patara, its destination. Paul and his friends then boarded another ship that lay ready to sail to Phoenicia. Before long they were on their way again.

Again they had the wind with them. To their left they saw the green coast of Cyprus peeking above the horizon, but Cyprus disappeared quickly.

It was not long before they saw the harbor of Tyre before them. There was a one-week layover in Tyre. Paul used that week to visit the congregation that had been established there. The believers in Tyre already knew what awaited Paul in Jerusalem and they warned him not to go on.

But when the week was over, he left anyway. The whole congregation, including the women and children, saw him off at the dock. They all kneeled together by the shore to pray. After that he said goodbye to them, and they went home.

The sea journey was almost over, for the ship docked at Ptolemais. From there Paul and his friends walked along the coast to Caesarea. They went to the house of Philip, the evangelist, who was one of the seven original deacons of the church in Jerusalem. Philip was the man who had baptized the Ethiopian official. The weary travelers stayed at Philip's house for a while and got to know the local congregation.

One day while Paul and his friends were at Philip's house, Agabus appeared. Agabus was the prophet who had brought the dark tidings of the coming famine in Antioch years before.

Agabus walked up to Paul and took his belt. He then tied his own hands and feet and declared, "Thus says the Holy Spirit: 'The man to whom this belt belongs will be bound by the Jews in Jerusalem and delivered into the hands of the Gentiles.'"

All who heard those words were frightened by them. Even Paul's companions, including Luke, begged him not to go to Jerusalem. But Paul answered, "Why are you weeping and making it so hard for me? I am prepared not just to be bound but to *die* in Jerusalem for the name of the Lord Jesus."

When they failed to change his mind, they finally gave up and said, "The will of the Lord be done."

Not long after that, Paul and his friends set out for Jerusalem, accompanied by certain brothers from Caesarea. Paul was calm, just as calm as his Master when He went to Jerusalem knowing that death awaited Him there. As long as he was in his Master's care, Paul knew he was safe.

196: An uproar in the temple

People were streaming into Jerusalem to celebrate the Feast of Weeks. They came from all the surrounding regions that were still faithful to the temple, the sacrifices and the laws of Moses. The Jews who did not believe in Jesus, those who opposed Paul's work, were now represented in Jerusalem in great numbers.

Paul quickly realized that they recognized him. They watched him as he walked through the streets with Trophimus of Ephesus and his other friends. He knew how much they hated him, but he did not let it upset him. He had come to Jerusalem to serve God. The elders of the congregation had received him with joy. They had rejoiced when they heard what great things God was doing among the Gentiles.

Paul spent a great deal of time in the temple to be alone with God. He made it clear that he did not despise the temple, as some of the Jews said he did.

Paul's enemies found him even in the temple. Jews from the vicinity of Ephesus saw him in the outer court and shouted with indignation and rage. How did that apostate who ate and drank with Gentiles *dare* to come into the holy temple?

They rushed toward him and seized him. They cried out for help from their friends, explaining that Paul was the wicked man who went all over the world turning the people away from God. Now he had gone so far as to desecrate the temple by bringing in Gentiles.

The accusation about the temple was not true. The Jews jumped to this conclusion because they had seen Paul in the city with Trophimus, who was a Gentile.

Paul was not given an opportunity to defend himself. The whole city was in an uproar. The people formed a mob and dragged him out of the temple. The gates were closed immediately so that he would not be able to enter the temple again.

The whole angry, screaming mob, which grew continuously, surrounded him on the temple square. Blows rained down upon him. Paul would have to die—that was all there was to it. The people would kill him right then and there as a criminal!

Suddenly some loud commands were heard. Swords and shields flashed among the people as Roman soldiers opened a path through the crowd. They shoved the Jews back and surrounded their victim.

Claudius Lysias, the commander of the Roman soldiers in Jerusalem, was there too. He had received word that Jerusalem was in an uproar and had sent his soldiers to quell the disturbance.

His soldiers had saved a man from the fury of the Jews. He told the soldiers to bind the man with two chains. Then he asked the people who the man was and what he had done wrong. But he could not understand a word of the babble and shouting with which the Jews answered. Therefore he had the prisoner brought to the Roman barracks.

It all happened so quickly that the Jews did not quite realize what was going on. When they saw Paul being led away, it dawned on them that he would escape their wrath. They charged at the soldiers and tried to tear him free. "Away with him!" they cried.

They were blinded by their hatred of Paul. They flailed at Paul so furiously that the soldiers carried him up the steps of their barracks in order to save him.

At the top of the steps he was safe. The Jews would not dare attack him there. The soldiers put him down.

Before they could lead him inside, Paul politely asked the commander if he could speak a few words to the people. The commander looked at him in amazement. "Do you speak Greek?" he asked. "Aren't you the Egyptian who started a riot here a while back?"

When the commander heard who Paul was and where he had come from, he granted his request. Perhaps he would find out from Paul's speech what he had done wrong and why the people hated him so much.

197: Citizen by birth

There stood Paul, on the same spot where his Master had once stood. His Master, too, had faced a raging mob crying out for His blood.

He motioned with his hand and waited for the crowd to be silent. Then he addressed the people in Hebrew. In very simple terms he told them his life story. There was no better defense he could present than to let them all hear that he had only done what God had told him to do.

He told them how he used to persecute the Christians and how he had been converted by Jesus on the road to Damascus. He told them about his return to Jerusalem, and also how the Lord had spoken to him in the temple. The Lord had commanded Paul to leave Jerusalem because He wanted him to preach to the Gentiles.

Up to this point the crowd listened quietly, but when Paul started talking about the Gentiles, the uproar broke loose with renewed force. Was God's salvation for the *Gentiles*? How could Paul be sent by

God if he said such things? He was no better than an accursed liar! God's blessings were for Israel alone. "Away with him!" they shouted. "He does not deserve to live!"

They were so angry that they didn't know what to do next. They screamed, waved their garments, and threw dust in the air.

The commander watched what was going on, but he had not understood a word Paul said because he did not know Hebrew. He concluded that Paul must be guilty of some horrible crime.

His patience was gone, so he ordered that Paul be brought into the barracks and whipped to get the truth out of him. The commander was determined to find out why the people were so angry at Paul.

Paul did not hear him give this command. But when the soldiers strapped his wrists together and fastened the strap high on a pole so that Paul would be stretched out to be whipped, he realized what was going on. He was not about to accept it without protest.

He asked a captain who stood by and watched, "Are you allowed to whip a Roman citizen without giving him a hearing?"

That was not allowed at all! The soldiers could even be punished for it. The captain hurried over to the commander and said anxiously, "What are you doing? This man is a Roman citizen!"

That frightened the commander. He went over to Paul. "Tell me," he said, "are you a Roman citizen?"

"Yes," Paul answered calmly.

The commander in his magnificent uniform looked at Paul suspiciously. He did not know what to think of this simple prisoner who stood with his hands strapped to a pole high above his head. It did not ap-

pear that this simple man would have enough money to buy Roman citizenship.

Not hiding his doubt, he said to Paul, "I became a Roman citizen by paying a great sum."

Paul answered proudly, "I am a Roman citizen *by birth!*"

At once the straps were undone. The commander hardly dared to think what might happen if it became known that he had bound a Roman citizen. From that moment on, he treated Paul well.

198: A quarrel in the Sanhedrin

The next day the commander ordered that the Sanhedrin should be summoned to hear Paul's case. He even planned to attend the hearing himself, for he wanted to know what accusation the Jews would bring against Paul.

The dignified judges assembled with anger and bitterness in their hearts. How sorry they were that they had not managed to murder their enemy the day before! They realized that it would not be easy to find an accusation against Paul that they could use to have him put to death.

Paul stood before them calmly and courageously. He knew that all those men hated him, but he looked at them with clear eyes and said, "Brothers, I have a completely clear conscience before God. I am not ashamed of what I have done."

When Ananias, the high priest, heard those words, he was beside himself with rage. Ananias could not say the same for himself, for he was an evil man. He was more evil than the former high priest, Caiaphas, and he was more crude than any of the other judges.

Did that apostate dare to speak so boldly here? "Hit him in the mouth!" Ananias cried out to the Sanhedrin members who stood closest to Paul.

To strike a prisoner was strictly forbidden. Paul's eyes flickered with rage when he heard that cowardly command. Could that crude man be a judge? Then he was one of the ones whom Jesus had called whited sepulchers. He may have *looked* pious and righteous, but his heart was false and full of sin.

Paul said, "May God strike you, you whitewashed wall! Do you think you can judge me according to the law after you give an order to strike me, which is contrary to the law?"

Paul was not struck after all. But some members of the Sanhedrin asked, "Who are you to scold God's high priest?"

When Paul heard that, he regretted what he had said. Ananias was not wearing his official garments, and he had not conducted himself like a high priest. That was why Paul had not accorded him the recognition to which he was entitled.

The apostle offered them a noble apology. "Brothers," he said, "I did not know that I was addressing the high priest, for it is written, 'You shall speak no evil about the rulers of your people.'"

By this time Paul realized that he could not expect justice from these men. They would try to trap him in his words in order to find some accusation to bring against him.

Paul then used a trick to avoid being condemned falsely. He knew that there were two parties that could not stand each other in the Sanhedrin—the Sadducees and the Pharisees. The Sadducees said that there was no resurrection, but the Pharisees did believe in the resurrection of the dead.

They seized every opportunity to argue this point with each other.

Therefore Paul cried out, "Brothers, I am a Pharisee, and the son of Pharisees. I am being tried here because I believe in the resurrection of the dead."

As soon as he said this, the members of the Sanhedrin took up their old battle again, forgetting the purpose for which they had come together. The Pharisees forgot their hatred of Paul as they argued about the resurrection and denounced the Sadducees. Soon there was a lively quarrel underway. The Sadducees grabbed Paul, ready to murder him, but the Pharisees protected him.

The Roman commander was also present. He feared that Paul would be torn to pieces, and so he hastily summoned his soldiers. They rescued Paul from the hands of the Jews for the second time.

The hearing before the Sanhedrin had accomplished nothing. The commander still didn't know what crime his prisoner was guilty of, but he did understand that it had something to do with those mysterious Jewish laws. Paul was not a criminal under Roman law. Still, the commander decided not to release Paul, for he would be safe only in prison.

That night, Paul was alone in his cell. The man who had wandered all over the world and would gladly have made further journeys was now trapped like a bird in a cage. Outside the cage were enemies who sought his life.

Things were looking dark for Paul. It would not be at all strange if he began to lose hope. Still, he was not lonely, for the Lord appeared to him during the night and said, "Take courage. Just as you have testified about Me in Jerusalem, you must also testify about Me in Rome."

Although he was still a prisoner with enemies surrounding him, Paul knew he was safe. The Lord's promise would protect him against all attacks from his enemies.

199: On to Caesarea

Paul's enemies did not know that he was under the Lord's protection. More than 40 Jews, bent on revenge, met the next day and swore an oath that they would not eat or drink until they had put Paul to death.

They went to the chief priests and made a deal. One of them would go to the Roman commander and ask him to bring Paul before the Sanhedrin again the next day. The Jews would then see that Paul was killed on his way to the Sanhedrin's meeting chamber. They would ambush him in one of the small, winding streets. Even if he was surrounded by Roman soldiers, they would give up their lives to attack him. That's how much they were consumed with hatred.

Once more God saved His servant's life. This time He did not use a dramatic miracle, as He had done in Lystra when Paul was stoned. He did not use an angel or a strong hero. Instead he used an ordinary boy who was probably not much older than twelve. The boy was a son of Paul's sister, who lived in Jerusalem.

No one knew how the boy discovered the plot. Perhaps he overheard something while hiding in a dark corner.

When the boy discovered what was going on, his cheeks burned with indignation. His young heart rebelled against this wicked plan. He loved his uncle, the heroic figure who made long, difficult journeys to foreign lands. He immediately decided to do whatever he could to save Paul's life.

He did not stop to consider that it was dangerous to interfere. The Jews might put him to death when they found out that he betrayed them.

The boy ran through the streets of Jerusalem to the Roman barracks. Panting, he climbed the steps and told the guards that he wanted to speak to Paul. His eyes were so earnest that the guards went off to make inquiries. His request was granted, and soon the boy was able to tell Paul what he had heard.

Paul was not afraid of death; in fact, he was prepared to die for Jesus. But if he could evade that cowardly attack, he would do so.

He thought about Jesus' words that he had heard during the night. He saw the hand of God protecting him in all of this.

He called the captain and said, "Would you please bring this boy to the commander? He has something important to tell him."

. The captain obliged, and the commander received the boy in a friendly way. He took him by the hand, drew him aside, and asked, "What is it that you wish to tell me?"

The boy was bold and straightforward. "The Jews have decided to ask you to bring Paul before the Sanhedrin again tomorrow so that they can question him further on a certain point. Don't agree to this, for more than 40 of them await an opportunity to attack him. They have sworn not to eat or drink until they have killed him. They are all standing ready, waiting for their chance. All they need is for you to say yes."

When the commander heard this, there was an earnest look in his eyes. He admired the boy for being so brave. He dismissed the boy and told him not to let anyone know that he had warned the commander.

That same day Claudius Lysias took

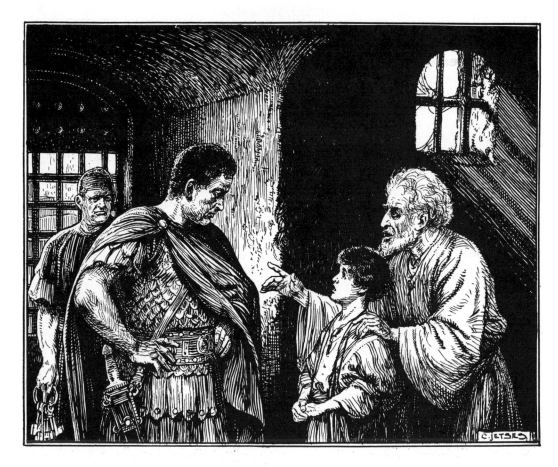

some measures to make sure that Paul would be safe. He ordered 200 soldiers, 200 spearmen, and 70 horsemen to prepare for duty. At three o'clock that night Paul was awakened, put on a horse, and led through the quiet, dark streets of Jerusalem, accompanied by the Romans. They marched through the darkness until daylight dawned. The foot soldiers then returned to the barracks of Jerusalem, but the horsemen went with Paul all the way to Caesarea.

In Caesarea Paul was brought before the governor, Felix, who lived in the palace Herod had built. The soldiers gave the governor a letter that Claudius Lysias had written. Paul was to remain in that great marble palace and have his hearing there.

Paul remained a prisoner, but his life was no longer in danger. The wicked plan of the Jews had failed. When they approached the commander with their cunning request, they were told that they would have to go to Caesarea if they wanted to question Paul again!

They must have been beside themselves with rage. Now there was no way for the 40 Jews to keep their oath!

Somewhere in Jerusalem there was a boy with a special joy in his heart. That boy had performed a great deed in the service of God's Kingdom.

200: An appeal to Caesar

Five days after Paul was brought to Caesarea, a sizable number of leading Jews appeared before the governor to bring accusations against the prisoner. Even the high priest Ananias was with them. The journey was not too long for him if there was some prospect of putting his enemy to death. He was even willing to put up with the humiliation of going into the house of a Gentile.

Ananias had a lawyer with him, a man named Tertullus. Tertullus did the talking. He accused Paul of desecrating the temple and creating an uproar. Paul was corrupting the people, he argued.

The Jews had no proof for their accusations, and Paul did not have a hard time defending himself. An uproar? It was no more than twelve days ago that Paul had arrived in Jerusalem, and no one had seen him addressing the people. Desecration of the temple? Paul had gone into the temple to offer sacrifices. That was when the Jews seized him and dragggged him away. Moreover, his accusers had not been able to name any other misdeeds when he stood before the Sanhedrin.

The Jews were speechless. It was true: they had found nothing. The reason for all the excitement at their meeting was the fierce argument about the resurrection from the dead.

Felix, the governor, was convinced from what he heard that Paul was innocent. But he did not dare pronounce him innocent and let him go, for he was afraid of the Jews.

But he could not condemn Paul either. Therefore he postponed judgment and declared that he wanted to talk with Claudius Lysias before making up his mind about the case.

Paul was again placed under heavy guard, but the captain of the guard was ordered to make sure that Paul was well treated. From then on the Christians in Caesarea could visit him as often as they wished and bring him anything he desired.

After a few days Paul was led before the governor again. This time there were no accusers to face; the only person with Felix was Drusilla, his wife. She was a daughter of King Herod Agrippa, the one who had murdered James, and she had embraced the faith of the Jews.

Felix and Drusilla were curious. They wanted to know what faith in Christ was all about, for the new faith was spreading all over the world. Some Roman soldiers in Caesarea had even embraced it. Paul was happy to enlighten them.

He had spoken to a governor once before—Sergius Paulus, who obtained eternal joy as a result. Would the same thing now happen with Felix? Paul knew the man and was aware what a wicked life he had led. Still, wasn't the gospel for sinners?

Paul talked about the righteousness that all who belong to Jesus should aim for. Felix didn't like to hear such talk, for he knew that he was a cruel, dishonest man. He could not even bear to look Paul in the eye, for it had been unjust of him not to release Paul.

Paul also talked about modesty and chastity. Anyone who wishes to be a disciple of Jesus must hold his evil desires and passions in check. A Christian must be ruled not by his own sinful heart but by Jesus alone.

Felix began to feel uncomfortable. He looked at Drusilla out of the corner of his eye, remembering how he had lured her away from her lawful husband.

When Paul began to talk about the coming judgment and the day when Jesus would return on the clouds of heaven to judge the living and the dead, it was too much for Felix. He trembled at the thought that he would someday have to appear before the heavenly Judge.

Felix therefore interrupted Paul and said, "That's enough for today. Someday when I have some time, you can tell me more."

Felix really did summon Paul on other occasions, but he did not ask him anything else about faith in Christ. He asked if Paul had any wealthy friends, for he hoped that Paul would offer him some money. He made sure Paul realized that he would be freed in exchange for money.

Paul did not want to buy his freedom, although he yearned to be free again. For two years he remained a prisoner. Then Felix was called to Rome and replaced by another governor. Because he wanted to do the Jews a favor, Felix left Paul behind as a prisoner.

The new governor was Festus. Like Felix, he was not an honest and courageous judge. He feared the Jews and wanted to remain friends with them at all costs.

As soon as Festus entered Jerusalem, the high priests and the leading Jews approached him. Their first request was that he let Paul come to Jerusalem for another hearing. They had already made their plans: they would murder Paul on the long, lonely road between the two cities.

Festus may have understood what they had in mind. He refused their request, but he did allow them to come to Caesarea.

Before long they stood before Paul as his accusers again. They made a number of grave charges, but they had no proof. Paul defended himself and maintained, "I have not done anything against the law of the Jews or against the temple or against the emperor." The new governor then came to the same conclusion as Felix: Paul was innocent. Even so, Festus did not acquit Paul.

Festus was perplexed by Paul's case. He did not know what to do. Should he give in to the wishes of the Jews? Would it really be so awful if Paul was murdered? Then he would be rid of that troublesome case.

Finally he asked Paul, "Are you willing to go to Jerusalem for a trial conducted in my presence?"

Paul's eyes blazed with indignation against the governor and against the Jews. For two years he had been held prisoner, although he was innocent and none of the charges against him had been proven. He had had enough. He should not have to put up with such treatment any longer.

Because he was a Roman citizen, he always had the option of appealing to Caesar. If he did so, no governor could pass judgment on him. Then he could only be judged by the emperor.

Paul answered proudly: "I am standing before Caesar's tribunal, which is the proper place for me to be tried. I have not done anything against the Jews, as you know perfectly well. If I deserve death, I would not resist the death sentence. Because I have done no wrong, I will not allow anyone to hand me over to the Jews to win their favor. I appeal to Caesar!"

After considering the matter with his counselors, Festus replied, "You have appealed to Caesar, and to Caesar you shall go!"

201: Ambassador in chains

When Paul finally appealed to Caesar, he created more problems for Festus. Festus would have to send the emperor a report and tell him what Paul had done wrong.

Just as Festus was thinking about this matter, he received a visitor to whom he could turn for advice—King Herod Agrippa II, the brother of Drusilla. King Agrippa ruled the northern part of the land. With him was his sister, Princess Bernice, who was a member of his household.

Festus laid the question of Paul before King Agrippa. Agrippa knew the Jews and was familiar with their religion. He had also heard of a man named Jesus, who was dead according to the Jews but said by Paul to be alive. He did not dare pass judgment on Paul without learning more about him. Therefore he said, "I would like to hear that man myself."

Festus answered, "You shall hear him tomorrow."

The next day was the most important day in King Agrippa's life, for there was much more than earthly power and human happiness at stake. He sat in the audience chamber next to Festus and Bernice, surrounded by great pomp. Officials of the court and leaders and prominent men of the city were also present.

Paul was led into this glittering assembly. He was pale from his imprisonment, and there were chains on his wrists. He looked poor and insignificant in those magnificent surroundings. Yet he stood there with a calmness befitting a king. In his eyes was a peace that not even imprisonment had been able to take away. He was an ambassador of the Most High God—an ambassador in chains.

King Agrippa said, "You may speak for yourself."

Paul began. Once more he told his life story. After all, what better defense was there? His life was the best proof that Jesus had risen from the dead and was seated as King on His throne in heaven.

When Paul talked about his King, his eyes shone with excitement. He forgot about himself and his legal position. All that mattered to him was telling these rich people with their poor sinful souls about Jesus. •

The great apostle was preaching again. He was fighting for King Agrippa's soul and for the souls of the others who were listening to him intently. He talked about the prophets, with whom Agrippa was familiar. He explained that they had foretold what was to happen to the Messiah. His suffering, his death, his resurrection from the dead—it had all been foretold.

When he talked about the resurrection of the dead, Festus interrupted him roughly. The Romans, those unbelieving pagans, branded anything that went beyond their understanding as foolishness. Resurrection of the dead? Anyone who believed such a thing was out of his mind! "You're talking nonsense, Paul," Festus declared. "All your learning is driving you insane."

Paul replied calmly, "Most excellent Festus, I am not talking nonsense, but the sober truth. The king knows about these things, and therefore I can speak boldly to him. I cannot believe that these things would be new to him. After all, the events of which I speak did not take place in some forgotten corner."

Turning directly to Agrippa, Paul said, "King Agrippa, do you believe the prophets? I know that you believe them!"

The king answered with a smile, "Do you think you can make a Christian out of me in such a short time?"

He said it in a friendly way, but it was meant as a warning. Behind that warning the king was hiding the uneasiness in his heart.

Paul then raised his bound hands before the king. In a fiery way he said, "I would be willing to pray to God to make you and all who are here today just like me—except for these chains, of course. I would beg Him to do it quickly and abidingly."

That was Paul's final, powerful assault on all those chained hearts.

The prisoner was led away again. The king stood up, and the others followed his example. They paused for a moment and said to each other, "This man has not done anything to deserve death or imprisonment."

Agrippa said to Festus, "This man could go free if he had not appealed to Caesar."

202: Off to Rome

The great day had finally come for Paul, the day he had waited for so long. He was on his way to Rome!

He had been a prisoner in Caesarea for over two years. Now the doors finally swung open for him, and the soldiers led him to the harbor. He was still a prisoner, but his friends Luke and Aristarchus were allowed to accompany him.

His companions were waiting for him at the harbor in Caesarea. The bound prisoners stood together in a large group, surrounded by their guards. Among them were thieves, murderers and revolutionaries from cities and towns all over

the land. They, too, were on their way to Rome, but they were going there to die. The emperor needed them for his own enjoyment and that of his officials. The prisoners would be torn to pieces by wild animals in an arena.

It was with such a group, including rough sailors and heathen soldiers, that Paul was to make his journey to Rome.

The boat set sail and headed north. The plan was to go from one coastal point to another. Julius, the captain, was in charge of the soldiers. He was friendlier to Paul than to the other prisoners. When the ship arrived in Sidon the next day, he allowed Paul to go ashore for a while and visit the believers there. Overwhelmed by the warm, loving reception he received, Paul came back on board. The journey continued.

A raw, boisterous wind began to blow from the north. The ship changed its course and sought protection under the high coast of Cyprus. Then it sailed west along this island and set out across the open sea to Myra.

There Julius found a better ship that would be sailing directly to Italy. It was a big ship carrying a lot of freight. The ship was carrying Egyptian grain from Alexandria to Rome.

The journey continued as the ship sailed westward from Myra. It made little progress because of the prevailing winds. When the ship was beyond Asia Minor and lost the protection of the high mountains, it became all but impossible to sail farther in the right direction. Therefore there was another change of course: the ship sailed south and sought protection behind the great island of Crete. Soon it was in a large, beautiful bay known as Fair Havens. There the anchor was thrown overboard.

Paul and his companions had made very little progress by this point. They could have been in Rome already—that's how long they were underway. Yet they weren't even halfway there. The month of September was already gone, and now the fall storms and dark skies would be coming, making further travel by sea almost impossible.

The whole journey began to look doubtful. Wouldn't it be better to stay anchored by Crete and wait for better traveling weather in the spring?

Julius, the captain of the soldiers, discussed this matter with the ship's captain and navigator. Paul joined them in their discussion. He did not know a great deal about sailing, but he did know the One who controls the winds and the waves. Paul had heard His voice speaking to him in his heart. Therefore he gave them a warning: "Men, I can see that this journey will lead to damage and great loss, including the cargo, the ship, and even our lives."

The navigator and the ship's captain did not pay any attention to Paul. They were experienced seamen and would not let themselves be thrown off stride by his speculation. The bay was open to winds from all directions and was not a suitable place to spend the winter. A short distance to the west, at Phoenix, was a harbor as calm and still as a pond. They decided it would be better to head for Phoenix.

Julius had more confidence in the ship's captain and navigator than in Paul. The weather seemed to be on their side too, for a gentle south wind sprang up just then, the kind of wind that usually comes in the spring. The anchor was hoisted, the sails were set, and the ship continued its journey, sailing toward a safe harbor.

203: Paul's assurance

The favorable weather did not last long. It seemed as if the storm had hidden for a while in order to lure the ship into its trap.

Suddenly the storm jumped up and threw itself at the ship. A raging northeaster swept down from the hills of Crete and dragged the ship along. The ship could not possibly advance against that wind; instead it was dragged along by the wind.

The sailors struggled and did what they could to reach the harbor. Finally they gave up as the ship was driven along on the angry, raging sea with its rolling mountains of water. The lifeboat danced along behind the ship, tugging at the rope that connected it with the ship.

When the ship was near the island of Cauda the sailors managed to get hold of the lifeboat and bring it on deck. Then they lowered heavy cables under the bow and brought them back around the ship. They fastened them tightly to hold the groaning planks and beams together. It was highly dangerous work, for the weather was getting worse and worse.

The ship swayed and danced like a ball on the waves. It was being driven west toward the Syrtis, the great sandbank that extended into the Mediterranean Sea north of the African coast. If they ran aground on the Syrtis, all would be lost. Therefore they threw much of the cargo overboard the next day, and on the day after that they threw the ship's tackle overboard as well.

Then there was nothing more they could do. They were helpless before the storm and the waves. For days they saw neither the sun nor the stars. The sky was as gray as the water. The days were dark, and the nights impenetrably black. The storm whistled and howled without interruption. The waves beat against the ship and drove it on to some unknown destination.

The soldiers, sailors and prisoners huddled together in despair. The differences between them had disappeared. Now they were only human beings in need, people who had almost no hope of deliverance.

After they had gone without eating for a long time, Paul stood up in their midst, looking as calm and peaceful as if there were no storm that could shake him up or harm him. He spoke some encouraging words to them: "If only they had listened to me and stayed by Crete! Then we would have been spared all this hardship and loss. But take courage, for not one of us will lose his life, although the ship will be lost."

They all stared at Paul in disbelief. He continued, "This very night an angel of the God to whom I belong and whom I worship stood by me. He said, 'Do not be afraid, Paul, for you must appear before the emperor. God grants you the safety of all who are traveling with you.' Therefore, men, take courage, for I trust my God. I know it will turn out just as the angel said. We will run aground on some island."

What strange words those were! An angel had found this small ship in the midst of the storm? Was there a God who would sent a comforting message to a single human being and preserve the lives of all on board for the sake of one man?

Paul's shipmates did not know what to make of his words. Still, those words were all they had to cling to. In time it would become clear that Paul had spoken the truth.

204: Shipwreck

On the fourteenth night of the storm, the sailors heard a new sound above the roar of the wind and the waves. It seemed to be the sound of heavy breakers washing up on some shore. They took soundings and found out that the water was about twenty fathoms deep. A little later it was only fifteen fathoms. This confirmed their suspicion that they were nearing land.

Quickly they threw out four anchors from the stern, for they did not want to be dashed to pieces against some rocks. The ship slowed down and then tugged at the ropes, but the anchors held. At last the ship was at rest. Everyone on board waited for morning.

The sailors went to the bow, telling the others that they wanted to throw out anchors there too. The truth of the matter, however, was that they planned to abandon the ship in an effort to save their own lives. Hastily they lowered the lifeboat into the water.

Paul saw what was going on and warned Julius, the captain of the soldiers. What would become of the soldiers and the prisoners if there were no sailors left on board? Paul said, "If the sailors do not remain on board, we cannot be saved."

The soldiers acted quickly. They cut the ropes by which the lifeboat was lowered from the ship. The empty lifeboat fell into the foaming waves and drifted away in the darkness. Now it was impossible for the sailors to abandon ship. The people on board would all live or die together.

Their lives hung in the balance now, and they were more afraid than ever. Again Paul encouraged them. In the gray early morning light, he stepped into their midst and encouraged them to eat so that they would be strong when they faced the difficult day ahead. "It will help you," he said, adding, "Not one of you will lose a single hair from his head."

Then he took bread and gave thanks to God in their presence. His voice was full of trust, and they strained to hear him above the sound of the wind and the waves. He broke the bread and ate calmly. His calmness then began to catch on; they all took courage and followed his example by eating.

When they were finished eating, someone counted the people on the ship. There were 270 men on board the tossing ship.

Strengthened physically and spiritually, they began to make the ship lighter by casting grain into the sea. That way the ship would sit higher in the water and might be able to pass over sandbanks and rocks without running aground or being dashed to pieces. The ship might yet make it to the shore.

No one on board was familiar with the land under the moving clouds. But they did spot a small bay with a beach. They decided to try to steer the ship toward it.

They hauled in the anchors and let the sea drive the ship. They loosened the rudder and hoisted the foresail to the wind, aiming the ship toward the beach.

Suddenly there was a bump and a lurch that sent them all flying. The ship creaked and shook, and then it lay still. They had run aground on a shoal, and the bow of the ship was stuck. The stern, however, had been broken by the force of the waves. It was a miracle that no one had been thrown overboard. They all huddled together on the bow.

Somehow they had to get to land. It would be impossible to keep a close eye on all the prisoners, so the soldiers suggested that they be put to death. Then no one would escape during the swim to the shore.

Julius, who wanted to spare Paul's life, rejected this suggestion. He ordered all who could swim to jump overboard first and try to get to land. The others followed when the ship was smashed to pieces under their feet. They thrashed around in the foaming water, reaching for a beam, a plank or a piece of driftwood. Panting, they clung to the wood.

In this way they drifted or swam to shore. When they stood together on the shore, frightened but safe, they saw that not one was missing. God's Word spoken through Paul had been fulfilled.

205: Malta

The land where Paul and his companions finally found safety was an island named Malta, which lay to the south of Italy.

They learned this from the inhabitants of the island, who came hurrying over when they saw strangers on the shore. They were very friendly to the shipwrecked travelers. They even made a bonfire for them in the shelter of some rocks. This gave the trembling, half-drowned men a chance to warm themselves and dry their clothes until lodgings could be found for them.

The sky threatened rain, and there was a menacing wind. Most of the men from the ship were numb with cold and could hardly move.

Paul, again showing his concern for others, gathered some more dry wood for the fire. He began to separate the branches and throw them on the fire one by one.

Suddenly, a viper reared up, driven out of hiding by the heat of the fire, and bit Paul's hand.

When the islanders saw it, they were frightened, for they knew that the viper's bite was fatal. They looked at Paul fearfully and said to each other, "This man is surely a murderer. Some goddess is striking him down because he escaped from the sea."

They watched him very closely, convinced that his arm would swell and that he would fall down dead before them.

Paul simply shook off the viper and let it fall into the fire. The poison had no effect on him. The Savior spared His servant's life because Paul was to testify about Him in Rome.

When the islanders saw that nothing happened to Paul, they changed their view of him and declared that he was a god.

The ruler of the island lived near the shore. His name was Publius, and he had room for many guests at his estate. He took in the shipwrecked travelers and showed them genuine hospitality. They stayed with him for three days.

God rewarded Publius for this kindness. His father lay sick in bed with fever and dysentery and was very weak. When Paul heard about it, he went to the man and prayed for him. Then he laid his hands on him and healed him.

When the news of this miracle spread across the island, people came from all directions, bringing their sick to Paul. God gave him the power to heal all of them.

The travelers stayed on the island for three months. After the people provided them with everything they needed, they boarded a ship from Alexandria that had spent the winter in Malta. The ship was named after the twins Castor and Pollux, the sons of Jupiter and the protectors of sea travel. But those who had traveled with Paul had enjoyed the care of a much better Protector.

The rest of the journey went well. Soon they reached Sicily and spent three days in the harbor of Syracuse. After that they sailed along the island until they came to Rhegium, at the southernmost tip of Italy. Then the south wind drove them on to Puteoli in just a few days. At Puteoli they would disembark for Rome.

The sea journey was finished. The prisoners had been brought safely to Italy. Along the shore of the beautiful bay where the ship lay anchored they could see the white marble villas of Herculaneum and Pompeii. Behind them, high and threatening, was a smoking volcano—Mount Vesuvius.

For Paul, even more glorious than this beauty was the surprise that there were Christian brothers in Puteoli. Julius was happy to give him permission to visit the Christians. For seven days Paul stayed with them. Then, strengthened by this encounter, he set off on the last leg of his long journey to Rome.

206: A welcome in Rome

The broad Via Appia, the queen of highways, lay shining in the spring sun. Caravans traveled along that road laden with all sorts of goods for sale. Armed soldiers marched by. Important Romans looked down from their chariots at the processions of slaves marching toward Rome.

Everyone headed toward Rome from the south marched along the smooth pavement of this famous road. Also walking along this road, under armed guard, was a procession of prisoners from Palestine. One of those prisoners was Paul.

Paul was now close to Rome, the city of millions, the heart of the powerful world empire. But there was worry written on his face, and his feet felt heavy. Now that his destination and fulfillment of his life's dream was so close, Paul seemed to be losing courage.

He was not afraid for his life. He was not thinking about himself but about the church he would encounter in Rome. He had written that church a long, instructive letter while he was in Corinth.

Was any congregation in as much danger as the one in Rome, which was surrounded by evil, sin and temptation? The Roman Christians lived in the city of the wicked emperor Nero. Nero had murdered his own mother and surely would not spare the Christians when he got to know them.

How would Paul be received by the church in Rome? Would the Christians there be willing to accept the chained prisoner as an ambassador of Christ?

Two days away from the city, in the forum of Appius, people came to meet the procession. They were tired and dusty from their long journey. They stopped near the prisoners and looked through the rows in great excitement.

"Is Paul among them?" they asked expectantly. They were Christians from Rome who had already received word from Puteoli that the great apostle was on his way. They had hurried at once to meet him. A day's journey farther, at Three Taverns, there were more Christians waiting to greet Paul.

This reception moved Paul deeply. All his worries and fears disappeared in the face of this love and faithfulness on the part of the church in Rome. He thanked God and took courage.

His children in Rome, whom he loved more than he loved himself, had been kept safe in the midst of all the dangers! God had not allowed his congregation to be destroyed.

The ambassador of the Lord entered Rome as a simple man, bound and accompanied by a gang of criminals. But he walked through this powerful world-city with a smile on his face. He knew that the iron power of the Roman empire would bow before his Lord someday.

The stone that Daniel had seen in Nebuchadnezzar's dream was heading for the statue. It would smash the statue and fill the entire earth.

207: Unhindered

Julius, the captain in charge of the soldiers, had brought the captives to Rome through many dangers. He led them to the Pretorium, the hall of justice, and turned them over to the commander there.

Again it became clear that God was looking after Paul, for he was not locked up with the other prisoners. Perhaps the commander in Rome decided to be kind to Paul because of the letter written by Festus, the governor. Or perhaps he was influenced by what Julius told him about the shipwreck and the journey.

Paul was given permission to rent a house, where he would stay by himself. The soldier who guarded him would always be with him, of course. He remained a prisoner, but he was allowed to work for his Master.

Three days after his arrival in Rome, Paul invited the leading Jews of the city to come and see him. They came to his house and looked in amazement at the soldier who stood behind Paul's chair and was chained to him.

Paul explained to the Jews how he wound up in Rome chained to a soldier. It was not because he had committed any crime but because the Jews in Jerusalem had been opposed to the thought of him going free. He also explained that he had appealed to Caesar because of the Jewish opposition. He had not done so to bring accusations against his own people. He was in chains because he preached about the hope of Israel, the Son of David.

The Jews in Rome had not heard any bad reports about Paul and did not hate him, as the Jews in Jerusalem did. They said to him, "We would very much like to know what your ideas are. We know that the sect you belong to is running into opposition everywhere."

They made an appointment to come to his house another day and talk. Thus in Rome, too, Paul began by talking to the Lord's covenant people about the Kingdom of God.

He spent that day, from early morning to late evening, trying to persuade them that Jesus is the Redeemer. He explained the writings of the prophets to them and also talked about the law, doing his best to bring them to faith.

But the result in Rome was the same as everywhere else. Some believed, but most resisted him stubbornly.

It was very sad. They didn't seem to be listening to what Paul said. They had ears just like anyone else, but they seemed to be deaf. Although they had eyes, they were blind to deliverance in Christ.

When Paul saw that, he thought about the punishment that Isaiah had already announced to Israel—the judgment of hardening that would come over the Jews when they rejected the Messiah. He warned the Jews in stern language and prophesied that God would pour out on the Gentiles the salvation that the Jews rejected.

Paul's words were in vain and only led to an argument. He was still arguing with them when the meeting broke up.

For two years Paul stayed in Rome in his own rented house, where he was allowed to receive anyone who came to visit him. For two years he preached the Kingdom of God and taught about the Lord Jesus Christ, boldly and unhindered. No one stood in his way.

Paul was happy, although he was a prisoner. He knew that he would be free in time and that no one could hurt him.

The soldiers who took turns guarding Paul quickly realized that he was not an ordinary prisoner but bore his chains for the sake of Christ. Even some important Romans believed, as the congregation in Rome grew in number.

Paul also made contact with other congregations, which he could not visit in person. His friends Luke, Timothy, Tychicus, John Mark, and many other faithful fellow laborers were with him. From all sides he received reports about what was happening. Like a father, he continued to watch over the congregation and exercise leadership through his fellow workers and his letters.

208: Philemon and Onesimus

It was most likely during his two years in Rome that Paul wrote his letter to the congregation of Colossae, a city near Ephesus. He also wrote to the Ephesians, sending them a general letter that was intended for all the congregations in their vicinity. And he wrote a tender, warm letter to the Philippians, who were sending him gifts of love.

It was from Rome that Paul wrote his letter to Philemon, who was a leading Christian in Colossae. It was only a short letter, but it was very valuable. Almost nowhere else are Paul's love and concern for his spiritual children manifested as clearly as in this letter.

Philemon had a slave named Onesimus. Onesimus ran away from his master one day because he desperately wanted to be free. He wandered farther and farther from Colossae, hounded continually by the fear of being caught and sent back to his master. His master would surely punish him severely, he reasoned. Finally he went into hiding in Rome. He did not tell anyone who he really was; he kept it a dark secret. No one would be able to find him among the thousands who lived in that great world-city.

Yet, Someone found him, Someone whose eye sees everything.

On a certain day Onesimus was at Paul's house, where he heard the chained apostle talking about Jesus. He listened in silent amazement. The message of Christ's love was wonderful comfort for his anxious, tormented heart.

Onesimus grew to love Jesus. The man who didn't want to be a slave now became a slave of Christ, who had bought him with His blood. Onesimus now belonged to

Jesus, body and soul. Only then did he learn what true freedom is.

After that his frightening secret allowed him no rest. He spent a great deal of time with Paul and did whatever he could for him. He loved the old, gray apostle like a father. Finally he could not keep his secret from Paul. He told him everything, knowing in advance what Paul would say. Paul would tell him that since he had reconciled himself with God, he should also reconcile himself with his master. Onesimus would have to go back to Philemon, who had a lawful claim to him.

That's just what Paul said. It was hard for Paul, for he had grown to love Onesimus, who did so much for him. Still, they *had* to go their separate ways, for it was God's will.

It was then that Paul wrote his beautiful letter to Philemon. He wrote the letter to make it easier for Onesimus to return.

"I am writing to you on behalf of Onesimus, my child," wrote Paul. "I have become his father during my imprisonment. Earlier he was not useful to you, but now he is very useful, both to you and to me. As I send him back to you, it is as if I am sending you my own heart. Perhaps that's why he has been away for a while, so that you would have him back for good. You have him now no longer as a slave but as a beloved brother.

"If you feel yourself to be bound to me, receive him as you would receive me. If you suffer any loss as a result or owe anyone anything, charge it to me. I, Paul, am writing this in my own handwriting; I will repay it. I write to you in the full confidence that you will listen to me. In fact, I know that you will do even more than I am asking of you.

"Meanwhile, prepare a guest room for me, for I am hoping—thanks to your prayers—to be given back to you soon."

209: A crown of righteousness

It is almost certain that Paul was not disappointed in his hope that he would eventually be set free. After about two years he was apparently released. His accusers still had not come from Jerusalem to explain what he had done wrong.

Then the aged eagle spread his wings once more. He may even have gone to Spain, which was what he had planned to do some years earlier when he was in Corinth.

But it is more certain that he went east again and visited the island of Crete, the large island he had sailed by as a prisoner. He also visited Philippi again, and Troas, and Miletus, and Corinth. No doubt he went to Asia Minor to call on Philemon and Onesimus.

During this journey east, he wrote two more letters—one to Timothy, who was laboring in Ephesus at the time, and one to Titus, whom he had left behind on Crete. But it was in Rome that God relieved the aged hero of faith of his duties.

In the year 64, a horrible fire swept through Rome. It lasted nine days and destroyed most of the city. The Christians were later blamed for this catastrophe. In the great persecution that then struck the Christians in Rome, Paul was taken prisoner again. He appeared all alone before the cruel emperor and his judges, just as Jesus once stood alone before Pilate.

At the first hearing Paul was not condemned. He was sent back to prison with Luke, who stood by him faithfully.

It was then that he wrote his last letter—another letter to Timothy, in Ephesus. In this letter he reported on his hearing before Nero: "At my first defense no one stood by me; they all deserted me. Still, I hope it will not be held against them. The Lord stood by me and gave me strength so that the message would be fully proclaimed by me. The Gentiles all had a chance to hear the message."

From this letter we also learn how lonely the aged warrior was near the end, and how much he yearned for his friends. "Do your best to come to me soon," he wrote. "Only Luke is with me. Get Mark and bring him along." We are moved as we hear the apostle say, "When you come, bring the cloak that I left in Troas with Carpus, and also the books, especially the parchments. Do your best to come before the winter."

The end of Paul's letter testifies to his great trust in God: "The Lord will protect me against all evil attacks and bring me safely into His heavenly Kingdom. To Him be the glory in all eternity. Amen!"

We do not know if Timothy reached Paul in time.

Paul died for his Master in the same way that James died. He was beheaded with a sword, which was the form of execution prescribed for Roman citizens.

Paul had fought the good fight and had run his course to the end. Many earthly rulers had tormented him during his life by unjust treatment. But Paul knew that the Lord, the righteous Judge, already had a crown of righteousness ready for him. "And not just for me," he wrote in his last letter, "but for all who long for His appearing."

210: Faithful unto death

We do not know much about the life and work of the remaining apostles. At first they remained in Jerusalem for some years, but later they went out into the world, obeying their Master's command.

Two letters of Peter are left, letters he wrote to the churches in Asia Minor. We do not know where Peter fled when the angel of the Lord released him from his prison cell in Jerusalem.

Some time later, at a meeting of the apostles, Peter was in Jerusalem again. After that he went to Antioch, and perhaps also to Corinth. Finally he traveled to Rome. In all likelihood he died there on a cross.

John lived to be very old. He lived long enough to see Jesus' prediction of Jerusalem's destruction fulfilled. In the year 70, the Romans destroyed the city after a horrible siege. The trouble had started when the Jews rebelled against the Romans.

The Christians had already fled by the time the war began. They found refuge in the city of Pella, which was beyond the Jordan. At that time John was probably busy preaching in Ephesus.

John lived in Ephesus for a long time and gave leadership to the churches of Asia Minor by his preaching and his letters. When he was very old, he was exiled to the small island of Patmos which was not far from Ephesus.

Even when John was alone, God was near him. In glorious visions he was allowed to see what was in store for the church of Jesus Christ. He described what he saw in a book that has been handed down to us—the book of Revelation, which is the final book of the Bible. It is a very beautiful book, but also a difficult and strange book. No one is able to understand it fully.

Still, the book of Revelation has been of comfort to believers all through the ages. The book makes it clear that although the church of Jesus Christ will suffer a great deal, it will never be rooted out. It might appear at times that God's enemies are free to do as they please, but in the end Christ will overcome them and rule eternally as King.

Two of the apostles, Matthew and John, wrote accounts of Jesus' work in the form of a "gospel." Luke, the physician, also described the life and work of Jesus in a "gospel," as did John Mark, the son of Mary. What John Mark wrote was probably based on what he heard from Peter.

Matthew wrote for the Jews. He saw Jesus as the Messiah in whom all the Old Testament promises are fulfilled. Mark wrote for the Romans. He viewed Jesus as the great King to whom all the powers are subject. Luke, the physician, described Jesus as the merciful High Priest who came to take away our suffering and sadness. And John depicted Jesus as the Word of God, as God's voice in the world, as the Son of God to whom all men must listen in order to learn God's will.

The four gospels together form one beautiful story about Jesus, just as four lamps together light up a room.

Luke also wrote a book known as "The Acts of the Apostles." Most of the book is devoted to the work of Paul.

We do not know what became of the other apostles—Philip, Andrew, Bartholemew, or Nathanael, the Israelite in whom there was no guile. We do not know what

happened to Thomas, the melancholy disciple, or what he did with his faith in his Lord and God.

We do know that all the apostles obeyed the command of their Master. Wherever they went, they preached the gospel. No amount of hatred or persecution could hold them back from their glorious work. They were faithful unto death and received the crown of life.

211: By faith

Next to the path stands a small flower in bloom—a daisy. No one pays much attention to it, but it has a sweet smell as it holds its head high and reaches for the sun. It's just a small flower, and people walk right past it without noticing it. Sometimes they even step on it.

Yet that little daisy is a divine miracle. It survives rain and hail and angry storms. When the winter cold comes, the daisy seems to die. But hardly does the spring sun warm the earth when a new daisy rises from the soil, looking just as joyous as the daisy the year before. All around the little plant other plants spring up—its offspring. They rise from the seeds that the storm scattered. Thereby God's wisdom and love are made known to all who have eyes to see.

What an amazing power it is that preserves the little daisy from all dangers! God has given a special strength and endurance to that little plant He created.

The church of Jesus Christ has also been planted by God upon the earth. Therefore it endures all oppression and cannot be rooted out, however much God's enemies may rage.

There is also an amazing strength in the

church, a power of endurance that protects the church from all dangers. God has placed that power in the hearts of all who truly love Him. That divine power binds them to God so that they can never be separated from Him. Because of that power, which we call faith, we can be sure that the church of the Lord will never be wiped out.

By faith the apostles preached after they received the Holy Spirit on Pentecost, not fearing the threats of the synagogue.

By faith Stephen testified courageously before his judges and prayed for his enemies when he was being stoned.

By faith Peter healed a cripple, made lame Aeneas walk, and raised Dorcas from the dead.

By faith Paul made his great journeys and bravely defied all dangers. Five times he was whipped by the Jews, and three times he was beaten by the Romans. He was stoned once, and three times he was shipwrecked. By faith he endured all this, for Christ's sake.

By faith preachers continued to carry on the work after the era of the apostles. The church spread ever farther across the earth. Almost everywhere there were people who lived by faith.

The believers endured some difficult times. They were tormented, oppressed and even put to death in all sorts of ways. But the blood of the martyrs proved to be the seed of the church. As the martyrs kneeled on the scaffold, their eyes shone with joy because they were allowed to die for their Savior and would soon see Him face to face. When the flames began to consume their bodies as they were tied to the stake, they could sometimes sing joyfully, by faith.

Even when they were put to death, their faith did not die. That faith lived on in more and more hearts, right to our own day.

Today missionaries are still fanning out across the world to bring the gospel to pagans. To all who truly desire God they bring the message that salvation is possible, through grace and by faith. The missionaries leave their homeland behind, and often their families as well. They endure hardship and danger because of their love for Christ. Their faith gives them strength.

No one who lives by faith can be silent about the Savior.

One day there will be no people left on earth who have not heard the voice of Jesus. Then Jesus, the Finisher of our faith, will return. He will appear on the clouds of heaven to judge the living and the dead.

When He comes, will He find faith on earth? The flame of faith will be burning in many hearts because He feeds that flame through His Spirit.

The believers will then enter eternal glory with Him.

Only the Father knows exactly when that will be. But we can be sure that the day is coming closer and closer.

Jesus will come as suddenly and unexpectedly as a thief in the night.

He will come as the Bridegroom, and He will bring His bride, the church, into His Father's house. All who belong to Jesus by faith yearn for that day. They pray, "Come, Lord Jesus. Yes, come quickly!"

The church of the Lord has already suffered a great deal and will probably undergo much more suffering before the great day comes. But those who love Jesus need not be afraid. All they need do is cling to Him in faith. Then they will never be separated from Him.

Who will separate us from the love of

Christ? Will persecution, or distress, or oppression, or hunger, or nakedness, or danger, or the sword? No! In all these things we are more than conquerors through Him who loved us. We can rest assured that neither death, nor life, nor angels, nor powers, nor present, nor past, nor height, nor depth, nor any creature will be able to separate us from the love of God, which is in Christ Jesus, our Lord!